Child Development

Child

Development

SUEANN ROBINSON AMBRON
Stanford University

Rinehart Press / Holt, Rinehart and Winston   *San Francisco*

A Leogryph Book

Project Manager: Jim Martin

Contributing Editors: Peter Salwen and Dawn Sangrey

Art Director: Andrew Mudryk

Photo Researcher: Alycia Smith Butler

Line Art: Vantage Art and Howard Friedman

Production Editor: Rodelinde Albrecht

Composition: Bodoni Book and Helvetica by York Graphic Services

Cover: Design by Ladislav Svatos/Graphicon, Ltd.

using photos by Philip Teuscher

Literary Credits

Part 1 opener
pages 3–4
From CHILDREN OF VIOLENCE, Volume II, *A Proper Marriage* by Doris Lessing. Copyright © 1952, 1954, 1964 by Doris Lessing. Reprinted by permission of Simon and Schuster and of John Cushman Associates, Inc.

page 57
From "The Origin of Personality" by A. Thomas, S. Chess, and H. Birch. Copyright © 1970 by Scientific American, Inc. All rights reserved.

Part 2 opener
pages 63–64
Reprinted by permission of Charles Scribner's Sons from LOOK HOMEWARD, ANGEL by Thomas Wolfe. Copyright 1929 Charles Scribner's Sons; renewal copyright © 1957 Edward S. Aswell, Administrator, C. T. A. and/or Fred W. Wolfe.

pages 116, 127, 128, 129, 130
From PSYCHOLOGY OF INTELLIGENCE by Jean Piaget, translated by M. Percy and D. E. Berlyne. Copyright © 1950 by Routledge and Kegan Paul, Ltd., London, England. Reprinted by permission of Routledge and Kegan Paul, Ltd.

Credits continued on page 491.

CONTENTS

Part 1
BIRTH AND BEFORE

I
Prenatal Development

7

GENETIC INFLUENCES

8

Mechanisms of Heredity

Cell Division
Gene Dominance
Sex Determination
Mutations

Inherited Characteristics

Physical Features
Defects
Mental Disorders
Personality
Intelligence

STAGES OF GESTATION

20

Preimplantation Period
Period of the Embryo
Period of the Fetus

PRENATAL ENVIRONMENTAL INFLUENCES

24

Teratogens

Diseases
Chemicals
Radiation

2

Birth and the Neonate

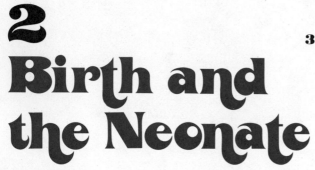

LABOR

Stages of Labor

Complications

Drugs During Labor

Anoxia

Childbirth in the Hospital

PREMATURITY

PHYSICAL CHARACTERISTICS OF THE NEWBORN

Part 2
INFANCY

3

67

Physical Development

4   103

Perception and Learning

5

125

Cognition and Language

**SENSORIMOTOR
INTELLIGENCE** **126**

Managing Emotions

**APPROACHES TO CHILD
REARING**

Changing Views

Attention

Discipline

CHILD ABUSE

**CULTURE AND
UPBRINGING**

Class Differences

**Child Rearing in
Other Cultures**

Features

Part 3
THE PRESCHOOL YEARS

7

8 237

Cognition and Language

9

Personality and Society

Part 4
MIDDLE CHILDHOOD

10

Frustration and Aggression

Delinquency

Sociopathic Personality

11 333
Learning and Cognition

12
361

Home, Peers, and School

THE HOME   362

Autonomy and Control

One-Parent Homes

Siblings

THE PEER GROUP   369

Group Norms

Games

Solidarity Against Grownups

Group Variables

> Leadership

Status in the Group

Friendship

Socialization and the Peer Group

Racial Awareness and Prejudice

THE SCHOOL 380

Teaching Methods

Teachers

Part 5
ADOLESCENCE

13

393

Growing into Adulthood

14

Culture and Identity

Epilogue　461
The Study of
Child Development

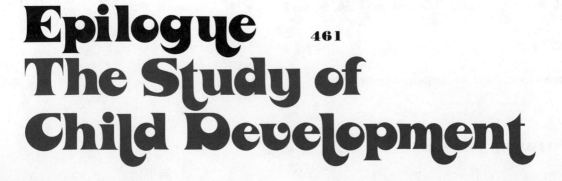

PREFACE

PURPOSE OF THE BOOK

This text is designed for introductory child development courses at the college level. The aim of the text is to give the student a comprehensive introduction to the principles of child development and at the same time to familiarize him with the concepts he will be working with if he pursues the subject in advanced courses. The text's fifteen chapters integrate the dimensions of physical, cognitive, personality, and social development into each major stage of the child's life—prenatal development and birth, infancy, the preschool period, middle childhood, and adolescence. The text presents all the basic concepts of child development, yet it can be thoroughly covered in one semester.

The book is specifically designed to bridge a large gap left by existing child development texts. Child development is an important course not only in psychology programs but also in other disciplines, including education, nursing, and home economics. Most psychology programs offer it as an intermediate course, requiring a course in introductory psychology as a prerequisite. In the other programs, however, the child development course may be the student's first encounter with psychological subject matter, while the only textbooks available have been those designed for an intermediate course. Thus the encounter may be unnecessarily difficult. This text seeks to remedy this situation by controlling the level of difficulty throughout, by introducing each technical term with a clear, complete definition, and by giving practical concrete applications and illustrations of the theoretical principles. The book constantly strives to promote student understanding by presenting child development as the fascinating subject it is.

ADVANTAGES

After providing a solid foundation in modern psychological and developmental theory and research, the text places less emphasis upon the methods of research than upon practical implications of research findings. Thus, while not ignoring methodology, the book stresses results for what they tell the student about the individual children they meet every day. Students in nursing, education, home economics—even parents and prospective parents—immediately understand the bearing of work in child development upon their own fields and interests.

The organization of the book further supports its pragmatic orientation: each of the five major parts corresponds to the practical need to deal with individual children at their own stage of development. This approach also engages the student and enables him to see how the material relates to him and the world outside the classroom. The student experiences some of the warmth and joy of working with children; "subjects" become real, memorable human beings rather than numbers in a table.

Another advantage of the book is its eclectic approach. The text draws from many disciplines in addition to psychology—biology, ethnology, medical research, sociology, and anthropology are employed—enabling the student to see the developing child in all his dimensions. Although the book focuses on the development of American children, it also utilizes examples from other cultures to point out similarities and differences in the development of children throughout the world.

ORGANIZATION OF THE BOOK

The book is divided into five major parts and an epilogue. Each major part covers the physical, cognitive, personality, and social development of the child in one of the broad stages of growth:

Part 1, Birth and Before, discusses the influence of inheritance and tells what happens to the individual between conception and birth. A section in Chapter 1 describes modern abortion methods. Chapter 2 details the birth process and describes the characteristics of the newborn.

Part 2, Infancy, contains four chapters on the period from birth to about two years of age. Chapter 3 deals with the baby's physical organs and motor abilities and with his feeding and sleeping requirements. Chapter 4 shows how his perception develops and presents findings on infant learning. The baby's cognitive and linguistic progress are examined in Chapter 5, and the social influences that mold his personality are discussed in Chapter 6.

Part 3, The Preschool Years, takes the child from age two to five or six. His physical and perceptual development is described in Chapter 7, his growth in cognition and language in Chapter 8, and his emotional and social relations in Chapter 9.

Part 4, Middle Childhood, follows the developing person through the grade school years to pubescence. Chapter 10 describes his growth in body and personality and discusses some of the personality problems that may arise in this period. Chapter 11 examines cognitive and moral development and presents some cases of the diagnosis and treatment of reading and learning troubles. Chapter 12 treats the child's social relations at home, with peers, and at school.

Part 5, Adolescence, describes the physical changes that occur at puberty and discusses their effects on the individual's personality and social life. Chapter 13 tells how he reaches a mature level of cognitive and moral development; Chapter 14 explores the issues of identity and alienation.

The Epilogue traces the emergence of the study of child development and tells how modern research is done in the field.

OUTSTANDING FEATURES OF THE BOOK

Readability. The purpose of a textbook is to transmit and register ideas and information, to induce the student to see old things in new ways and think about what he sees. To achieve this purpose, the text must be clear, comprehensible, and interesting to the student.

The readability of this book is promoted, first of all, by careful organization: topics follow logically one from the next, and each one is given an accurately descriptive heading. Second, the text is written to present even the most abstract concepts in prose that is alive, energetic, and easy to retain. Numerous and colorful examples have been used to illustrate, emphasize, and clarify ideas. Finally, where important technical terms are introduced, they are printed in boldface type, defined immediately in the text, and defined again in the glossary at the end of the book. The most central terms are featured in typographically emphasized "definers" at the point of their first mention in the text.

Stage Charts. Because the developmental theories of Erikson, Piaget, and Kohlberg flow from one period of development into the next, the student needs to be oriented to the theory as a whole each time he picks up the thread. To enable him to "find his place" in the theory, special charts are inserted at the appropriate points in the text. These charts show the entire theory in outline form and focus on the stage being discussed by means of a concise descriptive text.

Highlight Features. Distributed throughout the text in every chapter are several distinctive features that highlight a topic of particular interest at that point in the discussion. Where the patterns of infant sleep are being discussed in the text, for example, a feature on biological clocks is inserted; where changing views on child rearing are being discussed, a feature reviews some recent baby books. These highlight features capture the reader's interest and indicate the breadth of child development's sources and applications.

Introductions to Major Periods. Each of the five major parts of the book—Birth and Before, Infancy, The Preschool Years, Middle Childhood, and Adolescence—is introduced by a short text that makes the experience of the parent or the child at that stage concrete and palpable. These introductions, excerpts from well-known novels and autobiographies, convey the wholeness of the person and situation—a valuable grounding in everyday reality to balance the necessarily analytic material presented in the chapter texts.

Illustrations. Educators have shown that visual material is gaining importance as a teaching tool in today's classroom. Accordingly, this text uses numerous illustrations, including many that have been executed by a noted medical illustrator. The photographs, many of which were commissioned especially for this book, give the student the conviction that child development is about real children.

Summaries and Further Readings. At the end of every chapter is a summary containing the kernels of the most important ideas presented in the chapter. The summaries, which are organized into a series of short, coherent paragraphs, provide handy reviews for the student. Also following each chapter is a list of further readings that will lead the interested student to more information about specific points that have aroused his curiosity. Each reading is annotated to give the student a fuller idea of the reading's content than he could deduce from its title alone.

Glossary. A glossary at the end of the book provides the student with a child development dictionary in miniature, defining all the important terms used in the text.

Supplements. Teachers will find the accompanying Instructor's Manual helpful in arranging their curricula. The Manual contains suggestions on topics for class discussions, subjects for student term papers, and sample questions for examinations. The accompanying Study Guide contains review questions and independent projects involving student observation and experimentation.

ACKNOWLEDGMENTS

The creation of a book that clearly and accurately describes child development from birth through adolescence is a sizable undertaking. The contributions of many people helped to complete this project. Jim Martin has been a superb editor and has coordinated the details of the book's development. The contributions of colleagues who have read and criticized the drafts of various chapters have been invaluable. Vince Chiappetta and Aphra Katzev reviewed the first chapters, and Shirley Feldman made useful comments on the chapters dealing with adolescence. Deborah Burke and Felicia Lui provided research assistance, and Peter Salwen and Dawn Sangrey made significant editorial contributions. Finally, I wish to thank my husband Brian for his encouragement and patience, our friend Lynette Leahy for helping to mother our child, and our infant daughter Meghan for adding so much joy to our lives.

Part 1
BIRTH
AND
BEFORE

When her mother had left, Martha cupped her hands protectingly over her stomach, and murmured to the creature within that nothing would be allowed to harm it, no pressure would deform it, freedom would be its gift. She, Martha, the free spirit, would protect the creature from her, Martha, the maternal force; the maternal Martha, that enemy, would not be allowed to enter the picture. It was as one independent being to another that Martha spoke; and her hands on her flesh were light, as if even this pressure might be an unforgivable imposition.

To Douglas she forcibly outlined the things they must avoid in this child's future. First, even to suggest that the child might be one sex rather than another might have deplorable results—to be born as it chose was its first inalienable right. Secondly they, the parents, must never try to form its mind in any way whatsoever. Thirdly, it must be sent to a progressive school, where it might survive the processes of education unmutilated—for Martha felt, like so many others, progressive schools were in some way outside society, vacuums of progress, as it were. If this last necessity involved their sending the child at an early age to a country where there *was* a progressive school, then so much the better; for a child without any parents at all clearly had a greater chance of survival as a whole personality.

To all this Douglas easily agreed. The ease with which he did agree disconcerted Martha slightly; for her convictions had after all come from the bitterest schooling, which he had escaped. He did remark at one point that the war might make it difficult to do as they liked about schools, but she waved this aside.

Douglas was very satisfied with Martha. There had been moments in the last few weeks when she had seemed unreasonable, but that had all vanished. She was now gay and amenable, and the whole business of having a baby was being made to appear as a minor incident, to be dealt with as practically as possible. Practicality was the essence of the business, they both agreed; and the completed cradle, a mass of icy white satin and lace, was a frivolous note of contrast to the sternness of their approach. For Martha, who was prepared to spend infinite emotional energy on protecting the child from her emotions, it was a matter of principle that the physical requirements should be as simple as possible. She took one look at the lists of things supposed to be needed for a small baby, and dismissed them with derision, as Alice had already done. By the end of a fortnight after she knew she was pregnant, she already had everything necessary to sustain that child for the first six months of its life. They filled a small basket. The child might be born now, if it chose. Martha even had the feeling that the business was nearly over. For she was once more in the grip of a passionate need to hurry. Impatience to be beyond this milestone was a fever in her. The five months between now and the birth of the child were nothing—five months of ordinary living flashed by so fast they were unnoticeable, therefore it was possible to look forward to the birth as if it were nearly here. Almost, it seemed to Martha that strength of mind alone would be enough to rush her through those months; even her stomach might remain flat, if she were determined enough.

In the meantime, she continued to live exactly as she had done before. She would have scorned to abdicate in any way, and in this Alice agreed with her: the two women, meeting at some dance or drinking party in the evening, congratulated each other on not showing anything; retiring into comfortable

distortion would have seemed a complete surrender to weakness.

Almost at once, however, and it seemed from one day to the next, the wall of Martha's stomach pushed out in a hard curve, behind which moved the anonymous but powerful child, and Martha's fingers, tentatively exploring the lump, received messages that strength of mind alone was not enough. Besides, while Alice and she, the centre of a group of approving and envious people, insisted gaily that no fuss whatsoever was to be made about these children, that they were not to be allowed to change their parents' lives—and in their own interests, at that—it was obvious that both were very jealous of their privacy. Husbands and friends found these women admirably unchanged; during the daytime, they retired, and were irritable at being disturbed.

The moment Douglas had gone to the office, Martha drifted to the divan, where she sat, with listening hands, so extraordinarily compelling was the presence of the stranger in her flesh. Excitement raced through her; urgency to hurry was on her. Yet, after a few minutes, these emotions sank. She had understood that time, once again, was going to play tricks with her. At the end of the day, when Douglas returned from the office, she roused herself with difficulty, dazed. To her it was as if vast stretches of time had passed. Inside her stomach the human race had fought and raised its way through another million years of its history; that other time was claiming her; she understood the increasing vagueness of Alice's eyes; it was becoming an effort to recognize the existence of anything outside this great central drama.

From Doris Lessing, *A Proper Marriage*
© Copyright 1952, 1954, 1964 by Doris Lessing.
Reprinted by permission of Simon & Schuster, Inc.

1 Prenatal Development

For the third time in one day, Aunt Catherine has had to break up a fight. Erik and Elva, supposedly on their best behavior while staying at her house, have been bickering almost constantly. "They get it from their father," Grandma says. Their mother, Grandma's child, was always sweet and compliant.

"No, it's the way they're being brought up," Aunt Catherine says. "There's no discipline in that house."

What is it that makes Erik and Elva the way they are? What makes them tall for their age, addicted to strawberry ice cream, good in spelling, impossible to put to bed, clumsy with dishes, and rough with the cat? Did they inherit these characteristics in their genes, as Grandma thinks (the bad ones of course coming from their father), or is Aunt Catherine right, and everything the result of what they have been fed, permitted, and taught?

Grandma and Aunt Catherine can argue the matter all afternoon, as philosophers and scientists have argued it since the beginning of history. The debate, usually titled "Nature versus Nurture," continues today, and not just in living rooms but in academic journals as well.

Scientists have, however, been able to clarify some of the terms of the debate. They have discovered that a person's inheritance is not "in the blood," as people used to say, but in every cell of his body. Each cell contains a nucleus, and each nucleus has a set of chromosomes bearing thousands of genes that make up the person's genetic potential. No two people ever born have quite the same combination of genes, except identical twins.

A person gets his unique combination of genes at the moment he is conceived, and nothing will ever change it. If he lives to be a hundred years old, he will die with exactly the same combination. But environment starts to influence his development the very next moment *after* conception and will continue to do so all the rest of his life.

When a baby is born, she has already been subject to environmental influences for nine months. Science has reliably identified some of the characteristics that are primarily the result of her genetic makeup and some that have been decisively influenced by her environment; and there are many more characteristics that cannot be solely attributed to either influence. In any case, whenever it is known that the baby was born with a particular characteristic, even if it will not become apparent until later, it is called a **congenital** characteristic. If the baby is born blind, for example, her blindness is called a congenital defect, but it may be due to syphilis in the mother, which affects the developing baby in her womb, or it may be due to a genetic factor.

A **gene** is the hereditary material that governs one trait, and indeed some traits, such as eye color and blood type, seem to be determined almost entirely by one gene. Environment has little effect on these traits. Many other traits, however, are affected not only by the environment of the organism but by the combined influence of several genes. Thus, most genes operate in the environment of all the other genes in the individual's makeup. But taking this genetic pattern as an immensely complex whole, it can be said that heredity endows the person at conception with the potentiality to develop in a certain direction. Without this potentiality no development can take place, not even in the most favorable environment.

The genetic pattern, however, is no more than a potentiality. In a completely adverse environment it will disintegrate because the cells containing it will die, and in an environment that is unfavorable in certain ways it will fall short of its full development in corresponding ways. Thus, both a sound genetic pattern and a favorable environment are necessary for healthy development. Both affect the individual in so many ways that it is impossible except in a few cases to estimate which factor has had the greater influence.

GENETIC INFLUENCES

Half of a person's genetic material comes from his father and half from his mother. These two halves come together to form a unique combination of genetic potentialities when the sperm fertilizes the egg. In the nucleus of the fertilized egg, or **zygote**, are the materials that bear the pattern for a new person, one who is different from his parents and yet like them. Exactly what are these materials?

ZYGOTE

The first cell in which the father's genes are joined with the mother's is called the **zygote.** It takes its name from the Greek expression for "yoked" or "joined together."

Outwardly the zygote still looks like an unfertilized egg. The egg is so much larger than the sperm that it can absorb the sperm without showing it. Inside, however, the unfertilized egg has only twenty-three chromosomes, whereas the zygote has forty-six—the twenty-three that were in the egg originally and the additional twenty-three contributed by the father.

Less than two days after the sperm unites with the egg, the zygote divides into two cells. Then these two cells each divide again, and the process of division goes on, forming in nine months a new human being.

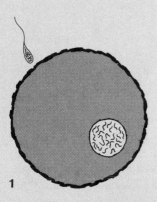

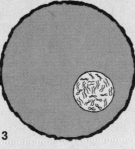

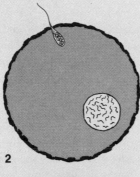

1 The unfertilized egg has twenty-three chromosomes.

2 The sperm brings twenty-three chromosomes from the father.

3 The zygote has forty-six chromosomes.

Monozygotic twins are genetically identical.

Fraternal twins can be of different sexes and have eyes of different colors.

Every individual carries two genes for the same trait, one from his father and one from his mother. Sometimes both genes give the same direction for the determination of the trait, and in this case the individual is said to be **homozygous** for that trait. If the trait in question is eye color, for example, and both of an individual's eye-color genes call for blue eyes, then the individual is homozygous for eye color. He is equally homozygous if both his genes call for brown eyes.

When one of his genes calls for brown eyes and the other for blue eyes, the individual is said to be **heterozygous** for eye color. Such an individual will have brown eyes because the gene for brown eyes is dominant over the gene for blue eyes. While this is usually (but not always) true of eye color, there are some traits in which neither gene is dominant.

In a few rare cases the cells dividing from the zygote become separated into two masses and develop into two individuals. These two individuals are called identical twins, or **monozygotic twins.** Fraternal twins, on the other hand, develop from two different zygotes—two eggs each fertilized by a different sperm.

Monozygotic twins are also closer than fraternal twins throughout the prenatal period. They usually develop together in one amniotic sac, both bathed by the same amniotic fluid, whereas fraternal twins usually have separate amniotic sacs.

Except for monozygotic twins, it is impossible for any two people to have exactly the same heredity. The study of monozygotic twins is important, therefore, in estimating the influence of heredity relative to that of upbringing.

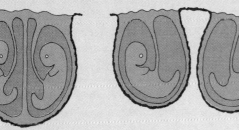

Mechanisms of Heredity

All life is based on complex organic molecules known as proteins. Proteins of one sort or another not only make up much of the substance of our body tissues—blood, skin, nerves, and muscles—but it is the interaction among proteins of different sorts that carry on the vital processes of living organisms. The proteins themselves are made up of simpler compounds called amino acids. There are only about twenty amino acids involved in the structure of most proteins; like the letters of the alphabet, the amino acids are few in number but are capable of endless recombination, so the number of proteins they can make is astronomical. The precise placement and combination of amino acids in a protein determine its structure and function in the body.

What does this have to do with heredity? A baby is conceived when a sperm (the male cell) fuses with an egg (the female cell) in the fallopian tube of the mother. There fertilization takes place: the nucleus of the sperm is engulfed by the egg, and the nuclei of the two germ cells are combined to become the nucleus of the zygote, the first cell of the new organism.

The most important material in that nucleus is a substance called deoxyribonucleic acid, or DNA (Figure 1.1). The DNA in the nucleus of a fertilized egg constitutes the genetic "blueprint" for a new, unique individual. How is this possible? The DNA is a relatively simple molecule—much simpler, for example, than most proteins. It is made up of a sugar, phosphates, and only four other components. But the arrangement of these four components forms a kind of code that provides the pattern for the development of the fertilized egg by determining the placement of amino acids in a protein.

Technically, therefore, it is not quite correct to speak of inheriting blue eyes or large feet. What we inherit is a set of biochemical instructions. If all goes well and those instructions are carried out through the amino acids in body-building proteins, we may indeed have blue eyes or large feet.

For all their simplicity, the DNA molecules are numerous and can act as a pattern for the formation of many proteins. The part of the molecule that results in the formation of a single trait in the developing person is called a gene. Most of a person's traits, however, are influenced by several genes. Thus, our knowledge of inherited characteristics, except in a few clear-cut cases, is extremely limited and tentative. This is especially true of the inheritance of such characteristics as intelligence and personality.

Nevertheless, for most purposes we are justified in thinking of a gene as a segment of a DNA molecule that directs the development of a single trait. It can be thought of as a location on the DNA molecule, like a dot on a map. When we speak of the gene for eye color, we are referring to the part of a DNA molecule that directs the synthesis of proteins affecting eye color.

The DNA molecules in our bodies are on rodlike structures called chromosomes in the nucleus of each cell. Although we have thousands of traits, our cells normally contain only twenty-three pairs of chromosomes with one chromosome

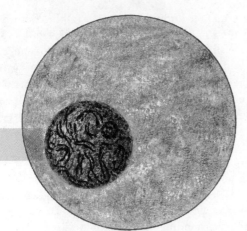

Figure 1.1. At left, a human cell. The dark mass within the cell is the nucleus in which are contained 46 chromosomes. Below, an enlargement of some chromosomes. They contain a basic chemical of heredity known as deoxyribonucleic acid, or DNA.

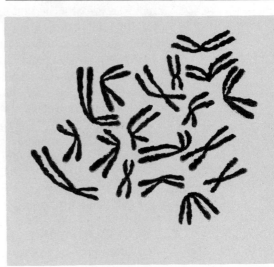

At left, a portion of a DNA molecule. (The illustration is theoretical since DNA has not been observed even through the most powerful microscope.) At each level of this spiral are pairs of chemicals. Their particular arrangement throughout the molecule determines the kind of protein that will be formed.

in each pair coming from the mother and one from the father. Both chromosomes in a pair contain factors for the same traits, so there are two factors for each trait. But the two factors may have different effects: one blood-type gene, for example, might be for type A blood and the other for type O. These differing forms of any given gene, which give different instructions for the form a characteristic should take, are known as the **alleles** of that gene. The tremendous number of possible combinations of alleles means that every human being is conceived with a unique genetic endowment.

Cell division

Our body cells constantly divide and produce new cells in order to maintain growth and good health. This process of cell division is known as **mitosis**. It continues throughout our lives as new cells emerge to replace old ones that wear out and are absorbed into the surrounding tissues and fluids. Cell division occurs most rapidly when a child grows and, later in life, when the body is recovering from an injury, such as when new skin is formed to heal a cut.

Cell division begins when the chromosomes replicate to form a second set of chromosomes exactly like the original. Then this set separates from the original, is surrounded by a membrane, and becomes the nucleus of a new cell. The new cell produced through mitosis has the same number of chromosome pairs as the parent cell.

Human sperm and egg cells are produced by a slightly different process of cell division known as **meiosis,** or reduction division. Meiosis, like mitosis, begins with the replication of the original chromosomes. But the ensuing cell divisions result in four cells instead of two. Each new cell has only half the number of chromosomes found in the parent cell. In this way, the sperm cell and the egg cell end up with twenty-three *single* chromosomes instead of twenty-three *pairs* of chromosomes. This is important because, if the sperm cell and the egg cell each carried twenty-three chromosome pairs, the zygote resulting from their union would have forty-six chromosome pairs instead of the normal twenty-three and probably would not live.

Gene dominance

What happens when the two alleles an individual receives from his mother and father contain differing instructions for the development of the characteristic they govern? In many cases the answer to this question lies in the principle of gene dominance and gene recessiveness.

One example of this principle is found in eye color. The allele that instructs the body to produce pigment for the iris (the only pigment possible being brown) is sometimes paired in the zygote with an allele for unpigmented irises (which look blue). The baby will be born with pigmented eyes because the effect of his allele for unpigmented eyes will be suppressed by the presence of the allele for pigmentation. Thus, the brown allele is called dominant and the blue recessive. Later, when this individual grows and his own germ cells are formed, the chromosome

13

Figure 1.2. Alleles for eye color on a pair of chromosomes. The dominant allele (B) is paired here with the recessive allele (b); the individual will have brown eyes. If the alleles were BB, the individual would also have brown eyes. Only if the alleles were bb would he have blue eyes.

pairs will separate in meiosis and 50 percent of the germ cells will carry the recessive gene. Figure 1.3 illustrates this case and every other possible combination for blue eyes and brown eyes. The figure shows, for example, how it happens that some mixed couples (one parent with brown eyes and one with blue) have no children with blue eyes while other mixed couples have as many blue-eyed children as brown-eyed ones.

Complete dominance, however, is rather rare among inherited traits. More often the effects of both alleles appear in the individual. This condition is referred to as codominance or incomplete dominance. Sometimes an individual will show the effect of one allele more than the other, but neither will be completely dominant. Incomplete dominance is characteristic of many hereditary diseases in man, including sickle-cell anemia, Parkinson's disease, diabetes, and gout.

Some inherited traits are polygenic; many genes are involved in the formation of the trait, rather than only one pair. Our chins and teeth are examples of features

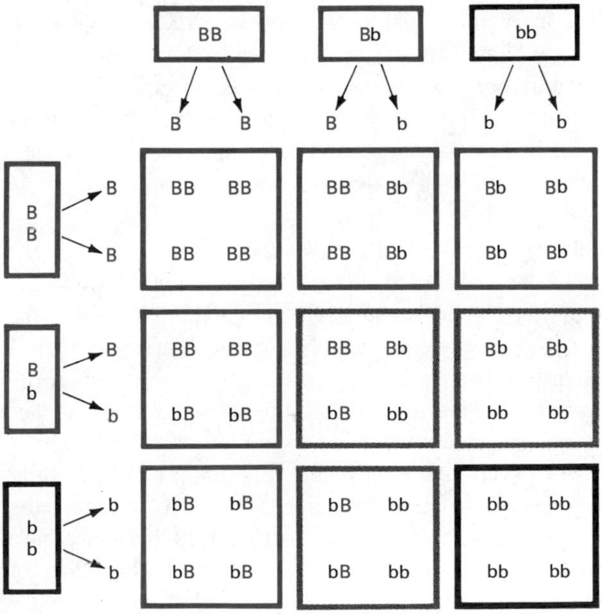

	BB		Bb		bb	
	B	B	B	b	b	b
B B → B, B	BB	BB	BB	Bb	Bb	Bb
	BB	BB	BB	Bb	Bb	Bb
B b → B, b	BB	BB	BB	Bb	Bb	Bb
	bB	bB	bB	bb	bb	bb
b b → b, b	bB	bB	bB	bb	bb	bb
	bB	bB	bB	bb	bb	bb

Figure 1.3. Inheritance of eye color. B is the allele for brown eyes; b is the allele for blue. Take a parent of any of the three possible combinations of alleles—BB, Bb, or bb—cross him with another parent of the same or different combination, and find the combinations their off-spring will have. Note that the parents' alleles divide in meiosis before mating, so the number of possible combinations in the offspring is not 1 × 1 but 2 × 2.

whose development is affected by several genes. Because many of our traits are polygenic, it may not be easy to claim that a child has "his mother's nose" or "his father's eyes." The genetic origins of these traits may be far more complex.

Sex determination

We have seen how such physical traits as eye coloring are passed on through genes from parents to children. But what determines whether a child is female or male? The answer, again, depends on the laws of inheritance, but in this case the mechanism involved is relatively simple: for human beings, sex is determined by a single pair of sex chromosomes. One of these is called the X chromosome, and the other, which is usually found only in males, is a smaller one called the Y chromosome.

At conception, an egg cell from the mother is fertilized by a sperm cell from the father. All egg cells and some sperm cells—about half of them—carry the X chromosome. The other sperm cells carry the Y chromosome. When a sperm cell carrying an X chromosome unites with an egg cell, the zygote has the combination of XX because all eggs carry the X chromosome. An XX zygote will normally develop into a female baby. When a sperm cell carrying the Y chromosome unites with an egg, the resulting zygote has the combination of XY and will normally develop into a male.

The general rule, then, is for all zygotes to be either XX females or XY males. But there are exceptions to this rule: they usually originate in some accident during meiosis which causes the egg or sperm to carry an abnormal number of X or Y chromosomes. The abnormality will then be transmitted to the fertilized egg. Thus, it has been found that females can, in rare instances, have an XXX, XXXX, or some other combination; males can have an XXY, XYY, or other combination. All of these are abnormalities, and persons having them will often suffer from confusion of gender, mental retardation, physiological defects, or sterility. One of these combinations, the XYY (with a double dose of the male sex chromosome), has been tentatively linked to unusually aggressive behavior. Fortunately, these abnormalities are extremely rare.

The X chromosome sometimes carries what are called sex-linked recessive traits. Some well-known examples are red–green color blindness, night blindness, muscular dystrophy, and hemophilia. Experiments have shown that the genes for these conditions appear only on the X chromosome. Since the female (XX) has two X chromosomes, she will express these recessive traits only if she carries the genes on *both* of her X chromosomes. This does not happen except in very rare instances; thus, women usually do not suffer from sex-linked diseases like hemophilia. But they may serve as carriers for such conditions. The male (XY) has only one X chromosome, which he receives from his mother. If that X chromosome carries a sex-linked recessive gene, the male will develop that trait because there are no corresponding genes on his Y chromosome that could mask the effect of the recessive gene on the X chromosome.

Mutations

Under normal circumstances, our genes are exact duplicates of the ones we received from our parents. But it is possible for changes to occur in our genetic material, and these changes may alter our physical structure, our biochemistry, even our behavior. Such alterations, known as **mutations**, are rare, and of those that do occur, the majority cause only invisible and insignificant changes. Some of them, however, have a harmful, even lethal effect.

Some mutations occur spontaneously. Others result from radiation from natural sources, such as ultraviolet rays in sunlight. But scientific research has established that other factors can increase the rate at which mutations occur. The survivors of the bombing of Hiroshima and Nagasaki suffered from an abnormally high number of mutations from radioactivity. Chemical dyes, antibiotics, X rays, and food preservatives are also suspected of inducing mutations. Many scientists are currently studying the effects of such drugs as LSD (lysergic acid diethylamide) and marijuana in causing mutations, but the results so far have been inconclusive.

Inherited Characteristics

We have already spoken of characteristics such as color blindness and blood type as inherited traits. But it is not really traits that a person inherits, only genes; these genes give him the potential to develop particular traits under certain environmental conditions. Remembering that heredity never acts alone but is always interacting with the environment, we can examine some of the cases in which heredity is known to have a decisive effect on the individual's development.

Physical features

The genes that a person inherits from her parents have a great influence on her physical appearance. Her eyes, hair, and skin coloring, her height and bone structure—all are results of the hereditary process. In some cases, the instructions contained in the person's genes may be counteracted by the effects of disease, nutrition, or other environmental factors. But normally the genetic influence predominates.

A classic study (Kallman and Sander, 1949) of monozygotic (identical) twins, who are identical in their genetic makeup, provided some striking examples of the inheritance of physical features. Although all the persons included in the study were over sixty years of age, each one was remarkably similar to his or her twin. The twins tended to show the same degree of graying of hair, the same kinds of eye and tooth changes, and the same extent of enfeeblement. Often they died within weeks of each other. In the most extraordinary case recorded, twin sisters became blind and deaf in the same month and died only five days apart.

Of course, some traits seem more affected by hereditary factors and others more by environmental conditions. Another study (Newmann, Freeman, and Holzinger, 1937) found that the height of monozygotic twins remained very close whether they were brought up together or separately. On the other hand, the weight of monozygotic twins brought up separately differed more than the weight of those who grew up in the same environment. Evidently weight is more easily affected by environmental factors than height.

However, even height can be influenced by nonhereditary conditions. Children of immigrants to the United States are, on the average, taller than their parents. Perhaps they have benefited from better diets, or from the prohibition of child labor. Certainly such a marked change in a whole group of people must have been the result of improved environmental conditions rather than of genetic change.

Defects

Sometimes the hereditary process passes along the potential for serious diseases or metabolic defects. Diabetes, glaucoma, hemophilia, and certain forms of muscular dystrophy can all be inherited. In many of these disorders, the action of the genes causes a failure in the body's production of some necessary enzyme. Without the proper amount or form of this enzyme, the metabolic process is disrupted; harmful substances build up in the blood and tissues and interfere with the normal process of growth and development.

One hereditary defect that has been in the news in recent years is sickle-cell anemia. The sickle-cell trait is caused by the inheritance of a mutant form of the normal gene. The mutant gene causes one wrong amino acid to be placed among the 300-odd amino acid molecules that make up hemoglobin, the material in red blood cells that enables them to transport oxygen throughout the body. Red blood cells with this abnormal hemoglobin cannot function properly, but because the mutant gene is recessive, an individual who has received a mutant allele from one parent and a normal allele from the other parent may enjoy nearly normal health. Only a clinical examination of his red blood cells will reveal some abnormal cells. When both of a person's alleles are the mutant type, however, he will develop severe sickle-cell anemia during childhood because none of his hemoglobin will be normal, and he will usually die of anemia before adolescence.

Geneticists first became interested in this disease when it became known that most of the Americans that it victimizes are black. After various investigations, it became clear that sickle-cell anemia is most prevalent in areas of the world where falciparum malaria abounds, such as central Africa, Sicily, southern Italy, and certain parts of Asia.

Further research suggested that the mutant gene has another effect: individuals with one mutant and one normal allele apparently have greater resistance to malarial fevers than individuals who do not carry the mutant gene at all. For the population of regions in which falciparum malaria is widespread, the mutant gene's protection against malaria outweighs the possible damage of the abnormal hemoglobin. This is not true, however, in the United States, where malaria is not a serious threat.

An effective treatment for sickle-cell anemia is still being sought, but many other genetic diseases can be treated with drugs or by modifying the patient's diet. Diabetics, for example, can enjoy good health by taking insulin and carefully avoiding certain foods.

One of the newer methods of coping with genetic diseases is genetic counseling. Before a couple decides to have children, they can have their genealogy studied in order to learn whether they carry genes that are likely to transmit defects to their offspring. For example, a woman who knows that congenital blindness has occurred in her family might be afraid to bear children, but with genetic counseling she could learn whether she too is likely to carry the gene that leads to this defect. Through such counseling, the fears of some prospective parents could be eased while others might learn that having children would be unwise.

Mental disorders

There are many kinds of mental disorders that can be inherited through the genes. Some fall under the general description of brain damage, which can result when the body, following genetic instructions, does not produce enzymes that the brain needs for proper functioning. These injuries are sometimes minimal, but sometimes they are fatal. They may be readily apparent, as with hemiplegia, in which one side of the body is paralyzed; or they may be disguised for a while, as with certain learning disorders that do not become apparent until the child reaches school age.

Some types of cerebral palsy can also be inherited. This is a disorder in which some of the child's muscles cannot be controlled by his brain. They may be spastic or rigid, but they will not respond to the normal messages sent by the brain.

Another well-known form of retardation is Down's Syndrome (mongolism). This defect, whose symptoms include very low mentality, can be found in about one of every 500 babies born in the United States; it occurs most frequently in the children of very young mothers or mothers over forty years of age. It is not caused by a mutant gene, but by the failure of the paired chromosomes to separate properly when an egg or sperm is formed. It is thus similar in origin to the sexual abnormalities discussed earlier. A victim of Down's Syndrome can be recognized by an unusual skin fold in the corner of the eyes, a broad nose, and a protruding tongue. The average life of the child is ten years.

Genetic factors may also contribute to diseases that we classify as mental illnesses. Often the causes of such mental disorders are unclear, and scientific authorities differ as to whether they result from hereditary or environmental factors. This is especially true in the case of schizophrenia, perhaps the most commonly diagnosed mental illness in the United States. Some studies of monozygotic twins (Kallman, 1938) point to a strong hereditary factor associated with schizophrenia, but other research links the illness to stresses in family life and unusual tendencies in the nervous system.

Personality

It is difficult to measure precisely the effects of heredity on an individual's personality. Certain environmental factors—including nutrition and the dynamics of family life—can have an obvious effect on personality, but the influence of heredity can also be demonstrated.

Figure 1.4. Monozygotic twins. Heredity obviously accounts for many similarities in monozygotic twins. To judge from their expressions, however, these twins do not have identical personalities.

An important aid in determining the effects of genetic inheritance on personality is the study of twins. In some cases, monozygotic twins brought up separately show remarkable similarities in personality and behavior. One study (Rosanoff, Handy, and Plesset, 1937) cites a pair of twin girls who were adopted separately during infancy. Both were feeble-minded and fell into patterns of sexual promiscuity, leading to illegitimate pregnancies. Both were eventually admitted to the same institution at the age of twenty, under different surnames. Only later did anyone realize that they were twin sisters.

In an interesting account published recently (Lindeman, 1969), the researcher found striking similarities between twins separated shortly after birth and brought up in very different circumstances. While Tony had the security of a large, warm, Italian Catholic family, Roger was moved from one foster home to another and finally ended up living with relatives of his Jewish father. Yet at age twenty-four, when the brothers discovered each other by chance, they showed amazing similarities, from their attitudes toward religion and work to such minor details as the way they held a cigarette or coffee cup. One had volunteered for military service just eight days before the other.

Emotional disorders may also be transmitted through genetic inheritance. One study of twin pairs (Eysenck, 1964) has shown that in adult criminal behavior and alcoholism, monozygotic twins are twice as likely to follow similar patterns as are fraternal twins. Other research has indicated that monozygotic twins brought up separately will often have similar tendencies toward crime and schizophrenia.

These twin studies suggest that the effects of heredity on personality must be significant. Yet there are also cases of monozygotic twins who show marked differences in their behavior and personality traits. Often this can be tied to dissimilarity in home background, as in the case of Berta and Herta. Berta, brought up by an adoptive mother in an affluent and overprotective home, was a quiet, shy girl. Herta, on the other hand, grew up in the home of her psychopathic father and soon was getting into trouble and providing other evidence of an unstable personality.

Even when monozygotic twins are brought up together, they may develop personality differences. Frequently, one twin becomes physically dominant during childhood and begins to assume a leadership role more easily. This pattern took place in the lives of Doreen and Eileen. At birth, Doreen weighed over six pounds, whereas Eileen weighed only a little more than four. During childhood Eileen came to rely heavily on her larger twin sister and fell into a role of being the "sweet" twin. By the time they were grown, Doreen had become very active and was involved in volunteer teaching and horseback riding. Eileen was much more inhibited, and had no boyfriends until after Doreen had married (Shields, 1962).

Intelligence

The study of the influence of heredity on intelligence is both complex and controversial. In part, this is because there is no commonly accepted definition of intelligence. Does intelligence mean the ability to acquire knowledge, the capacity to think creatively, an aptitude for abstract and intellectual reasoning, or the ability to adjust to changing conditions? Is a gifted poet intelligent, even if she cannot solve simple mathematical problems? Is the person with a great deal of "common sense" more intelligent than a highly educated but somewhat naive research chemist?

There are no simple answers to such questions, but intelligence tests have nonetheless been devised and administered to millions of people. The results show a correspondence between heredity and the ability to perform in IQ tests. One classic example (Muller, 1925) is the case of Jessie and Bessie. These twins were separated at the age of two weeks and did not meet again until they were eighteen. Although they each grew up in ranching and mining communities, Jessie's home environment was much more affluent. She was able to complete high school, whereas Bessie was forced to move from place to place with her less affluent family and finished only four years of schooling. Despite these differences in family background, when they took standard intelligence tests at age thirty, the scores of the two twins differed by only two points. Interestingly, it was Bessie, the relatively uneducated sister, who had the higher score.

Other classic studies have substantiated these conclusions. Perhaps the most striking finding (Newmann, Freeman, and Holzinger, 1937) is that monozygotic twins brought up in different homes scored more nearly the same on intelligence tests than did fraternal twins who grew up together.

In the light of such evidence, it cannot be denied that heredity has a strong influence on the type of intelligence measured. Some investigators have proceeded to estimate, primarily on the grounds of twin studies, just how much heredity contributes to a person's intelligence and how much is contributed by the environment. The educator Arthur Jensen put the figures at 80 percent for heredity and 20 percent for environment. This estimate led him to argue that if the aim of compensatory educational programs is to boost children's IQ scores, they are futile (Jensen, 1969).

Partly because this conclusion invites racist interpretations, it was hotly debated in public as well as academic arenas. One of the most telling replies came from the psychologist Urie Bronfenbrenner (1972), who attacked Jensen's estimate that the influences on a person's intelligence are 80 percent genetic. Bronfenbrenner found that the twin studies used by Jensen did not justify any estimate at all because they involved too many uncontrolled factors. He pointed out, for example, that when monozygotic twins are separated and brought up in different homes, the homes are often quite similar in cultural environment. Other investigators (Newmann, Freeman, and Holzinger, 1937) had previously speculated that intelligence was only 50 percent or less determined by heredity, and a later analysis (Fehr, 1969) arrived at about the same figure.

Jensen's argument that compensatory education can never make people much smarter because intelligence is determined mainly by heredity has been opposed by using Jensen's own methods to arrive at the estimate that a person's height is 90 percent genetically determined (Gage, 1972). If this had been known in 1800, the conclusion would have been that no amount of improvement in health and nutrition would ever make people much taller—and yet the average height of people in Western countries has increased by several inches since then.

STAGES OF GESTATION

The prenatal phase of human life lasts an average of 266 days. During these nine months, the zygote divides into as many as 200 billion cells. The fetus grows within the mother's uterus until it is strong enough to sustain life outside of her womb.

There are three principal stages of gestation. The first, the **preimplantation period**, lasts from ten to fourteen days. During this period, all cells are exact replicas of the zygote. When the tiny cell mass, or blastocyst, has implanted itself in the wall of the uterus, the **period of the embryo** begins. Differentiated tissues and important body systems—such as the circulatory and digestive systems—begin to develop. The embryo stage lasts about six weeks, usually until the end of the eighth week of pregnancy. Then the **period of the fetus** begins. During the thirty weeks of the fetal stage, all the individual body systems develop toward readiness for birth, and the fetus as a whole grows dramatically in size.

Preimplantation period

Cell division begins on the first day after conception. While the zygote is splitting into new cells, it moves through the mother's fallopian tubes toward the uterus (Figure 1.5). The embryo is nourished at this time by the yolk of the ovum.

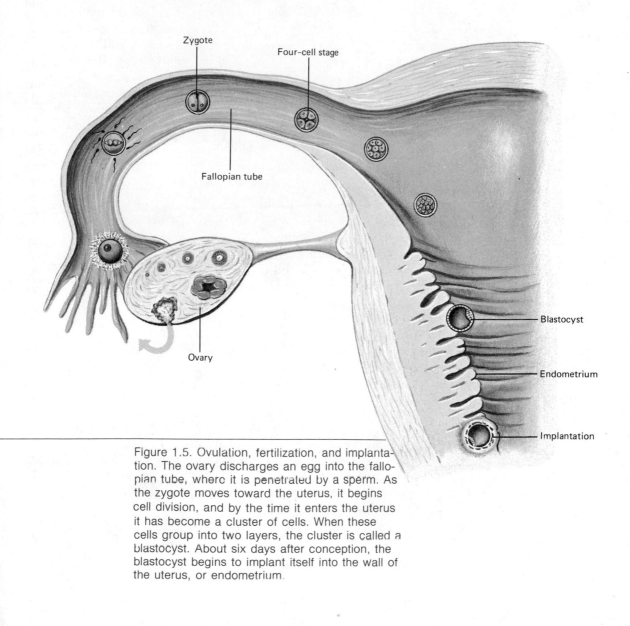

Figure 1.5. Ovulation, fertilization, and implantation. The ovary discharges an egg into the fallopian tube, where it is penetrated by a sperm. As the zygote moves toward the uterus, it begins cell division, and by the time it enters the uterus it has become a cluster of cells. When these cells group into two layers, the cluster is called a blastocyst. About six days after conception, the blastocyst begins to implant itself into the wall of the uterus, or endometrium.

By the time the embryo arrives at the uterus, it may contain as many as thirty-two cells. The process known as differentiation is about to begin, when the cells of the embryo will separate into groups according to their future roles. Two distinct layers of cells are formed as the embryo reaches what is called the blastocyst stage. The outer layer eventually forms the housing and life-support systems for the fetus, including the placenta, the umbilical cord, and the amniotic sac. The inner layer of the blastocyst will become the baby. At this point the blastocyst is a hollow ball, with many of its cells massed at one end.

The blastocyst floats for some time in the uterus. By about the sixth day after conception, it begins to implant itself in the uterine wall. This is a critical point in gestation, for if the blastocyst does not implant itself properly and at the correct time, the cell mass will die before it can reach the embryo stage. But if all goes well, the blastocyst will be firmly embedded about two weeks after conception.

It may be that the intrauterine device, or IUD, has its contraceptive effect at this point. Exactly how the IUD prevents conception is not known, but if it stimulates chemical or mechanical reactions in the uterus aimed at ejecting the foreign body, the same reactions could keep the blastocyst from becoming implanted.

Period of the embryo

During this forty-six day period, the embryo grows to a length of over one inch. By the end of the embryo stage, many body systems will be in operation, and the embryo will show the beginnings of a human appearance.

The embryo takes nourishment and oxygen and releases waste products, such as carbon dioxide, through the **umbilical cord,** which links the embryo with the placenta. The umbilical cord contains three blood vessels so that the embryo's blood can circulate to and from the placenta.

The **placenta,** which eventually grows to a size of six to eight inches long and more than one inch thick, is a disk-shaped mass of tissue that serves as a two-way filter between the bloodstreams of the mother and the embryo. Here the embryo deposits its waste products and receives oxygen, amino acids, sugar, fats, and minerals from the mother's bloodstream, but the cells of the placenta prevent any actual mixing of the embryo's blood with the mother's.

The same time that the embryo is being nourished, the **amniotic sac** is developing into a protective chamber. By the end of the eighth week, this sac completely surrounds the embryo. The watery fluid inside keeps the embryo from being jostled by any sudden movements of the mother. The amniotic sac also keeps the embryo at a constant temperature.

During the embryonic period, three layers of cells are differentiated. The outer layer, or ectoderm, develops into sensory cells, skin, and the nervous system. The middle layer, or mesoderm, becomes the excretory system, muscles, and blood. The inner layer of the embryo, the endoderm, forms the digestive system, lungs, and thyroid gland.

By the end of the third week in development, the embryo's heart is beating,

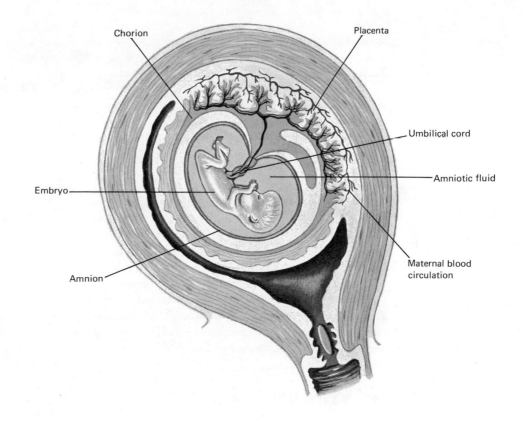

Figure 1.6. Embryo. The umbilical cord links the embryo with the placenta. The mother's blood and the baby's blood, though kept separate by the placenta, exchange oxygen, nutrients, and wastes through it. The fluid in the amniotic sac protects the embryo from shocks and helps to regulate its temperature.

and its nervous system is forming rapidly. After the fourth week, the legs are curled, and the eyes have appeared as dark circles. During the fifth and sixth weeks, arms and legs can be seen. After eight weeks, all of the major body organs are present. The liver is making blood cells and the kidneys are removing waste products. The mouth, nose, eyes, and head are clear and distinct. The head is roughly half the body size at this time. Fingers and toes are blunt, and ribs show under the skin.

The eight-week time span of embryonic development is a particularly vulnerable period in human growth. The embryo can very easily be affected by chemicals,

drugs, hormones, or viruses in the mother's system. Rubella (German measles) is a common danger during this stage of pregnancy.

Period of the fetus

The fetal stage begins in the ninth week of pregnancy and continues until the birth of the baby, usually about thirty weeks later.

The mother first feels the fetus move in the third and fourth months of pregnancy. It can open and close its mouth, swallow, and make certain head movements. It may even suck its thumb. The fastest growth period for the fetus is the fourth month, when it almost doubles in length, reaching six inches from crown to rump. Limbs become sensitive to touch, and a heartbeat can be heard with a stethoscope.

After five months, the skin of the fetus is fully developed. Hair, nails, and sweat glands are apparent. The fetus sleeps and wakes. In the sixth month, the eyelids are open, and the fetus can open and close its eyes. It may now weigh as much as twenty-four ounces. During the seventh month, the eyes can distinguish light from dark. The brain has more control over body systems than before, and an infant born prematurely at this time has a fair chance of survival. In the last two months the fetus gains about eight ounces per week.

In recent years, scientists have done extensive research on fetal development. The goal of these efforts is to prevent deformities and save the lives of babies endangered by prenatal problems. It may someday be possible to perform surgery and give blood transfusions to babies in the uterus.

PRENATAL ENVIRONMENTAL INFLUENCES

Environment begins to influence the individual as soon as he or she is conceived. As the zygote undergoes mitosis, the new cells become part of their own environment, and through their particular physical and chemical influence, they guide and control the development of further new cells. Different genes are activated or suppressed in each cell, so that while one group of cells is developing into brain tissue, another is giving rise to the heart, another to the lungs, and another to the skeletal system. Meanwhile, the lump of cells is surrounded by the larger environment of the mother's uterus, and this environment is surrounded by the mother and the world she lives in.

Securely implanted in the wall of the uterus, the embryo is bathed in amniotic fluid, kept at a constant temperature, and protected from physical shock. The uterine environment is remarkably effective in protecting and nourishing the growing child. The great majority of women have uncomplicated pregnancies and give birth to healthy babies.

For many years, in fact, it was believed that the baby in the uterus was completely insulated from all outside influences, but now we know that is not entirely true. Environmental influences ranging from radioactivity and stress in the outside world to drugs, hormones, and viruses in the mother's bloodstream can affect prenatal development. Even though the placenta acts as a filter, keeping the blood of the mother and the fetus from mixing, a number of potentially dangerous substances can pass through it. And, of course, if the mother's blood lacks the nutrients required by the growing fetus, it may not develop fully.

Lack of proper nourishment or the introduction of harmful substances will affect the fetus in different ways at different stages of prenatal development. This

Figure 1.7. The fetal stage. When the circulatory, muscular, and nervous systems and the major physical structures of the body are present in their rudimental form, the embryo enters the fetal stage. In the third month, the fetus is able to open and close its mouth and swallow. After the fifth month, hair, nails, and sweat glands are apparent, the fetus sleeps and wakes. By the seventh month, the eyes can distinguish light from dark; the fetus is sufficiently developed to have a 50 percent chance of surviving birth.

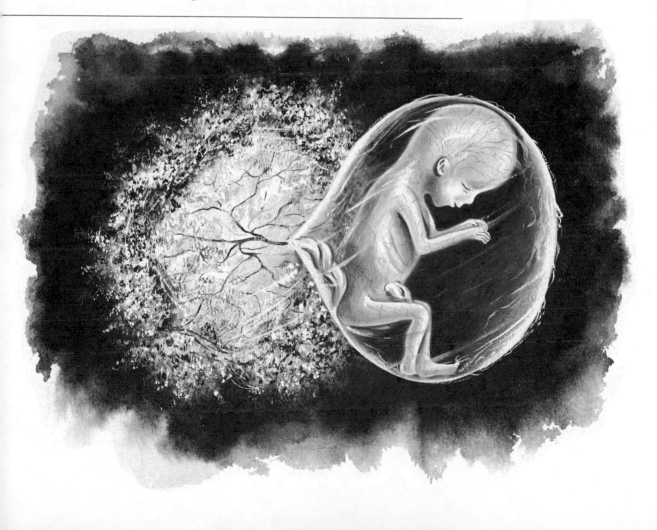

is because the body organs and parts develop at different speeds but through definite phases. First they go through a phase of rapid multiplication in the number of cells. Then there is an increase in both the number of cells and in cell size. In the third and final phase of development, cell size continues to increase rapidly but cell division slows down.

The second phase, when a body part or organ system is growing most rapidly, both in cell number and size, is known as the **critical period** of development for that part or system. If an environmental factor, such as a chemical or virus, interferes with growth during the critical period, development will be permanently affected. The organ does not have another chance to develop, as the third phase begins at a preset time, even if the developmental potential has not all been achieved.

The effect of environmental influences will vary, therefore, in accordance with the stage of prenatal development in which the environmental factor is encountered. During the first three months of pregnancy, tissues and important body systems are beginning to develop in the embryo. Adverse influences during this period will affect the basic structure and form of the body. Physical development can be arrested and irreparable malformation may occur. For example, women who took the drug thalidomide during the first three months of pregnancy gave birth to many children with deformed limbs and other serious defects, but it did not appear to have adverse effects when it was taken toward the end of pregnancy.

Thus, congenital defects due to prenatal environmental factors, like those due to genetic factors, range from relatively minor problems, such as slightly retarded growth, to such major ones as severe mental retardation or physical deformity.

Teratogens

When it was discovered that the development of the unborn can be affected by many outside influences, scientists went to work to find out exactly how. The scientific study of congenital abnormalities caused by prenatal environmental influences is known as **teratology,** and the environmental agents that produce abnormalities in the developing fetus are called **teratogens**. A teratogenic agent may be a chemical such as a drug or hormone, a virus or other organism, or radiation. The effects of some teratogens, particularly newly developed drugs, are just becoming known. As medical researchers discover new teratogens and their effects, it may become possible to eliminate many congenital defects.

Diseases

In rare cases infants have been born with cases of smallpox, malaria, measles, chicken pox, or mumps that have been transmitted from the mother. The placenta cannot filter out extremely small disease carriers such as viruses; they are able to migrate through the placenta and infect the fetus.

German measles, or rubella, is the most widespread of the viruses that have a teratogenic effect. If a pregnant woman contracts rubella in the early months of pregnancy, she is likely to give birth to a child with a congenital abnormality. Heart disease, cataracts, deafness, and mental retardation are among the abnormalities caused by rubella. There is no direct correlation between the severity of the disease in the mother and its effect on the fetus; women who have had mild attacks of rubella have given birth to babies with severe abnormalities.

In recent years, a rubella vaccine has been developed, and school-age children have been innoculated to prevent spread of the disease. Girls who are not innoculated are advised to catch rubella so as to eliminate later danger in their pregnancies. Pregnant women who have not had rubella cannot take the vaccine because the vaccine itself causes a mild case of rubella.

Other viruses—mumps, polio, and influenza—also have teratogenic effects, but the probability that these viruses will harm the fetus is not as great as with rubella, and the defects they cause are not as serious.

Disorders not caused by a virus can also have teratogenic effects. Women suffering from diabetes are six to ten times as likely to give birth to infants with congenital malformations as nondiabetic mothers, and their infants often have respiratory difficulties soon after birth. Diabetes in the mother can be controlled with proper medical care, however, and the threat of damage to the fetus can be greatly reduced.

Women who develop toxemia (blood poisoning) during pregnancy frequently give birth to premature babies or to babies smaller than average for their gestational age—that is, age since conception. If untreated, toxemia can be fatal to both mother and child.

Toxemia is one of several diseases that can cause anoxia in the baby. **Anoxia** is a condition in which the brain of the baby does not receive enough oxygen to allow it to develop properly. Anoxia can cause the child to be born with certain forms of epilepsy, mental deficiency, and behavior disorders. Reading disorders, which affect some 10 percent of normally intelligent school-age children in the United States, have also been linked to anoxia. These problems, when they are caused by brain damage during the prenatal period, can never be adequately treated in later life.

Chemicals

Chemicals can cause a wide range of congenital abnormalities. The severity of the abnormality depends on the amount of chemical the mother is exposed to, the developmental stage of the fetus, and the period of time over which the mother's exposure to the chemical takes place. A pregnant woman should guard against exposure to all chemicals during pregnancy, but she must be particularly careful about taking drugs.

Most of the drugs that can interfere with prenatal development have been identified only within the last ten or twenty years. Certain drugs used in the treatment of cancer are known to cause malformation in babies; others used for the treatment of thyroid malfunction in pregnant mothers have caused goiter and other symptoms in the newborn child. Even such a seemingly harmless drug as

TERATOGENS

Agent	Critical Period	Effects
Diseases Rubella	First month: 50 percent chance of causing defect Second month: 22 percent chance of causing defect Third to fifth month: 6 to 10 percent chance of causing defect	Death; heart disease; malformations of heart, eyes, head; retardation; deafness
Mumps	First three months	Death, malformations of heart
Poliomyelitis		Poliomyelitis
Hepatitis		Hepatitis
Syphilis	After fifth month	Fetus aborted, stillborn, or premature; deformities of head
Diabetes[a]		Abnormally high proportion of stillbirths; missing vertebrae and other skeletal abnormalities
Drugs Insulin (large doses, as in shock therapy)	First fourteen weeks	Death, malformations
Tolbutamide (for diabetes)		Death, malformations

tetracycline, an antibiotic which is commonly prescribed for colds and flu, is now known to cause minor congenital abnormalities of the baby's skeleton and teeth.

Pharmaceuticals are not the only drugs that can affect the baby prenatally. Women who are addicted to heroin, morphine, or methadone give birth to addicted babies. Soon after birth, the babies show symptoms of withdrawal—fever, tremors, convulsions, difficulty in breathing, and intestinal disturbances. The severity of infant withdrawal depends on the period of the mother's addiction, the size of her doses, and how soon before delivery she last took the drug. Some infants die during

Thalidomide	First two months	Deformities
Streptomycin, tetracycline (antibiotics)	Throughout pregnancy	Deafness[b]
Anticonvulsant drugs for epilepsy	Throughout pregnancy	Cleft lip, cleft palate, cardiac defects
Aspirin (large doses)		Fetus aborted, growth retarded[c]
Nicotine	Eighth month Throughout pregnancy	Increased fetal heartbeat; prematurity; stunted growth Possible increase in congenital heart disease
Heroin	Throughout pregnancy	Addiction in the newborn
Radiation X rays	Early months	Defects in central nervous system; mental retardation; possible increase in rate of cancer
Radiation from nuclear explosion	Early months	Leukemia, cataracts, retardation

[a]Women often develop diabetes during pregnancy.
[b]Not firmly established.
[c]In laboratory animals. Increased effects in association with benzoic acid, a common food preservative.

SOURCES:
Wilson, J. G. Environmental effects on development and teratology. In Assali, N. S. (Ed.), *Pathophysiology of gestation*. New York: Academic Press, 1972.
Rugh, R. and Shettles, L. B. *From conception to birth*. New York: Harper & Row, 1971.

withdrawal. The effects of heroin, morphine, and methadone addiction on the later growth and development of the infant, if he survives, are not yet known.

The teratogenic effects of LSD have not yet been fully researched. One investigator (Kato, 1970) gave LSD to four pregnant rhesus monkeys, and all four showed temporary chromosomal damage. One of the offspring showed no adverse effects, but the other three died soon after birth. Unfortunately, a study of four monkeys proves little about monkeys and less about humans.

Research on the use of marijuana during pregnancy has also been inconclusive.

In 1974 researchers released the preliminary findings of a study that seemed to provide the first clear evidence that marijuana might be dangerous to the health of both mother and fetus. They found that white blood cells taken from regular users of marijuana were less effective in fighting viruses in a test tube than white blood cells taken from nonusers. (Nahas, 1974).

Nicotine may trigger chemical reactions in the mother's body that are transmitted through the placenta to the fetus. After a pregnant woman smokes a cigarette, fetal heartbeat almost always increases, but there is no evidence of permanent heart or circulatory system impairment in babies born to mothers who smoke. However, women who smoke are twice as likely to have premature babies as women who do not smoke. This may be a reaction to nicotine, or it may be due to certain factors in a woman's personality or body chemistry that cause her to smoke and at the same time bring about premature birth.

Radiation

The effects of prenatal exposure to radiation were tragically demonstrated by the babies born after the atomic explosions in Japan during World War II. If a woman in her first twenty weeks of pregnancy was within a half mile of the center of the explosion, her chances of delivering a normal baby were very small. Expectant mothers farther from the center of the explosion gave birth to babies with congenitally dislocated hips, malformed eyes, heart disease, leukemia (cancer of the blood), and mental retardation.

Exposure to X rays and other small, controlled amounts of radiation is not known to damage the fetus. Larger doses of therapeutic radiation, such as those required for the treatment of cancer, may be injurious to the fetus and can sometimes cause spontaneous abortion. There really seems to be no completely safe level of radiation; even the various levels of natural radiation found in different parts of the world can be correlated with the higher or lower chances of babies born in those parts of the world to have congenital abnormalities.

Anxiety in the Mother

If a mother is extremely anxious—about her pregnancy, her abilities as a mother, or any other problem in her life—the unborn child may be affected. Mothers who are relatively free of emotional stress, on the other hand, tend to give birth more easily, and their babies usually develop normally. Although the baby's nervous system is separate from the mother's, strong emotions in the mother such as rage, fear, and anxiety cause a great increase of hormones and other chemicals in her bloodstream. These substances pass through the placenta wall, and it is believed that they can reproduce the mother's physiological state in the fetus.

One researcher (Sontag, 1944) found that the bodily movements of the fetus increased considerably when the mother was undergoing stress. He suggested that if this stress is prolonged or often repeated, it could have enduring consequences for the child. Excessive stress in the seventh to tenth week of pregnancy—when the roof of the mouth and the bones of the upper jaw are forming in the fetus—may

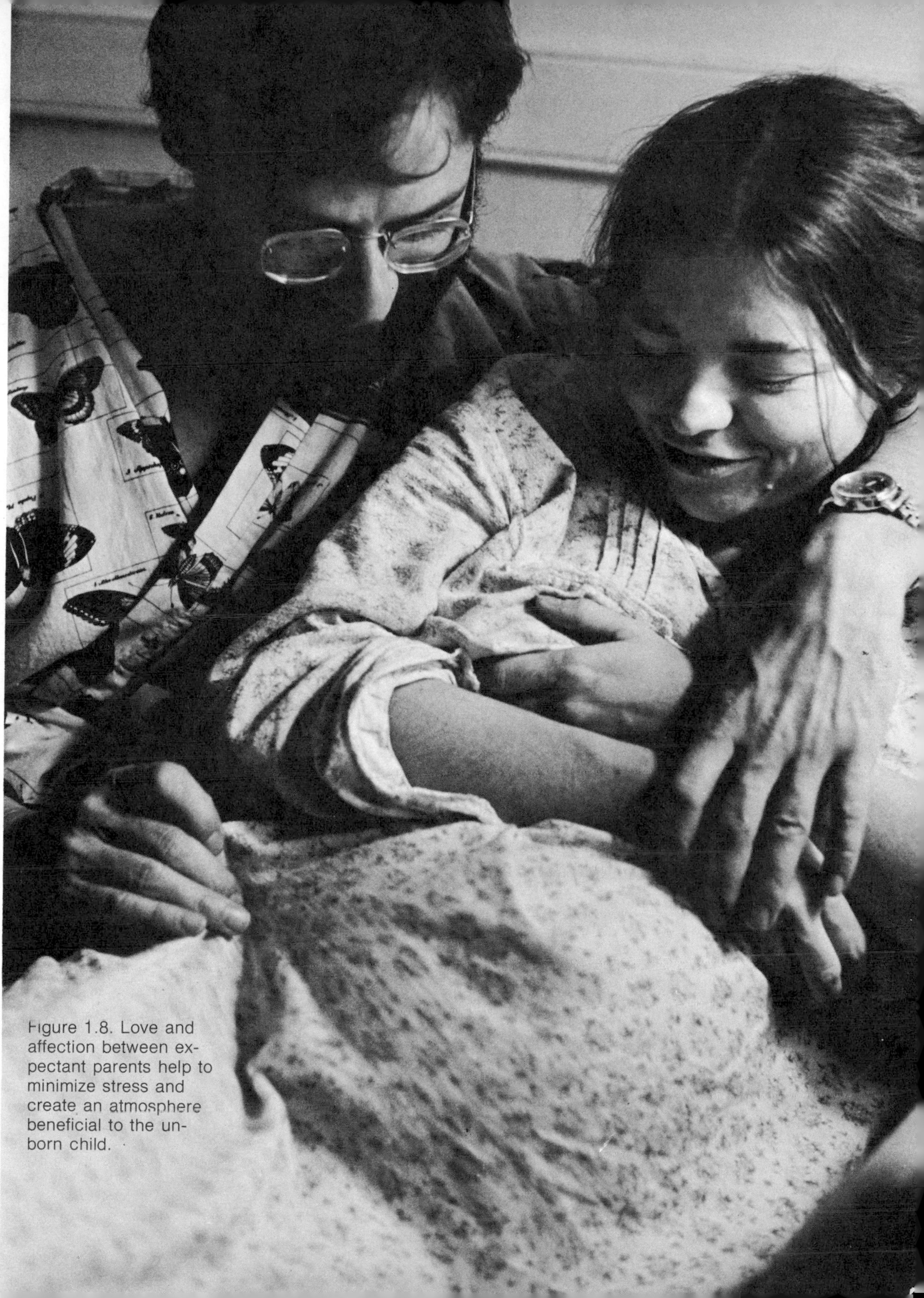

Figure 1.8. Love and affection between expectant parents help to minimize stress and create an atmosphere beneficial to the unborn child.

be a factor in causing cleft palate and harelip. Later in pregnancy, stress is less likely to cause physical abnormalities.

The Rh Factor

The Rh positive factor, an inherited, genetically dominant trait, may cause the blood types of the mother and the child to be incompatible. If such incompatibility exists, it can harm the child and endanger his life. This can happen only when the mother's blood is Rh negative and the child's is Rh positive. Fortunately, 85 percent of the American population is Rh positive, so this occurs very seldom.

When antigens—certain proteins in the blood that cause normal immunologic reactions—pass from the bloodstream of the fetus through the placenta and into the mother's bloodstream, the mother's blood manufactures antibodies to combat them. The antibodies in the mother's blood then circulate back into the fetal bloodstream and attack his red blood cells, thus depriving him of oxygen. Miscarriage, stillbirth, or death soon after birth may result. If the infant survives, he often suffers brain damage or partial paralysis.

This condition in the child is called *erythroblastosis*. Erythroblastosis occurs only once in 200 pregnancies. Firstborn children are not threatened, as the mother's blood has not had time to produce a large amount of antibodies, but the risk increases with each pregnancy. In the past, erythroblastosis was always fatal, but now medical techniques can minimize the harmful results of Rh incompatibility. After the birth of the first child, the mother can take an injection to reduce the buildup of antibodies in her blood. If this is not done and the woman becomes pregnant again, a doctor can measure her antibody count and induce labor when the count becomes too high. Immediate and complete blood transfusions to the newborn infant will eliminate the mother's antibodies from his blood.

The Mother's Diet

Only in recent years has the mother's nutrition been considered important to the development of the fetus. Doctors and researchers realized that pregnancy puts additional demands on the mother's body, but they used to assume that the fetus's nutritional needs would be met first, even at the mother's expense.

The current opinion, however, is that the prenatal development of the fetus and its growth and development after birth are directly related to maternal diet. Women who follow nutritionally sound diets during pregnancy give birth to babies of normal or above-normal size. Their babies are less likely to contract bronchitis, pneumonia, or colds during early infancy. Their teeth and bones are better developed, and their mothers have fewer complications during pregnancy and on the average spend less time in labor.

But if the mother's diet is low in certain vitamins and minerals when she is pregnant, the child may suffer from specific weaknesses. Insufficient iron may lead to anemia in the infant, and a low intake of calcium may cause poor bone formation. If there is not enough protein in the mother's diet, the baby may

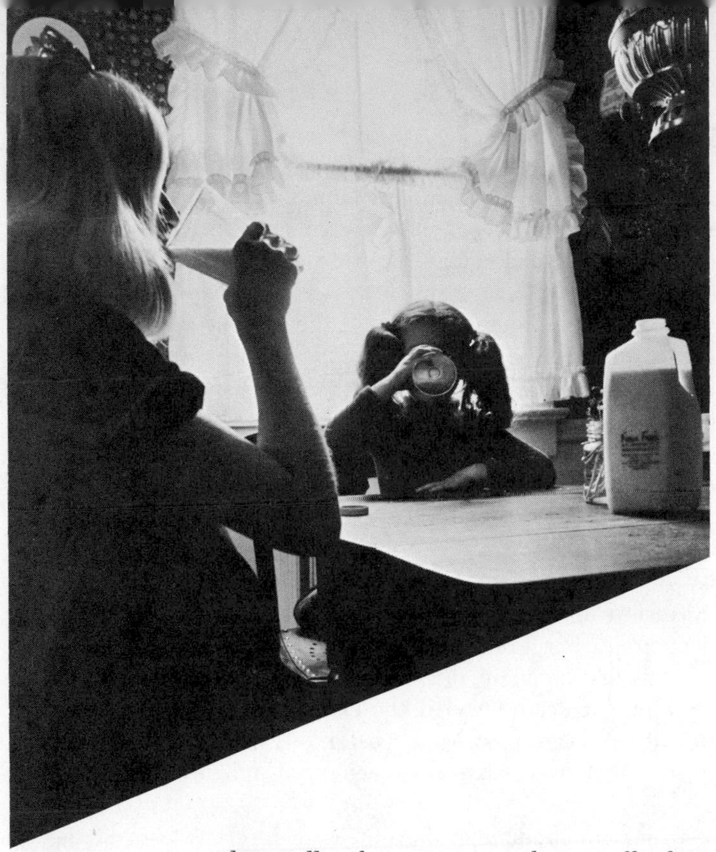

Figure 1.9. Proper nutrition is essential not only to the growing child but to the unborn child as well. Milk is a good source of vitamins and body-building proteins and calcium.

be smaller than average and may suffer from mental retardation. Iodine insufficiency may cause cretinism (a form of mental retardation).

Lack of B vitamins in the mother's diet may impair mental functioning in the child. Shortages of vitamins C and D may lead to physical abnormalities. On the other hand, overdoses of certain vitamins can also do harm: too much vitamin D can cause mental retardation and physical defects. Rats and mice given excessive doses of vitamin A early in pregnancy gave birth to offspring with physical abnormalities, and the same doses given later affected attention span and motivation.

One study (Vore, 1973) links malnutrition in the prenatal period and infancy to deficits in the development of the central nervous system and the brain. These deficits reduce the child's ability to learn, and the damage cannot be repaired. In view of world food shortages, it would seem that the prospect is for millions of babies to be born with permanently impaired mental abilities.

ABORTION

Abortion is no longer illegal in the United States, but many people's religious and ethical beliefs are still offended by it. Most states prohibited abortion, except in special cases, until the U.S. Supreme Court nullified all but the most lenient state laws. Now the only legal requirements are that the abortion be performed by a licensed physician in a hospital or clinic and that it be done before the pregnancy advances beyond a specified number of weeks.

Abortion was not prohibited in the United States until about 1800. Before then, most people accepted the British common-law concept that abortion is not a crime if it is performed before quickening—the first feeling of fetal movement, which usually occurs in the sixteenth to eighteenth week of pregnancy. Abortion was first prohibited for medical reasons. The aim of the new laws was to protect the life of the mother, for in those days, before bacterial infection could be controlled, abortion posed a far greater threat to the mother's life than childbirth.

Nowadays, with modern antiseptic and surgical techniques, abortion in the early months of pregnancy is safer than childbirth. The opposition to abortion now is based on moral and religious, not medical, grounds.

Abortion Methods

Women have used a variety of techniques to induce abortion, many of them ineffective and all dangerous. For example, they have taken ergot and quinine sulfate. But if these drugs are taken in doses large enough to induce abortion, they frequently cause injury or death. And if the child is born despite the drug, he is often deformed. Other drugs—estrogen, castor oil, calomel, herbs, and a number of purgatives and irritants—have also been tried and proved ineffective and often injurious.

One of the oldest means of inducing abortion is to insert foreign bodies or substances into the uterus. Knitting needles, chopsticks, wires, and other instruments sometimes perforate the wall of the uterus and lead to death by infection or hemorrhage. Boiling water, soapsuds, alcohol, lye, and other substances in the uterus burn the tissues or cause hemorrhage or shock, even death. Women still try to induce abortion by lifting heavy objects, jumping from high places, and riding horses. This does not work, but it can injure the mother or the fetus.

The technique used by a physician in a legal abortion depends largely on the stage of pregnancy. Until recently, the most widely used technique for the termination of pregnancy in the first twelve weeks was *dilation and curettage* (D&C). Under this procedure, the cervix is dilated with instruments until the opening is large enough to allow the insertion of a curette, or scraping instrument, which removes the embryo from the wall of the uterus. This technique is still widely used and can be performed under a local anesthetic.

Suction curettage, also known as vacuum aspiration, is now the technique most frequently used to terminate pregnancy during the first twelve weeks. As with D&C, the cervix is dilated, and then a vacuum suction device is inserted to remove the contents of the uterus. This procedure is also performed under a local anesthetic. It reduces the risk of perforating the uterus and reduces the likelihood of blood loss and trauma.

During the twelfth to sixteenth weeks of pregnancy, a *hysterotomy* is sometimes performed. The uterus is opened surgically from above, and the fetus is removed. Usually the woman must spend several days in the hospital.

Because hysterotomy is a major operation and must be performed under general anesthesia, many physicians advise their patients to wait until the sixteenth week of pregnancy and undergo the safer *salting-out* technique. In this procedure, a hypodermic needle is inserted into the uterus and some of the fluid is removed from the amniotic sac. Saline solution is then injected into the sac to kill the fetus and induce labor. Labor begins in twelve to sixteen hours, and the women expels the fetus naturally. Salting-out is performed under local anesthesia.

Menstrual extraction is one of the newest techniques for terminating very early pregnancies. Feminist groups and some physicians consider it the safest and the least expensive method of early abortion. Instead of waiting ten days until a pregnancy test can be given, a woman whose menstrual period is late can go to her physician's office for menstrual extraction. A thin, flexible plastic tube is inserted into the undilated cervix, and a syringe attached to the tube is used to suck out the contents of the uterus, including the fertilized egg if one is present. Legally speaking, menstrual extraction is not abortion if it is done before pregnancy has been medically verified.

In recent years, medical researchers have been seeking an abortion-inducing drug. One group of drugs—the prostaglandins—looks promising. In 1971 several countries, including the United States, began testing prostaglandins. Other drugs may be found if the prostaglandins prove unsatisfactory, but in any case it will probably be several years before an abortion pill or injection is available.

References

Bronfenbrenner, U. *Influences on human development.* Hinsdale, Ill.: Dryden Press, 1972.

Eysenck, H. J. *Crime and personality.* Boston: Houghton Mifflin, 1964.

Fehr, F. S. Critique of hereditarian accounts of "intelligence" and contrary findings: a reply to Jensen. *Harvard Educational Review,* 1969, *39,* 571–580.

Gage, N. L. IQ heritability, race differences, and educational research. *Phi Delta Kappan,* January, 1972, 308–312.

Jensen, A. R. How much can we boost IQ and scholastic achievement? *Harvard Educational Review,* 1969, *39,* 1–123.

Kallman, F. J. *The genetics of schizophrenia: a study of heredity and reproduction in the families of 1,087 schizophrenics.* New York: Augustin, 1938.

Kallman, F. J., and Sander, G. Twin studies on senescence. *American Journal of Psychiatry,* 1949, *106,* 29–36.

Kato, T. Chromosome studies in pregnant rhesus monkeys macaque given LSD-25. *Diseases of the Nervous System,* 1970, *31,* 245–250.

Lindeman, B. *The twins who found each other.* New York: Morrow, 1969.

Muller, H. J. Mental Health traits and heredity. *Journal of Heredity,* 1925, *16,* 433–448.

Nahas, G. G. et al. Inhibition of cellular mediated immunity in marihuana smokers. *Science,* Feb. 1, 1974, 419–420.

Newmann, H. H., Freeman, F. N., and Holzinger, K. J. *Twins: a study of heredity and environment.* Chicago: University of Chicago Press, 1937.

Rosanoff, A. J., Handy, L. M., and Plesset, I. R. The etiology of mental deficiency with special reference to its occurrence in twins. *Psychological Monographs,* 1937, *48* (4), no. 216.

Shields, J. *Monozygotic twins: brought up apart and brought up together.* London: Oxford University Press, 1962.

Sontag, L. W. Difference in modifiability of fetal behavior and physiology. *Psychosomatic Medicine,* 1944, *6,* 151–154.

Vore, D. A. Prenatal nutrition and postnatal intellectual development. *Merrill-Palmer Quarterly,* 1973, *19,* 253–260.

SUMMARY

1

Every individual is influenced by both genetic and environmental factors even before he is born. The individual's genetic potentialities are inherited from his parents, but the combination of genes he receives is unique. A gene is a part of a chromosome that directs the formation of a single trait. Chromosomes are found in the nucleus of every living cell.

2

Inherited characteristics include physical features, such as eye and skin color, and certain rare diseases. Traits such as mental illness, intelligence, and personality may be affected by inheritance, but in many cases the evidence is inconclusive.

3

In gestation, the zygote develops into a fully formed baby through three stages. During the short preimplantation period, the zygote enters the uterus while undergoing cell division. When this tiny cell mass embeds itself in the uterine wall, the embryo stage begins. When tissue differentiation and system development are essentially complete, the embryo enters the fetus period and grows rapidly until it is ready for birth.

4

Environmental agents that adversely affect an individual's development before birth are called teratogens. Some teratogens are diseases that infect the mother and injure the child. Others are drugs or chemicals that cross from the mother's bloodstream into the child's. A third type of teratogen is radiation, such as X rays and nuclear particles, which originates outside the mother's body.

5

Legal abortion in the United States now makes it possible for women to terminate pregnancy with full medical protection. Techniques vary according to stage of pregnancy.

FURTHER READINGS

Apgar, V. and Beck, J. *Is my baby all right?: A guide to birth defects.* New York: Trident, 1972.

In one out of every sixteen births, a baby is born with a defect that will significantly affect his life. Apgar and Beck explain the causes of both genetic and environmental birth defects. The intricate steps of development that take place in the human fetus, and how the pattern can go wrong, are carefully described by the authors.

Hall, R. E. (Ed.), *Abortion in the changing world.* (Vol. I.) New York: Columbia University Press, 1970.

This is a collection of the proceedings of an international convention on abortion. The papers do not debate the controversy but present knowledge and information about abortion. The approach is interdisciplinarian.

Montagu, A. *Human heredity.* Cleveland: World, 1963.

The author not only explains what is scientifically known about the science of heredity but clarifies the heredity/environment issue. The second half of the book is a discussion of common physical and functional traits which are inherited genetically.

Scrimshaw, N. S. and Gordon, J. E. (Eds.), *Malnutrition, learning, and behavior.* Cambridge, Mass.: The M.I.T. Press, 1968.

A collection of papers presented at an international conference on the effects of malnutrition on learning and behavior. The results of studies on both experimental animals and children are presented. Retardation of physical growth and development due to protein deficiency is a problem of massive proportions in underdeveloped countries as well as urban and rural poverty areas in the industrialized nations.

Watson, J. P. *The double helix: a personal account of the discovery of the structure of DNA.* New York: Atheneum, 1968.

DNA is the molecule of heredity, and Watson's discovery has been called by many scientists the most significant since Mendel's. Watson received the Nobel Prize for the work he describes in this book, and he manages to tell a great deal, as well, about the general creative process itself.

Zimmerman, D. R. *Rh: the intimate history of a disease and its conquest.* New York: Macmillan, 1973.

The behind the scenes story of the defeat of Rh—one of the most dramatic medical achievements of twentieth-century medicine. The individual contributions of each of the researchers, from the naming of the disease to the development of the Rh vaccine, are told with a sense of excitement.

2 Birth and the Neonate

The large majority of mothers and babies have always come through childbirth in good health and spirits; otherwise, we would not be here to tell about it. Although the hospital is the preferred setting for childbirth, it is not because giving birth threatens the mother's health. Of course, even the most sophisticated medical techniques cannot produce an instant baby, without fuss or bother to the parents. But that is not the aim; in fact, most doctors believe that delivery is easier, and mother and child get off to a better start, when the parents involve themselves in preparing for childbirth. This involvement, they believe, can contribute much to making childbirth a happy experience.

Medical attention greatly reduces the chances that complications in childbirth will mar the experience. We have all heard about several kinds of complications—a mother's pelvis being too narrow to allow the passage of the baby's head, for example, or a baby coming out bottom first instead of head first, as most do. We should not forget, however, that although there are many kinds of complications, they are all quite rare. Most of them can be foreseen and prepared for, and in a hospital there are ample resources for dealing with even the unforeseen ones.

Although these facts are well known, prospective parents must never be allowed to lose sight of them. No one needs unwarranted worries, and prospective parents have a special interest in keeping themselves worry free. We have seen in Chapter 1 how excessive anxiety on the part of pregnant women is suspected of having undesirable effects on their babies. It is also believed that the greatest intensifier of pain in labor is the mother's fear (Wiedenbach, 1967).

Many parents combat anxiety and fear by participating in a program known as **natural childbirth.** They read factual material on childbirth, attend lectures, and discuss what they learn with other prospective parents. They also practice breathing routines and exercises that prepare the mothers for labor and give the fathers an opportunity to demonstrate their moral support.

Popular report sometimes pictures advocates of natural childbirth as opposing the use of anesthesia or other drugs in labor, but this is not accurate. Whether or not to use drugs—and how much—is a decision that must be left to the mother and her physician. However, many women prefer to remain conscious and bring voluntary effort to bear in the delivery. This can facilitate delivery and give the mother a great sense of accomplishment.

Natural childbirth preparation equips a woman with a number of valuable defenses against pain. With knowledge, confidence, and the techniques of rhythmic breathing, there is more chance of controlling the situation and not succumbing to fear. Moreover, the husband becomes part of a team rather than a bystander; this creates a deeper sense of sharing and may make the transition to parenthood much easier for both.

LABOR

Is this labor? Has the time come at last? Many mothers ask themselves this question more than once in the late weeks of pregnancy. Sometimes they feel a contraction and then nothing further happens. Such contractions are known as Braxton Hicks contractions; experienced mothers say real labor contractions cause more discomfort,

Figure 2.1. Natural-childbirth training. The prospective father and mother both learn exercises and breathing techniques in preparation for a delivery in which she will be "awake and aware." The training sessions include demonstrations of the effectiveness of the techniques: here the father pinches the mother's ankle to simulate labor pains while she practices breathing techniques that enable her to tolerate the pain more easily.

recur with more regularity, become gradually more frequent, and are intensified by walking. But such things are easy to imagine.

Other signs that, if accompanied by contractions, may or may not herald the beginning of labor are an ache in the small of the back, abdominal cramps, diarrhea, indigestion, "show"—a small amount of blood-tinged mucus emerging from the vagina—and "water breaking"—a discharge of fluid from the vagina. Yet even the discharge of fluid, which is caused by the rupture of membranes, may occur some time before actual labor begins. No wonder so many women rush to the hospital only to be sent home again.

A doctor can settle the question by vaginal inspection. If the cervix, the opening at the bottom of the uterus, is starting to dilate, labor has begun.

Stages of Labor

Labor progresses through three stages: the stage of dilation, the stage of expulsion, and the placental stage. The first stage, **dilation**, may only be two hours long, or it may last sixteen hours or more. Each contraction, at first, is thirty to forty-five seconds in duration. The contractions are involuntary; the mother cannot start them or stop them at will, or make them come faster or slower. Their purpose is to dilate the cervix until it is wide enough to let the baby through—usually about four inches.

In the course of the first stage the contractions come more and more frequently, until finally they are only a minute or two apart. Each contraction also becomes longer; toward the end of the first stage they may last ninety seconds. The mother's mood also changes as the first stage progresses. At first she feels the contractions with a sense of jubilation or relief, for she has been waiting nine months for this moment. When she has spent some hours in labor, however, and the contractions are both longer in duration and quicker in succession, she may become serious and determined.

The father may assist in the phase of mild, brief contractions by helping the mother relax and by timing the interval between contractions. If they have practiced breathing techniques together, he coaches her. As the contractions become more intense, he gets her to the hospital; many hospitals now allow him to remain with her in the delivery room, where he may help her stay comfortable.

At the end of the first stage, there may be six or eight contractions that are acutely painful. The cervix has been stretched around the baby's head. The mother may feel ready to give up, but this phase is soon over.

In the second stage, **expulsion**, the involuntary contractions continue to be long in duration and closely spaced, but now the mother has a strong urge to bear down voluntarily with her abdominal muscles. In between contractions she may drift off into a state of forgetfulness, but she rouses with each new contraction and pushes down with all her strength. She sweats, flushes, and grunts, and the baby's scalp comes into view, only to disappear again when the contraction ends. Each time, however, more and more of the baby's head can be seen. When it comes out as far as its widest diameter, it stays out, and in a short time it is free. The

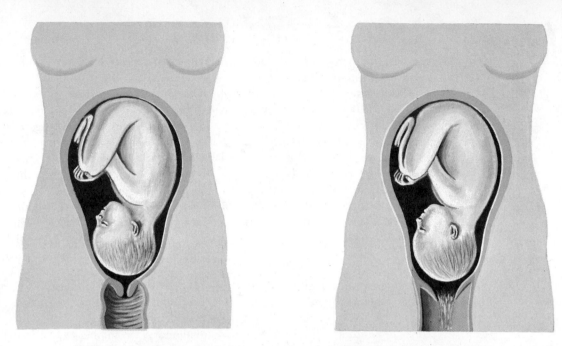

Figure 2.2. The cervix in late pregnancy and labor. Above left: the closed cervix is sealed with a plug of mucus during pregnancy so that nothing can enter the uterus from the vagina. Above right: breaking membranes release a flow of fluid through the cervix; this often marks the onset of labor. Below left: the cervix is dilated, or stretched, by the contractions of the first stage of labor. Below right: the cervix is stretched around the baby's head, molding it, just before delivery.

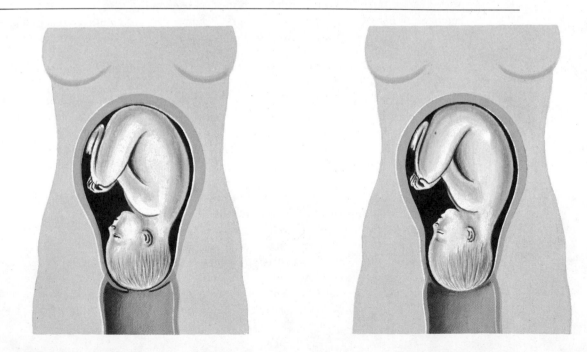

baby's head may be *molded*—elongated in shape due to passage through the cervix—but the soft skull bones that have been squeezed together soon recover their normal shape.

Some babies will give their first cry at this point. With the next contractions, the shoulders emerge, and the rest of the body slips out easily. The mother experiences a great feeling of release and elation.

When the baby has been delivered, the doctor holds him or her up by the feet. Fluid and mucus escape from the mouth and nose, and he gasps his first breath and utters his first cry if he has not done so before. The umbilical cord is clamped and cut. Then a nurse takes the baby, wrapped in a receiving blanket, to perform a series of procedures that vary from hospital to hospital. Typically, the baby is given drops in his eyes to prevent infection, both mother and baby are given plastic identification bracelets, and fingerprints of the mother and possibly footprints of the baby are taken. Finally, a series of tests known as the Apgar

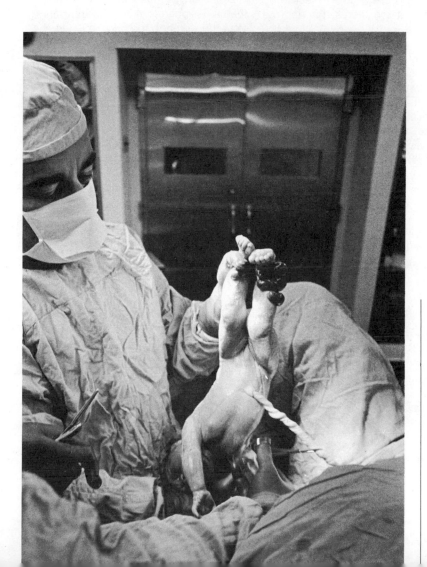

Figure 2.3. Cutting the umbilical cord. The baby has just emerged, and the physician holds him by the ankles to clear his nose and mouth of fluid. As soon as the baby has begun to breathe, the physician clamps and cuts the umbilical cord, severing the last physical connection between the newborn child and his mother.

"GENTLE" BIRTH

Our culture is full of powerful images that reflect the tremendous positive significance of birth. When Christians talk about religious conversion, they sometimes call it "being born again;" radical feminists may describe finding themselves as "giving birth to themselves;" the rock poet Bob Dylan has said, "He who's not busy being born is busy dying." In these images, birth is the fundamental creation, the coming to life.

But what about the physical realities of being born? How does it feel to be forced out of the uterus, through the vagina, and into the world? What are the newborn infant's impressions of the outside world in those first few minutes as he comes into it? At least one expert, French obstetrician Frederick Leboyer, believes that being born is a terrifying experience. And the terror of birth is multiplied, in Leboyer's view, by the insensitivity of modern delivery techniques to the feelings of the infant.

Most babies are born into an operating room full of blinding light, noisy bustle, and the excitement of people at the end of a long wait. Within minutes of his birth the child is assaulted by many hands: they wash him; they tag him; they weigh him; they even take his footprints. Some physicians still practice the traditional ritual of holding the newborn child by his ankles and giving him a slap to make him breathe. Leboyer feels that all this is a brutal introduction to life outside the womb.

He has developed an alternative method of delivery that is called "nonviolent" or "gentle" birth, a method that is designed to make the transition from the womb to the outside world as nonthreatening as possible. "Gentle" birth is a logical extension of natural-childbirth techniques, with the difference that natural childbirth focuses on the experience of the mother and father during labor and delivery, whereas Leboyer's method focuses on the experience of the baby.

The Leboyer technique includes a number of radical changes in the usual operating-room procedure. As soon as

rating are made to evaluate the baby's muscle tone, heart rate, breathing effort, color, and reflex response. The rating is made to assure that the baby is normal and needs no special immediate care. During the third or **placental** stage, the placenta and the attached membranes and cord, commonly called the **afterbirth,** are expelled from the uterus. Labor is now completed.

The length of the entire process varies greatly, as does the actual experience of labor. Fifteen hours is an average figure for the duration of birth from the first contraction to the expulsion of the afterbirth. But this average covers a spectrum of labor as long as twenty-four hours and as short as three hours or less. Labor is usually longer for first babies than for later ones.

Complications

Variations from the norm that may occur during the delivery of a baby can usually be dealt with successfully by the obstetrician and the hospital staff. The baby may, for example, come out bottom first in what is called a **breech presentation.** Sometimes one foot is the first thing to appear, and sometimes the umbilical cord

the infant begins to emerge, the physicians and nurses attending the birth lower their voices, and the lights in the operating theater are turned down. Everyone handles the baby with the greatest possible tenderness. As soon as he has slipped from the vagina, he is placed on his mother's belly and permitted to establish normal breathing before the umbilical cord is severed. After a few minutes, the obstetrician places the infant in a lukewarm bath, an environment very like the uterus from which he has just come. In this way the differences between the world of the first nine months and the world in which the child will continue to grow are minimized.

Leboyer has written a book that describes his delivery technique and a film showing an actual birth by his method. Both have been widely circulated in France, where the technique has aroused great controversy.

Each of us has experienced birth, and none of us remembers it, although it may be recorded in our unconscious memories. Sigmund Freud conjectured that the experience of birth, which he described as one of shock at being separated from the mother, could set the pattern for all our later feelings of anxiety (Freud, 1924). One of Freud's students, Otto Rank, further developed this notion of the "birth trauma." Rank felt that birth is such a terrifying experience that it leaves a lasting mark on every individual. Others have questioned this theory, noting, for example, that the newborn child's nervous system may be so undeveloped that it cannot yet register any experience as strongly and sharply as Rank (and Leboyer) suggest (Allport, 1961).

Leboyer's method has been practiced in France for seven years, but no comparative research has yet been done on the children who have been delivered by this technique. Some studies are now under way, and it will be interesting to see what differences, if any, are found between children delivered by traditional methods and those who enter the world by a "gentle" birth.

comes out alongside the head. The doctor must manage these variations with great skill if the baby is to be delivered unharmed. Caution is taken to examine the width of the mother's pelvis as soon as breech presentation is indicated. The fetal heartbeat is watched carefully during labor, and when there is cause for concern, a surgical operation known as a cesarean section is performed.

A **cesarean birth** is one in which the baby is delivered through a surgical incision made into the mother's abdomen and uterus. It is a safe operation for both mother and baby if no other harm has come to the fetus prior to delivery. Babies delivered by cesarean section do not have molded heads and look better in general than babies born normally. A cesarean section might be made for the simple reason that the fetus's head is unusually large or the space between the mother's pelvic bones is narrow. The operation might also be performed because of some danger for the fetus or some failure of an essential function in the mother. If a woman has had her first baby by cesarean delivery, it is usually repeated for the second baby; this avoids rupturing the uterine scar.

A common means of helping nature during birth is through the use of a tonglike instrument known as forceps. These concave, elongated tongs are inserted as two separate units into the vagina. Each is placed at an appropriate place on the baby's head; when the handles are joined, the baby's head can be rotated and pulled.

A forceps delivery may be required when the mother is so sedated that she cannot actively do the pushing required to deliver the baby during the second stage of birth. Danger signs from either fetus or mother could call for speeding up the delivery with forceps. Because forceps have caused damage to the baby's head in the past, doctors now generally avoid using them unless all conditions are favorable; otherwise, they opt for a cesarean section.

Drugs During Labor

What is good for the mother is not always good for the fetus. For decades the pains of labor have been eased with many types of drugs, from mild painkillers such as analgesics to general anesthetics that obliterate all sensation. Recently researchers have begun to take a careful look at the possible effects of these drugs on the fetus, especially in light of the extreme danger of some drugs taken earlier in pregnancy. A review of the various studies (Bowes et al., 1970) explains that most of the medication administered during labor crosses the placenta by diffusion. No study found that the drugs caused long-term harm to the fetus, but they did find more sluggish behavior in babies whose mothers took labor medication. These differences in visual attentiveness, weight gain, general brain activity, and sucking behavior generally fade away within a few weeks. Labor drugs thus seem to be safe, provided that the fetus has not been weakened by some complication of birth.

Anoxia

Anoxia, or the deprivation of oxygen, can cause severe brain damage. Mild incidents of anoxia have been blamed for minor cases of brain damage, learning disabilities, and behavior difficulties. The fetus can be subjected to anoxia before birth, as mentioned in Chapter 1. If the mother is anemic, for example, and her blood is deficient in iron, the oxygen-carrying capacity of her blood may be so low that oxygen in the blood of the fetus falls to dangerous levels. Anoxia can also strike the baby at birth, either by a rupture of the blood vessels in the brain or by a failure of the umbilical circulation to provide oxygen before the baby is ready to take her first breath. There are many things that can happen during birth to interfere with or cut off the umbilical circulation. The cord may be clamped and pinched, part of the placenta may become detached, the contractions may be so forceful that oxygen is delayed, or the mother's blood pressure could decline because of bleeding.

Whatever the cause, however, when the cutoff of oxygen is acute there is damage to the brain cells. Cerebral palsy, which sometimes results in paralysis of the arms or legs, in tremors of the fingers or in the face, or in an inability to use the vocal muscles, is due in many cases to natal or prenatal anoxia.

Neonates suffering a mild loss of oxygen at birth seem to be more irritable than usual for about the first week. Their muscular activity is more tense and rigid, and their response to visual stimulation and pain less sensitive (Graham et al., 1956). Studies that trace the effects of mild anoxia through childhood years indicate that these children score a little lower on tests of intellectual capability but that many catch up over the years. Some problems in motor coordination and attention seem to persist indefinitely (Ernhart et al., 1960).

Childbirth in the Hospital

Today it is not unusual to hear complaints leveled against some aspects of hospital care. This is in large part due to costs. Maternity costs are very high, considering that childbirth is not really an illness, and the combined bills of hospital and obstetrician can be a heavy burden for a family.

Moreover, doctors and nurses do not always have the time to minister to the more subtle psychological needs of a woman during labor and after delivery, particularly when their skills are needed for the more urgent cases of complicated births. Some women have prepared themselves for natural childbirth only to find that the policy of their hospital was not sympathetic to the practice, for which moral support is a necessary ingredient. Nor does every hospital encourage breast feeding, and a bewildered new mother may not get the extra care she needs for those awkward first feedings. More and more hospitals, however, are providing support for natural childbirth, and any good hospital provides a reassuring setting for giving birth and adjusting to motherhood. It can have rich significance in her memory of the event.

In response to some of the criticisms, the maternity policies of many hospitals have become more flexible. Fathers are allowed in the delivery rooms, they have almost unlimited visiting hours, and older children are allowed to visit with their mother in special areas of the hospital. Many nursery schedules are more informal than formerly, and some hospitals offer an arrangement known as "rooming in," where the newborn is kept with the mother rather than in a general nursery. This facilitates a more relaxed adjustment to the baby, greater ease in feeding him when he is hungry, and more education in baby care—often an awesome task for a new mother.

Some hospital administrators have plans for still further innovations. One idea is for the father to stay with the mother in the delivery room and then spend the remainder of the recovery period in an adjacent facility something like a motel with cafeteria service.

There is, nevertheless, a trend among some couples, most of them in the well-educated middle class, to avoid the hospital completely and have their babies in their own home. Most obstetricians frown on the practice; the possibility of birth complications and the occasional need for a blood transfusion or a cesarean section are sufficient reasons for their attitude. People who advocate home delivery do so partly for financial reasons, but they also believe that birth is an essentially healthy and joyous event and should take place in the warmth of the home where it can be shared and, indeed, celebrated by the whole family.

A far more significant development in the obstetrical field is the growing importance of the nurse-midwife as a helper for doctors who are too busy to give much attention to women without serious childbirth difficulties. The number of medical students adopting obstetrics as a specialty has been declining, and fewer of those who choose the field are interested in normal deliveries. Obstetricians seldom have time for more than the most perfunctory examination and tests for their patients during the prenatal period. They are rarely involved with a woman's choice of natural childbirth instructions; she usually takes courses on her own. Postnatal care and advice are almost unheard of, other than the standard checkup.

In contrast, the nurse-midwife, working under the supervision of a physician, provides a range of much needed services—family planning, instruction, counseling, and postnatal advice about baby care—and she performs all uncomplicated deliveries as well. There are a growing number of certified training programs and a growing number of deliveries by nurse-midwives in large hospitals—a fact that bears testimony to growing acceptance by the medical field and holds promise for optimum quality maternity care in the future.

PREMATURITY

Babies born prematurely are at a decided disadvantage physically and often in other ways as well. Later in life, many premature babies have problems with language learning or make poor scores on tests of general academic achievement.

A baby is considered premature if he is born at thirty-seven weeks of gestation or earlier (the normal gestation period is forty weeks). But it is often difficult to tell just when gestation began, and some babies are born small even after forty weeks in the womb. Small babies—those weighing under five and a half pounds—have many of the same disadvantages whether they were born early or simply born small. For this reason they are considered premature in either case. Premature babies can be measured and tested, especially for reflexes, to determine the exact dimensions of their prematurity.

The premature baby is not physically ready to adapt to the world outside the uterus. He has less fat to insulate his body and therefore less ability to keep warm. He may be lacking in immunity to infection and in the muscular strength necessary to expand his lungs for breathing. The capillary network in his lungs may also be inadequate to provide a sufficient exchange of gases. As soon as possible after he is born, therefore, he is placed in a warmed crib or an incubator. In many cases he is given oxygen at first, though too much of it for too long may result in blindness. Because his body, being underdeveloped, is delicate, he is not handled more than necessary (Wiedenbach, 1967).

Studies following the development of premature babies over a period of years have kept track of their motor and perceptual performance, their intelligence, and any behavior disorders they may show. One study (Fitzharding and Steven, 1972) found that by the school years there was a high incidence of speech defects and a variety of learning and school problems. Many of the children, however, had a normal intellectual potential, as indicated by their IQ scores. The researchers found that tutoring and the use of special teaching tools could overcome the learning problems of these children.

In another study (Scarr-Salapatek and Williams, 1973), the researchers concentrated on prematures born to disadvantaged mothers. Women living in impoverished conditions have the highest rate of low birth weight babies, and these babies grow up in conditions that give them little chance to overcome the handicaps that might have resulted from their prematurity. The researchers gave an experimental group of low birth weight babies more sensory stimulation and human contact than such babies normally receive, being isolated as they usually are for special physical care. Afterwards, the researchers visited the mothers of these babies regularly to give them intensive counseling on child care. The results showed that the early stimulation and subsequent attention did much to overcome the initial handicap.

PHYSICAL CHARACTERISTICS
OF THE NEWBORN

It takes a while for many babies to become beautiful. At first the skin of the neonate is thin, sensitive, and very ruddy in appearance. Some have little white bumps around the nose and on the cheeks; darker complexioned babies often have bluish colorations on the back or the buttocks. Some are born with a full head of hair as well as a fine down on the ears, the lower back, and the shoulders.

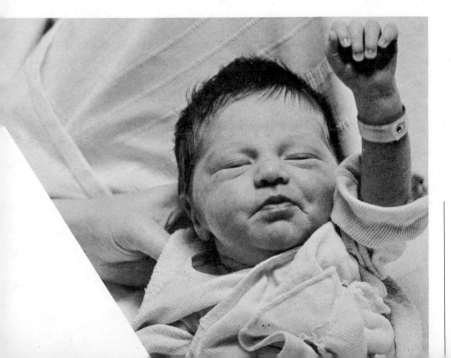

Figure 2.4. This three day old has a full head of hair and the puffy eyelids that often characterize a newborn baby.

The eyes of the newborn seem small. The lids are puffy, the eyes have a dull color, and the gaze has an absent, almost unseeing quality. Many babies have blood spots on the eyes for the first few days, due to pressure during delivery. The nose, too, often suffers some temporary distortion from having been pressed down during birth, and the head is molded.

The neonate's body has a frail look; he does not yet have the thick fatty tissue that gives a baby his soft roundness. He keeps his legs bent in at the knee with his feet flexed outward, which tends to give his limbs an awkward look. In fact, he looks his best when wrapped snugly in a receiving blanket.

Some newborns show the curious effects of the mother's hormones. Their breasts are large and may even secrete a few drops of fluid, which is called "witch's milk." Newborn girls have a small amount of vaginal discharge; occasionally this discharge is tinged with blood as if it were menstrual flow.

Many of these characteristics come as a surprise to first-time parents, but their baby's appearance changes rapidly for the better. Meanwhile, even more important changes are taking place inside the baby's body as he makes the transition from fetal life to independent functioning.

Respiration

The fetus receives a steady supply of oxygen through the umbilical cord; the newborn must breathe for himself. Normal breathing is a reflex action triggered by a chemical imbalance: an excess of carbon dioxide in the blood stimulates the respiratory center of the brain, and without thinking about it, we take a breath. This process, which prompts each successive breath, also prompts our first gasp. The oxygen level in the neonate's blood drops when the umbilical cord is clamped, shutting off his oxygen supply; the breathing reflex follows almost immediately. Squeezing through the birth canal has already prepared the lungs for their first breath.

As the neonate takes his first few breaths, his lungs expand. The smaller bronchi and the tiny lung buds, or *alveoli,* are at first collapsed or filled with fluid, so the first few breaths must be vigorous enough to expand them. With the opening of the alveoli, the capillaries unfold, and the way is opened for an increasing volume of blood to the lungs.

This adaptation does not occur all at once. Even during fetal life, a certain amount of blood is pumped through the lungs, but changes in the circulatory system are necessary before the lungs receive the entire output of the right ventricle of the heart.

The newborn breathes with his diaphragm in what is called abdominal breathing, rather than with his chest. He favors his nose rather than his mouth. The breathing of a newborn baby is often very uneven. Because control of the soft palate and the larynx is still immature, many babies make wheezing and snorting noises as they breathe.

Circulation

When the umbilical cord is clamped and cut, one major branch of the circulatory system, as it existed in the fetal stage, closes down. The main blood vessels to and from the placenta shut off shortly after birth.

As circulation through the umbilical cord stops, circulation through the lungs increases. In the fetal heart the pulmonary circulation—blood pumped to and from the lungs—is not separate from the general body circulation, as it is in an adult. There is an opening between the right and left auricles known as the *foramen ovale*, and a small shunting vessel known as the *ductus arteriosus* between the aorta and the pulmonary artery (see Figure 2.5). The foramen ovale permits incoming blood to flow into either auricle, and the ductus arteriosus permits blood pumped out by both ventricles to enter the general circulation. After the baby is born, however, the foramen ovale gradually seals up and the ductus arteriosus constricts and shuts off. When these closures are complete, the right ventricle pumps blood only to the lungs, as it does in an adult.

The newborn's heart beats rapidly, from 120 to 140 beats per minute. During the first weeks of life, the blood is very rich in hemoglobin, the substance that carries oxygen to the tissues.

Digestion

The neonate is well equipped to make the change from passively receiving nutrition from the mother's blood to actively seeking food with her mouth. She has a strong sucking reflex, and she has sucking pads on the inner surface of each cheek. After a day or two of sucking she develops what looks like a blister but is really a callus on the surface of the lip.

Babies are usually fed about twelve hours after birth, depending on the policy of the hospital. If the baby is breast-fed, the mother's milk begins to flow the second or third day after birth. At first the breast produces a substance called colostrum that provides an abundant supply of antibodies to the newborn. Whether on breast milk or bottle formula, the diet is usually supplemented by a sugar–water mixture for the first few days.

At birth the neonate's lower intestine is filled with a greenish black, sticky substance called *meconium;* this first stool is normally passed within the first twenty-four hours. The stool turns to a lighter, golden color after the last meconium is passed. The stools vary in number during the first days of feeding. Often, because of the overactivity of the reflex that stimulates the intestinal tract once the stomach is filled, the newborn will have a bowel movement after, or even during, each feeding. Weight loss of about half a pound in the first few days of life is normal.

Although the baby produces a surprising number of enzymes at birth, one enzyme in the liver known as transferase is deficient in almost 50 percent of newborns. This temporary deficiency results in mild jaundice—the skin takes on a yellow tint.

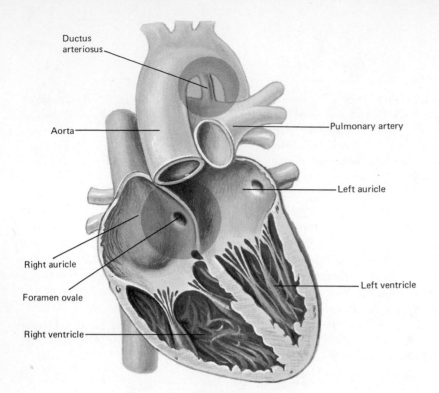

Ductus arteriosus

Aorta

Right auricle

Foramen ovale

Right ventricle

Pulmonary artery

Left auricle

Left ventricle

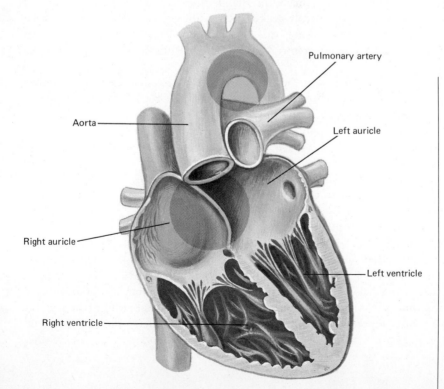

Pulmonary artery

Aorta

Left auricle

Right auricle

Left ventricle

Right ventricle

Figure 2.5. In the fetal heart (top), the foramen ovale permits blood to flow into either auricle, and the ductus arteriosus permits blood pumped out of either ventricle to enter the general circulation. A separate flow of blood to the lungs is not needed because the lungs are not in operation—the blood gets oxygen in the placenta. In the adult heart (left), blood flows from the right auricle to the right ventricle and then is pumped to the lungs, where it is oxygenated. Returning from the lungs to the left auricle, it flows to the left ventricle and then is pumped to the body by way of the aorta.

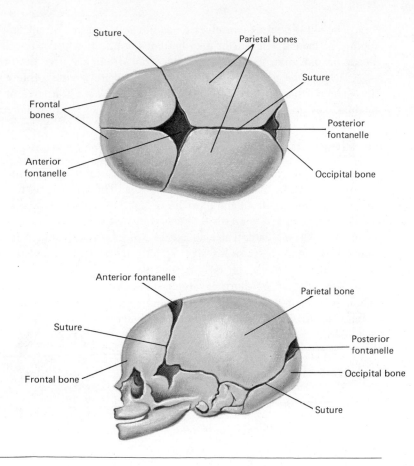

Figure 2.6. The fontanelles. The infant's skull bones are separated by the fontanelles, areas of tough connective tissue that do not entirely close until the child is about one year old.

Skeleton

The skeleton of the newborn has been enriched by the calcium received from the mother's body, but many bones are still mainly cartilage at birth. Some are only connective tissue, and bone formation takes place after the baby is born.

The main characteristic of the neonate's skeleton is its flexibility. The skull, for example, is made up of several bones that touch each other at certain places called the **sutures**, and other places are actually separated by soft areas of the connective tissue called the **fontanelles** (Figure 2.6). The largest of the fontanelles is near the top of the head. This is the last to close, around a year after birth.

The skull bones themselves are quite soft and are often molded temporarily to an egg shape during birth, then flattened and somewhat distorted when the baby sleeps on one side. None of these distortions remains after the first year.

Despite the general pliability of the neonate's bones, fractures occasionally do occur during the birth process. Most common are fractures of the collarbone; healing, however, is usually rapid, and the fracture requires no treatment.

Temperature Regulation

The adult body has a number of mechanisms to help it maintain its internal temperature while the air around it changes. The neonate is more vulnerable to his surroundings. Two of the most basic reactions—secretion of sweat to lose heat and shivering of the muscles to raise body temperature—are simply not yet developed in the neonate. The neonate is also at a disadvantage in maintaining his body temperature because his layer of fatty tissue is thin, and he does not benefit from insulation.

Although the newborn is largely dependent on others to make sure that he is not subjected to extremes of heat or cold, his body is not totally lacking in defense mechanisms. When he cries his body temperature is raised because the metabolism rate is increased.

Immunity to Infection

Before birth, the baby receives a valuable supply of antibodies directly from this mother, especially toward the end of pregnancy. These antibodies protect him at birth when he is suddenly confronted with an environment filled with germs, many of which invade his skin, his digestive tract, and his respiratory tract almost instantly. The protection of some of the mother's antibodies lasts for about a month in the baby, while others, against diseases such as measles, polio, and hepatitis, last from six to twelve months. The mother's antibodies protect the baby against most of the common infectious diseases, but the baby's immunity level will only be as high as the mother's.

The neonate starts immediately to produce his own antibodies. It is possible that antibodies derived from his mother could compete with his own ability to react to immunity injections, such as those for diphtheria, measles, and polio (Vlahović et al., 1973). When more information is available on this subject, it could be crucial in determining the formula and timing of the injections.

BEHAVIOR OF THE NEONATE

The most predictable behavior of the neonate is his repertoire of *reflexes*—involuntary motor responses to specific stimuli. Testing the newborn's reflexes is usually an important part of the physical examination he is given. Such tests aid in neurological evaluation and are valuable as a measure of prematurity.

A rather complex example is the embracing reflex, or Moro reflex, described by Ernst Moro in 1918. If the baby's position is suddenly changed or support seems to fall away, he will grimace and sometimes cry; he will also extend his legs and arms and then bring his arms up in a motion like an embrace. Most babies seem to lose the Moro reflex in about three months (Kessen, Haith, and Salapatek, 1972). Another reflex, the grasp reflex, is elicited by touching the baby's palm; he grasps hold of what has touched him. In the first weeks of life, many babies can hold their own weight by the strength of their grasp. One investigator (Prechtl, 1965) has suggested that these two reflexes may be related to the ability of baby monkeys to cling to their mothers. If a human baby's head is dropped at the same time as his palms are being stimulated, he grasps much more strongly than usual.

Stroke the sole of the neonate's foot, and his toes will usually spread outward in what is called the Babinski reflex. Later in life the normal reaction to this stimulus is just the opposite—the toes will curl downward. A number of reactions, however, appear to be precursors of later capabilities. For example, hold the neonate in an upright position so that his feet touch a solid surface, and he reacts with an automatic walking response, placing his foot down in a heel–toe sequence. This response is another reflex that is useful in determining prematurity; only the full-term neonate walks on the whole foot, whereas prematures walk on tiptoes.

The Babkin reflex is a response that can be demonstrated by pressing the palms of both the baby's hands. He reacts by opening his mouth, turning his head from the side to straight forward, and occasionally by raising his head.

The two responses associated with feeding are perhaps the most important reflexes. The first of these is the rooting reflex, which is produced by stroking the baby's cheek, his chin, or the corner of his mouth. He responds by turning toward the side that was stroked and searching restlessly with his mouth as if he were looking for something to suck.

The sucking reflex itself, the newborn's response when his lips are touched, is by far his most interesting and complex activity. When a baby sucks he is coordinating a number of activities with remarkable efficiency. He is using his cheeks to create suction and his tongue and palate to squeeze the nipple. He is at the same time synchronizing these two activities with swallowing, as well as with the breathing he does through the nose. The extensive research devoted to this response is quite understandable. It has been used as an index of various perceptual reactions and studied for its own complexity in connection with the newborn's learning and adaptive capacity.

Sensory Capabilities

The neonate perceives the world through many senses. He reacts to pain, heat, and cold—and certainly to touch. He responds to change in balance. He seems to distinguish certain kinds of sounds, smells, and even tastes.

Much of what a newborn perceives depends on what researchers call his "state": if he is asleep, the type of sleep; or if he is awake, the type of wakefulness and whether he is hungry or has just been fed. He will not perceive visible things if he is asleep, of course, but there are also states of wakefulness that seem to affect what he perceives or how he perceives it.

The reverse is also true: stimulation affects state. A sudden change of position, a startling sight or sound makes the neonate more alert and active. Rocking, on the other hand, can stop his crying and lull him to sleep. Researchers (Gordon and Foss, 1966) have speculated that rocking may have this effect because the newborn requires kinesthetic stimulation—the feeling of being bodily in motion— and further that this stimulation may help to regulate his internal temperature.

It has also been found (Pederson and Ter Vrugt, 1973) that the more vigorous rocking is, the more effective it is in controlling the infant's crying. Knowing this can make life easier for the mother; it may have implications for the social development of the infant as well. One psychologist (Ainsworth, 1971) has suggested that the security of the attachment between mother and infant may depend to some extent upon the mother's ability to promptly control the infant's crying.

Experiments for visual reactions have established that babies are born with the pupillary reflex—their pupils widen in darkness and narrow in brightness. They also seem to have visual preferences. They like figures with strong contrasts and a certain degree of complexity. In experiments where newborns have been shown a simple triangle, they seemed to spend most of their time looking at one of the angles (Salapatek and Kessen, 1973).

In experiments with smells, it has been found that the newborn seems to perceive changes in smell. He flinches from some sharp odors, such as ammonia or vinegar, but has no reaction at all to many other odors that adults find repulsive.

Learning

Many experiments have been designed to find out whether a newborn's impressions are recorded by his brain. In one study the baby's palms were pressed to produce the Babkin response, and at the same time a buzzer was sounded. After this was done many times, the experimenters were able to produce the response with the sound alone (Kaye, 1965). In another experiment a tone was repeatedly followed by a puff of air that made the baby blink his eyes. Later, the tone alone was sufficient to produce the blink (Little, 1971).

More complex experiments have used a combination of stimulus and response accompanied both by a signal, such as a tone, and a reward for good response, such as a squirt of milk in the baby's mouth. The use of a reward has had especially interesting results in experiments devoted to the sucking capabilities of the newborn. In one series of studies, which tested each of the two components of sucking separately—suction and compression of the nipple—the results showed that the newborn definitely reacts to feedback. He will adjust his sucking to obtain the most efficient flow of liquid, in a kind of adaptive learning (Sameroff, 1972).

It is generally felt that one of the best signs of learning in the neonate is the process called habituation, in which the baby seems to become familiar with a stimulus and has a decreasing reaction to it. Habituation is usually demonstrated by a two-step testing procedure. In the first step, a stimulus such as a checkerboard with four squares is presented several times, and the baby's response time is recorded. The second step consists of presenting a brand new stimulus, such as a 144-square checkerboard. The infant seems to grow bored with the first stimulus and perk up for the second, suggesting that in the course of the repetitions he has made some record of the first stimulus.

Individual differences

The experiments cited in this chapter have yielded many important generalizations about the neonate, but it must not be forgotten that these generalizations describe only a normal range among the babies studied, not every baby. Even before the start of an experiment, a researcher may have to eliminate many perfectly normal babies from the sample because they are not cooperative subjects. In one experiment, for example, trials were made with ninety babies, but only thirty were finally used in the results (Friedman, 1972). The others were rejected because they fussed, they cried, or they were too drowsy or irritable.

TWO TEMPERAMENTS

Donald exhibited an extremely high activity level almost from birth. At three months, his parents reported, he wriggled and moved about a great deal while asleep in his crib. At six months he "swam like a fish" while being bathed. At twelve months he still squirmed constantly while he was being dressed or washed. At fifteen months he was "very fast and busy"; his parents found themselves "always chasing after him." At two years he was "constantly in motion, jumping and climbing." At three he would "climb like a monkey and run like an unleashed puppy." In kindergarten his teacher reported humorously that he would "hang from the walls and climb on the ceiling." By the time he was seven Donald was encountering difficulty in school because he was unable to sit still long enough to learn anything and disturbed the other children by moving rapidly about the classroom.

Clem exemplifies a child who scored high in intensity of reaction. At four and a half months he screamed every time he was bathed, according to his parents' report. His reactions were "not discriminating—all or none." At six months during feeding he screamed "at the sight of the spoon approaching his mouth." At nine and a half months he was generally "either in a very good mood, laughing or chuckling," or else screaming. "He laughed so hard playing peekaboo he got hiccups." At two years his parents reported, "He screams bloody murder when he's being dressed." At seven they related: "When he's frustrated, as for example when he doesn't hit a ball very far, he stomps around, his voice goes up to its highest level, his eyes get red and occasionally fill with tears. Once he went up to his room when this occurred and screamed for half an hour." (Thomas, Chess, & Birch, 1970)

Babies develop at their own individual speed. What is more, they are born with their own temperament, and they manifest this individuality almost immediately. Some babies are born more irritable than others. Some react more vigorously to lying naked on their backs when they are being changed. They may act more determined when they are hungry or may be more petulant when they cannot latch onto the breast. Some babies are placid and easily contented; others are active and easily ruffled or distressed. They may show, for example, less tolerance for stomach distress and as a result may cry more. Very soon, however, each baby brings her individual temperament into interaction with the environment. Her parents may accept her nature and try to channel either her restlessness or her placidity in a desirable direction; or they may be frustrated by her behavior, perhaps comparing her to an older sister. This interaction will be just as important as the kind of temperament she starts out with.

For many years psychologists interested in discovering how personality is formed concentrated most of their attention on the child's early environment. Recently, however, investigators (Thomas, Chess, and Birch, 1970) have identified certain characteristics of temperament that are apparent at birth. The investigators rated a number of babies for these characteristics and then followed the development of the children for more than ten years. They found that parents, trained observers, and teachers agreed in their ratings of individual children as high, medium, or low in nine characteristics: (1) motor activity, (2) regularity of such functions as eating and sleeping, (3) acceptance of something or someone new, (4) adaptability of behavior, (5) sensitivity to stimuli, (6) intensity of responses, (7) general cheerfulness and friendliness, (8) distractibility, and (9) attention span and persistence.

The investigators also found that in many children these characteristics had the tendency to form typical clusters. The three types of temperament formed by these clusters were called "easy," "difficult," and "slow to warm up." However, 35 percent of the children studied could not be classified in any of the three types.

Some of the characteristics seemed to become less prominent as the individual developed and adapted to circumstances. They remained present, however, and occasionally popped up again in new situations. In only a few of the children studied were there permanent changes in characteristics. It is possible too that inconsistency in temperament may itself be a basic characteristic of some children.

Although the temperaments of "difficult" and "slow to warm up" children seldom show any basic change, it was found that taking plenty of time with the child, respecting his temperament, and using special handling tactics can induce the child to learn appropriate behavior, get along with other people, and meet new demands. For example, a very active child cannot be expected to sit quietly and contentedly through a long automobile trip. Frequent stops during the trip should be made to let him get out and run around. Similarly, if a nonadaptable child rejects a new food, his parents should offer it again day after day until he comes to accept it; otherwise he will learn that by being obstructive he can always have his way.

In general, the investigators concluded that any demand that conflicts strongly with a child's temperamental characteristics may put the child under severe stress. Thus, parents and teachers who understand the child's temperament, and know what he can and cannot do, may be in a position to avoid many problems in development and behavior.

References

Ainsworth, M. D. S. Developmental changes in some attachment behaviors in the first year of life. Symposium presented at the biennial meeting of the Society for Research in Child Development, Minneapolis, April, 1971.

Bowes, W. A., Brackbill, Y., Conway, E., and Steinschneider, A. The effects of obstetrical medication on fetus and infant. *Monographs on Social Research in Child Development*, 1970, *35*, 4.

Ernhart, C. B., Graham, F. K., and Thurston, D. Relationship of neonatal apena to development at three years. *Archives of Neurology*, 1960, *2*, 504–510.

Fitzharding, P. M., and Steven, E. M. The small-for-date infant. II. Neurological and intellectual sequelae. *Pediatrics*, 1972, *50*, 50–57.

Friedman, S. Habituation and recovery of visual response in the alert human newborn. *Journal of Experimental Child Psychology*, 1972, *13*, 339–349.

Gordon, T., and Foss, B. M. The role of stimulation in the delay of onset of crying in the newborn infant. *Quarterly Journal of Experimental Psychology*, 1966, *18*, 79–81.

Graham, F. K., Mantarazzo, R. G., and Caldwell, B. M. Behavioral differences between normal and traumatized newborns. *Psychological Monographs*, 1956, *70*, No. 427 and 428.

Kaye, H. The conditioned Babkin reflex in human newborns. *Psychonomic Science*, 1965, *2*, 287–288.

Kessen, W., Haith M. M., and Salapatek, P. H. Human infancy: a bibliography and guide. In P. H. Mussen (Ed.), *Carmichael's manual of child psychology*. 3rd ed. New York: Wiley, 1970.

Little, A. H. Eyelid conditioning in the human infant as a function of ISI. Paper presented at the meeting of the Society for Research in Child Development, Minneapolis, April, 1971.

Pederson, D. R., and Ter Vrugt. D. The influence of amplitude and frequency of vestibular stimulation on the activity of two-month-old infants. *Child Development*, 1973, *44*, 122–128.

Prechtl, H. F. R. Problems of behavioral studies in the newborn infant. In D. S. Lehrmann, R. A. Hinde, and E. Shaw (Eds.), *Advances in the study of behavior*. Vol. I. New York: Academic Press, 1965.

Salapatek, P., and Kessen, W. Prolonged investigation of a plane geometric triangle by the human newborn. *Journal of Experimental Child Psychology*, 1973, *15*, 22–29.

Sameroff, A. J. Learning and adaptation in infancy: a comparison of models. In Reese, (Ed.), *Advances in child development and behavior*. 1972, *7*, 169–214.

Scarr-Salapatek, P., and Williams, M. L. The effects of early stimulation on low birth-weight infants. *Child Development*, 1973, *44*, 94–101.

Thomas, A., Chess, S., and Birch, H. The origin of personality. *Scientific American*, 1970, *233*, 102.

Vlahović, V., Rede, T., Beleznay, O., Pavésić, D., and Raćki, V. Factors affecting the development of serum immunoglobulin levels in infants. *Pediatrics*, 1973, *52*, 2, 206–213.

Wiedenbach, E. *Family-centered maternity nursing*. New York: Putnam, 1967.

SUMMARY

1   Natural childbirth is a program enabling prospective parents to prepare themselves for the experience of having a baby. They study and discuss the stages of childbirth with other parents, practice breathing routines and exercises, and in this way increase their confidence.

2   Labor progresses through the three stages: dilation, expulsion, and the placental stage. Complications are unusual, and a hospital is equipped to handle them. Though anesthesia administered during labor is known to cross the placenta, it appears that these drugs do not cause any permanent damage to the neonate. Anoxia at birth may be caused either by ruptured blood vessels in the brain or delay before the baby begins breathing. When the oxygen loss is acute, there is damage to brain cells.

3   Although premature babies have not fully developed their physical systems for adapting to the world outside the uterus, early stimulation and special care can help them overcome the initial handicap.

4   The neonate makes several physiological adjustments to become an independent organism. The respiratory center in the brain reacts to a chemical imbalance in the blood, and this triggers breathing. Once the umbilical cord is cut, circulation through the lungs increases, and the heart gradually develops to its mature form. The sucking reflex enables the neonate to adapt to the breast or bottle.

5   The neonate possesses a repertoire of reflexes, including the embracing reflex, the grasp reflex, and two reflexes associated with feeding—rooting and sucking. Newborns can learn many responses and show adaptive learning in their sucking behavior.

6   Individual babies develop at their own rate, which is determined in part by their individual temperament. Studies have identified several specific characteristics of temperament that become apparent practically from birth. These characteristics tend to fall into typical clusters, enabling researchers to classify children as "easy," "difficult," or "slow to warm up."

FURTHER READINGS

Bradley, R. A. *Husband-coached childbirth.* New York: Harper, 1965.
    A handbook on natural childbirth directed to prospective fathers. The author has presided at more than 7,000 births with fathers cooperating and aiding in the birth of their children. The book emphasizes the joys of having a baby rather than being delivered of one.

Dick-Read, G. *Childbirth without fear: The original approach to natural childbirth.* (4th ed.) Wessel, H. and Ellis, H. F. (Eds.) New York: Harper, 1972.
    The English obstetrician Dick-Read wrote this book in 1944, and it changed the course of obstetric history. He has proven from his own experience as a physician that childbirth is a natural physiological process not meant to be painful. The book contains a history and rationale of natural childbirth and an explicit step-by-step guide for expectant mothers.

Forbes, T. R. *The midwife and the witch.* New Haven: Yale University Press, 1966.
    The combination of fear, awe, and mystery surrounding childbirth has given rise to dozens of superstitions and folk tales which are recounted by the author, an obstetrician. Half the book is devoted to the history of midwifery and its relationship to witchcraft. Illustrated with old woodcuts of births assisted by midwives.

Montagu, A. *Life before birth.* New York: New American Library, 1964.
    A famous anthropologist examines myths and facts about the influences during pregnancy which effect the unborn child. Montagu feels that the interval between conception and birth is far more important to subsequent growth and development than we have realized.

Richardson, S. A., and Guttmacher, A. (Eds.), *Childbearing: Its social and psychological effects.* Baltimore: Williams and Wilkins, 1967.
    The purpose of the book, as stated by its authors, is to review studies of reproduction which have a social science orientation. The articles included are concerned with psychological stress during pregnancy, the relationship of social class to pregnancy, and cross-cultural studies of pregnancy and child bearing.

Part 2
INFANCY

Sometimes, pulling himself abreast the high walls of his crib, he glanced down dizzily at the patterns of the carpet far below; the world swam in and out of his mind like a tide, now printing its whole sharp picture for an instant, again ebbing out dimly and sleepily, while he pieced the puzzle of sensation together bit by bit, seeing only the dancing fire-sheen on the poker, hearing then the elfin clucking of the sun-warm hens, somewhere beyond in a distant and enchanted world. Again, he heard their morning-wakeful crowing clear and loud, suddenly becoming a substantial and alert citizen of life. . . .

His crib was a great woven basket, well mattressed and pillowed within; as he grew stronger, he was able to perform extraordinary acrobatics in it, tumbling, making a hoop of his body, and drawing himself easily and strongly erect: with patient effort he could worm over the side on to the floor. There, he would crawl on the vast design of the carpet, his eyes intent upon great wooden blocks piled chaotically on the floor. . . .

One day when the opulent Southern Spring had richly unfolded, when the spongy black earth of the yard was covered with sudden, tender grass and wet blossoms, the great cherry tree seethed slowly with a massive gem of amber sap, and the cherries hung ripening in prodigal clusters, Grant took him from his basket in the sun on the high front porch, and went with him around the house by the lily bed, taking him back under trees singing with hidden birds, to the far end of the lot.

Here the earth was unshaded, dry, clotted by the plough. . . . Against the high wire fence there was the heavy smell of hot dockweed. On the other side, Swain's cow was wrenching the cool coarse grass, lifting her head from time to time, and singing in her strong deep voice her Sunday exuberance.

In the warm washed air, Eugene heard with absolute clearness all the brisk backyard sounds of the neighborhood, he became acutely aware of the whole scene, and as Swain's cow sang out again, he felt the flooded gates in him swing open. He answered "Moo!" phrasing the sound timidly but perfectly, and repeating it confidently in a moment when the cow answered.

Grant's delight was boundless. He turned and raced back toward the house at the full stride of his legs. And as he went, he nuzzled his stiff mustache into Eugene's tender neck, mooing industriously and always getting an answer. . . .

"Why, what on earth are you doing, Mr. Grant?"

"Moo-o-o! He said 'Moo-o-o!' Yes he did!" Grant spoke to Eugene rather than to Eliza.

Eugene answered him immediately: he felt it was all rather silly, and he saw he would be kept busy imitating Swain's cow for several days, but he was tremendously excited, nevertheless, feeling now that that wall had been breached. . . .

Thus, later, he saw the first two years of his life in brilliant and isolated flashes. His second Christmas he remembered vaguely as a period of great festivity: it accustomed him to the third when it came. With the miraculous habitude children acquire, it seemed that he had known Christmas forever.

He was conscious of sunlight, rain, the leaping fire, his crib, the grim jail of winter: the second Spring, one warm day, he saw Daisy go off to school up the hill: it was the end of the noon recess, she had been home for lunch. She went to Miss Ford's School For Girls; it was a red brick residence on the corner at the top of the steep hill: he watched her join Eleanor Duncan just below. Her hair was braided in two long hanks down her back: she was demure, shy, maidenly, a timid and blushing girl; but he feared her attentions to him, for she bathed him furiously, wreaking whatever was explosive and violent beneath her placidity upon his hide. She really scrubbed him almost raw. He howled piteously. As she climbed the hill, he remembered her. He saw she was the same person.

3
Physical Development

At birth we have all our limbs, organs, and senses; we can breathe, cry, suck, and swallow; we even have a temperament of our own. We still have a long way to go, however, before we will be able to hit a home run, write a term paper, and get a driver's license. No other animal—not even elephants or whales, who have plenty of growing to do—must go through such a long period of development before they are able to survive in the world without assistance from adults. At times during this period our development seems to proceed at a rather leisurely pace, and at other times we grow astonishingly fast along every dimension. The fastest development takes place during infancy, the first two years of life.

Rapidly as the body grows in infancy, it develops according to orderly and predictable patterns. One pattern is its tendency to develop first at the head and then the rest of the body, part by part, moving downward in what is called a *cephalocaudal* sequence. Even in the fetus, the head forms first. The arm buds form before the leg buds, the nervous system grows from the brain downward, and the facial muscles develop before other muscles because they are closer to the brain. Accordingly, a baby has a well-developed sucking reflex before he can do much of anything else. He gradually gains control of his head, neck, and trunk muscles, in that order. He learns to use his arms before he can control his legs. The cephalocaudal growth pattern helps explain why a child sits before he can stand and crawls before he can walk.

The nervous system also grows from the spinal cord outward, illustrating the second sequential pattern: development occurs first at the center of the body and later at the extremities, or in a *proximodistal* direction. First the baby can control his trunk and then his arms, hands, and fingers; first his hips and then his legs, feet, and toes. Proximodistal growth explains, for instance, why a baby is able to reach out in a somewhat random way for a large object long before he is able to pick up something small with his fingers.

Another pattern of general development is that a baby's physical responses move from a general reaction to a controlled, specific one. For example, when a young baby sees something he wants (a toy, say, or his bottle), he expresses his pleasure and desire by widening his eyes, panting with excitement, wiggling all over, and waving his arms madly at the object. The older baby, who is no less pleased and excited, simply smiles and reaches for the object.

There are also approximate times when certain new features should appear, and quantitative ranges of normal development. It is important to distinguish normal development from any truly irregular situation because many abnormal conditions can be corrected if detected early and given proper medical treatment or physical and dietary therapy. To put it simply, a knowledge of growth patterns enables parents to know when to worry and—almost as important—when not to. The range of ages when a given development normally occurs is in most cases quite broad, so there is usually no reason to worry when a baby does not achieve a development at the age "most" babies do.

How does one assess whether a child is "normal" in his development? Usually by comparing his growth or abilities to those of other children of the same age. Most aspects of the physical growth of children have been extensively studied and measured. The vast amounts of statistical data amassed in these studies have been used to arrive at averages—the average age at which a child learns to walk or gets his first tooth; the average weight, height, head circumference of the one year old; and so on.

The average is usually what you arrive at by adding up all the figures in a study and then dividing the sum by the number of figures. Strictly speaking, however, this is what scientists call the *mean.* The word *average* is sometimes applied also to the statistical measures known as the *median* or the *mode,* and in many cases it is important to know which of these measures is being used. It is equally important to know what the word *average* does not mean: it is not a synonym for *normal.* If one reads, for instance, that the average age at which a child first walks without assistance is thirteen months, one must not assume that all babies who walk sooner or later than that are abnormal. With walking, as with practically every other motor skill and index of growth, a wide range of variation is normal. Each child has a unique hereditary endowment that, in a healthful environment, will unfold according to an individual pattern. The *rate* of growth and maturity will be different for each child although the overall *pattern* of development may be similar.

MEAN, MEDIAN, AND MODE

The results of an experiment or study in child development are often expressed in such terms as **average, mean, median,** or **mode.** Let's suppose, for example, that we have collected data about the heights of 1,000 two year old babies. We can use our figures to construct a curve showing the number of babies in our sample who had reached any given height. The point *M* on the graph has special significance. It indicates the *mean height* of the babies, the statistical average obtained by adding the heights of all the babies and dividing by the total number, 1,000. It also indicates the *median height,* the point at which exactly half the babies were shorter and half were taller. Finally, it indicates the *mode,* the particular height reached by the greatest number of babies.

Such a curve is described as a "normal" or "bell-shaped" curve. When statisticians speak of a "normal" distribution, they mean one like this, in which most individuals fall within a relatively well-defined range. In a normal distribution, the mean, the median, and the mode either coincide, as in our example, or they fall close together.

For many characteristics, however, the distribution is not "normal" in this sense. We might, for example, take another sample of 1,000 children, this time between the ages of one and six, and determine the age at which each child spoke his first sentence. Our new curve might be one that would be described as *skewed,* or asymmetrical. Because most children learn to speak sentences early in the preschool years, most of the scores fall toward the left-hand side of the graph, and the mode, the median, and the mean fall at quite different points along the curve. Curves may be skewed either to the right or to the left, depending on how the values are distributed.

Other studies may yield even more complex distributions. For example, we could take a third sample of children and gather the figures on the rate at which they gain weight during a crucial period of growth—from about ten weeks after conception to about one year of age. The curve would be *bimodal* because there are two peaks of weight gain, one at about the thirty-fourth week of prenatal development, and the other during the fifth to tenth weeks after birth.

In each of these examples most values fall within a rather well-defined *range.* The "normal" situation is for children to vary, sometimes rather widely, in their rates of development. If a child falls at the extreme end of a curve, it may be a warning that something is wrong. In such a case the parents clearly should seek professional advice. But if your one year old has not yet shown her first tooth, don't worry. Nature never meant for us all to be alike.

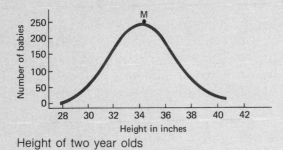

Height of two year olds

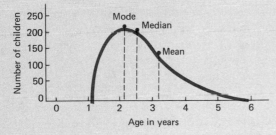

Age of speaking first sentence

Growth from conception through birth

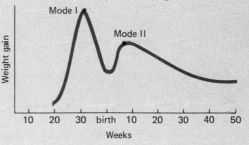

GROWING

Most people equate growth with an increase in height and weight. These are, of course, the most obvious signs, but there are also less apparent kinds of growth in the infant. Muscles increase not only in size but in specialization; as bones harden, the skeleton is transformed from a gelatinous mold into a sturdy frame; the brain cells grow and become specialized. These changes are subtle and sometimes related. The bones of the skull, for example, overlap during delivery to permit birth. Within a short time after birth they have been pushed back into place by the growing brain, though they have not yet grown together. Eventually, by about a year and a half, growth of the cranium will sufficiently catch up with brain growth to close the openings between the bones of the skull.

Increases in weight and height are only a rough index of total growth because different parts of the body mature at different rates. As the body grows, new tissues and structures emerge, differentiate, and specialize in function—all in an orderly manner. This differentiation and specialization, along with growth, prepare the organs, organ systems, and the total organism to function in new and more specific ways and at progressively higher levels. Of an individual's total weight at birth, 20 percent is muscle, 16 percent vital organs, and 15 percent nervous system. In the adult, these proportions are 43 percent, 11 percent, and 3 percent, respectively. The proportion of water making up the body drops from 75 percent at birth to 58 percent at age twelve. The tissues lying under the skin, mostly fat, increase rapidly in thickness during the first nine months of life, then decrease until the child is about two and a half. Boys, as they grow, tend to have more muscle; girls, more fat.

Growing children of the same age develop at noticeably different rates, and even great differences may still be completely normal. The untrained or overanxious eye may exaggerate these differences. Parents tend to become concerned when their baby, especially if he is their first, appears to be too small or late in teething or walking. In determining the child's so-called "normality," we must consider two factors: the child's individual growth rate and how it compares with other children of the same age. These factors yield information on just what is and is not normal growth, and they roughly predict how tall or heavy a child will be at maturity. If, for example, we know the relative pattern of growth for children and the amount of weight a child can expect to gain by a certain age, we can then assess the normality of his growth. What is important is the child's relationship to his age group, although it must be kept in mind that the normal growth patterns are based on studies that used mostly white, middle-class children as subjects.

Weight, in combination with height, is frequently plotted against chronological age to produce *growth curves*. Such curves are used to compare the individual child's growth patterns against those of the average rate of growth. The combination of weight and height is considered a more reliable indicator than weight alone, because height is irreversible, whereas a child may occasionally lose weight. The curves are also useful in determining body build, size, and periods of rapid growth.

The term *age equivalent* is defined (Stott, 1967) as the average age at which a child reaches a particular developmental stage. This can be applied to any variable for which age norms have been established: height, weight, skeletal or dental age, and sexual or organic maturity. For example, a one year old girl might be shorter and heavier than average. If her height is that of the average ten month old and her weight is that of the average thirteen month old, she would be described under this system as a twelve month old with a height age-equivalent of ten months and a weight age-equivalent of thirteen months. Age equivalents are a simple but useful device for comparing chronological, or actual, age with developmental age.

There are other more complicated means of measuring the relative growth and development of children. One way of statistically analyzing a child's development is to graph it. When any given physical characteristic is measured over a period of time and plotted on graph paper, it produces a characteristic curve. Examples are the relatively simple growth curves for height and weight; the Harris Curves, which measure different parts and types of body tissues; the Iowa Curves (Figure 3.1), based on height and weight measurements of fifteen hundred boys and an equal number of girls from mainly upper-income Iowa homes; the Wetzel Grid, which plots growth in terms of overall body size and shape; and the Fels Composite Sheet, which can be used to record height, weight, bone formation, age of walking, and other characteristics on a single graph.

Weight

Because it sums up all the increases in body size, weight is an important indicator of growth. Children grow faster during the first two or three years of their lives than they ever will again. A two year old weighs about one-fifth of what he will probably weigh at eighteen.

Parents and pediatricians have devised several rules of thumb for calculating what a baby's average weight gain should be. One formula states that an infant generally doubles his weight during the first five months, triples it by the end of the first year, and quadruples it by two and a half. Another method of calculation says that the average baby gains two pounds per month for the first three months and about one pound per month by the time he is six months old, then tapers off to two-thirds of a pound per month during the last quarter of the first year. Then he gains only a half pound per month during the second year of life. Neither of these guidelines for figuring the average weight gain of a child can be taken as a hard-and-fast rule; they only summarize what is shown in growth curves.

The child's rate of weight increase is determined not only by his heredity but also by what and how much he eats. To achieve their growth potential, babies and small children should be given a nutritionally sound diet and be allowed to eat more or less as much as they like. (There is little danger in the first few years of a child becoming obese from voluntary overeating; most fat babies become that way by being forced by overzealous parents to eat more than they really want.) As will be shown later in this chapter, poor nutrition in early childhood can have devastating and long lasting—sometimes even permanent—effects on all aspects of a child's development, not just on his weight.

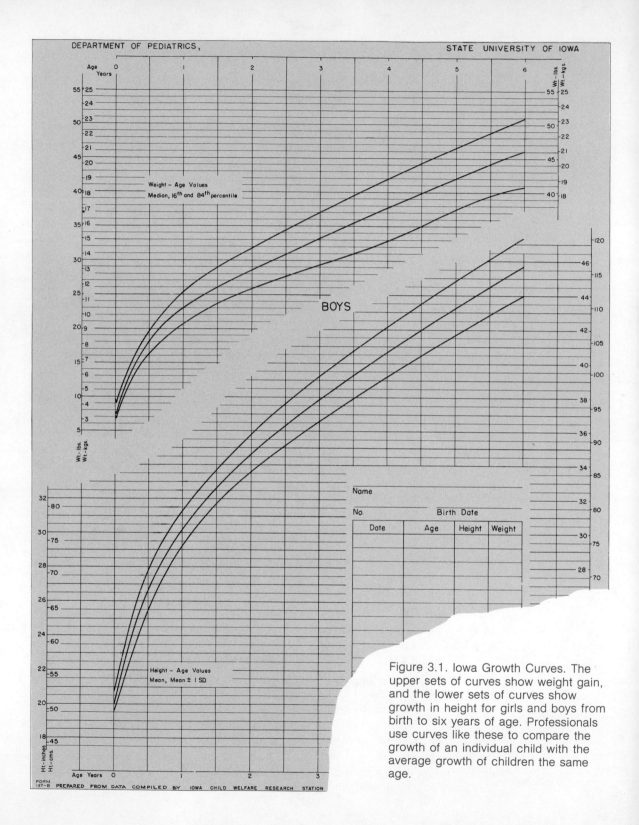

Age Years

Weight – Age Values
Median, 16th and 84th percentile

BOYS

Wt.- lbs.
Wt.- kgs.

Name

No.   Birth Date

Date	Age	Height	Weight

Ht.- inches
Ht.- cms.

Height – Age Values
Mean, Mean ± 1 SD

Age Years   0   1   2   3

FORM
197-B   PREPARED FROM DATA COMPILED BY IOWA CHILD WELFARE RESEARCH STATION

Figure 3.1. Iowa Growth Curves. The upper sets of curves show weight gain, and the lower sets of curves show growth in height for girls and boys from birth to six years of age. Professionals use curves like these to compare the growth of an individual child with the average growth of children the same age.

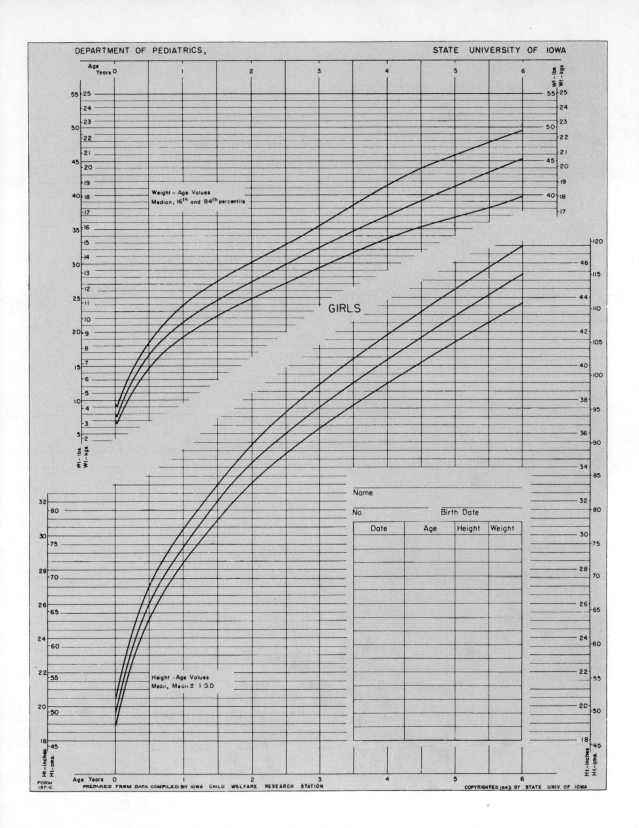

GIRLS

Weight – Age Values
Median, 16th and 84th percentile

Height – Age Values
Mean, Mean ± 1 S.D.

Name

No.   Birth Date

Date	Age	Height	Weight

Body Proportions and Height

Babies are astonishingly large-headed. About a quarter of a newborn's body length is head, compared with only one-eighth for adults. The circumference of the chest, which is smaller than that of the head at birth, takes about a year to catch up and become the larger. Legs grow from one-third of body length for babies to one-half at adulthood. Stem length (head to buttocks) and total length increase nearly equally during the first year, and then the legs begin to grow more rapidly.

The average length at birth is about twenty inches. Most babies grow nine or ten inches in their first year and are between thirty-two and thirty-seven inches tall at the age of two. As with weight, however, the rate of increase is much more important than the number of inches in determining normality. A more significant way of calculating height increases during the first two years of life, therefore, is by percentages: in the first three months a child increases his overall length about 20 percent, nearly 50 percent by one year, and almost 75 percent by age two.

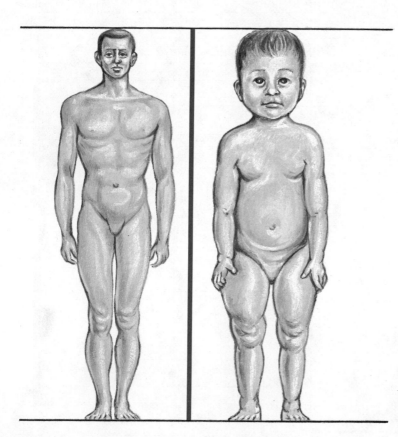

Figure 3.2. The body proportions of a one year old (right) are strikingly different from the proportions of an adult (left). The child's head is proportionally much larger, and his trunk and legs are much smaller, than the corresponding parts in the adult.

Skeleton

The developmental stages of the skeleton are very distinct and easy to observe, thanks to X-ray technology; comparative studies are available in X-ray "atlases." Variations in the skeletal growth of individuals may be great, and there seems to be little or no connection between the rate of skeletal maturation and other developmental processes.

At birth the skeleton is composed largely of cartilage and in appearance is somewhat like a puzzle whose pieces are on the verge of being locked into place. The large spaces that exist between most of the bones gradually decrease as the bones lengthen (Figure 3.3). The bones in the hands and feet of the newborn are far from coming together (in fact, there is usually only one real foot bone—in the heel—at birth; the rest are still in the cartilage stage); the pelvis is small and not connected to the thigh bones; the thigh and the bones of the calf are themselves not connected; the rib cage is open wider in front than it is in later life; and in general the bony frame of a baby is more open than that of the adult. The relatively large spaces between the bones give the infant's joints a pliability that gradually decreases as these gaps are closed by the growing skeleton. A six month old baby has no trouble, for instance, putting his foot into his mouth to suck his toes as a change of pace from his thumb, while most adults would find this a difficult and tiring (not to mention unrewarding) acrobatic feat.

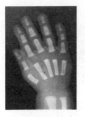

Figure 3.3. Maturation of the skeleton. These X rays of girls' hands show gradual development of the skeleton from birth to eighteen years, when the hand is mature. Notice that at birth there are no small bones in the wrist, but by eighteen years there are at least seven wrist bones.

Birth

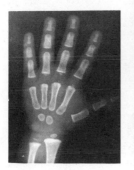

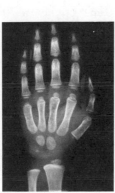

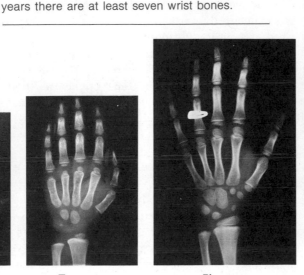

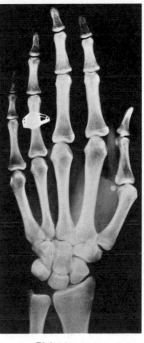

One year　　**Two years**　　**Five years**　　**Eighteen years**

Infants' bones contain more water and proteinlike substances than do mature bones and have a lower mineral content. It may appear that the softness of a baby's skeleton is advantageous, allowing the body to bounce. But young bones, though they do not fracture as easily, are more liable to deformity than they are later in life because they are less resistant to pressure and muscle pull. Because a child's bones are so malleable, it is vital that her diet (and that of her mother during pregnancy) be adequate. A deficiency of vitamin D, for instance, can produce the condition known as rickets, in which the strengthening of the bones is retarded. They bend permanently under the child's weight when she begins to stand and walk, resulting in such deformities as swayback, bowlegs, or knock knees.

Ossification, or bone formation, starts from a few locations and spreads outward from those locations. The primary ossification centers are apparent in fetal life but secondary centers appear after birth. When ossification is complete, the bones are mostly cartilage. The next step is *calcification,* the hardening of the bones through deposit of calcium salts. The degree to which the skeleton has already calcified at birth depends on the mother's own state of calcification, the levels of calcium and phosphorus in her blood, and the balance of calcium, vitamins, and phosphorus intake during pregnancy.

At birth the child has a rounded chest, high shoulders, and short neck. As he grows his chest broadens and flattens, and his ribs begin to slope downward. His shoulders drop, increasing the length of his neck. Before birth the fetus's chin usually rests on his chest, and his legs are doubled up against his abdomen. This hunched-over position causes the spine to form a curve like a C. As soon as the child is born, he starts to breathe for himself, and for this he must lift his head. From this point on, the neck and spine begin to straighten. Later, as the infant learns to sit up and then to stand and walk, the spine assumes the S-curve necessary for balance in an erect position. The spine, which is largely cartilaginous at birth, becomes less flexible as the vertebrae calcify. This is another factor in the preparation of the body for an upright posture.

The skull of the newborn contains forty-five separate bones. Some of them overlap to permit passage of the head through the birth canal, but the growth of the brain soon returns these bones to their original position. Later, many of the skull bones will fuse, but in the young baby some of the gaps between them are so large that they can be seen and felt even by an untrained observer. These large interstices are known as "soft spots," or fontanelles, and are really not as soft as many people believe, since they are covered by a very tough membrane. As the skull grows, the fontanelles close; they have usually disappeared by the time the child is a year and a half old.

Like the other bones of the body, an infant's skull bones are relatively soft. Therefore, if a baby always sleeps with his head turned toward the same side, the bones may flatten somewhat on that side. Some parents wonder if the slight irregularity in head shape caused by this flattening will develop into a permanent misshaping, but they need not worry; the shape of the skull gradually returns to normal as the baby gets older.

Teeth

Teeth begin to form when the fetus reaches its sixth week, and by birth all twenty baby teeth and a few permanent teeth are developing, although they will not begin to make their appearance until around the middle of the first year. During the prenatal period the crowns of the baby teeth (the parts that will show) form and calcify deep in the jaws. Even in these early stages a definite sequence of development is present, beginning with the calcification of the eight front teeth, four upper and four lower (Figure 3.4). Layers of dentine, a bonelike material, are deposited to form the core of the tooth, which is then covered with enamel to complete the crown. Most of the permanent teeth have begun to grow and calcify by the time an infant is six months old.

In a sense, the jaws of the infant and the young child are a kind of tooth-building factory. Not only do they contain the twenty baby teeth, but they are also producing the thirty-two permanent ones. This is still another of the many reasons that good nutrition is so important in the young child; a balanced diet, supplemented with additional vitamins and with fluoride, is essential to the development of sound teeth.

The baby teeth appear in a predictable sequence, but the age at which they erupt and the amount of discomfort that accompanies their appearance are extremely variable. The first teeth usually erupt between four and twelve months of age, with the average at seven months. A small number of babies are actually born with one or two teeth, while a few children do not get their first tooth until sixteen months; neither extreme is cause for alarm. The factors influencing the time and rate of tooth development are not completely known. There seems to be no relationship between the time of teething and a baby's general physical or intellectual development.

Some babies get their teeth with a minimum of fuss, while others fret and drool for months before each tooth emerges. Babies drool a certain amount anyway, but teething usually increases the phenomenon.

Sucking or mouthing food causes some teething babies enough discomfort to decrease their appetite somewhat. Some pediatricians recommend beginning weaning when a baby starts to teethe, since drinking milk or formula from a cup seems to irritate sensitive gums less than sucking on a nipple.

Figure 3.4. Development of the teeth. Twenty baby teeth appear in five stages, shown here from left to right, usually starting at about seven months of age. The infant's jaw contains the buds of some permanent teeth even before the first baby teeth break through the gums.

As the teeth grow, so does the face. The pattern of facial growth is established during the first three years and is marked by more or less proportionate increases in facial size. Influencing both the growth of the face and the position of the teeth is the growth of the jaws. The relationship between the upper and lower jaws determines efficiency in chewing and facial balance. The condition known as *malocclusion*—a word formed by combining *mal,* bad, and *occlusion,* closing— occurs either because the upper and lower jaws grow at different rates or because the position and spacing of the teeth are incorrect. This improper alignment of jaws or teeth can be caused by hereditary factors, such as unequal jaw growth, or by environmental conditions, such as thumbsucking or premature loss of teeth through accident or decay, or by both. Malocclusion produced by thumbsucking ordinarily corrects itself spontaneously, even after the preschool years, when the habit is discontinued. Fortunately, because of the plasticity of the growing jaw, other forms of malocclusion can be corrected by such orthodontic means as selective extraction of teeth, if the jaws are overcrowded, and the use of braces.

Muscles, Fat, and Skin

The infant is probably born with all the muscle fibers he will ever have. Muscle growth results from increases in the length and thickness of these fibers; and the structure, attachment, and nervous control of muscles also develop systematically. At birth the muscles represent one-fourth of body weight, a proportion that increases to two-fifths by maturity. The muscles grow in a cephalocaudal sequence, and therefore the young baby's best developed muscles are those in his eyes, mouth, and respiratory tract. On the whole, however, a child's large muscles function better than his small, fine ones. Throughout the entire growing period he is more skillful in activities involving large movements than in those requiring precision. His arms are better developed than his legs (though the legs may be fatter), whereas in the adult the thickest muscles are in the legs and back.

Overlying the muscles are two layers of tissue: the subcutaneous layer, which is chiefly fat, and the cutaneous tissues, which include skin, hair, and nails. A thick layer of fat pads the frames of infants and small children and gives babies their characteristic chubby look. The layer of fatty tissue thickens rapidly during a child's first nine months and then decreases until, by the time the child is five, it is normally only about half as thick as it was at nine months. The child's skin grows at the rate necessary to keep pace with his increase in skeletal size and his fat and muscle growth. The amount and rate of growth for head hair is highly variable among babies and young children.

Brain and Nervous System

The brain is the primary organ of the central nervous system. Along with the spinal cord, it controls all of the infant's reflex activity and the action of involuntary organs and mediates all voluntary movements, perception, and abstract thought.

EEG

The electroencephalograph (EEG) is a device that measures and traces the fluctuating electrical charges generated by the brain. These charges, often called brain waves, are usually picked up with plate or needle electrodes on the surface of the scalp. Records of the amplitude, frequency, and regularity or irregularity of the waves give the psychologist valuable information about brain functioning during both sleep and wakefulness. When the subject is awake but relaxed, for example, the tracing produced by an EEG is likely to show mostly regular waves of moderate voltage. As the subject becomes drowsy, the amplitude of the wave is reduced. Low-amplitude waves in a consistent pattern characterize deep sleep. There is another stage of sleep in which the EEG tracing suddenly changes to the patterns of alert wakefulness. This is termed *paradoxical sleep* or *REM sleep.* REM stands for "rapid eye movement"; in this type of sleep the person's eyes are moving rapidly under his eyelids, and he is dreaming vividly.

The most successful uses of the EEG have been in sleep research, the diagnosis of abnormal nerve conditions such as epilepsy, and the discovery of the functions of different parts of the brain. Scientists cannot tell what a person is doing or thinking by studying his EEG tracing, but with the help of the EEG they have discovered many interesting developmental phenomena, such as the unclear differentiation between sleep and wakefulness in newborn infants.

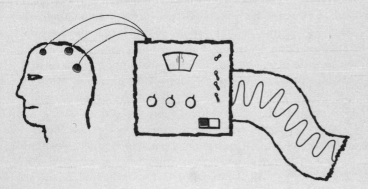

The infant possesses most, if not all, of the cells that will ever compose his brain, though the cells become larger and more specialized. At the age of one year, the brain has already reached 60 percent of adult weight, and the brain of a five year old is 90 percent the weight of an adult brain.

In the newborn child the brain functions chiefly to control such essential reflex behavior as sucking, swallowing, emptying the bladder, and coughing. These reflexes come from the midbrain and spinal cord, whereas voluntary control arises in higher brain centers. These higher centers are also the seat of sensation and intelligence. Gradually, as these higher centers assume some of the functions formerly controlled by the midbrain and spinal cord, many of the baby's reflexes start to disappear. For example, the walking reflex that a newborn demonstrates when held in a standing position originates in an entirely different area of the central nervous system from the part that controls the voluntary walking of the one year old.

By six months the child has acquired considerable control over voluntary movements. Different parts of the brain develop in accordance with these movements. First are the cells controlling the upper trunk, neck, and upper arm; those controlling the legs and head follow. By the age of one month the child can control his hands in addition to his arms, and by three months, his head.

The maturation of the nervous system does not depend on exercise or learning. For practical purposes, this means that a baby's development cannot be speeded up by training or practice. She simply cannot do things until her central nervous system is ready for her to do them. Thus, if a child is not yet ready to walk, no amount of coaxing or exercise will prompt her to do so.

Tracings of babies' brain waves made by an electroencephalograph (or EEG for short) show that all children have slightly different patterns of brain function, much in the same way that every person's fingerprints are unique. This individual variability in the function of the brain is undoubtedly related to individual differences in physical development as well as in intellectual ability and temperament.

MOVING AND MANIPULATING

The control a child achieves over his body depends on the structural readiness of his body and the functional readiness of his brain. Even during the prenatal period the muscles involved in grasping, sitting, and walking are exercised, but these motions cannot become voluntary until a sufficient maturation of the neuromuscular system (the nerves and the muscles they control) has occurred. Most of the child's basic physical accomplishments are achieved, on the average, during the first year and a half of his life. He will practice—and succeed at—using his arms and hands to procure and examine whatever attracts his attention; he will sit up to survey his surroundings; he will creep from one place to another to explore a larger world; he will stand up to view new vistas from what seem to him to be lofty heights; and, ultimately, he will demonstrate his growing independence by taking a few steps all by himself.

When one stops to examine this progression in the child's mastery of motor skills, two patterns become apparent. The first is the baby's will to gain greater mobility, to get around. The second is his need, which is more innate than imitative, to achieve the upright posture. The famous physician Benjamin Spock (1972) aptly describes this second drive as a celebration of "that period millions of years ago when man's ancestors got up off all fours." At the same time that the child learns to balance on his feet, he is also learning to manipulate things with great skill, which reflects another prehistoric development of man: "Our ancestors stood up because they had found more useful things to do with their hands than walking on them."

Sometimes one of these two drives—the desire for mobility and the need to become upright—takes precedence over the other. A baby who is an adept creeper may be too busy scooting around on his hands and knees examining his world to take the time to practice standing. The less proficient creeper, on the other hand, may spend a great deal of time practicing pulling himself to a standing position; because he has a greater need to learn to walk than the baby who gets around well on all fours, he may be an earlier walker. As a child learns one skill, he may temporarily slow down or even regress in his mastery of others. His rate of progress may also be affected by illness or by an accident, such as a fall, that frightens him.

A child's motor control depends on the maturation of his central nervous system, but when he is ready to perform, he should be encouraged to do so and given plenty of opportunity to practice. If he is not ready, he should be left alone, inasmuch as no amount of pushing can get him to do what he is not physically capable of doing. Forcing a baby to try a skill he is not ready for can result in misery and frustration for him; sometimes it may make him reluctant to try it when he *is* ready. One should always keep in mind that every infant is an individual who has his own rate of physical development and his own pace of learning.

Grasping

As we saw in Chapter 2, the grasping reflex is present at birth. The newborn's hand is actually strong enough in a reflex grip to support his body weight; as a vehicle of the will, however, it is useless. Many reflexes gradually die out during infancy (some protective reflexes, such as blinking, never disappear), and many others are replaced by learned, voluntary actions. The hand of the newborn responds reflexively, for example, to stimulation of the palm; the fingers close down in a grasp, but the thumb is flaccid and inoperative. About one month after birth the grasping reflex starts to become distinctly weaker, and by four months it is gone. At about the time it disappears, the child begins to reach out for things, and some time after the middle of the first year he can voluntarily grasp, transfer, and manipulate objects. Characteristically, the palm and side of the hand are used more than the fingers to pick up small objects during this period. This method is called the "palmar scoop."

As voluntary grasping develops and becomes more refined, coordination of hand with eye becomes important. The maturing child first reaches and misses, then reaches and touches, reaches and grasps without the ability to hold the desired object, and finally reaches, grasps, and manipulates.

After the child learns to grasp, he must learn to let go. Initially he drops an object because his hand relaxes involuntarily when his attention and muscular energy are diverted elsewhere, but by six to eight months he has usually learned to let go on purpose. This new skill often becomes a favorite game, with the child dropping a rattle or other object on the floor, having his mother retrieve it and hand it back, only for him to drop it again.

The child gradually gains control over his fingers and thumbs, and by eight or nine months the forefinger and thumb work smoothly in opposition. This enables the child to use his hands to pick up and hold smaller things, and by one year he can execute this manipulation skillfully on even very small objects. Many one year olds delight, for instance, as they crawl around, in picking up (and sometimes eating) tiny specks of dust and dirt.

Rolling Over

Rolling over is usually a baby's first maneuver with his whole body, and it cannot be accomplished until he has gained considerable control over his head, torso, and legs. To roll from front to back, the baby raises his head and one shoulder, arches his back, and twists, giving a shove with his legs, and over he goes. Many babies start to master this stunt at the age of about five months; a month or so later, they usually learn to roll from back to front as well. Rolling may become one of a child's favorite pastimes, and he will practice it for the sheer pleasure of the movement itself, without much conscious direction. Later, when the stunt becomes old hat, he will roll over with some other purpose in mind, such as reaching for a toy. Rolling over eventually leads to such complex maneuvers as pulling up into a standing position.

Sitting Up

As with rolling over, a child must gain strength in his neck and back and control over his head before he can sit up. The newborn baby demonstrates what is known as "head lag." Although he can usually raise his head from the mattress very slightly when lying on his stomach and may be able to turn it from side to side, when he is held upright his head is floppy and either drops backward or sags forward on his chest. As he practices raising his head while he is prone, however, his neck and shoulder muscles strengthen; eventually he is able to get his head and chest well off the bed and can hold his head erect when he is picked up.

When the child has gained enough control over the upper part of his body, sitting up follows naturally. Many babies can sit with the support of pillows by the age of four months if helped up into a sitting position. The noted child psychologist Arnold Gesell (1940) found that 20 percent of the four month olds in one study were able to sit with only slight support; at six months over half the group sat in this way, and about 20 percent could sit alone for several seconds. At an average of twenty-eight weeks, children can sit up briefly by themselves, leaning forward on their hands. By forty weeks the muscles of the back are usually strong enough for most children to sit straight and steadily for a fairly long period of time, and most have strong enough abdominal muscles to get to a sitting position on their own.

Creeping and Crawling

Although most babies can use their arms and legs to pivot themselves around on their stomachs by the middle of the first year, they do not usually begin to creep—that is, to get around on all fours—until they are over seven months old. A child may become remarkably adept at getting around this way, and even after he has learned to walk, he may occasionally revert to creeping as a more proficient means of locomotion. Although most children creep before they can walk, some do not. Creeping, therefore, may not be a necessary stage of motor development.

Babies have many different styles of creeping or crawling (technically, creeping is done with the stomach clear of the ground). Some do it on their hands and knees; others use the "crab-walk" method of hands and feet; some even creep on their hands, one knee, and one foot. When a baby starts to creep, he may not

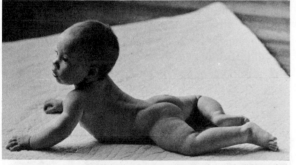

Figure 3.5. Getting up to creep. In the first picture (left) the baby is lying on her stomach with some of her weight supported by her hands and thighs. She bends one knee (lower left) and shifts her weight back onto that leg, raising her torso off the floor. Then she bends the other knee and pushes up with her arms until her weight is equally distributed between her hands and her knees (below). Notice how the toes are used for support in the final creeping posture.

go forward at first; he may go backwards, sideways, or in circles instead. Somehow, however, he usually ends up where he wants to go, and once he gets there, he may well demonstrate that he knows how to pull himself up to a standing position while holding onto a piece of furniture. This ability to pull up usually occurs about the same time creeping begins.

Walking

Walking is a tremendous milestone in a child's life. It enables him to expand his environment immensely and, by freeing the hands for manipulation, makes the possibilities for exploration almost limitless. Walking comes not only through learning but also through maturation of the skeletal and muscular systems and the neuromuscular mechanism. Well-developed sight and hearing are required to help the child keep his balance and steer his course. He must, after all, be able not merely to place one foot in front of the other, but also to see where he is going.

Most children can stand with support between eight and ten months and alone by one year. The average age of unassisted walking is between thirteen and fourteen months, although, of course, some children walk much earlier, others later.

A child's first independent steps are jerky and uneven. Her feet are spread and her toes turned outward. Her arms are held out for balance. She weaves as she walks, and she falls frequently. As she practices, she moves on to "toddling," a kind of flat-footed paddling about. Soon she becomes bold enough to undertake positively daring feats—climbing stairs, running, balancing on one foot. As her muscles grow stronger and her balance improves, her walking patterns also become more mature. By the time they are two and a half, most children walk quite well.

The healthy child normally demonstrates a great deal of enthusiasm and a genuine sense of accomplishment in her walking progress. Neither bumps nor falls deter her practice. Only illness or parentally induced timidity represent a serious obstacle to her mastery of this skill.

Self-Feeding

Sucking is one of the newborn's basic reflexes. Coordination of hand to mouth begins at around four months for most children, although some newborn babies are adept thumb or finger suckers (a talent many of them cultivated while still in the uterus). A baby's tongue and lips are acutely sensitive, and he uses them to explore almost everything he can get hold of. By six months the baby puts objects into his mouth all day long, but purely exploratory mouthing is on the wane by about nine months (although chewing on objects may continue throughout a baby's active teething period). It is replaced around one year by purposeful food-getting.

Coordination of hands and fingers also advances during this period, permitting the child to manipulate eating utensils. Mastery of these utensils comes gradually, however; it takes most children quite a while to learn how to fill a spoon and even longer to master the art of carrying it to the mouth without spilling the contents.

Figure 3.6. Standing up to walk. From a sitting position (upper left), the child shifts her weight to one hand, then to both hands, one leg, and one foot (above). She raises her torso up and balances on feet and hands in a creeping position (lower left), and finally stands by balancing on her feet alone before shifting her weight to one foot so that she can take a step (below).

A child may be quite content to be fed for some time, but once he decides to get into the act, he usually becomes adamant about it. Often he wants the independence of self-feeding before he has all the physical skills needed to accomplish it. He may tire before he has finished his meal and want and accept help. Most children are accomplished self-feeders by the age of three.

EATING

The infant experiences hunger as a generalized sensation of unpleasantness; eating brings about a generalized feeling of satisfaction. This association of food with pleasure is the basis of appetite. Both hunger and appetite are essential to development. The body will produce hunger, but if the child has unpleasant associations with food or feeding, he may resist eating, which can ultimately result in dietary deficiencies and emotional disturbance.

Diet

Nutrition may well be the most important factor in an infant's environment, affecting as it does his growth, functioning, and resistance to disease. Poor nutrition results in stunted growth. Children who are undernourished are ultimately smaller as adults than children who are adequately fed; even when an initially poor diet is improved in later childhood, the losses in growth potential are never fully recouped.

Because diet is so important, the subject of what and how much to feed a child has been given a great deal of attention. A classic experiment (Davis, C. M., 1935) in which children were allowed to select their own diet from a variety of natural, unrefined foods showed that the children ate eagerly and consumed astonishingly large quantities, then stopped with an air of finality. At the conclusion of the experiment, their appetites, digestion, and overall physical condition were well above average. Some of the implications of this study are still quite controversial, but it does seem clear that if a parent offers his child a diet of overall high nutritional value, he need not be worried about getting the child to eat precisely measured, meticulously selected portions of food.

The chief element in the diet of the very young child is, of course, milk (or some high-protein substitute, such as soybean emulsion). In feeding a baby, both his rate of weight gain and signs of hunger should be considered. Overfeeding, which has an adverse effect on health and eating habits, should be discouraged almost as much as underfeeding. Appetite varies with each child, and from day to day for any one child. A baby's appetite, weight gain, the interval he is willing to wait between feedings, and his response to new foods are all important in determining when so-called "solid" foods (that is, foods other than milk or formula, such as cooked cereal or strained vegetables and fruit) are introduced into his diet, and when portions of milk or solids should be increased.

Some parents, doctors, and nutritionists advocate introducing solid foods within the first month after birth. They argue that solid foods fill a baby more adequately and keep him from getting hungry too often; that the use of solid foods, with a wide variety of food sources, makes it possible to construct a better diet; and that solids stimulate the gums and allow the child to increase his chewing skills.

Others doubt that solids should be started so soon. They point out that the baby gets all the calories he needs and essentially all the nutrients he can digest from breast milk (supplemented with multivitamin preparation) or from a scientifically prepared formula; that he is more likely to develop food allergies when he is young; and that the imperfectly developed tongue reflex in the infant can cause the baby to cough and gag on solid foods.

One investigator (Davis, A., 1959) suggests that if hunger or nutritional requirements make it necessary to introduce solids before a baby is three or four months old and able to control his swallowing mechanism, he can be fed them by bottle. Mashed cereal or fruit, mixed with a large amount of milk or formula, can be sucked through a nipple with enlarged holes.

Once the child begins to eat solids, he can be introduced gradually and relatively simply to the foods that will eventually make up his mature diet. Most children accept new foods after experimentation. Their doing so results more from curiosity than from any nutritional craving; their attention is drawn to new textures and colors. Parental ingenuity and a concern for the child's comfort while eating are usually sufficient to encourage the acceptance of a new food. It is important that the utensils be suitable to the child's size and manipulatory abilities; a two year old finds it much easier, for example, to handle a small spoon than a large, heavy fork. He also likes his chair to be the right size for him.

Even more essential than utensils and furniture, of course, is the emotional climate that prevails at mealtimes. Children, and adults as well, have a heartier appetite and better digestion when a meal is a pleasant, serene event. For this reason, some pediatricians recommend that a baby not eat with the rest of the family until he is fairly proficient at self-feeding. Things can get rather hectic when a member of the family must feed himself and a small baby simultaneously; usually neither can really do justice to the meal.

By his second birthday a child can swallow and digest quite solid food and can usually feed himself with some skill. At this point he no longer needs special food and is ready to join the family at mealtimes. This privilege is not a license to permit his indulgence in the entire adult menu, however. Nutritionists consider lean meats and stewed fruits with mild seasoning appropriate for the growing child but discourage heavy indulgence in sweets and starches. Food requirements—both the right kind and the right amount of food—vary with a child's age, size, rate of growth, and level of activities. His diet should always include items from all of the four basic food groups—meat and dairy products, cereals, fruits, and vegetables. In addition, most doctors recommend supplementing the diet with a multivitamin preparation specially formulated for children. Giving the child small portions of food and permitting him to ask for more is preferable to serving large portions and expecting him to eat them all. Overeating in infancy is a start toward adult obesity.

Schedule

The initial considerations in building positive associations with food are likely to revolve around the eating schedule. Should feedings be systematically spaced, or should the child be fed on demand? When foods other than milk or formula are introduced, what should they be, and how much? These are among the most commonly raised questions; the way in which the adult handles them will strongly affect the developing food habits and attitudes of the young child.

It is probably safe to say that parents are infinitely more dogmatic about schedules, or the lack thereof, than any baby would ever desire; a tremendous controversy has raged over this matter of regularity versus flexibility. The two sides in the controversy can be briefly characterized as follows: the advocate of the regular schedule says that the infant should be fed at strict time intervals, every three hours during the first week or so of life and every four hours thereafter. This is based on what has been observed to be the average rate of digestion and pattern of hunger in the newborn. Adherents of the strict schedule usually also believe that a child should be encouraged to drink a given amount at every feeding, calculated according to his age and weight. On the other side are the practitioners of the so-called "self-demand" schedule, who say that a baby should be allowed to eat whenever he seems hungry and be permitted to drink as much or as little as he feels like at any given feeding.

Neither extreme is the best approach to scheduling. Spock (1972) hit the nail on the head when he said:

> When parents act as if the schedule is a matter of belief, like a religious or political conviction, it seems to me that the real point has been lost. The main purpose of any schedule is to do right by the baby. But another purpose is to enable the parents to care for him in a way that will conserve their strength and spirits. This usually means getting down to a reasonable number of feedings at predictable hours, and omitting the night feeding as soon as the baby is ready. Otherwise the parents won't be able to do as good a job with him in other respects. What's good for them will be good for him, and vice versa.

Because as the child grows his stomach is able to hold larger and larger amounts and can thus compensate for longer intervals between feedings, and because children have a tendency to develop regular habits of hunger if guided somewhat to do so, the best solution to the problem seems to be what has been called a self-regulating schedule. Self-regulation implies that a newborn's feedings are initially adapted to his needs and capacities; the tiny infant is more or less fed when and however much he wants. Gradually, however, parental regulation is introduced, and the baby eventually becomes content with feedings at fairly regular intervals. A self-regulation schedule prevents a small baby from having to cry for hours when he is hungry and later on encourages him not to mind terribly if he has to wait a bit.

Some investigators (Watson and Lowrey, 1967) contend that a healthy child will not develop feeding problems unless some adult has tried, usually in early infancy, to impose on him the adult's own ideas of how much he should eat. They recommend that, because the infant has the same physiological variations in appetite as an adult, he should be allowed to take more or less as much as he wants. They also caution against the forced introduction of solid foods, which might result later in the refusal of all foods. Almost all children have spells during which they refuse certain foods; such refusals should be respected. The lesson seems to be that parents should take it very slow and easy when trying to regulate a child's eating patterns. As long as they consistently offer their child a balanced, wholesome diet, occasional fluctuations in his appetite and temporary refusals of or cravings for certain foods seldom result in his becoming undernourished or overweight.

Breast or Bottle

In our culture, an infant is either breast- or bottle-fed, depending in most cases on his mother's preference. Either way, the mother (or other caregiver) establishes a degree of physical contact with and cooperation from the infant. Cooperation is essential. Stressful or abrupt feeding may disrupt the relationship and encourage the infant to associate feelings of discomfort with his mother and with the satisfaction of his physical needs.

The quality of the feeding relationship seems to matter a great deal more than the choice of feeding method. Thus the supporters of one or the other method of feeding have usually tried to convince us that their particular method is more gratifying for mother and child. Naturally, the choice depends on individuals. It also reflects the consensus of the women in a culture. In parts of Pakistan, women breast-feed their children freely and permissively until they are about two years old; in the United States what breast feeding there is—chiefly among the educated middle class—is likely to be "token," with feedings restricted, supplemented by the bottle, and discontinued after the first three months (Newton, 1972).

It has long been recognized that breast and bottle feeding are not biologically equivalent. The sucking technique, the speed of milk intake, and even the composition and taste of the milk differ. Moreover, the mother's physical state is greatly affected by nursing (Newton, 1972). The sucking of the infant stimulates the mother, causing a rise in the temperature of the mammary area and a contraction of the uterus. Nursing also inhibits the menstrual cycle. The bottle-feeding mother feels none of these effects.

The psychological or developmental results of breast and bottle feeding are more difficult to specify. A British study found that nursing mothers touch their babies more than bottle-feeding mothers—not because breast feeding required more handling but apparently because of attitudinal differences. Numerous studies have

Figure 3.7. One of the advantages of bottle feeding: father can do it.

suggested that breast feeding may be related to more positive attitudes toward infant and adult sexuality. Researchers (Masters and Johnson, 1970) found, for example, that nursing mothers generally resumed marital intercourse soon after pregnancy, and in another study (Sears, Maccoby, and Levin, 1957) they were found to be more than usually tolerant of masturbation and other sexual play in their children. While these and other studies indicate that the nursing mother is more mature and more accepting of her sexual role, results are sometimes conflicting. For example, one study found that breast feeders were more envious of the male sexual role (Adams, 1959), while another reported more discontent among the bottle feeders (Newton, 1972).

Experts do agree that breast feeding is not the best choice for all mother–infant pairs. Some mothers are unable to nurse; others find it painful for physical reasons, embarrassing for social reasons, or impossible because of a career commitment. Initial difficulties in nursing can make a new mother anxious about her ability to fulfill the maternal role; this may impede a feeding relationship that would have gone smoothly by bottle. While some mothers feel guilty about the choice of the bottle, most are quickly reassured by the baby's evident progress on formula. Indeed it appears that overall weight gain in the first six months is greater for bottle-fed infants in highly developed nations (Aitken and Hytten, 1960). While some studies report developmental differences as a result of infant feeding experiences, no clear conclusions can be drawn. It is difficult to isolate feeding effects because in our society even breast-fed babies do not live by breast alone.

Weaning

In our culture, weaning—the termination of the child's breast or bottle feeding—is usually initiated by the last quarter of the child's first year, though nowadays some mothers begin cup feeding much earlier. In a sense, though, weaning begins as soon as the baby starts to take vitamins from a medicine dropper, orange juice or fish-liver oil from a spoon, water from a cup—that is, as soon as the child begins to have some inkling that liquids also come in containers other than the breast or bottle.

Children differ in their readiness to be weaned. The child's natural curiosity about new food tastes, textures, and smells prepare him for weaning. When a baby shows signs of beginning to be bored with the bottle or breast—when, for instance, he starts chewing on the nipple, playing with his hands, or flirting with his mother as she is feeding him—it is a pretty good clue that he will find drinking from a cup an exciting new horizon.

All babies are born with a sucking instinct; they nurse to satisfy not only their hunger but also this instinct. Weaning cannot be successfully undertaken, therefore, until the child's craving for sucking has pretty well dwindled. The parent can assume that this has happened when signs of boredom with nursing begin to appear. The sucking instinct of some babies, however, is not quite satisfied in infancy, and they become attached more fervently than ever to the bottle or breast as they get older. Some bottle-fed babies also develop a passionate attachment to the bottle when it has been used in infancy as either a pacifier or a mother substitute. When a baby is put to bed with a propped bottle instead of being fed in his mother's arms until he becomes sleepy, the bottle gets all the credit for his feeling of well-being and therefore takes on undue importance.

Weaning can also be difficult if it is undertaken too late. The longer a child nurses, the more he comes to rely on it. It is, after all, a pleasant experience, and no clever child relinquishes his pleasures lightly. He may even want to have his cake and eat it too, taking some milk from the cup, which he finds fun and challenging, but continuing with the breast or his nice old bottle as well.

The process of weaning should be gradual. If a baby is forced to go "cold turkey," he may balk completely at cup feeding. The usual procedure is to start by feeding a small amount of milk from a cup at each meal. As the amount is increased, the quantity given by bottle or breast is decreased. Finally, only the cup is offered at one meal, usually the meal at which the baby has seemed least interested in nursing. Soon the second bottle or breast feeding can be omitted altogether, and shortly thereafter the cup can be offered exclusively at all three meals.

It is usually recommended that a breast-fed baby be weaned directly to the cup, bypassing the bottle stage altogether. Otherwise, the mother may have to go through the whole process twice, once in getting the baby accustomed to the bottle and the taste of cow's milk, and again when the shift to the cup is made. If, however, a mother wishes or is required to discontinue breast feeding before her baby is

Figure 3.8. Denver Developmental Screening Test. Bar graphs show the percentage of children who are able to perform the items tested.

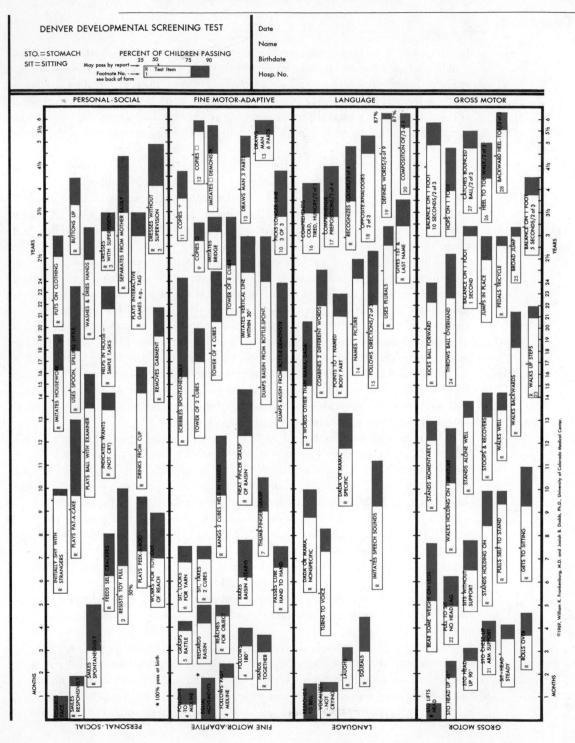

physically ready to drink from a cup, the introduction of the bottle will be necessary. If at all possible, this too should be done gradually.

Sometimes it is the mother who postpones weaning. She may be reluctant to end this emotional tie with her child, or she may worry that he will not get enough milk from the cup to stay healthy. Or she may just be afraid that the process will upset him. These last two fears are almost always unfounded. By the time they are ready to be weaned, most babies can do with considerably less milk than they are used to taking from the bottle or breast, and if children are weaned when they themselves indicate signs of readiness, they seldom become very upset.

Digestive and Dietary Disorders

It may be inaccurate to say that clothes make the man, but it is literally true that diet makes the child. Some children are not provided with adequate nutrition in their formative years, either because they simply do not get enough food or because they are not getting the right kinds. The effects of poor nutrition can be not only severe but long-lasting and even permanent. There are other children who are given adequate, well-balanced meals but who, for some reason, react poorly to something in the diet or have a generalized poor reaction to the whole digestive process. These problems, however, either are usually outgrown within a reasonably short time or can be remedied by altering the diet. Thus, the results of such disorders are seldom as severe or long-lived as those of malnutrition.

Practically all young babies do some spitting up during or after feedings. The muscle valve at the upper end of the stomach may not be well enough developed to hold down all the contents when a full baby is picked up or jostled. If the baby has swallowed air while nursing, some milk may lie on top of the air bubble; when the baby is burped, therefore, he will bring up not only the bubble but also a little milk. Infants also have occasional spells of mild indigestion or gas. None of these conditions is anything to worry about.

Colic

As it is usually used, *colic* is a catchall word that describes the symptoms of infants who have regular or prolonged bouts of paroxysmal crying during their first few months of life. More precisely, however, colic is a syndrome characterized by a distention of the abdomen, apparently resulting in severe pain and causing the baby to cry violently and continuously during the colicky period. Gas usually begins to distend the abdomen shortly after a feeding, and four hours of incessant crying is not exceptional. The trouble is most common during the late afternoon or evening. The condition tends to begin when the infant is only a few weeks old and is usually over or definitely on the wane by the time he is three months old.

Unfortunately, no one really knows what causes colic. X rays taken of colicky babies do not show any anatomical irregularities of the gastrointestinal tract. A number of researchers have hypothesized that an immature nervous system may be the cause of the condition. One recent investigation (Ferreira, 1960), seemed to show that babies whose mothers were under greater than average emotional stress during pregnancy were more likely to be colicky.

Almost as unfortunate as not knowing the cause of colic is the fact that there are no reliably effective remedies. Pediatricians occasionally prescribe a tranquilizer for a severely colicky baby (and sometimes for the nerve-racked parents as well), but generally babies simply outgrow the syndrome without medical treatment. Since colic seldom affects the baby's appetite (ironically, the colicky baby's screaming sometimes even serves to *increase* his appetite), the condition has no serious effect on a child's overall nutrition.

Allergies

A surprisingly large number of babies are allergic to one or more foodstuffs, some of the most common of which are eggs (especially the whites), citrus fruits, and, not least of all, cow's milk. The allergy usually manifests itself by digestive upsets, such as vomiting or diarrhea, or by a skin rash of some kind, frequently eczema or hives, when the offending food is introduced into the diet. When the allergic substance has been identified, it is eliminated from the diet. If it is an essential nutrient, some similar foodstuff that the child can tolerate is substituted for it. Even a milk allergy creates no real problem nowadays, since formulas made with soy protein instead are readily available.

Allergies may also be caused by airborne substances, such as dust, pollen, and pet hairs. This kind of allergy must usually be diagnosed by skin tests.

Although some people remain allergic to certain foods all their lives, others outgrow some or all of their infant allergies, often in a remarkably short period of time.

Malnutrition

Malnutrition occurs in infancy when substances vital to the growth and maintenance of the body are missing from a baby's diet or are present in insufficient quantity. Not only is malnutrition responsible for generally poor health, increased susceptibility to disease, stunted growth, and deformities of the body, but it can also impair mental development. Outright deficiency diseases, such as rickets (caused by an insufficient amount of vitamin D in the diet), scurvy (due to a lack of vitamin C), and beri-beri (from too little vitamin B_1), are less common in Western societies today than formerly, chiefly because of an increased use of vitamin supplements in the diets of babies and growing children. But a more insidious form of malnutrition, protein deficiency, is nearly as common as ever.

Proteins are normal constituents of almost all animal cells. In the child they serve the special function of providing building materials for the manufacture of tissues during growth. They also play an important role in the development of antigens necessary for the body to build up immunities to disease. An insufficient

Figure 3.9. This baby in Bangladesh will probably suffer permanent physical and intellectual damage if he survives, even if he gets a good diet from now on.

amount of protein in a child's diet causes underweight (not only because the protein itself is lacking but also because its lack depresses the appetite) and below normal growth of the skeleton and the nervous system. The subnormal growth of the brain results in depressed adaptive and intellectual capacity, and once the damage has been done, it can never be completely compensated for. Because high-protein foods tend to be among the most expensive, protein deficiency is most common among the children of poor families.

SLEEPING

The infant's waking hours are a time for alertness and activity. Observing the world and moving around in it provide him with knowledge of himself and his surroundings. His need for physical and intellectual activity is urgent and persistent throughout early childhood.

Just as the need for activity is fundamental, so is the need for rest. Rest conserves energy required for the growth and maintenance of the body. It may take the form of quiet play, relaxation, or sleep. When it is insufficient, hyperactivity may result; signs of emotional instability, such as excessive fussiness, overreaction to stress situations, and loss of acquired skills, may occur. Fatigue also increases a child's susceptibility to illness and accidents.

The amount and timing of rest vary with age. A young baby needs more rest and shorter intervals between rest periods than a toddler does. Preschool children need more rest than they will during their school years. Infants and young children whose environments are not overstimulating are usually able to rest when they need to. As a child's abilities increase and his experiences widen, he tends to resist relaxation and rest; slowing down simply becomes more difficult.

Sleep is a positive rather than a negative body function. It is a time of readjustment of the whole body mechanism, including the nervous system, rather than a mere cessation of bodily activity. During sleep the brain continues to function, but at a lower level; other activities, such as heart rate, respiration, and metabolism, also decrease.

As the baby develops, she begins to spend more time awake than asleep. During the first few weeks of life, the average number of hours spent sleeping is between sixteen and seventeen, and neither sleeping nor waking periods are sustained for long. Occasionally a newborn baby sleeps as long as eight hours at one time, but the average amount of time, day or night, is four or five hours. The longest wakeful period seldom exceeds two hours. From the end of the first month to about three months, the average total sleeping time in a twenty-four hour period shortens to fifteen hours, with a corresponding increase in the waking periods. Most babies also start to consolidate their sleep periods and to straighten out their daytime and nighttime hours; when the middle-of-the-night feeding is given up, they begin to sleep through the night. This is without doubt one of the milestones in the child's development that is most eagerly anticipated by her parents.

BIOLOGICAL CLOCK

Rhythmicity is a crucial organizing principle of behavior and health; even in very young babies a relationship can be detected between regularity and ease of adjustment. We "set" our entire body by the time we go to sleep at night. Regular hours of sleeping help keep us in tune with ourselves and with the rest of society.

As the hours go by each day we change noticeably. Our mental acuity, the keenness of our senses, our vulnerability to stress or infection, even subtle signs of vitality and idiosyncrasies of behavior all show distinct rhythms. As the wheel of consciousness shifts from day into night, from waking into deep sleep, we can see how much we change. The contrast between our most alert periods and our oblivious moments is only one indication of the rhythmic change taking place in our physiology every twenty-four hours.

One study (Kastner and Kastner, 1968) has concluded that everyone is governed by preset time patterns that he is born with. Scientists call these forces "biological clocks." Among the most familiar of these forces, though still not completely understood, are those that control the timing of animal hibernation, bird migration, and the blooming of flowers. In humans, disturbance of inner rhythms has been related to diseases of the joints, of certain internal organs, of the salivary and sweat glands, and other parts of the body. Such periodic mental and emotional states as elation, excitement, depression, insomnia, and an abnormal craving for food also appear to be related to body rhythmicity.

By six months a fairly definite pattern of wakefulness has been established, usually during the day. By the time a child is one, most of her required sleep is obtained at night, but one or more daytime naps of from one to three hours are still necessary. The child should continue to take naps during the day as long as she seems to need them. Some children continue to benefit from a daytime nap as late as the fifth year.

In the early months of life, the child's sleep is relatively shallow, although there are some indications that the more frequent her feedings and the more satisfied she is, the quieter she will remain while asleep. The young baby wakes because of internal proddings, especially of hunger; often her awakening is abrupt and accompanied by a sharp cry. In brain activity, as recorded on the EEG, there is often little difference between the sleep and wakefulness of the infant.

An older baby's sleep is more like an adult's, characterized by heavy and light periods. During the heavy periods, the baby is almost motionless, her breathing is quite regular, and she makes very little sound or facial movement. During the lighter sleeping periods she moves more, her respiration is much less regular, and she makes faces and noises. She may sigh, groan, sneeze, pass gas, and even fuss or whimper a little—all without waking up. Older babies wake more smoothly and fall asleep more easily than young infants. By about sixteen weeks the waking mechanism is usually functioning so well that crying upon awakening is uncommon. The conditions under which a baby sleeps most restfully are also like an adult's. A firm mattress, warm but not overly heavy coverings, and good room ventilation are desirable. Absolute quiet is not essential. In fact, a baby may sleep more soundly when there is a constant, low level of background noise than in a perfectly silent household where she may be awakened by some loud or unexpected sound.

Both sleep and rest are influenced by the individual child's temperament, activity level, and home environment. Some children need more sleep than others. Some vary from day to day in the amount of sleep they require; others are consistent. Some sleep less at night and take longer daytime naps, and some have the reverse pattern. Sleep also varies in depth and integratedness; some children are relatively sound sleepers, others light. Conditions that tend to disturb sleep—such as indigestion, a wet or soiled diaper, and other bodily discomforts; changes in the environment; and fear or undue excitement—may affect one child more than another.

It is difficult to draw general rules about the total amount of sleep a baby requires. For optimum health and growth, the child must have whatever circumstances dictate as adequate for him. As in feeding, adults should set reasonable guidelines according to the child's ever increasing maturity. Constant but not rigid regularity, with definite routines for getting ready for bed and the association of the bed with sleep, will help guide the child into good sleeping habits.

References

Adams, A. B. Choice of infant feeding technique as a function of maternal personality. *Journal of Consulting Psychology*, 1959, *23*, 143–146.

Aitken, F. C., and Hytten, F. E. Infant feeding: comparison of breast and artificial feeding. *Nutrition Abstracts and Review*, 1960, *30*, 341–371.

Davis, A. *Let's have healthy children.* (Rev. ed.) New York: Harcourt, 1959.

Davis, C. M. Self-selection of food by children. *The American Journal of Nursing*, 1935, *35*, 403–410.

Ferreira, A. J. The pregnant woman's emotional attitude and its reflection on the newborn. *American Journal of Orthopsychiatry*, 1960, *30*, 553–561.

Gesell, A. et al. *The first five years of life.* New York: Harper, 1940.

Kastner, J., and Kastner, M. *Sleep: the mysterious third of your life.* New York: Harcourt, 1968.

Masters, W. H., and Johnson, V. E. *Human sexual inadequacy.* Boston: Little, Brown, 1970.

Newton, N. Battle between breast and bottle. *Psychology Today*, 1972, *6*, 68–70, 88–89.

Sears, R. R., Maccoby, E. E., and Levin, H. *Patterns of child rearing.* New York: Harper, 1957.

Spock, B. *Baby and child care.* New York: Meredith, 1972.

Stott, L. H. *Child development: an individual longitudinal approach.* New York: Holt, 1967.

Watson, E. H., and Lowrey, G. H. *Growth and development of children.* (5th ed.) Chicago: Year Book Medical Publishers, Inc., 1967.

SUMMARY

1   The first two years of an individual's life are the time of his most rapid development. Although every child develops at his own rate, each grows in orderly and predictable patterns: cephalocaudally—from head to tail—and proximodistally—from trunk to extremities.

2   As the infant grows, his skeleton solidifies through calcification, and his neck and spine straighten in preparation for upright posture. Baby teeth and permanent teeth are being produced simultaneously.

3   A child achieves increasing control over his body as his muscles and brain develop. In his progress toward mastery of motor skills, the child feels a need for greater mobility, especially in an upright posture. Walking indicates advanced learning and successful coordination of several complex mechanisms.

4   A properly diversified diet, an appropriate emotional climate, a sensible feeding schedule, and gradual weaning contribute to the child's healthy growth. Minor digestive disorders like colic and food allergies are usually outgrown without medical treatment. Malnutrition, however, can cause permanent damage.

5   Sleeping is a positive body function that allows a readjustment and balancing of the body. The infant gradually increases his daily proportion of time spent awake and consolidates his sleeping hours. Experimental evidence with the EEG has shown that with growth, the child's sleep becomes more like an adult's, alternating between heavy and light periods.

FURTHER READINGS

Breckenridge, M. E., and Vincent, E. L. *Child development: Physical and psychological growth through adolescence,* Philadelphia: Saunders, 1960 (4th ed.). This book presents a clear and comprehensive description of the many facets of physical development, including a lucid discussion of the emotional, nutritional, and environmental factors that affect growth; the growth of each organ separately; and illustrative case studies and work projects.

Caplan, D. (Ed.), *The first twelve months of life: Your baby's growth month by month.* New York: Grosset and Dunlap, 1973. This is a lavishly illustrated, well-written guide to the growth and development of infants. Caplan, Director of the Center for Infancy and Early Childhood at Princeton, presents a compendium of psychological and medical advice. There is a growth chart for each period under the headings: motor, language, mental advances, and social advances.

Church, J. *Three babies: Biographies of cognitive development.* New York: Random House, 1966. This is a record of the lives of three babies from birth to age two written by their mothers. Flesh and blood babies are described, living and developing in the material, emotional, and symbolic center of family, neighborhood, and society.

Gesell, A. et al. *The first five years of life: A guide to the study of the pre-school child.* New York: Harper, 1940. A classic longitudinal study of children based on careful observation and tests. Of special interest are personal-social behavior, motor characteristics, language, and adaptive behavior. This is a standard reference for expected patterns of growth.

Gunther, M. *Infant feeding.* Chicago: H. Regnery, 1971. Dr. Gunther is qualified both as a researcher and a practicing physician to write with authority on infant feeding. Viewing breast feeding as the basis of infant feeding, she offers a full explanation of all the processes involved in lactation.

Kragman, W. M. *Child growth.* Ann Arbor, Mich.: The University of Michigan Press, 1972. This is a discussion of motor growth, adaptive response, language, and personal and social development and includes prenatal development and the newborn child. It discusses pathology due to genetic inheritance and poor nutrition. This is a short book, packed with information in readable form. Charts and graphs.

Rand, W., Sweeny, M., and Vincent, E. *Growth and development of the young child,*
Philadelphia: Saunders, 1953.
The physical growth process is described from prenatal life to full maturity. Especially
interesting are the chapters on meeting the physical needs of the growing child,
which discuss the effects of warmth, nutrition, and sleep, on physical growth.

Tanner, J. M. *Education and physical growth,* New York: International Universities
Press, 1970.
This concise book gives a quick overview of physical development from birth to
early adolescence. It discusses the principles of physical development, the course
of growth, the development of the brain, and factors that affect growth. The information is up to date and presented in clear, nontechnical terms.

4
Perception and Learning

To us it is obvious that the tiny infant gets hungry several times a day, sees and feels the nipple, sucks it, and presently feels satisfied. It is very practical, moreover, for the caregiver to understand the matter in just these terms. But a newborn's hunger cry sounds the same as his cry of pain, and we have no reason to suppose that he distinguishes between the two feelings. Still less can we suppose that he categorizes his experiences as either feelings or perceptions or that he sees much difference between his foot and his blanket. In fact, it may be some weeks before he realizes that the arms that cuddle him, the breast that feeds him, and the two eyes that hover over him are all parts of the same entity, not automatic responses to his needs for cuddling, feeding, and stimulation.

How do we know what the infant realizes and perceives? Science has no window on his mental processes, but ingenious experiments have been devised to find out what he does and does not respond to. The response measured may be a smile or an eye movement, or it may be a change in heartbeat or breathing. In one study of visual perception (Ahrens, 1954), for example, several two month old infants were presented with different arrangements of dots, angles, and bars drawn on cardboard, and the experimenters watched them to see when they would smile. It turned out that the dots evoked the most smiles, which suggests that an infant builds his perception of facial features beginning with the eyes.

In a somewhat more sophisticated experiment (Fantz, 1961) the researcher placed the infants in an enclosed "looking chamber." Lying on their backs, the infants faced a target area about a foot away. The objects shown, one at a time, were three black and white patterns (a face, a piece of newspaper, and a bullseye) and three colored circles without patterns. Eye motions were observed through a hole in the top of the enclosure, and the length of time an infant would first look at a pattern was clocked with a stopwatch. The face pattern proved to hold their attention for the longest period.

Another experiment (Bridger, 1961, 1962) tested the hearing of infants one to five days old. A device for measuring heartbeat was attached to the infant and then a pure, steady tone was sounded. Startled at first, most of the infants registered a faster heartbeat. After several trials their heartbeat remained steady when the tone was sounded; they grew used to it. Then a different tone was sounded, and the heartbeat sped up. The researcher concluded that the infants could tell the difference between the two tones.

NONVISUAL SENSES

To some extent it can be said that a baby learns to see, but his nonvisual senses—hearing, touch, taste, and smell—seem to develop and become meaningful to him without practice. A crying baby, for example, will probably quiet down the first time he is picked up and rocked. Of course, he was rocked a great deal before he was born, and there is no reason to doubt that he felt it.

His mother's heartbeat was also familiar to him before birth and apparently continues to soothe him during babyhood. It has been observed (Salk, 1962) that in most cases when a mother picked up her baby, she placed him against her left side, where her heartbeat is easiest to hear. Women who had never borne any children of their own showed no preference for placing babies on either side. Perhaps babies rapidly teach their mothers that they are happier where they can hear the heartbeat.

Hearing

Babies can hear at birth. Not only can they tell high-pitched sounds from low-pitched ones, they even seem to sense the direction from which a sound is coming, since they move their heads toward the source (Leventhal and Lipsitt, 1964). Experiments have also shown that babies begin early to listen to people's voices. Some infants only twenty weeks old were found to discriminate between the syllables "bah" and "gah" (Moffitt, 1971).

But it is important to recognize that the way a baby reacts to sounds depends on the conditions in which he hears them. A mother knows that her baby may be startled and frightened by a loud noise when he is alone in his crib but remain quite undisturbed by a similar noise when safe in her arms. This sense of security is transmitted from mother to child long before he has any notion of the concept "mother" or even recognizes her as a specific, unique person.

Taste and Smell

Taste is completely absent at birth but develops rapidly in the first two weeks. The first tastes a baby learns to tell apart are sweet and bitter—and he greatly prefers sweet. Salty tastes seem to be halfway along the desirability scale; the baby will accept them when he is hungry but reject them in favor of milk or glucose when these are offered. Well-fed babies learn to discriminate more carefully among foods than do babies who are not so well fed, and the substitution of water for milk may elicit a surprised lift of the eyebrows by the ripe age of ten days.

The sense of smell is present in primitive form at birth. Newborn infants seem to be insensitive to faint odors but show a distinct aversion to sharp, unpleasant smells like ammonia. Using changes in breathing rates as a measure of response, a pair of researchers (Engen and Lipsitt, 1965) established the newborn's ability to discriminate among certain distinctive odors. They presented their subjects ten times with a combination of two scents, noting their diminishing breathing rate as the novelty wore off. When they subsequently exposed them to only one of the two components, the breathing rate shot up once more; the babies reacted to it as a new stimulus, giving evidence that they had noticed the difference.

Tactile Perception

One aspect of tactile perception, the infant's sensitivity to pain, increases rapidly right after he is born. Throughout infancy, the head is more sensitive to pain than the arms and legs, and girls are more sensitive than boys. Sensitivity to heat and cold varies greatly among individual babies, but all of them show some response

Figure 4.1. This water is cold! The tactile sensation of cold water in a bathtub can elicit an unmistakable response from an infant.

to external temperature changes as well as to internal change, such as formula that is too hot or too cold.

Tactile perceptions are a delight to the baby from the moment she first stuffs her fist into her mouth or grasps her feet with her hands. A little later, the realization that these are *her* fingers and *her* toes lends further zest to her explorations.

Soon the method of investigating by touch and taste is firmly established. It will be practiced on building blocks in the playpen and mud pies in the garden with equal intentness. Gripping and handling objects is necessary to the infant's motor development, and handle them she does, especially when she is able to get around on her own.

Some time between the eighth month and her first birthday the baby learns to crawl, and her world suddenly changes. She becomes a part of her surroundings in entirely new ways, ways previously made impossible by her immobility. Like all of us, she finds travel extremely broadening. It certainly changes her view of familiar objects, though she may not realize for many weeks that the chair whose underside she is exploring is the same object she has always seen from the crib.

But this is only the beginning. Sooner or later, without any prompting, the little girl discovers that crawling need not be confined to a single level. She can pull herself up by the leg of the coffee table, crawl onto the top, and view the living room from this new eminence; or she can crawl up the stairs and enjoy an even more dramatic view by looking down through the bannister staves. This is also the time when hands and heads get stuck in openings big enough to get into but not out of. Tactile experience sometimes comes at a price.

But such mishaps, frequent though they are, do not dampen the child's enthusiasm for exploration. Despite her own fears and the hazards involved, she will learn to stand up and walk. It is not unusual for a mother, awakened by a sound, to rush into her baby's room and find her standing in the crib, clutching the bars, either sound asleep or barely awake, almost as if practice at walking cannot be suspended even for a night.

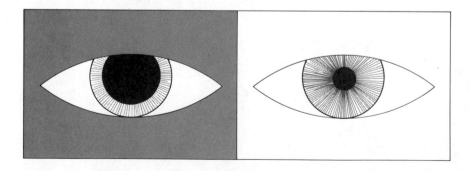

Figure 4.2. Pupillary reflex. The pupils of the newborn automatically contract in bright light and dilate in dim light.

SIGHT

Much more is known about the sight of an infant than about the other senses. There are several different processes necessary to vision; in order for a person to see well, all of these processes must operate properly. They do not all work well at birth, but they soon improve.

The *pupillary reflex* (Figure 4.2) is one of these processes. It consists of an automatic narrowing of the pupil of the eye in bright light and a widening in dim light. Babies exhibit the pupillary reflex almost immediately after birth, even if they are premature. Therefore we know that the newborn baby can distinguish between light and dark, although during the first two days only gross changes, from very bright light to totally dark and back again, activate the reflex. It takes a few weeks to respond to subtler changes.

Visual coordination (Figure 4.3) is the ability of the ocular muscles to turn the eyes in the direction of an object. It is achieved when the baby can follow a moving object with his eyes, which most of them do a few weeks after birth.

One study of visual coordination in infants (Nelson, 1968) not only established that babies 42 to 133 days old could follow lights that flashed on one after another in a row, but also indicated that some of them had caught on to the game. When the last light had been turned off, they looked back at the first bulb and waited for it to flash on again.

Figure 4.3. Visual coordination. An infant soon learns to follow a moving object with his eyes.

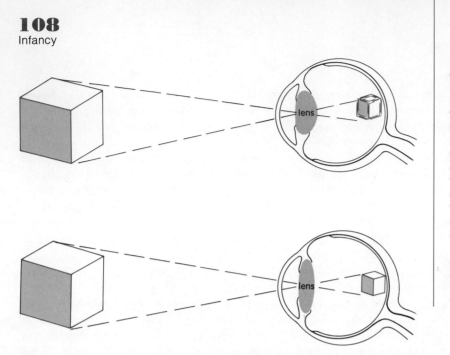

Figure 4.4. Accommodation of the lens. The image of an object will not be focused sharply on the retina unless the lens is flattened or allowed to return to its more globular shape, depending on the distance of the object from the eye. Some cameras can also be adjusted for distance, and for the same purpose: to produce a sharp image on the film. But camera lenses are not flexible, and so the adjustment must be made by moving the lens closer to or farther from the film.

The infant's next step in refining his visual perception is the achievement of *convergence*—focusing both eyes to produce a single image. Babies start making rough attempts at convergence in their first hours of life but do not perfect it until the end of the second month. It is achieved through practice. The eye movements, erratic at first, gradually speed up; they grow smoother and more refined until, after about eight weeks, the infant has achieved binocular (two-eyed) vision as good as an adult's.

But he still has much to do to bring about clarity of vision. During the first three months his vision is blurry because the muscles controlling his eye lenses cannot yet adjust the lens curvature to focus the light rays sharply on the retinas. This adjustment is called *accommodation of the lens* (Figure 4.4). It begins in the second month and is fully developed by the third or fourth month.

Even then, however, the baby's visual perception can hardly be called equivalent to the adult's. The neural pathways and visual receptor mechanisms are not yet fully developed. Around the age of eight weeks the little girl may smile in apparent recognition at her mother or father bending over her, but experiments indicate that recognition is partial at best. Her eyes cannot yet absorb the complete face before her, only the forehead and eyes. The clear recognition of something familiar is still some weeks away.

Objects of Attention

Indications are that while the baby is very young, his perceptions are organized along very different lines from the adult's. His perceptive frame of reference changes, however, almost from month to month.

During the first three months an object must have relatively flamboyant characteristics to attract the baby's attention—such characteristics as movement, sound, sharp color contrast, or distinctive contours and patterns. The youngest babies seem interested in very simple patterns, older ones in more complex designs.

One well-known experiment showed that familiarity is at least as attention catching as complexity (Haaf and Bell, 1967). Four drawings were shown to a group of four month old boys. The first drawing resembled a human face; the second was the outline of a face with an eye missing and lines and squiggles filling the outline at random. The third drawing was a face outline that was blank except for a nose; and the fourth had no facial features at all, only the outline filled with the same squiggles as the second drawing.

The babies paid most attention to the first drawing, the most recognizable face, even though it was less complex than the drawings with squiggles. The second drawing was also second in the amount of attention it attracted, apparently because it was a face lacking only one eye.

The experimenters concluded that in this instance what interested the babies most was neither complexity nor amount of detail, but "faceness." Their general conclusion was that babies' attention is attracted to objects that look familiar. In different contexts, however, novelty is often quite as effective an attention getter as familiarity, especially when it is combined with movement. This may account in part for the fascination that television has for some babies, long before they understand any words. Something in the television receiver moves, and that is enough to make it more interesting than the chairs and paintings in the same room.

Depth Perception

The ability of a baby to perceive depth during the first year has been established by a famous experiment using a "visual cliff" (Gibson and Walk, 1960). Six month old babies were placed on a raised plank wide enough to serve as a crawlway. The babies did not actually crawl on the plank, however, but on a sheet of plate glass that rested on the plank. The glass was much wider than the plank. Under it on one side was a checkerboard pattern on the same level as the plank, and on the other side the same pattern three feet or so *under* the plank. An adult would perceive this side as a cliff dropping off from the plank.

So did the babies. They could feel the plate glass that covered the apparent depth with their hands and knees, but they still could not be induced to venture off the center crawlway on the "cliff" side, even when tempted to do so by their smiling, beckoning mothers. Then the checkerboard bottom was raised to within a few inches of the glass, making the depth much less fearful. Nevertheless, the babies continued to trust their own depth perception more than their mothers' entreaties to cross.

How such judgment is acquired is not clear. Some authorities maintain that babies have built-in depth perception at birth; others believe they are taught by the experience of seeing objects at various levels and distances.

THE WORLD PERCEIVED

During the first weeks of life the baby evidently exists in a world without continuity, inasmuch as he has not yet perceived the repetitiveness of events or any cause and effect relationships. Thus each perceptual impression is novel and isolated, an event belonging exclusively to the moment, without past or future.

After a while he begins to see connections between some of these separate events. He can perceive them as configurations, though without much awareness of the details of which they are composed. Soon he is associating certain "demand qualities" with certain configurations, and these in turn arouse associated feelings. His mother's face, for example, carries the demand quality of huggability, while a rattle has the demand quality of shakeability. These ever-broadening configurations have been called **schemata** (plural of **schema**) by the Swiss psychologist Jean Piaget.

Which impressions the infant will respond to most vigorously is a matter not only of developmental level but also of individual predisposition. This preference may well be the first indication of a specific talent; a marked response to sounds, for example, may indicate a musical bent. In any case, there is a wide range of variation in individual perceptual reactions and adaptations. The infant's individual emotional constitution also affects his perception. Each infant in the act of perception is attaching a personal and unique meaning to some object or event, and each new experience that can be related to an object known before will add new associations to that object. Some of these associations will be emotional, and the emotional overtones will enter into and alter the perception. Emotional associations are part of every infant's growing perceptual development.

Perhaps one of the most essential accomplishments in the infant's perceptual and mental development is his realization that objects are the same from occasion to occasion and continue to exist in the meantime. According to Piaget, infants before the age of six or eight months conclude that objects they cannot see do not exist. They stop looking for an object as soon as it is hidden from sight. When the object reappears, the infant acts as if it were a new object, not the same one as before. He understands only gradually that it *is* the same, and therefore that its existence is permanent.

The amount of emotional involvement an infant can invest in an object or event is limited by its impermanence. There may be some exceptions to this rule; a few vital objects, such as the child's parents, may have some permanence at an early age, but even they can be forgotten. This accounts for the dismaying experience of many a new father who, on returning from a three-day business trip, finds himself no longer recognized by his offspring.

The full knowledge of the separate existence of things beyond his awareness does not become evident to a young child until he is well into his second year. At that time, peekaboo games turn into more sophisticated hide and seek adventures; and out of the new ability to find hidden objects or persons grows the realization that they continue to exist even when not seen.

SCHEMA

A **schema** is an organized pattern of behavior. The infant's first **schemata** (plural) are reflexes; sucking is probably the most complex schema he is born with. Soon, however, his schemata are expanded and modified by learning and experience. The two month old regularly brings his hand up to his mouth and sucks his thumb; this habit, which is partly learned, is a new schema derived from the primitive sucking schema.

There is little noticeable difference between what an infant knows and what he does. We cannot say he recognizes the figure of a face until he shows that he can distinguish it from squares and circles. When he demonstrates this, Piaget explains it by saying that he has formed a schema of a face. *Schema* is a useful term in Piaget's theory of cognition because it means any distinct unit of what an individual knows and does. As this unit is built up from past experiences and actions, much can be learned by observing it accommodate new experiences and actions.

Sensory schemata may be thought of as ideas or mental representations although, according to Piaget, a child under eighteen months of age never thinks of things that are not materially present to him. The schemata that tiny babies have of objects they recognize probably contain only the essential features and little detail. A three month old's schema of a face may be simply an oval outline and two eyes. New experience, however, is constantly being assimilated into the original schema, and it elaborates rapidly. The mother's face becomes associated with warmth, the breast, the taste of milk, and eventually with the child's own utterance of "Mama."

Schemata are formed from associations of many kinds. The baby's own shaking of the rattle is part of his schema of the rattle; being picked up and hugged is part of his schema of grandmother. The emotions the baby feels in conjunction with these experiences are also integral features of his schemata.

Perception and Environment

It has been known for some time that when the infant's surroundings do not provide sufficient stimulation, her maturation may be retarded, sometimes even impairing her intelligence and mental health. A favorable environment, rich in intellectual as well as emotional stimulation, is therefore an important factor in full development of the child's potential.

The child's surroundings can be divided into a physical and a psychological environment; but the two are closely interdependent, and nowhere is their interaction more evident than in matters of perceptual development. Even the adult personality undergoes profound and traumatic changes under conditions of sensory deprivation, as in imprisonment or isolation. This must hold true all the more for a small child, who has not yet built up the inner resources to counteract external deprivation.

From babyhood on, the child avidly reaches out for sensory experience and ways to integrate the perceptual stimuli she receives. This hunger for discovery grows along with her as she leaves the crib and begins to crawl. By the time she reaches the toddling stage, she is exploring the world every waking moment, disemboweling toys and furniture, emptying garbage pails and medicine cabinets, and eating thumbtacks, wallpaper, and detergents with equal relish.

Many mothers, worried about their breakable treasures, move more and more things to higher and higher shelves, but the toddler soon learns how to get at them. It is reasonable to deprive a child of the sensory stimulation of shattering a crystal vase or plastering the wall with catsup and mustard, but she can be restricted too severely.

One observer (Fraiberg, 1959) has written about a little girl named Barbara who was reared by an overly strict grandmother and forbidden to touch any but a very few of the objects in the home. Barbara's fear of punishment was so strong that she refrained from the exploration normal for her age. As a result, she suffered not only perceptual retardation with regard to objects, but also a pronounced disturbance in learning to talk and relate to other people. At four years old she was in psychotherapy. She recovered only after the therapist gave her the environment she should have had at two, complete with love, freedom from fear, and a wealth of objects to explore and handle.

Orphanages have for many years served as a dismal testing ground for deprivation. It was discovered in orphanages, for example, that infants reared in a bare, purely functional institution grow up with a below normal interest in their environment. Their feelings of attachment to the few objects that are a part of their environment, such as toys, are also lower than normal (Provence and Lipton, 1962). Their instinct for discovery remains dormant because the objects in their environment provide less than adequate stimulation to their senses. As a result, they learn how to relate to the external world much later than infants reared at home. Often this impairment persists to some extent throughout life, making them less capable of meaningful personal and object relationships.

INTELLIGENCE

Intelligence is a complex concept whose exact formulation has proved elusive. Although the various definitions given for intelligence have much in common, there is still disagreement as to whether it is a single function or consists of several independent abilities. Over the years a number of its components have been isolated and assessed through the use of intelligence tests, but it cannot be said that intelligence is what these tests measure because the tests are different from each other and because no individual gets the same score throughout his life on any one test.

Psychologists also disagree about whether intelligence is a hereditary attribute or an ability that is learned and affected by the individual's environment. Within the range of human intelligence—between the gifted and feebleminded—there is enough variability, even in the course of one individual's development, to invalidate the notion of intelligence as a single, constant ability.

The measurement of infant intelligence started in the United States with the work of Arnold Gesell, who began a monumental study of infant behavior in the early 1920s. By 1925, he had published his first series of behavior and ability norms (averages for certain ages) and subsequently expanded them in a number of later editions. In its entirety, his work presents a richly detailed picture of childhood from birth to ten.

Many further studies of mental development in infancy followed Gesell's methods and findings. The enormous effort expended in the development, standardization, and application of these schedules for infant behavior had two aims. First, the studies describe the regular changes in behavior that children display as they grow. The second and potentially more important use is as a diagnostic tool. Psychologists continue to try to improve the test scales in the hope that by detecting key variations in an infant's normal development they will be able to foresee certain difficulties, such as reading and learning problems, that may become all too apparent later in the child's life.

Among the many studies that followed Gesell's work was the Berkeley Growth Study, which traced the intellectual development of a group of sixty-one children from birth to adulthood. The Berkeley Growth Study is an example of a longitudinal study, which accumulates data about the same individuals over a long period of time. This kind of study contrasts with the cross-sectional study, which deals with a large group at one particular time.

At least two valuable insights came as a result of the Berkeley Growth Study. It was discovered that intelligence is by no means constant and that testing intelligence in the very young is inexact. The study also revealed the phenomenon that led earlier investigators to the erroneous conclusion that IQ is constant for any one individual. Tests given a month or so apart yielded fairly consistent scores, but as the time intervals between test and retest increased and the babies matured, the scores varied more and more. In addition, great differences in individual mental growth patterns were found, especially during early infancy. These differences were

IQ

A person's IQ, or intelligence quotient, is widely assumed to give a reliable indication of his mental capacities. Most IQ tests give an individual a simple numerical score: a "normal" IQ is about 100, and 98 percent of the people who take the tests fall in the range between 60 and 140. Beyond those extremes are found only the 2 percent who are either "feebleminded" (below 60) or "geniuses" (above 140). Intelligence tests are routinely given to most of us by schools and the armed forces, and many companies now give IQ tests to prospective employees. Yet, although these tests are given to almost everybody and the scores used for many purposes, very few people have any clear idea of what IQ tests actually measure.

The ancestor of modern IQ tests was the *Binet-Simon Scale,* developed by the French psychologists Alfred Binet and Theophile Simon and first used in 1905. The scale was administered by asking school children to answer a list of questions that became more difficult as the list went on. The point beyond which the child could no longer answer the questions determined his *mental age.* The scale became widely used in France and was soon adapted for use in other countries.

One of the most important adaptations was carried out by Lewis M. Terman at Stanford University. Terman intended to revise the test to make it suitable for use in the United States, but he not only rewrote large portions of it but devised a new formulation for expressing the test results. He determined the individual's age and then divided this score by the individual's chronological (actual) age. This usually resulted in a decimal fraction, which he eliminated for the sake of simplicity by multiplying by 100. The final score was the individual's intelligence quotient.

IQ is a more revealing measure than mental age because it expresses the individual's abilities as compared with others his age. A four year old with a mental age of five, for example, is said to have an IQ of 125. Since it was first published in 1916, the Stanford-Binet test, as it is called, has become the single most widely used IQ test.

Later refinements were added to the test. Performance components were added to the original verbal problems in order to test the intelligence of infants and preschoolers, whose verbal abilities are limited. Alterations were made in the statistical procedures, to give a more accurate reading of the test results. Testing adults has been a problem, since mental age does not increase in any obvious way after the late teens. The Stanford-Binet test tried to allow for this by using a cut-off age; anyone over age sixteen was assigned the chronological age of sixteen. A number of other tests, especially those developed by David Wechsler, have been used to obtain more accurate measures of adult intelligence.

But what exactly do intelligence tests measure? Some critics argue that a high IQ only indicates an ability to do well on IQ tests: in other words, nothing. By following the careers of thousands of people with high and low IQs, however, it has been found that IQ tests do have a certain amount of *predictive validity* as indicators of success in school. But when it comes to things like getting a good job and keeping it, or meeting the demands of everyday life, IQ tests seem to have very little predictive value. So many different factors go into what we call "intelligence" that a person of very high mental abilities may well get a low IQ score.

A task in an intelligence test.

so great, in fact, that Nancy Bayley, a psychologist who made many contributions to the study of infant intelligence testing, concluded that each child may be a law unto himself (Bayley, 1955).

The behavior measured in infant IQ tests is mostly perceptual and motor. For example, the Cattell Baby Test for infants aged two to thirty-two months includes the following items: at three months, the infant can follow an object being swung around his head, and at sixteen months, he can put beads in a box.

Two other widely used tests are the Gesell Development Schedules and Bayley's Scales of Infant Development. The Bayley Scale, which consists of 163 items, is considered one of the best standardized tests in the field. A standardized test is meant to sample mental abilities in such a way that an individual's score will state his position relative to the average person of the same age and from the same general population. The Bayley Scale provides an "age placement" for each of the 163 items, referring to the age in months at which 50 percent of the children were capable of performing that particular task. For example, the age placement for building a tower of two cubes is about fourteen months; that of reaching a toy with a stick is seventeen months, and that of building a six-cube tower, twenty-two or twenty-three months.

Despite the widespread use of several of these infant tests, researchers (Stott and Ball, 1965) performing a quantitative analysis of them have concluded that there is "a great lack of consistency among and within the scales . . . in terms of factor content and meaning, thus pointing up the need for more consistent and adequate test scales." Many researchers are currently trying to devise better tests.

LEARNING

Although humans have many innate, or reflex, reactions—blinking, sneezing, and crying, to give three examples—much of our behavior is learned. **Learning** is the process by which a person acquires or modifies a habit or pattern of behavior. It happens in response to a specific set of circumstances (stimuli), which may or may not have been arranged on purpose. An infant's learning, like an adult's, is a reaction to his environment. An infant who is picked up only when he cries may cry just to get attention, but start picking him up when he smiles, and he may soon learn to smile more often.

At what age do babies begin to learn? Both the Cattell and the Gesell infant intelligence scales contain the test item "anticipating the bottle" at the three-month level. Anticipation is expressed by sucking movements at the mere sight of the bottle. The inescapable conclusion is that even at that tender age learning has already taken place: the baby has learned what to expect when he sees that object.

There is, of course, a great deal of interest in the question of how babies learn. It is apparent even to the casual observer that babies frequently learn by doing what they have observed someone else do. Piaget reported an amusing incident of imitation in his own daughter at sixteen months:

> Jacqueline had a visit from a little boy [about her age] whom she used to see from time to time, and who in the course of the afternoon got into a terrible temper. He screamed as he tried to get out of a playpen and pushed it backward, stamping his feet. Jacqueline stood watching him in amazement, never having witnessed such a scene before. The next day, she herself screamed in her playpen and tried to move it, stamping her foot lightly several times. . . . (Piaget, 1950).

Yet there is little experimental data pertaining to learning through imitation in children of this age group; most of the existing studies used older children as subjects.

To researchers working in infant learning, it is also obvious that there is a basic similarity between the human baby's response and that seen in many test animals. The basic principle in these reactions is that a specific response can be evoked by presenting a particular stimulus—that is, by managing the subject's surroundings in a specific way. This was called **conditioning**. A response is considered unconditioned (innate) if it is determined by inborn factors. Perspiration is an example of an innate response because it will appear in any human being when the proper stimulus—overheating—is presented. But a conditioned (acquired) response depends on learning. Two models of this type of learning—classical conditioning and operant conditioning—have been advanced.

Classical Conditioning

In dogs, salivation is an unconditioned response to food. All dogs salivate when they start to eat. The Russian psychologist Ivan Pavlov, working at the turn of the century, constructed an experiment in which he rang a bell every time he brought his dogs food. After he had done this several times, the dogs began to salivate whenever they heard the bell, even if no food was present. Thus Pavlov *conditioned* the dogs to salivate at the sound of a bell.

The same process can influence responses in humans. For example, a baby may cry as soon as he sees the doctor because several times before, the doctor stuck the baby with a needle. The neutral stimulus (the doctor) is associated with the unconditioned stimulus (the needle) again and again until the doctor alone evokes the same response (crying) as the needle.

Russian psychologists continue to investigate the mechanisms of classical conditioning. In a study using children eighteen to thirty-six months of age (Degtiar, 1962) children were conditioned to respond to the visual cue of a lamp and the auditory cue of a bell; these stimuli signaled that it was time for pleasurable activity, such as playing or eating. Interestingly, it was found that many of the children were able to respond to the stimulus when it was generalized to the *word* "lamp" or "bell" rather than the sight or sound of the object.

Operant Conditioning

The discovery that responses could be predictably produced and altered—that behavior could be changed—ushered in a new era in the study of learning processes both in animals and in humans. In the 1930s, the psychologist B. F. Skinner devised the learning method known as **operant conditioning.** One important difference between classical and operant conditioning is that in classical conditioning the subject's behavior is entirely responsive—the baby sees the doctor and then he cries. In operant conditioning, on the other hand, the response precedes the stimulus—a rat presses a lever and then he gets food, or a man does a day's work and then he gets paid.

A 1959 experiment (Rheingold, Gewirtz, and Ross) used operant conditioning to teach three month old infants to vocalize. The researcher immediately rewarded any random vocalization the infant made by smiles, pats on the tummy, and conversational cooings. In just six days of conditioning there was a measurable increase in vocalization. When the rewards were stopped, vocalization dropped back to its pre-experimental level.

Operant conditioning depends more on what follows than what precedes it. As Skinner (1968) has written:

> Operant behavior, as I see it, is simply the study of what used to be dealt with by the concept of purpose. The purpose of an act is the consequences it is going to have. Actually, in the case of operant conditioning, we study the consequences an act has had in the past. Changes in the probability of response are brought about when an act is followed by a particular kind of consequence.

This consequence is called reinforcement. It can be positive (pleasant) or negative (unpleasant). In the case of the child who knows he will get a lollipop if he puts his toys away, the lollipop is a positive reinforcer.

Reinforcement

The element of reinforcement has proved especially important in the operant learning processes of young children. **Reinforcement** is the reward that motivates learning. It rests on the fundamental tenet of psychology that when an action is followed by a satisfying consequence, that action tends to be done more often. If the satisfying consequence is merely the avoidance of punishment, the technique is called *negative* reinforcement. A child who refuses to cooperate in a play group may be punished simply by being left out. If this teaches him to cooperate, he has been conditioned by negative reinforcement.

On the other hand, paying extra attention to a child, even in the form of severe punishment, may *positively* reinforce the undesirable behavior if gaining attention is his primary goal. This is the case when a teacher reprimands one of her pupils for disrupting the class and he responds by being even more disruptive.

IN EXTREMIS

I saw my toes the other day.
I hadn't looked at them for months.
Indeed, they might have passed away.
And yet they were my best friends once.

When I was small, I knew them well.
I counted on them up to ten
And put them in my mouth to tell
The larger from the lesser. Then
I loved them better than my ears,
My elbows, adenoids, and heart.
But with the swelling of the years
We drifted, toes and I, apart.

Now, gnarled and pale, each said, *j'accuse!*—
I hid them quickly in my shoes.

A type of reinforcement that works particularly well with infants is primary reinforcement—a stimulus that satisfies a basic, unlearned drive and is intrinsically satisfying, like candy. The infant's need to be picked up and hugged has also been used successfully as a primary reinforcer. In a recent experiment (Vernon, 1972), mothers of infants under one year old were instructed to anticipate their babies' needs as much as possible. They were also asked to change their former practice of picking the babies up only when they cried; they started to pick them up when they were in a good mood as well, and cuddled them especially when they were laughing or smiling. At the end of four weeks the average number of crying incidents per day was less than half what it had been a month earlier. The mothers also reported that their babies laughed much more than before and appeared decidedly happier and more outgoing.

Another widely used type of reinforcement is *conditioned* reinforcement, rewards we learn to appreciate for what they can get us, not for their intrinsic value. Money is an obvious example of a conditioned reinforcer. Coins may interest an infant because they are bright, but a little later the child learns that offering them to the man in the ice cream truck brings the primary reward of ice cream. Infants learn very rapidly to value the *social* reinforcers—attention, affection, and approval. At the beginning of life a baby probably does not know it when he is the object of someone's attention. But as attention is repeatedly associated with the satisfaction of his needs, it begins to call forth a pleasant emotion in its own right. The same is true of affection, of which the baby usually receives a great deal together with the satisfaction of his wants and the accompanying attention.

Approval assumes its reinforcement value a little later than attention and affection, inasmuch as it requires some verbal comprehension. Nonetheless, the small infant can pick up at least some of the nonverbal cues denoting parental approval, such as smiles, stroking, and an approving tone of voice. Actually, these social reinforcers often occur simultaneously. You cannot give a child approval, for example, unless you are paying attention to him.

The efficacy of reinforcement in shaping the learning of even the youngest babies was demonstrated in a study (Lipsitt, Kaye, and Bosack, 1966) of babies aged only thirty-five to ninety-five hours. The infants gradually increased their rate of tube sucking by reinforcement with a sugar solution.

Changes in behavior and changes in frequency of behavior are affected by processes other than learning. The physiological maturation that accompanies growing up is one such process. Furthermore, children do a lot of learning that cannot be described as any sort of conditioning. Much of what they learn to do is first observed and then imitated.

READINESS FOR CERTAIN TASKS

Comparative psychology, the study of similarities between human and animal behavior, has made an important contribution to the study of the infant's developmental stages: the discovery of *critical periods*. For many species there are measurable periods lasting from a few days to a few weeks that are crucial to the learning of certain behavior. During these periods the organism apparently has reached the precise degree of maturation needed to assimilate the environmental stimulus that will result in the new behavior. If the specific environmental stimulus is not available during this time, that particular behavior will either not develop at all or will appear late and in defective form. For example, if baby geese are not imprinted by a mother figure in the first forty-eight to seventy-two hours of life, they never can be. In humans lack of vocal stimulation during the critical period may retard the child's ability to communicate with others.

Experimental data confirms the existence of critical periods in the social development of other animal species, but there is little reliable research dealing with critical periods in humans. Studies of institutionalized children, who have almost by definition been deprived of many kinds of environmental and social stimuli, do indicate late learning and often missed stages of psychological and cognitive development in these children. Yet such studies are not conclusive evidence of the existence of critical periods in human development; these children have had so many deprivations that it is impossible to lay the blame for their abnormal development on any single factor.

Nevertheless, the concept of the critical period underlies much of our present-day theory of child development. Piaget's theory of cognitive development, for example, assumes a succession of stages, each of which is dependent on the achievements that took place during the preceding stage. Some psychologists suggest that these critical periods for learning are linked to the maturation of the neuro-muscular system, or to some kind of hormone balance. The critical period for a certain stage of development will therefore vary according to the individual, and no definite timetable can be given. The stages and tasks may be common to all babies, but the ways in which the stages are met and the tasks mastered are as unique to each child as his fingerprints.

References

Ahrens, R. Beiträge zur Entwicklung des Physiognomie- und Mimerkennens. *Zeitschrift zur experimentalen ange-wandten Psychologie*, 1954, *2*, 412–454.

Bayley, N. On the growth of intelligence. *American Psy-chologist*, 1955, *10*, 805–817.

Bridger, W. H. Sensory discrimination and autonomic function in the newborn. *American Academy of Child Psychiatry*, 1962, *1*, 67–82.

Bridger, W. H. Sensory habituation and discrimination in the human neonate. *American Journal of Psychiatry*, 1961, *117*, 991–996.

Degtiar, E. N. Comparative characteristics of physiological conditions during the formation of a stereotype in the first and second signal system. *Zhurnal Vysshei Nervnoi Deyatelnosti*, 1962, *12*, 63–68.

Engen, T., and Lipsitt, L. P. Decrement and recovery of responses to olfactory stimuli in human neonates. *Journal of Comparative Physiological Psychology*, 1965, *59*, 312–316.

Evans, R. *B. F. Skinner: the man and his ideas.* New York: Harper, 1968.

Fantz, R. L. The origin of form perception. *Scientific American*, 1961, *204*, 66–72.

Fraiberg, S. H. *The magic years: understanding and handling the problems of early childhood.* New York: Scribner's, 1959.

Gesell, A., and Ilg, F. L. *Child development.* New York: Harper, 1949.

Gibson, E. J., and Walk, R. D. The "visual cliff." *Scientific American*, 1960, *202*, 64–71.

Haaf, R. A., and Bell, R. Q. A facial dimension in visual discrimination by human infants. *Child Development*, 1967, *38*, 893–899.

Leventhal, A. S., and Lipsitt, L. P. Adaptation, pitch discrimination, and sound localization in the neonate. *Child Development*, 1964, *35*, 759–767.

Lipsitt, L. P., Kaye, H., and Bosack, T. N. Enhancement of neonatal sucking through reinforcement. *Journal of Experimental Child Psychology*, 1966, *4*, 163–168.

Moffitt, A. R. Consonant cue perception by twenty- to twenty-four-week-old infants. *Child Development*, 1971, *42*, 717–731.

Nelson, K. E. Organization of visual-tracking responses in human infants. *Journal of Experimental Child Psychology*, 1968, *6*, 194–201.

Piaget, J. *Psychology of intelligence* (Percy, M., and Berlyne, D. E., transl.). London: Routledge and Kagan Paul, Ltd., 1950.

Provence, S., and Lipton, R. C. *Infants in institutions.* New York: International Universities Press, 1962.

Rheingold, H., Gewirtz, J., and Ross, H. Social condition-ing of vocalizations in the infant. *Journal of Comparative Physiological Psychology*, 1959, *52*, 68–73.

Salk, L. Mothers' heartbeat as an imprinting stimulus. *Transactions of the New York Academy of Science*, 1962, *24*, 753–763.

Skinner, B. F. *Technology of teaching.* New York: Appleton-Century-Crofts, 1968.

Stott, L. H., and Ball, R. S. Infant and preschool mental tests: review and evaluation. *Monographs of the Society for Research in Child Development*, 1965, *30*, No. 101.

Vernon, W. M. *Motivating children.* New York: Holt, 1972.

121

SUMMARY

1   The newborn does not distinguish the boundary between himself and the outside world. It is by means of his sense perceptions that he begins to construct a notion of himself and his world.

2   Infants can distinguish sounds at birth and tastes within the first two weeks of life. The tactile senses are active soon after birth and the sense of touch is an important mechanism for learning to discriminate among objects, textures, and materials.

3   Sight is a complex learning experience because the mastery of seeing requires physical development as well as skill in using the eyes, coupled with an ability to understand what is being seen. Studies show that the first objects infants see are faces, and they are probably first attracted to the eyes. One year old children have an organized sense of depth perception.

4   The infant learns to organize the data received by his senses into a structure that Piaget calls a schema. Schemata become associated with an emotional context which then is integrated into the schemata. Schemata acquire permanence, and the young child weaves her own schemata into a sense of history and continuity. Young children deprived of an opportunity to use all their senses may suffer an intellectual and emotional impairment that can never be totally corrected.

5   Psychologists have devoted much effort to the study and measurement of intelligence in children. It is now known that intelligence varies for an individual over time and that test results for an individual child are not necessarily descriptive of the child's ability. Motor and perceptual abilities are the factors most child IQ tests measure.

6   Conditioned learning takes place when an environmental stimulus becomes associated with the physical response of a person or animal the best known example being Pavlov's dog. Skinner introduced the concept of operant conditioning in which a reinforcement follows the desired response.

7

Reinforcement is positive when it is desired by the subject and negative when a punishment. Most important in the learning processes of social animals such as human beings are social reinforcers, either positive or negative: praise or blame, attention or neglect, inclusion or rejection.

8

Children learn by imitation. The lesson for the child may be intended or accidental, suggesting that those in charge of young children had best set a good example.

FURTHER READINGS

Guilford, J. P. *The nature of human intelligence.* New York: McGraw-Hill, 1967.

> Guilford, a distinguished psychologist, states that the major aim of this book is to give the concept of "intelligence" a solid theoretical framework. This is a careful presentation with an excellent section on testing in developmental psychology.

Isaacs, S. *Intellectual growth in young children.* London: G. Routledge, 1930.

> This volume is based on research records of children at a school in Cambridge, England, in the 1920s. The data gathered from this group of children is analyzed under the theoretical problems of discovery, reasoning, and thought. Written with many quotations from the children's conversations.

Lavatelli, C. S. and Stendler, F. *Readings in child behavior and development.* (3rd ed.), New York: Harcourt, 1972.

> The papers collected in this book were selected for their presentation of important concepts in child development and for their relevance to students today. Of particular interest are the sections dealing with learning in infancy and conceptual and cognitive development.

Skinner, B. F. *Walden II.* New York: Macmillan, 1948.

> This is a novelized version of Skinner's utopia, fashioned by a benign creator. The conditioning of the children for a lifetime residence in Walden II makes for an interesting chapter, especially since this book has stimulated the establishment of several real Waldens.

Watson, J. B. *Behavior: an introduction to comparative psychology.* New York: Holt, 1967.

> To find out what behaviorism is, read this book, because John B. Watson defined it, shaped it, promoted it, and coined its terminology. Stimulus and response, reward and punishment, and the entire mechanics of conditioned learning are laid out. This book was originally published in 1914.

White, B. L. and Watts, J. C. *Experience and environment: major influences on the development of the young child.* Englewood Cliffs, N.J.: Prentice-Hall, 1973.

> A report on a major research undertaking at Harvard on the development of intellectual and social competence from birth to the age of six. The data is based on observations in the homes of the children being studied. The researchers were interested in the development of language, the senses, abstract thought, and social competence. Interesting case studies are included as well as a full discussion of the methodology and testing used.

5
Cognition and Language

"He said 'Daddy' today!"

Cognition is knowing. Sometimes the term *cognition* is used to mean a kind of knowing that is more definite, more certain, and more lasting than immediate sense perception. Sometimes it is used to mean the parts or dimensions of knowing that can be distinguished from emotion. Sometimes it seems to include the entire breadth of mental life. According to one list (Kagan and Kogan, 1970) cognition includes imagery, perception, thought, reasoning, reflection, problem solving, and all verbal behavior.

The study of these functions in very young children has only just begun. In fact, most of the work on infant cognition has been done since 1960, although Jean Piaget, the most influential figure in the discipline, published his first books on children from 1923 to 1932.

Piaget regards cognition as a form of biological adaptation—the organism's constant effort to bring about a harmonious interaction between his own schemata and the outer world. It is a "system of living and acting operations" that strives for equilibration, or a balancing between what the individual knows and what he perceives in the world (Piaget, 1950).

SENSORIMOTOR INTELLIGENCE

Piaget describes the cognitive processes of infants as **sensorimotor intelligence**, for until an individual is about two years old, his mental life is completely given over to regularizing his sensations and controlling his motor activity. There are six stages in the period of sensorimotor intelligence, the last of them ending around the child's second birthday. Cognitive development in the sensorimotor period is a gradual and continuous process, but the order of the six stages is always the same. Each stage occurs in proper sequence and is a necessary preparation for the next. No child, however, is a "pure" example of one stage or another; one aspect of the infant's behavior normally advances faster than another.

Much of Piaget's early investigation of infant behavior was carried out by observing his own three children—Lucienne, Laurent, and Jacqueline. He used no scientific instruments or laboratory procedures, his aim being to learn as much as possible about infants in their native surroundings. Although his early observations were limited to the three children, they were carried out over a much longer

PIAGET'S PERIODS OF COGNITIVE DEVELOPMENT

Sensorimotor Period (birth to 24 months)

Stage 1 (birth to 1 month)

Egocentric perceptions: makes no differentiation between self and other objects. Reflex activity.

Stage 2 (1 to 4 months)

Shows curiosity and primitive anticipations. Beginning of hand-mouth coordination. Begins to make differentiations as a result of own sucking and grasping actions.

Stage 3 (4 to 8 months)

Increased manipulation and contemplation of objects. Begins to imitate and construct perceptual classes and relations. Repeats rewarding activities. Development of eye-hand coordination.

Stage 4 (8 to 12 months)

Imitates and anticipates more actively. Uses familiar actions or responses to deal with new situations.

Stage 5 (12 to 18 months)

Perception and behavior become more exploratory and experimental. Discovers new ways to solve problems and attain goals. Begins to understand that external objects have independent existence.

Stage 6 (18 to 24 months)

Beginning of imagination and speech.

Preoperational Period (2 to 7 years)

Concrete Operational Period (7 to 11 years)

Formal Operational Period (11 years on)

period of time than would have been possible in the laboratory and were often supplemented by informal experiments to test the child's development. Piaget was a remarkably thorough, cautious, and sensitive observer and was closely aided by his wife, a trained psychologist.

Piaget used the terms *assimilation* and *accommodation* to describe the two processes that work toward equilibrium and gradually promote the infant from one step to the next. Assimilation results from the organism's tendency to use a structure in more than one way. The structure known as the sucking reflex, for example, is specifically adapted to the nipple, but the infant seeks to exercise it on anything he can get in his mouth. A blanket, a thumb, toys, or a pacifier will serve as "nourishment" for his need to suck. And when he uses a blanket in this way, he assimilates it—makes it similar—to other suckable objects.

As soon as certain actions prove successful, the infant begins to modify them to make them more effective. This modification of an action to improve the way it meets the environment is what Piaget terms accommodation. It is exemplified by the breast-fed infant's learning to search for the nipple with increasing effectiveness. In Piaget's observation of his son:

> As soon as his cheek comes into contact with the breast, Laurent [at twelve days old] applies himself to seeking until he finds drink. His search takes its bearings immediately from the correct side, that is to say, the side where he experienced contact. . . . [At twenty-six days of age] Laurent . . . feels the nipple in the middle of his right cheek. But as he tries to grasp it, it is withdrawn four inches. He then turns his head in the right direction and searches. . . . This time he goes on to touch the nipple, first with his nose and then with the region between his nostrils and lips. . . . He raises his head in order to grasp the nipple.

Reflex Stage

The human infant is born with certain sensorimotor reflexes, such as orienting reactions to sound and light, crying and sucking, the impulse to close his or her hand around something placed in it, and a general crying and thrashing about in response to any loud noise, sudden bright light, or abrupt movement.

But even at this earliest stage—roughly from birth to one month of age—the baby does not function by reflex alone. The lifelong process of learning by experience begins almost immediately. One of his first accomplishments is to expand his sucking response. At birth, his lips begin to suck as soon as they are touched; two weeks later he sucks much more efficiently and practices sucking between feedings. His original instinct is generalized to the sucking of rattles and blanket corners.

This is not to say, however, that the infant cannot differentiate between the genuine article and imitations. Before the end of his third week he has usually caught on to the fact that, while many soft substances provide relief from the trials of life, only one of these suckable objects results in the joys of a full stomach.

Primary Circular Reactions

During the second stage—from one month through four months of age—a gradual process of discrimination sets in. The infant begins to repeat simple activities, such as opening and closing his fists, purposefully rather than accidentally. Other actions are discontinued out of the same sense of purpose; a little girl may, for instance, continue to suck the corner of the blanket but discard her rattle. Her perceptive explorations grow less haphazard, more goal oriented: she looks in order to see, touches in order to feel.

At this stage the infant begins to develop such reactions as bringing the hand to the mouth. By initiating these movements she is rewarded with a pleasurable result in terms of her own body. She then learns to obtain the result by repeating the pattern of movements, beginning a "circular" process of reward, reinforcement, and repetition.

The infant also begins to anticipate future events. For example, when placed in an appropriate position she anticipates nursing by initiating sucking movements. As Piaget records:

> [When Laurent] is put in my arms in position for nursing, he looks at me and then searches all around . . . but he does not attempt to nurse. When I place him in his mother's arms without his touching the breast, he looks at her and immediately opens his mouth wide. . . .

The first signs of curiosity begin to appear at this stage, as well as evidence of some interest in unexpected events. The child also shows some signs of expectancy by watching the spot where an object has disappeared.

Secondary Circular Reactions

The circular reactions of the previous stage revolved almost exclusively around the baby's own body, whereas those that make their appearance in the third stage—from the fourth through the eighth month—involve the environment to an increasing extent as the baby learns to crawl.

This is the time when the child begins to evolve a concept of objects and to classify objects into groups. The secondary circular reactions, such as accidentally causing a rattle to sound and then trying to reproduce the result, show that the infant has learned that he and external objects are separate entities whose interaction he can bring about at will. For example, having found that it is fun to make the rattle sound, and doing so repeatedly, the infant will realize that *he* can produce the sound by shaking the rattle. Now there is no holding him: dizzy with the sense of power, he will perform this miracle over and over again, gurgling with joy. There is no longer anything accidental or tentative about this particular action; it is the deliberate performance of a specific act to bring about a specific result.

On the thirteenth day of his son's fourth month, Piaget observed:

Figure 5.1. What exactly is an object? This one always falls when you drop it. Leave it on the floor while you're doing something else, or even hide it completely from sight, and it's there again—or still—when you come back to it.

In the evening . . . Laurent by chance strikes the chain while sucking his fingers . . . he grasps it and slowly displaces it while looking at the rattles. He then begins to swing it very gently which first produces a slight movement of the hanging rattles and a faint sound inside them. Laurent then definitely increases by degrees his own movements: he shakes the chain more and more vigorously and laughs uproariously at the result obtained. On seeing the child's expression it is impossible not to deem this gradation intentional.

The infant can now perceive the difference between a slight movement of his own and a more vigorous one, and he distinguishes between the loud and soft sounds of the rattle. He notes the relationship between sound and movement.

The infant's object concept—the knowledge that an object exists even though he cannot perceive it at the moment—is initially acquired by coordinating schemata with one another and realizing that there is a relationship between them. The schema of the seen rattle, for example, is coordinated with that of the heard sound. Then, out of the building blocks of object concepts, he forms more and more schemata. As a result, he arrives at the first of four new abilities that Piaget recognized as specific to this stage. Because he can now conceive of objects, he can also *anticipate* where they will land when he drops them.

The second new ability is called *interrupted prehension.* When the baby loses an object while reaching for it, he will continue to make reaching movements with his hands. Then comes *deferred circular reaction*—the spontaneous resumption of an interrupted action. For instance, the infant is playing intently with the zipper on his playsuit when the chiming of a clock distracts him. At an earlier stage he would have shifted his attention to the clock and forgotten the zipper; now his attention soon returns to the zipper, and he resumes playing with it. Lastly, the power of *identification* expands to the point where the infant is able to recognize a partly covered object of which he can see only an exposed side.

All these new abilities also indicate the development of a sense of object permanence and, related to it, a rudimentary form of general space perception. He becomes more interested in the relations of objects to each other and no longer relates every object exclusively to himself. Vaguely he begins to understand that there is a big world full of objects and he is part of it but not the whole.

Coordination of
Secondary Reactions and Schemata

At the fourth stage—from the eighth through the twelfth month—the infant first displays intention as the primary motivating agent for beginning an activity. In the earlier stages, some accidental result of his actions had given direction to his further activity; now he starts with an intended result clearly in mind. When confronted with an obstacle, he will not, as before, keep repeating a futile action. Instead he now activates the new faculty of originality—not, as yet, by discovering a totally novel solution, but by successfully applying an action previously used in a different context to the new situation confronting him. Through the process of generalized assimilation, an action learned under past circumstances is thus expanded to include new situations that are different, yet sufficiently similar to make the action appropriate in both cases.

During this stage there is also a great advance in the skill of imitation. The baby is now capable of making much more meaningful connections between the actions of a model, such as his mother, and corresponding actions of his own. In addition, he begins to imitate actions that he cannot see himself perform and that have not aroused his interest before—such as lip movements and vocal sounds.

Any new action, such as smacking the lips or waving the hand—if at all within the baby's capabilities—now excites the urge to imitate to a much greater degree than during preceding stages. Piaget notes the following:

> Jacqueline began by making a slight noise with her saliva as a result of the friction of her lips against her teeth, and I had imitated this sound at the outset. [She] was moving her lips as she bit her jaws. I did the same thing, and she stopped and watched me attentively. When I stopped she began again. I imitated her. She again stopped and so it went on. . . .

Imitation may at first be very approximate, but the baby's attention span has lengthened quite a bit by now, and she is often willing to practice with surprising patience and perseverance to master a new skill. In this as in other areas, she exhibits a growing sense of the organization of things with respect to herself as well as to her surroundings. She begins to be able to anticipate events that are not the result of her own actions, because she has become aware of the independence of objects from herself and of a certain systematic predictability in the way people and objects behave.

Tertiary Circular Reactions

The fifth stage—from the twelfth through the eighteenth month—has been called "the climax of the sensorimotor period" (Ginsburg and Opper, 1969). All the abilities learned in earlier stages are now expanded and applied to increasingly complex situations. The infant now becomes systematically adventurous in his

Figure 5.2. A shadow is a curious thing. It follows you everywhere, yet you can't pick it up. It mimics your shape and motions, though sometimes it's longer than you are, sometimes shorter, and sometimes all gone. Where does it go? Could it be lost forever?

explorations of the environment. He is much readier than formerly to try novel solutions to problems and to learn by trial and error. For the first time he shows curiosity about an object for its own sake and seems intent on learning everything he can about it. In this stage, his interest in novelty is an end in itself. Piaget observed that Laurent, while playing with the soap dish, accidentally dropped it. The novelty of the situation immediately caught the child's interest, and he attempted to repeat the event, dropping the soap dish several times in succession.

Experimentation with new means for achieving a goal is also characteristic of this stage. When Lucienne was one year and five days old, Piaget arranged the following problem for her: a pivoting box was placed on a table and atop the box, just out of the infant's reach, was a toy bottle. In Piaget's own words:

> Lucienne at first tries to grasp the box, but she goes about it as though the handkerchief were still involved. [Grasping a handkerchief was a previous problem.] She tries to pinch it between two fingers, in the center, and tries this for a moment without being able to grasp it. Then, with a rapid and unhesitating movement she pushes it at a point on its right edge. . . . She then notes the sliding of the box and makes it pivot without trying to lift it; as the box revolves, she succeeds in grasping the bottle.

At first the child attempted to pinch the box, a maneuver she had used successfully to obtain the handkerchief. Then, by trial and error, she was able to accommodate her behavior and discover a new method. By pushing the box, Lucienne was able to bring the bottle closer. Her actions were directed both by the goal and by previous schemata that gave her an understanding of what was happening.

Invention

Now we have reached the great divide—the transition to thought.

Until now, the infant's mental processes have been evoked by actions and have manifested themselves entirely through actions. There has been for all practical purposes, no "action-free" cognition. All this changes during the tremendous mental revolution that takes place during the sixth stage, which occurs in the second half of the second year: the child gains the ability to imagine things. This amounts to no less than a change to a higher plane of reality—the one on which he will spend the rest of his life. From now on, he can transcend the strictly immediate situation in thought.

This truly enormous change often first appears in play. The child may be engaged in the enjoyable game of throwing alphabet blocks out of the playpen, one by one, for Mommy to pick up and bring back. One day, quite suddenly, this familiar pastime may take on a new dimension that will cause Mommy to catch her breath: this time, when the last block is thrown out, the game does not end. Without breaking the rhythm of his movements, the baby once more bends down with an outstretched hand, straightens up, lifts his arm and throws—an *imaginary* block.

This totally new dimension of cognitive functioning—imagination—quickly enters into all his activities. From now on when he confronts a problem, he will no longer charge into immediate action to reach a solution through trial and error. What he will do, though at first on a very primitive level, is what an adult does when tackling an obstacle. He will first envision a solution and then act to bring about the result he has anticipated in imagination.

Piaget called the next major period in the development of cognitive functioning the "preoperational" period. This period, which starts at the age of two years and ends at seven, will be discussed in later chapters. Piaget points out, however, that sensorimotor cognition does not stop when a child reaches his second birthday; much of the behavior associated with it continues long afterward.

Piaget also recognizes that the development of each new stage is gradual and that the age of its appearance varies from child to child, depending on environment as well as the child's own potential for cognitive growth. It is not surprising, then, that a recent experiment (Kagan, 1972) suggests that children may begin to form hypotheses before they are a year old.

It is essential to Piaget's theory, however, that the stages always occur in the same order. This may not have much practical importance in infancy, when cognitive development is very rapid, but it can make a crucial difference in planning curriculums at school. Pupils may skip grades, but they cannot skip a stage of development, and instructors can take advantage of this knowledge by adapting their materials and methods to the way the child learns at each stage.

LANGUAGE

Only weeks after birth, a baby has begun to make a few basic gestures and sounds. He gains an approximate notion of certain key expressions, tones of voice, and words. Soon he is spending hours babbling and cooing to himself, though he does not yet speak or understand language systematically. When he cries he is not trying to tell us what he is crying about—in fact, he may not really know what is bothering him. He depends on his parents to figure out what is wrong and set it right.

This arrangement soon changes. The baby's gestures become more precise; he begins to use a few words. Now, instead of simply waving his arms about, he may reach out or point to the bottle or toy he wants; instead of simply crying or murmuring, he may say the word—"mama," "up," "bye-bye"—that makes his meaning relatively clear. He starts to work at using sounds to make himself understood.

With this change the task of bringing him up becomes much easier, not only because he can now understand his mother's wishes more clearly, but also because

COGNITION

For most purposes we use the word *cognition* as a synonym for *knowing.* A typical psychological dictionary defines cognition as "a general term covering all the various modes of knowing—perceiving, remembering, imagining, conceiving, reasoning." Thus cognition is distinguished from other aspects of mental life: from feelings such as fear and anger; from desires or needs for food, warmth, and affection; and from intentions to carry out some action. It would seem that the modes of cognition—remembering, imagining, and reasoning—are abilities that develop as a person makes the transition to thought, and yet Piaget describes the infant's earliest mental activities as cognitive processes although he does not believe that thought begins until age two. How can there be cognition before some form of thought?

To understand how this can be, it may help to remember that Piaget began his career as a biologist and never lost sight of the biological basis of cognition. For Piaget, the infant's cognition before he develops the capacity for thought is entirely on the sensorimotor level: his mental processes always come in response to some present physical stimulation, either from outside—holding a toy, or being fed or tickled—or from inside—hunger, or a desire to be cuddled or rocked. We can understand Piaget's position more clearly if we look, for a moment, at the biological basis of cognition.

Scientists do not yet understand all of the brain's workings, but they have traced some general patterns. There seem to be certain parts of the brain where sensory impulses are received, sorted, and coordinated, and other parts that store the huge amount of information received. Cognition might be described as the process by which the brain registers and files all this information. Although the brain apparently takes in practically every bit of information that comes to it, only a fraction of it is readily available to our immediate consciousness. The rest stays with us, and is added to continuously throughout our lives, though we cannot "think" about it.

In Freudian terms, we might think of the mind as including three different but overlapping territories: the *conscious,* the *preconscious,* and the *unconscious.* Conscious thought consists of whatever we might be doing or thinking of at the moment. Preconscious thoughts are those which are available to our memory, although we may not "have them in mind" at the moment—knowing where we were at noon yesterday, or feeling hungry or jolly without quite realizing it. The unconscious is the great mass of information that is not accessible to our awareness. The contents of the unconscious mind surface sometimes in dreams. We also see evidence of it when we have nervous habits that we are unaware of until others point them out. Indeed, those mannerisms that seem most obvious in others are often the very things we do not notice in our own behavior.

Thus it seems that cognition can be going on without our even paying attention to its objects, much less thinking about them. This "thoughtless" cognition is the only cognition that infants—and probably most animals—are capable of, and yet they know a great deal. "Thoughtless" cognition continues after the dawn of thought and does not stop even in adulthood; thinking as a mode of knowing only adds to it.

the acquisition of language has a powerful effect in itself. It almost seems as if the knowledge of words brings with it a magical control over the environment. One observer (Fraiberg, 1959) notes, for example, that the child's mastery of the expression "bye-bye" very often coincides with much easier acceptance of his parents' departures. Similarly, acquisition of the phrase "night-night" seems to make the nightly ordeal of having to go to bed a little more bearable.

A somewhat similar control of consequences through words can be observed in the toddler happily transforming her nursery wall into a crayon rainbow, to the accompaniment of rhymthmic head shaking and the incantation of "no-no, no-no." Out of such rote repetition there gradually emerges real understanding of the meaning behind the words. A few weeks later the toddler may again approach the wall with her crayons, mutter "no-no," and sadly turn away.

Study of Language Learning

Our knowledge of how children learn language is still sketchy, but tremendous advances have been made in the past fifteen or twenty years. An essentially new science has appeared—*psycholinguistics.* Psycholinguists explore the area where psychology and linguistics overlap: the learning, use, and understanding of language. In their studies they naturally rely on the findings of linguistics and psychology, but they also use material from such other fields as anthropology, neurophysiology, and ethology.

Traditionally, research in language learning has been hampered by two major obstacles: the multiplicity of languages, and the fact that none of us has the faintest recollection of how he learned to speak—perhaps for the very reason that memories cannot persist in the absence of linguistic tags. We all know how greatly the spoken or written word helps in forming and remembering a mental image or even a feeling. Small wonder, therefore, that our earliest, wordless years are blanks in our minds.

We get an inkling of the wealth of early linguistic knowledge lost to us when we consider the normal youngster's extraordinary attention to detail. As soon as he has words enough to let us know, he amazes us with the astounding acuteness of his observations. Publishers of children's books have learned this to their sorrow from the mothers and nursery teachers who transmit such comments as "Why does the king's crown have four peaks on page three, and five peaks on page eleven?" and "How could the little girl get lost in the dark when there's a moon in the picture?"

Multiplicity of languages, on the other hand, has become an aid rather than an obstacle to progress in recent years. Psycholinguists have lately discovered that a number of universal factors underlie children's acquisition of speech, no matter what their native tongue. The words differ from language to language, but the ways in which infants use them are astonishingly similar. We know, for instance, that in at least six languages infant speech is characterized by the same type of syllable duplication to describe the same types of objects and that diminutives are formed in predictable ways. Thus, the English "choo-choo" corresponds to the German "Töf-töf" (car), the English "doggy" to the German "Hundi."

Figure 5.3. A reading lesson. Words go with objects and pictures of objects.

"He said 'Daddy' today!"   "Here's Daddy!"   "Daddy!"

"Daddy?"   "Who's that?"

"Say goodnight to Daddy."   "DADDY!"

Studies (Brown, 1970; Slobin, 1973; and Ervin-Tripp, 1973) further indicate that the stages children go through while progressing from baby talk to adult communication are roughly identical, regardless of native tongue, socioeconomic class, and ethnic background. In addition, it seems that children everywhere talk about the same things while undergoing these developmental stages. They all speak of objects and situations; they make demands; and they use mostly nouns and verbs; they talk *to* themselves a great deal but never *about* themselves or interpersonal relationships.

Thanks to the data accumulated by such cross-national studies we now have a fairly detailed plan of the linguistic route from birth through infancy. Let us look at some major milestones along this route.

The first sounds infants make are crying or screaming, shortly followed by babbling. One researcher (Engel, 1973) has postulated another, intermediary stage—a period of humming. In daily records of her son's vocalizations, kept from the time of his first cry, she noted that his humming sounds, which were quite different from singing, soon assumed sentencelike upward and downward intonations. After a period of apparently haphazard practice, he began to invest them with meaning. A pointed finger accompanied by a level-pitched "mmm" indicated that he was pointing the object out to her. When he actually wanted to have it, his pitch rose in a manner similar to the adult query or request intonation: "mmm?"

The researcher believes that early screaming and crying, while certainly forms of expression, cannot be considered real language; neither can gurgling, which is merely the pleasure-denoting equivalent of crying. Babbling, which follows in the wake of cooing, is in her view the first true attempt at linguistic expression. She points to an interesting sequence as the basis for this belief: babbling first appears at a time when the infant already understands the meaning of a few spoken words; it disappears as soon as language has been mastered, having then outlived its usefulness. Significantly, it often reappears in later life when linguistic expression is in some way reduced or impaired, as in stuttering or while learning a foreign language—or while taking an essay exam.

Crying

Babies use crying to indicate their displeasure at a relatively limited number of states of pain or general unease. These states are usually hunger, thirst, and being in pain from colic or teething. Being wet is a less frequent cause of crying. Soiled diapers generally cause greater discomfort to mother than offspring, unless the condition is compounded by diaper rash. In short, if he is well fed, a crying baby is most likely in pain, and it is unjust to grow suspicious of his motives when he promptly stops crying on being picked up.

Have you ever suffered through a night of raging toothache, barely able to wait for morning to call a dentist, only to find the pain gone as soon as you get out of bed? If so, you know that some forms of toothache are worse in a horizontal than a vertical position. Teething seems to be one of them; and a child probably does not stop crying from pure diabolic glee at having got you out of bed at

3 A.M. but because the pain goes away when you pick him up. The same may be true of the discomfort caused by a gas bubble, which gets dislodged as you pick him up and pat his back.

Ignoring prolonged crying also entails the risk of missing a potentially important warning. A touch of hoarseness in the crying, for instance, may herald a croup attack. These sometimes develop and worsen with frightening speed, and—especially in very young babies—require immediate medical attention.

Elements of speech

Speech may be divided into two basic elements: sounds and intonations. Since intonation can and does take place independently of speech sounds, it is of particular interest in tracing the linguistic development of infants from birth to two years. In an extensive study of the subject (Tonkava-Yampol'skaya, 1973), researchers asked these questions: Does the cry of a newborn infant have any intonational structure? What are the intonations in the cooing and babbling of infants during the first year of life? Can they be shown to have a communicative value? What are the characteristics of the intonational repertory of infants during the second year?

The study revealed that during the first month communication is largely limited to disagreeable sensations. Cooing with a placid intonation first appears during the second month; vocalizations of happiness and laughter appear during the third. During the seventh month the infant learns to convey a wish through a requesting intonation, whereas he may not master a questioning one until his second year.

Imitation

The study of intonations suggests that imitation is an important factor in the child's acquisition of language. Acoustical analysis of infant vocalizings revealed a closer and closer approximation of the babies' speech sounds to the intonations they heard from the adults around them. Interestingly, only one intonation seems to require no learning: "The intonation of discomfort in adults fully coincides with its counterpart in children from the immediate postnatal period onward. . . . after acquiring the communicative value of an intonation of discomfort during the first month of life, the intonational pattern in the cry of a newborn infant then retains its form and meaning throughout the entire subsequent lifetime" (Tonkava-Yampol'skaya, 1973).

Another observer (Engel, 1973) also accords imitation a vital role. According to her experience with her own child, language begins with the sounds of "m" and "b," which emerge during the humming period. These consonants become associated with a vowel—usually "a," which is the one that results most naturally from simply closing and opening the mouth while voicing these consonants.

The first of these wordlike formations was produced by Engel's son as "am" (meaning "I'm hungry"), although the more usually observed sequence is "ma" (meaning the same thing). These and similar syllables are first emitted in short sequences rather than singly (ma-ma, da-da, bye-bye). Later they proliferate and expand through imitation—first by ear alone, then by ear and eye combined: the baby not only imitates the sound he hears his mother make but tries to copy it more accurately by imitating the lip movements that produce it.

Recent research (Bloom, Hood, and Lightbown, 1974) suggests that imitation is a major tool used by the child to expand his understanding and use of language. Thus a child learning the word *eat* will imitate the phrase "eat apple." Later, when he is learning the word *red*, his imitation will take the form "red apple"; he will not imitate the word *eat* again because he has already learned it. The child's language is not imitative of what he already knows well; instead, he imitates words, and later grammatical structures, that he is in the process of learning. His imitation is on the frontier of his knowledge.

Sound Components

The basic sound components of any language are **phonemes**—the smallest units of sound that have meaning in the language. The English language uses about forty-five different phonemes. Examples are the "b," "e," and "d" of "bed." If we change one phoneme, we get a different word—"red," for example, or "bad." The phonemes of a language are the contrasting units that allow us to tell the difference in meaning between one utterance and another. They are analogous to, but not identical with, the letters of the alphabet.

To make a language, phonemes must be arranged into larger units called **morphemes.** A morpheme is the smallest part of a word that conveys meaning and cannot be further subdivided without destroying meaning. Thus, some morphemes are in effect words (bed, work), and these are called *free morphemes* because they can be used by themselves. However, if we add anything to alter their meaning in any way, we create words consisting of two morphemes rather than one (beds, worked). Because these endings are not meaningful unless combined with a meaningful morpheme, they are called *bound morphemes.* From morphemes the child progresses to the formation of words, at first simple and then more complex, and from there to the creation of meaningful word sequences, called phrases and sentences. For this last step the child needs *grammar* and *syntax*—the set of rules that govern the creation of sentences in any given language.

Linguist Noam Chomsky, who developed a theory of what he calls transformational grammar, has prompted many psycholinguists to focus their attention on how these linguistic rules are acquired by the child. Is the child born with certain innate semantic predispositions? If so, through what processes are they activated and expanded? Chomsky believes that the infant has a basic sense of grammar long before he begins to make any use of it.

The one year old understands a good deal more language than he can produce. During the second year the gap between comprehension and performance begins to narrow, but it will be a long time before it is fully closed. The one year old who can say "mama" probably understands two or three more words fully. By the age of two, the average infant knows 200 words or so, but his speaking vocabulary still lags behind by a wide margin.

Two-Word Sentences

At around eighteen months the infant emerges from the stage in which a single word stands for a whole sentence. Now two words are used in combination to convey meaning. The sequence of the words is that of adult speech, but the intermediate words are missing. The infant is evidently trying to imitate adult language, but at this stage of cognitive development he cannot yet reproduce it completely or accurately.

One researcher (Braine, 1963) who observed the emergence of two-word sentences in her own children has divided this embryonic grammar into two classes of words: *pivots* (or operators) and *X words*. Pivots are words that are singled out for constant repetition in any number of combinations; then after a time a particular pivot seems to have been practiced enough and is replaced by a new one. X words are all other words at the child's command. They do not occur as often or persistently as pivots, nor are they necessarily part of a combination. Pivots are always used in combinations and are always used in the same position, either initial or final.

The researcher's son Gregory provided an example of pivots and X words in action. His third word combination happened to be "see hat," which was followed by "see sock," "see horsie," and "see boy." *See* was the first word in ten of his first thirteen word combinations.

Figure 5.4. Understanding language comes before speaking it. Children understand more of what they hear than they can say themselves.

Other general pivot favorites are "my," "pretty," "all gone," and "more." The word "more" can have especially wide applications, such as "more Grampa?" on meeting the second set of grandparents.

As the above examples indicate, most pivots are not nouns, whereas most X words are nouns. In the next phase of two-word sentence construction, X words become more important, and an increasing number of the two-word units consist of nouns in both first and second position, such as "daddy office."

Complete Sentences

Beyond this point in the child's linguistic development there is no single accepted theory. Experts are sharply divided as to what accounts for the development of the ability to form complete, grammatical sentences. One researcher (Slobin, 1968) sees the explanation in a combination of reinforcement, expansion, and imitation. For example, the sound of the starting car centers the toddler's attention on his father's usual morning departure. He says "Daddy office." His mother nods smilingly (reinforcement) and replies, "Yes, Daddy has gone to the office" (expansion). The same situation is likely to occur again the next morning and the next; and with each repetition of this playful sequence associated with his mother's smiling face, the child comes closer to the realization that the idea "Daddy office" should be expressed as "Daddy has gone to the office." Since he loves to imitate her, he will shortly switch from his version to hers.

A very different view is expressed by other psycholinguists. One investigator (Brown, 1966), on the basis of his own longitudinal studies, points out that what parents reward (and therefore reinforce) is not grammatical accuracy but factual accuracy, and that children acquire correct grammar quite early despite lack of reinforcement—indeed, parents often seem rather to reinforce the errors by repeating their offspring's "cute" mistakes:

> When Eve said: "Mama isn't a boy. He is a girl," the answer was: "That's right." Eve used the wrong pronoun but mother knew what she meant and what she meant was true. On the other hand, when Adam said in perfect English, "Walt Disney comes on, on Tuesday," his mother said, "That's not right," because Walt Disney doesn't. (Brown, 1966)

This parental tendency, the researcher concludes, "makes rather paradoxical the usual product of child training—a speaker who is highly grammatical but not notably truthful."

Theories of Language Learning

How, then, do we learn to speak grammatically? Every theory that has been advanced to explain language acquisition has been severely criticized. The question of language learning is fiercely debated today, with almost every conceivable position finding its champion; data from anthropology, biology, psychology, lin-

LANGUAGE AND THOUGHT

Our thinking, and the language we use to give form to that thinking, are two sides of the same coin. The attitudes we learn as children are reflected in, and reinforced by, the grammar and vocabulary we learn at the same time.

Reformers recognize that to change people's attitudes we often have to change their use of language. The women's movement, believing that traditional attitudes are tied to traditional terminology, works to change words, urging people to use terms like *businessperson, chairperson,* and *Ms.* in place of *businessman, chairman,* and *Mrs.* The new usage is intended to redefine sex roles, and thereby to hasten social progress. Similarly, civil rights leaders in the 1960s came to feel that the word *Negro* perpetuated their subordinate position by recalling a history of servitude. They substituted the word *black* for *Negro* to promote a new, positive image, and began to think in new terms: "Black is beautiful."

The use of new words to shape people's ideas about the roles of women and blacks in our society may owe something to a theory developed by the linguist Benjamin Lee Whorf. The *Whorfian hypothesis,* as it is called, maintains that the grammatical structure of our language, and the vocabulary we are taught, impose rather narrow limits on the kinds of thoughts we can allow into our minds; once the language is learned, a door is shut, in effect, against new perceptions.

After studying the languages of the Hopi Indians and the Jivaro of South America, Whorf concluded that the language we use shapes our thinking and behavior. He said that every language contains concepts, embodied in words and word patterns, that are peculiarly its own, and that this produces a special world view. The implication for child development is that we unwittingly impose our own world view on our children simply by teaching them to speak our language.

Whorf's hypothesis has been attacked because it is unprovable, but it has been a springboard to further study of the relationship between language and culture. His findings have become part of a growing body of knowledge called *sociolinguistics,* which explores the influence of language on society.

Does thought change language? Or does language change thought? Think of words like *moonwalk, ecology,* and *detente,* which have recently become part of our vocabulary. In each case the idea comes first, but the word, once it is in circulation, helps shape our further thinking.

In the novel *1984* George Orwell shows us a monolithic society whose rulers impose on it an artificial, narrow language, Newspeak. Orwell suggests that the most effective way to manipulate people is to control their language. The citizens in *1984* not only have no way to think about personal freedom, or to question the authority of Big Brother, but by losing their natural language they have been cut off from the past; in ignorance of their own history, they are trapped, physically and intellectually, in a sterile and seemingly indestructible dictatorship.

The totalitarian societies of recent times have tried, to some extent, to transform Orwell's fiction into fact, but the results have been inconclusive. No Big Brother has lived long enough to impose his brand of Newspeak on several generations of subjects, and so language was never brought completely under control. Until this is done, it will be impossible for us to know whether control of language always means control of thought.

guistics, and even mathematics are cited as evidence for each theory. We will not try to choose between them but simply set forth the main lines of reasoning.

One group of researchers emphasizes reinforcement and imitation in language acquisition. This approach, commonly called the *empiricist* approach, is probably the prevailing modern view. The empiricist position is closely associated with the behaviorist learning theories of psychologists C. L. Hull and B. F. Skinner. In *Verbal Behavior* (1957) Skinner tried to explain all language as simply a special form of behavior that could be explained thoroughly in terms of stimulus and response. As the title suggests, language is to be regarded as essentially a set of habits that the child learns in adaptation to outside circumstances. Language originates as behavior aimed at obtaining food, comfort, and other needs, and it never loses this basic character no matter how elaborate and sophisticated it becomes. However, this is where the theory seems to run into trouble: highly sophisticated speech is difficult to explain by the empiricist approach.

One empiricist (Mowrer, 1960) has introduced the concept of *mediation*, or a tendency to react similarly to stimuli that are similar but not identical, in an effort to bridge the gap between simple conditioning and the higher mental processes. According to this modification of the empiricist theory, it is by mediation that we understand the symbolic significance of words and sentences and use them freely and expressively.

The *rationalist* approach of Chomsky and others questions the ability of empiricist theory to explain language development. This position is also referred to as *nativist*, because it maintains that the ability to learn and use language is innate, or native, to the human brain. Support for this position comes from many different sources. One theorist (Miller, 1964), for example, points out that "the magnitude of the learning task and the speed with which children accomplish it [are] impressive arguments that children must be naturally endowed with a remarkable predisposition for language learning." Another theorist (Lenneberg, 1964) has listed some biological facts that suggest that language ability may have evolved as a uniquely human trait. For example, children of all cultures learn language at about the same age and tend to learn it in similar ways. Our tendency to learn language is so strong that many learn it despite blindness or deafness. In addition, a number of "language universals" have been discovered independently by different linguists (Chomsky, 1957; Greenberg, 1963). As one rationalist (Lenneberg, 1964) has said, "Although language families are so different, one from the other, that we cannot find any historical connection between them, every language, without exception, is based on the same universal principles of semantics, syntax, and phonology."

Their conclusion is that these universal principles are built right into the human brain in the form of what Chomsky calls an "innate schema." This allows the child to hear and absorb language as it is spoken by himself and others and to sort out the bits and pieces of speech into a formal system, even without formal instruction. The speaker may never even be conscious that he is speaking his language according to a set of rules but, according to Chomsky, "it seems plain

INSTINCTS

A house is in flames, the children trapped inside. Breaking through the ring of firemen, the mother rushes into the house, risking her own life to save her children. What makes her do this? Is it the "maternal instinct"? If this is really the explanation for her behavior, how much of what she does in less dramatic moments is also controlled by instinct? Most new mothers smile and feel a flood of novel (but somehow familiar) emotions when they first see their baby. Later they feed, clean, play with, talk to, and discipline their children. But how much of this, if any, is instinctive?

For many years the scientific study of instinct was shaped by a somewhat arbitrary distinction between instinctive behavior and behavior that is learned. But most researchers no longer accept this distinction; they believe instead that all behavior results from an interplay between inborn tendencies and what the individual learns from the environment.

This was not always true. In 1902 William James defined instinct as "the faculty of acting in such a way as to produce certain ends, without foresight of the ends, and without previous education in the performance." He went on to list the "basic human instincts," and included locomotion, vocalization, pugnacity, secretiveness, modesty, and cleanliness. Other authors vied with James to add more and more items to the list, proposing such "instincts" as self-abasement and self-assertion. By the 1930s it was obvious that instinct theory had become so overused that it no longer explained anything.

As behaviorist theories came to dominate psychology in the 1930s and 1940s, the term *instinct* was more or less abandoned. After all, there was overwhelming evidence that punishment and reward could make a human (or an animal) do almost anything. Also, many of these "instincts," which were supposedly present in all human beings, did not seem to exist in other cultures. The behaviors that did seem to be universal were connected with psychological needs for food, drink, movement, and sex. The behaviorists preferred to think of these behaviors as arising from physiological *drives*.

Comparative psychologists, who study animals of many species, were among those who began to make the notion of instinct useful again. Very broadly, they describe an instinct as a predisposition, built into an individual's nervous system, to behave in certain ways. An animal will act out an instinctive behavior when a particular stimulus, called a releaser, is present in the environment. Instincts are build into a species during the course of evolution because they are adaptive for the species.

Instinct alone cannot explain much human behavior. In most animals instinctive behavior is stereotyped. Human instincts, if they exist, are shaped much more by learning. Aggression, for instance, is expressed not only by fighting and shouting, but also by arguing, doing well in school, or even withdrawing. For man, an instinct is an inherited tendency to learn some kinds of behavior with special ease.

Perhaps our most important instinct is the ability to adapt our behavior to the needs of the environment through learning. Instincts that may have been necessary to our cave-dwelling ancestors would certainly not help us much in twentieth-century America; we shed much of our instinctive legacy as we became civilized.

But perhaps some of this legacy remains. According to Chomsky, we have an instinctive ability to learn to talk—language, in some form, is a "biological property" of the human brain. When Piaget suggests that every normal child passes through a series of developmental stages in a predetermined order, he too seems to be saying that much of our development is built in; in other words, instinctive. Freud also stressed the instinctive element in human behavior. All of these theories are controversial, but most researchers accept at least part of each of them.

that language acquisition is based on the child's discovery of what from a formal point of view is a deep and abstract theory—a generative grammar of his language. . . ." This theory has the advantage over the empiricist view that it takes into account the fact that normal language use is creative, innovative, and appropriate to its social context (Chomsky, 1965). According to the nativist view, it is the mastery of grammar that makes these qualities possible, and the basic rules of grammar exist in the brain before language is learned, waiting to be activated by learning and experience.

A number of other researchers (Berko, 1958; Brown and Fraser, 1963; Ervin, 1964) have accepted the major aspects of nativist theory but have remolded it in important ways. The result is what is called the *rule learning* approach, which attempts to modify nativism in a way that accepts the importance of imitation, maturation, and comprehension. They point out that, ironically, the correct use of language by a child is not good evidence that he is using (or understanding) grammar; he may say "I saw it" rather than "I seed it" because he has been taught to say that particular sentence correctly or because he is imitating an adult. Brown and Fraser suggest that the best evidence that a child is using a grammar to produce sentences is the occurrence of systematic *errors* in his speech:

> So long as a child speaks correctly, it is possible that he says only what he has heard. In general we cannot know what the total input has been and so cannot eliminate the possibility of an exact model for each sentence that is put out. However, when a small boy says, "I digged in the yard" or "I saw some sheeps" or "Johnny hurt hisself," it is unlikely that he is imitating.

These researchers tried to determine the actual, as opposed to the ideal, grammatical rules used by young children by observing children's systematic errors and their use of made-up words. They concluded that quite early in their language learning, children infer general grammatical rules from the language around them. The first rules are simple, forming a "provisional grammar" that is actually a simplification of adult grammar. With age, maturation, and experience, the child's grammar becomes more detailed and complete and finally becomes quite similar to adult grammar. In this way the child comes to master his native language.

References

Berko, J. The child's learning of English morphology. *Word, 14,* 1958.

Bloom, L., Hood, L., and Lightbown, P. Imitation in language development: If, when, and why. *Cognitive Psychology,* July, 1974.

Braine, M. D. S. The ontogeny of English phrase structure: The first phase. *Language,* 1963, *39,* 1–13.

Brown, R. The dialogue in early childhood. Unpublished paper, Harvard University, 1966; quoted in Slobin, D. *Imitation and grammatical development in children.*

Brown, R. The first sentences of child and chimpanzee. In *Psycholinguistics: Selected papers.* Glencoe, Ill.: The Free Press, 1970.

Brown, R., and Fraser, C. The acquisition of syntax. In Cofer, C. N., and Musgrave, B. S. (Eds.), *Verbal behavior and learning: problems and processes.* New York: McGraw-Hill, 1963.

Chomsky, N. *Aspects of the theory of syntax.* Cambridge, Mass.: M. I. T. Press, 1965.

Chomsky, N. *Syntactic structures,* The Hague, Netherlands: Mouton, 1957.

Engel, W. v. R. The development from sound to phoneme in child language. In: Ferguson, C. A., and Slobin, D. I. (Eds.), *Studies of child language development.* New York: Holt, 1973, 9–12.

Ervin, S. M. Imitation and structural change in children's language. In Lenneberg, E. H. (Ed.), *New directions in the study of language.* Cambridge, Mass.: M. I. T. Press, 1964.

Ervin-Tripp, S. M. Imitation and structural change in children's language. In Ferguson, C. A., and Slobin, D. I. (Eds.), *Studies of child language development.* New York: Holt, 1973.

Fraiberg, S. H. *The magic years: Understanding and handling the problems of early childhood.* New York: Scribner's, 1959.

Ginsburg, H., and Opper, S. *Piaget's theory of intellectual development. An introduction.* Englewood Cliffs, N.J.: Prentice-Hall, 1969.

Greenberg, Joseph H. (Ed.). Universals of language. Cambridge, Mass.: M. I. T. Press, 1963.

Holt, E. B. *Animal drive and the learning process.* New York: Holt, Rinehart and Winston, 1931.

Kagan, J. Do infants think? *Scientific American,* 1972, *226,* 3, 74–82.

Kagan, J., and Kogan, N. Individual variation in cognitive processes. In *Carmichael's manual of child psychology,* 3rd ed., 1970.

Lenneberg, E. H. A biological perspective of language. In Eric H. Lenneberg (Ed.), *New directions in the study of language.* Cambridge, Mass.: M. I. T. Press, 1964.

Lenneberg, E. H. (Ed.). *New directions in the study of language.* Cambridge, Mass.: M. I. T. Press, 1964.

Miller, G. A. Language and psychology. In Eric H. Lenneberg (Ed.), *New directions in the study of language.* Cambridge, Mass.: M. I. T. Press, 1964.

Mowrer, O. H. *Learning theory and the symbolic process.* New York: Wiley, 1960.

Neisser, U. *Cognitive Psychology.* New York: Appleton-Century-Crofts, 1967.

Piaget, J. *Psychology of intelligence* (Percy, M., and Berlyne, D. E., transl.). London: Routledge and Kagan Paul, Ltd., 1950.

Skinner, B. F. *Verbal behavior.* New York: Appleton-Century-Crofts, 1957.

Slobin, D. I. Cognitive prerequisites for the development of grammar. In Ferguson, C. A., and Slobin, D. I. (Eds.), *Studies of child development.* New York: Holt, 1973.

Slobin, D. Imitation and grammatical development in children. In Endler, N., Boulter, L., and Osser, H. (Eds.), *Contemporary issues in developmental psychology.* New York: Holt, 1968.

Tonkava-Yampol'skaya, R. V. Development of speech intonation in infants during the first two years of life. In Ferguson, C. A., and Slobin, D. I. (Eds.), *Studies of child language development.* New York: Holt, 1973.

Vygotsky, L. S. *Thought and language.* Hanfmann, E., and Vakar, G. (Eds. and transl.), Cambridge, Mass.: The M. I. T. Press, 1962.

148

SUMMARY

1 Piaget describes the way infants think as sensorimotor intelligence and distinguishes the development of thinking into six stages based on the biological adaptation of the infant to harmonize what he knows with what he perceives of the world.

2 Piaget sees the development through the stages of the sensorimotor period as gradual and continuous but inflexible in respect to the sequence—each stage being a preparation for the next.

3 The infant progresses through the stages by assimilation and accommodation. Stage 1, the Reflex stage, is a development of the innate reflexes. Stage 2, Primary Circular Reactions, is based on the circular process of reward, reinforcement, and repetition, and involves the infant's learning about his own body. Stage 3 is the Secondary Circular Reaction stage from the fourth to the eighth month, in which the baby learns about his environment and how to act upon it. Stage 4, Coordination of Secondary Reaction and Schemata, takes the infant through to one year of age. In this stage he starts an action intentionally, learns by imitation, and can predict systematically how objects and people will behave. Stage 5, the Tertiary Circular Reactions Stage, marks a greater curiosity for the sake of pure learning and a propensity for experimentation. Stage 6, Invention, signifies a transition to symbolic thought. The young child can manipulate his environment with his imagination independent of physical objects or a specific setting.

4 Learning his own language is a task which parallels the sensorimotor stages and continues well past the second birthday. Psycholinguistics, a relatively new discipline, is devoted to the study of the acquisition of language skills by children. Studies show that no matter what the language, infants use sounds in similar ways.

5 Infant vocalizing is first limited to crying, followed by the happier sounds of cooing, with laughter and babbling through the third month. A regular sequence can be distinguished cross-culturally.

6 Imitation is also important in the acquisition of language; young children will not only try to imitate the sound but try to copy the lip movements of experienced speakers. Children imitate sounds primarily during a learning process.

7

Linguists have named the basic sound components of speech, phonemes. Morphemes, composed of phonemes, are the smallest units of sound which have meaning. The child acquires phonemes first and then morphemes. At this point he must learn the rules of syntax and grammar—an important aspect of psycholinguistics.

8

The child's first sentence generally consists of two words which, for the individual child, are invariably used in the same order, showing evidence that children conceptualize language in terms of a system. There is no agreement among psycholinguists as to how children learn to talk in complete grammatical sentences. When parents reinforce a correct sentence, there may be ambiguity as to whether the grammar or the context is being praised.

9

The empiricist approach associated with B. F. Skinner emphasizes the behaviorist view that language is an adaptation to the environment and good usage will be rewarded. The rationalists, followers of Noam Chomsky, whose system is sometimes called the nativist approach, see the ability to learn as a predisposition of the species, an innate schema existing in the brain before language is learned.

FURTHER READINGS

Beard, R. M. *An outline of Piaget's developmental psychology for students and teachers.* New York: Mentor, 1969.

No one in recent years has made a greater impact on educational thought and research than Jean Piaget, but few read his books. This is largely due to the fact that he is not always the clearest writer. Dr. Beard's outline is a lucid account of the major features, carefully arranged and expressed without hiding the genuine complexity of the issues.

Cunningham, M. *Intelligence: Its organization and development.* New York: Academic Press, 1972.

Cunningham formulates a unified theory that explains Piaget's stages of sensorimotor intelligence from reflex behavior through the emergence of cognition, interpreting Piaget's observations in terms of an information-processing model. Cunningham's model of intelligence is useful for problems in developmental psychology and can be adapted for the computer sciences.

Elkind, D. *Children and adolescence: Interpretive essays on Jean Piaget.* New York: Oxford University Press, 1970.

Although Piaget, the Swiss psychologist, has been studying the development of children's thinking for fifty years, it is only in the last decade that professionals in education and psychology have come to recognize the importance of his contributions. David Elkind worked with Piaget in Geneva, and in this book he explains the entire body of Piaget's work in a clear and absorbing fashion. He introduces the volume with a personal recollection of Piaget.

Hopper, R., and Naremore, R. C. *Children's speech.* New York: Harper, 1973.

The goal of this book is to explain how children learn how to talk. Since children learn to talk as naturally as they stand up and walk, specific aspects of the development are singled out and then placed in a matrix of events. There is a section on communication patterns of minority-group children and the problems of speech therapy.

Lewis, M. M. *Language, thought and personality.* New York: Basic Books, 1963.

Dr. Lewis presents the day-to-day changes in the speech, language, thought, feelings, and social behavior of children from their birth. The data are drawn from studies of both normal and retarded children. The latter, in particular, afford a new understanding of linguistic development in normal children.

Spitz, R. A. *No and yes: On the genesis of human communication.* New York:
International Universities Press, 1957.

Spitz examines in minute detail some of the earliest infant behavior in order to
discover the roots of verbal and nonverbal communication. He draws on his knowledge of deprived children, comparing normal and abnormal development to establish
his theory. Of particular interest are his observations of nonverbal communication
in infants.

Social Relationships

A baby derives his sense of himself largely from others. As his mother strokes his tummy and back, and as he reciprocates by smiling and gurgling, he gains a sense of his physical self. As one psychologist (Murphy, 1972) puts it, "All these actions provide sensations which gradually become organized into a cognitive map of himself—perhaps with the feeling 'There is such a lot of me and all so luscious.' "

But not all babies come to feel they are "all so luscious." Some babies apparently do not establish a firm sense of self, either as a separate physical being or as a social person capable of relationships. An infant treated as if he is not there may grow up to feel that he is a nobody—or "has no body" (Laing, 1960). A battered baby, if he grows up at all, may feel that he is irredeemably bad. In the first few months of life the baby is in the precarious position of establishing himself as a being in the world. The psychiatrist R. D. Laing (1960) vividly pictures the dilemma of the newborn:

> There it is, a new baby, a new biological entity, already with its own ways, real and alive, from *our* point of view. But what of the baby's point of view? Under usual circumstances, the birth of a new living organism into the world inaugurates rapidly ongoing processes whereby within an amazingly short time the infant *feels* alive and has a sense of being an entity, with continuity in time and location in space.

How does this happen? The infant learns that he is an entity because someone touches him. He learns that he is the same person from day to day because things happen to him regularly. He learns that his arms and legs are part of him—that he does not disappear forever under a peekaboo blanket—because somebody plays with him. In short, the infant's feeling for himself and his world cannot be taken for granted; it is entirely dependent on the care and attention he receives in the first year of life.

ATTACHMENT

A new mother expects that when the newborn baby is placed in her arms, an intimate personal relationship begins. Indeed the infant seems equipped from birth to demand his mother's love and attention. Soon he cries to bring his mother or father to him; he cries to be picked up, fed, and otherwise stimulated; and often

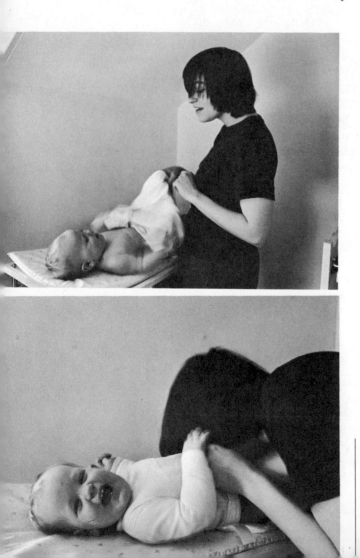

Figure 6.1. Changing a baby's diapers gives him stimulation; tickling even more.

as not he cries when put down. At six weeks the infant will smile at his mother and grasp her face and clothing. At four months he will babble and initiate cuddling and other intimate games.

All these behaviors are doubtless gratifying to a parent who spends a lot of time in child care. But despite the early signs of attachment, infants under six months of age do not really recognize or relate to their caregivers as separate human beings. Though the infant may cry when his mother or father turn their attention to something else, nearly anyone who provides the desired stimulation or satisfaction will quickly be accepted as a substitute. Early attachment is *indiscriminate;* the baby seeks stimulation rather than any particular person.

It is usually at about seven months or so that a special attachment develops, usually to the mother (or mothering figure) but sometimes toward others as well. Although there is some variance in the age of onset, nearly 90 percent of all infants form special attachments by the end of the tenth month (Schaffer and Emerson, 1964). Now the infant cries loudly when his mother disappears, even if there are many other people present to provide comfort and stimulation. When his mother is present, the infant tends to engage in an array of attachment behaviors directed exclusively toward her—exchanging glances, seeking physical contact, vocalizing, and so on. When mother leaves, the infant will orient himself to the door. If he can, he will follow on all fours.

At this stage, the infant is in the process of developing his first meaningful attachment to another person. This is in fact a social relationship, one that involves all the possibilities of warmth and rejection, care and neglect. The quality of the mother–child relationship is from the outset the determining factor in development.

Attachment in Other Species

It appears that mother–infant attachments occur in other animal species as well as among humans. Since animal young develop much more quickly in every way, they form attachments earlier than humans do. A particularly early and striking form of attachment is found in certain flock animals, such as geese, chickens, ducks, and swans. These birds are able to walk very soon after hatching, and they are instinctively programmed to follow the first moving object they perceive, which in most cases is the parent bird. The newly hatched goose, for example, displays an inflexible following response that attaches him to the parent bird. There seems to be a short period during which the following response can be fixed, or **imprinted**, in the young goose. If mother goose is not present, the infant will follow whatever does appear—even if it happens to be a six-foot honking scientist. Konrad Lorenz, the famous researcher and writer on animal behavior, has succeeded in attaching goslings to his own person and to a variety of mechanical decoys.

In numerous experiments, researchers have found that birds imprinted on humans or other inappropriate objects are unable to perform normally in their own species. At mating time, for example, some experimental geese and ducklings preferred their human caretakers to birds of their own species. If attachment is not made at the critical point, and to the appropriate object, permanent behavioral abnormalities may result.

Imprinting of this clear-cut variety does not seem to take place in higher animals. Nevertheless, striking attachment behaviors have been observed in many species. For example, a baby monkey clings tightly to his mother's hairy abdomen, giving evidence of strong attachment within the first two weeks of life. In most species, a disruption of the attachment produces some disturbance in the young and possibly in the mother too. An infant monkey who does not have the opportunity to cling to the soft belly of his mother—or to something very similar—will develop without normal social and sexual responses. A baby sheep removed from its mother at birth will not be able to follow the flock when he is returned to pasture. And a mother goat will be unable to recognize or feed her young if she has been separated from them during the critical period immediately after birth.

MOTHERING

Attachment in the human baby is unquestionably more complex than attachment in other animals. Nevertheless, there are some similarities. First, in all species studied so far, attachment takes place at about the time the young become mobile and only slightly before they display a fear of strange objects or animals. The human infant, for example, becomes attached to his mother at about four to six months and learns to creep at about seven to nine months. His fear of strangers is usually manifested a month or so later (Schaffer and Emerson, 1964). Some researchers have suggested that imprinting in geese and attachment in human infants can take place only before the onset of the fear response, which occurs independently. But it seems more likely that the development of the attachment—the recognition of the mother as a special object—is itself what makes other beings seem strange and frightening.

Both animals and humans suffer some harm when their attachments are disrupted or altered. We have seen that sheep and goats grow up with social and sexual peculiarities as a result of having failed to make a primary attachment. Studies of institutionalized human infants have shown that comparable difficulties are experienced by children who receive little or no mothering.

Several animal experiments have become important precisely because they suggest the effects of poor mothering and inadequate attachment. The most famous of these is, in a sense, an attempt to discover the very basis for attachment. What accounts for the firm and healthy relationship between the mother and the newborn?

For many years, it was assumed that feeding was the answer. The infant clung to his mother and eventually came to prefer her because it was she who extended the breast or bottle. The striking studies conducted by psychologist Harry Harlow (1959, 1966) were designed to test this assumption. Harlow constructed two surrogate, or substitute, monkey mothers. One was a body made of bare chicken wire; the body of the other was covered with soft cloth. A feeding bottle could be attached to either one. Each baby monkey had both kinds of surrogate mother, but some were fed only by the wire mother, and others only by the cloth one.

If mother–child attachment were based primarily on feeding, the baby monkeys should have become attached to whichever surrogate mother had the bottle. Instead, Harlow found that *all* the monkeys developed the classic clinging attachment to the cloth-covered mother surrogate, preferring her presence between feedings and in stressful situations. The wire mother was ignored except at feeding time.

These experiments clearly demonstrated that tactile stimulation, as manifested in the clinging response, was the critical bond between mother and infant. Nevertheless, the comfortable cloth surrogate was not, in the end, an adequate mother, for "her" babies did not develop normally. Most of the female monkeys, at maturity, were unable to nurse their own young, and a few were even vicious toward them. Apparently feeding and tactile contact do not of themselves constitute adequate mothering for monkeys. Anyone who has observed a live monkey mother busily cuddling and grooming her young knows that primate mothering is complex behavior. It is especially so in the human.

Attachment in Humans

It was once assumed that babies inevitably become attached to whoever feeds, changes, bathes, powders, and dresses them. But human infants, like monkeys, have needs above and beyond the alleviation of physical distress. One study of sixty infants (Schaffer and Emerson, 1964) found that more than a third of them did not choose as their first specific attachment the person who usually performed these routine tasks. In fact, in 22 percent of the cases studied, the person chosen did not even participate in daily care, though she was usually a close relative or someone else the baby saw regularly.

FATHER

I always wanted to have a family. I wasn't prepared at first, but I just settled down. I never wished I wasn't a father.

My wife was seventeen and a little frightened when our daughter was born. I helped with the diapering, bathing, and feeding. I'd sit up with the baby and rock her. Now my kids and I have a friendship.

I don't treat Bridget and Mickey any differently. They get the same. We go bike-riding or to the movies together. They come to me with their schoolwork, their problems. They can trust me.

Every year I bring them to the plant where I work so they can see why I work and what I do. I want them to get good educations and decent jobs, but I don't make choices for them. I just want to know what my kids are doing.

I haven't seen my father since I was eleven.

—Andy Crayton, 34, assembly line worker and father of Bridget, 11, and Mickey, 10. Reprinted with permission from *Ms.*, May 1974.

Mothering, of course, is not something that can be done only by a mother. More and more, fathers are taking an active role in caring for infant children—feeding, bathing, diapering, and playing with them. In families where the mother works (and in families where a working father is the only parent), children develop important emotional attachments to other mothering figures—grandparents, aunts and uncles, older brothers and sisters.

It seems that mothering is a matter of social stimulation as well as physical care. If a mother (or other caregiver) props a bottle in an infant's mouth and leaves him sucking, a physical need is being met, but that is all. The infant needs social stimulation if he is to develop an attachment to the caregiver. When the mother strokes and smiles at her infant during the feeding session and at other times, a relationship is formed.

Physical Contact

Like monkeys, human infants have an inborn need to cling. The newborn infant will grasp any finger that touches his small palm. Later he will show his attachment by clinging to his mother's skirts, burrowing into her lap, or pulling on her hair. The extent to which mothers encourage and supply this physical contact is an important factor in the infant's social development.

Particularly crucial is the *quality* of the mother–infant contact. Is the baby picked up only in the course of routine feeding and diaper change? Or is he held for the sheer pleasure of it? Is he cradled in the arms of a tender, confident mother or held in a nervous, impersonal way? There are many differences between mother–infant pairs, and researchers believe that the subsequent social patterns of the infants can be traced to these differences. One researcher, for example, (Ainsworth, 1972) found that when mothers held their babies relatively long and sometimes when it might not be expected, the babies appeared to be particularly relaxed and "well-rounded." They enjoyed being picked up—so much so that they sometimes initiated the contact by extending their arms. Nevertheless, these babies responded positively and cheerfully to being put down. Other infants, who were held more frequently but for shorter periods, did not respond so positively to being picked up and were likely to fuss when put down. When a mother was abrupt or insensitive in her pick up, the infant tended to squirm in protest and to cry loudly when released.

Some researchers—and many parents—have suggested another possibility: that physical contact between the mother and baby is at least partly influenced by the baby himself (Bell, 1968; Schaffer and Emerson, 1964). A mother who approaches two successive babies with the same general inclinations may nonetheless find that her first baby is a "cuddler" who delights in being held, while her second child is restless in her arms, eager to be put down to explore his toys and surroundings. Maternal behavior does not seem to account for such differences in infants, nor have any relevant social or environmental factors been isolated as causes. It seems that some infants are biologically predisposed to seek a high degree of physical contact—from mother, father, stuffed dog, or security blanket. Others are naturally more goal- or task-oriented and dislike situations that cuddle them, confine them, or otherwise restrict their energies.

Smiling

Smiling, like physical contact, is an early means of communication between mother and child. In fact, nearly everyone smiles at a baby, hoping she will smile in return. New fathers even gather before the hospital nursery window imagining smiles on the faces of their newborn infants. A smile is important because, in our culture, it initiates a social relationship.

An infant may be seen to smile when she is only a few hours old, but it is not yet a social smile. When the infant has acquired the generalized schema for the human face, she proves it by smiling at a face or facelike representation. Like most early attachment behaviors, the smile is at first bestowed indiscriminately. Until about seven to ten months, when the first specific attachment is formed, there can be no special smile for mother.

Nevertheless, the smile is from the start an important influence on the mother–child relationship. When the infant smiles, her mother is likely to interpret this as a sign of high contentment. A smiling baby is a virtual advertisement for motherhood: she makes any mother feel proud, contented, and singularly blessed. The mother will respond with babbling, frequent cuddling, and so on. A grumpy, serious baby may not inspire the same attention. Depending on her own temperament, the mother may be resentful, anxious, or full of self-doubts. She may tempt the baby nervously with toys or affection or may simply decide, whenever possible,

Figure 6.2. Reflex smile and social smile. A baby's early smiles are just a haphazard exercise of the facial muscles, like waving the arms and legs about. A true smile comes when the baby has something recognizable to smile at.

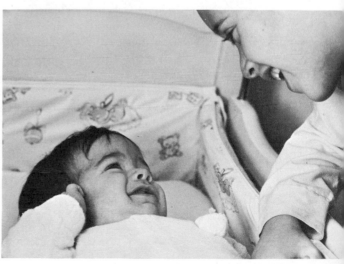

to leave well enough alone. The frequency of the infant's smile can contribute to the overall quality of the mother–child relationship.

The mother's responsive smile is equally important. It transforms the spontaneous smile of the infant into an exchange—the first real social interaction. In effect, the mother's smile shows the infant that he can have an impact on a person in his environment. Long before he can talk, he has discovered an important social tool. A smile will get him many things he likes—a smile in return, some cuddling, or talk and play.

The frequency of smiling behavior seems to be congenitally influenced. Some infants appear to be smilers almost from birth, while others do not smile even with strong encouragement. Among a group of newborn infants, the range is very wide, even for premature infants (Freedman, 1966). Despite these congenital differences, the infant's smiles will generally increase if his mother reinforces them with her own smile or some other stimulation. Mothers, too, however, vary in their tendency to smile, and in general responsiveness.

Basic Trust

The position of the newborn infant may be difficult for us to imagine. From the time of late childhood, we have been able to make realistic comparisons of our mother with other mothers, of our family life-style with other life-styles—saying, for example, "My mother is easy to talk to, but she's stricter than most," or "I don't have to take that from my parents—it's not the way things are done." An infant or very young child is absolutely unable to make such comparisons. He must accept as the real and total world the particular family situation in which he finds himself. His viewpoint is determined almost exclusively by mediating adults.

Noting this, the psychoanalyst Erik Erikson has characterized infancy as the period during which the child develops basic and long-standing expectations about his world. During infancy, the first psychosocial stage in Erikson's model, the great issue at stake is trust versus mistrust. Basic trust involves a positive orientation toward oneself, the world, and others. Mistrust is manifested in negative feelings, such as fear and insecurity.

According to Erikson, basic trust has its origins in mothering that combines "sensitive care of the individual needs and a firm sense of personal trustworthiness within the trusted framework of the culture's life style" (Erikson, 1968). When the infant's needs are met in a consistent and affectionate way, he is satisfied that his world is a safe place. He trusts his caregivers basically because of their consistent attentiveness toward him, but also because they convey a stable sense of their own worthiness.

When the infant's needs are not recognized, he is in an entirely different position. His world is chaotic, unpredictable. Sometimes his cries are met with milk and cuddling; sometimes he is ignored or pushed harshly aside. If he is left to cry for long periods, he cannot conclude, as we might, that his mother is neglectful, for he has no experience to judge her by. It is his *world* that seems neglectful of him. Perhaps it really is an arbitrary and unfriendly place, or perhaps he is someone who just does not get attention. Under such circumstances, the infant develops a basic mistrust of the world and a sense of his own unimportance.

Basic mistrust is soon manifested in behavior. When the infant is not regularly satisfied in his need for physical contact, nourishment, and so on, he reacts with prolonged crying. In Uganda, one researcher (Ainsworth, 1963, 1967) found that she could tell secure relationships from insecure ones (or trusting from mistrusting ones) on the basis of infant crying. Among a group of American infants she found that the amount of infant crying reflected the degree of responsiveness the mother had shown in the past. If a mother does not respond or responds too slowly to the infant's cries, he increases both the frequency and duration of his crying episodes (Ainsworth, 1972). It seems as if he no longer trusts that she will come right away.

Once the baby accepts the orientation of mistrust, his environment works to reinforce it. Constant crying behavior will undercut the infant's already precarious position. His mother now concludes that he is a bad or cranky baby who simply cannot be attended every time he cries. Other members of the family shout and curse at him; the neighbors bang on the walls. And when he is held, it is usually by some desperate person who hopes to shut him up.

The initial expression of mistrust—the constant crying—causes a further degeneration of relationships. The infant reacts by crying even more. He is self-defeating and will continue to be so. He is the toddler we see years later, crying in the supermarket: his mother slaps his face and then he wails. His behavior pattern begins to resemble that of many maladjusted adults, such as the neurotic who cannot trust relationships but continues to be demanding or possessive even when it is clear that his behavior drives others away. Basic mistrust leads to self-defeating behavior patterns, a reduced sense of self, and an inability to deal positively with others.

The Institutionalized Infant

A child with an unresponsive or inconsistent mother will cry for long periods in an attempt to attract attention. But what of a child who has no mother or regular caregiver, a child who is fed by a propped-up bottle? At first this child too will indulge in prolonged crying; but after a time he will do the only thing he *can* do. He will gradually reduce his crying and subside to a state of quiet indifference. When his demands are unmet, he becomes altogether undemanding. It is a tragic adjustment.

Human children cannot really grow up without some adult care. However, some children are placed as infants in institutions such as orphanages or foundling homes where they live more or less deprived of ordinary mothering. The quality of institutional care varies, of course. But in few if any institutions does the infant enjoy an intimate, long-continuing attachment to one adult. Were the infant able to become attached to a small group of caregivers, nothing in the literature indicates that he would be psychologically impoverished. However, few institutionalized infants develop any enduring attachments. In fact, they become as unresponsive to adults as their caretakers are to them. And they remain relatively uninterested in playmates and toys.

The probable effects of institutionalization have been suggested by experiments with the rhesus monkey (Harlow, 1962b). Harlow, who conducted the surrogate mother studies mentioned earlier, became interested in the whole question of monkey mothering as a result of his having attempted to raise fifty-six monkeys in isolation. In order to protect the monkeys against an infectious disease, Harlow separated them from their mothers almost at birth. Each was placed in a wire cage—alone, but within view of other laboratory monkeys. None was allowed any physical contact with his mother or with other young monkeys. The subjects might be said to have been "institutionalized" from birth—deprived of mothering and removed from normal family (or group) life.

Much to Harlow's surprise, not one of the monkeys developed normally. Although the rhesus monkey is a highly sociable animal, these monkeys were indifferent and sometimes aggressive toward one another. None mated or showed evidence of the playful cooperation that is characteristic of the breed. Some of the monkeys sat staring into space. Others engaged in repetitive and destructive behaviors—rocking or biting themselves, for example. A classic photograph shows one of Harlow's young monkeys curled up, face to floor, in a position that resembles nothing so much as a human schizophrenic, withdrawn into his own world amid the bustle of some hospital corridor.

Fortunately, few human babies are ever so severely deprived of mothering. Some, however, have been placed in orphanages or other institutions, and their development has been scientifically compared with that of children reared at home. Of course, institutionalized infants are not representative of the population as a whole. They tend to come from low-income neighborhoods and disorganized families—the kind of background that in our society is linked with lower intelligence scores and a variety of social handicaps.

In fact, several studies have found institutionalized children to be retarded in sensorimotor and social development. Differences appear only after three or four months of life, and the negative effects of institutionalization seem to increase with the length of stay in the institution. For example, the peak of smiling comes later in institutionalized infants, presumably because of lack of stimulation from caregivers (Provence and Lipton, 1962). Movement is sometimes inhibited, and resistance to disease is relatively poor, even when medical care is adequate (Spitz, 1945). Visual discrimination, reasoning, and concept formation suffer. Behavior is often disturbed. Most important, language learning is seriously, perhaps irreversibly, retarded. In some institutions, the infant is no more encouraged to babble than to cry.

It is not surprising that many institutionalized children are thought to be mentally retarded. Undoubtedly, many are. However, several studies suggest that when the conditions of institutionalization are bypassed or eliminated, such children experience a remarkable rise in IQ and in social capacities as well. A most interesting study was conducted (Skeels, 1966) over a period of thirty years. The subjects of the study were twenty-five children raised in an orphanage and classified as mentally retarded. Because mentally retarded children are seldom considered for adoption, the subjects reached the age of two without any significant life prospects. At that point, thirteen of the children, most of them girls, were transferred to another institution where each was adopted by an older mentally retarded child in a kind of "big sister" arrangement. Though the transferred children continued to live in an institutional setting, there was one important difference: each now had a caregiver or mothering figure. The children who remained in the original orphanage did not have this advantage.

Twenty years later, the transferred group was significantly higher in IQ than the orphanage group. Whereas only one member of the orphanage group had completed high school, almost half of the transferred group had attended high school, and one had even gone to college. All of the transferred children grew up to be normal, self-supporting adults, whereas four members of the orphanage group were still in institutions. These differences reflect not only the effect of the "big sister" relationships, but the fact that most of the transferred children were eventually perceived as normal and were adopted into a family setting. Clearly not all the children were simply and irreversibly "mentally retarded."

Often, children who lack a permanent home of their own may be placed in foster homes. For some children, this is an opportunity to participate in normal family life. But the foster parents are performing a service, and they are paid by a government or community agency for performing it; they do not adopt the child. This can make the arrangement precarious from the child's point of view. If the foster parents have a child or if one of them falls ill or if they simply find the child's behavior unacceptable for some reason, the child may be moved back to an institution or to another foster home. The child may also be moved because of action by his own family or by the placement agency. In fact, it is common for a foster child to be brought up in a series of homes in the course of his childhood. Despite its imperfections, however, the foster home environment has definite advantages over the institution for the child's development.

In general, institutionalized children transferred to a better institution or to a foster home show fewer personality disturbances and higher intelligence scores than children who remain in institutions. Comparisons of institution and foster children have shown that foster children were emotionally more secure and better adjusted, even when they spent their first three years of life in an institution (Goldfarb, 1945a). Foster children who were brought into the home as infants were decidedly better adjusted than children who spent the first three years in institutions (Goldfarb, 1945b). The latter were often transferred from one home to another because their behavior was found to be aggressive, unresponsive, or otherwise undesirable.

It might seem reasonable to conclude that the lack of a permanent attachment is the likely cause of retarded development in institutionalized children. There is evidence, however, that the lack of stimulation that a mother would normally

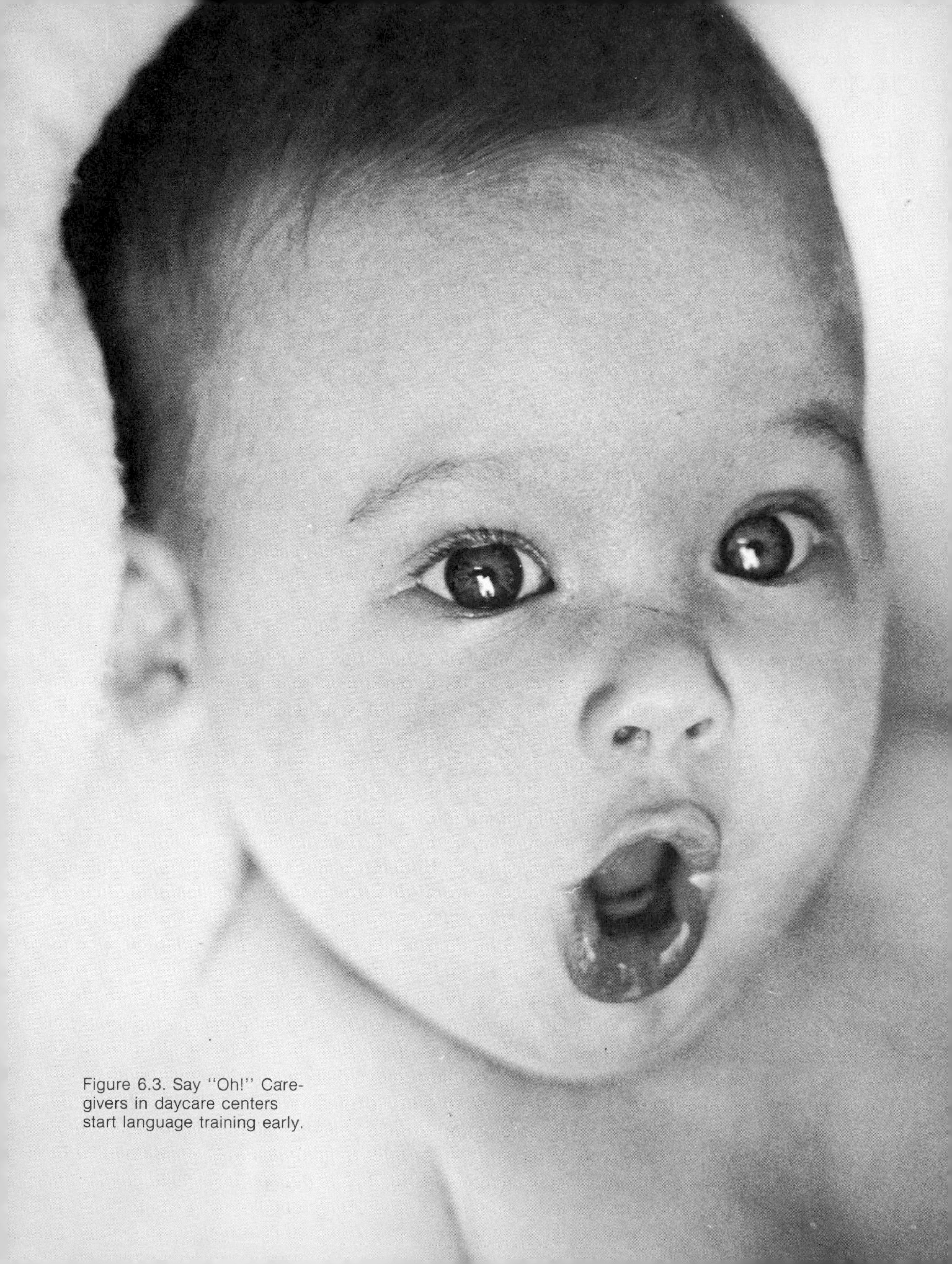

Figure 6.3. Say ''Oh!'' Care-givers in daycare centers start language training early.

provide may be a more important factor. The lack of a mothering figure, according to some studies (Rheingold, 1956), does not of itself cause retardation. Moreover, urban reading scores show that the simple presence of a mother does not prevent language deficiencies. It is conceivable that an institutionalized infant, given a stimulating developmental program, could be as advanced, or even more advanced, than an infant raised at home. This is in fact the goal of countries where to a large extent child rearing takes place in daycare centers and other collective settings. The Soviet daycare centers, for example, offer a very careful program for cognitive development (Bronfenbrenner, 1970). According to the official manual of the daycare program, the "upbringer" (or caregiver) gives special attention to language training:

> [She] carries the baby to different objects and shows him large, colorful, sound-making toys and windup toys; with children eight to nine months of age, she encourages them to pick out from a collection of many toys the one which she names; in order to acquaint the child with the names of adults and other children she plays hide-and-seek . . . The upbringer encourages the child to duplicate sounds which he already knows how to pronounce as well as new ones. and structures his babbling and imitation of simple syllables.

A child raised in such an environment would not be expected to be deficient in language. On the other hand, a child raised at home, but without this kind of individual stimulation, is likely to be quite backward in language skills. This realization has been one of the strongest considerations leading to the design of Head Start and other programs for preschoolers in the United States.

The possibilities for learning are immense, even when the mother is unavailable. The infant does need warm, human attention from one dependable person as well as sensory stimulation, but if a father or aunt or grandmother can meet these needs, a nurse or aide in a publicly supported childcare program could presumably do just as well, provided that the program was adequately designed and carried out.

ANXIETIES

From studies of institutional infants it is clear that the mother, or the stimulation usually provided by the mother, is essential to virtually all aspects of development. But the mother–infant relationship is also the source of the first anxieties that the infant experiences. For as soon as the infant is aware of his mother as a special person, he is at once in a position to lose her. And when he can discriminate the faces of his mother and other family members, he is confronted with the awful possibility of "strangers." Fear of separation and fear of strangers are part of every normal childhood.

Separation Anxiety

At a certain stage of his development—usually about ten months—the infant may be seen crawling persistently behind his mother, following her from room to room. But what happens when he cannot follow but only watch as his mother disappears?

He makes every possible attempt to regain his mother. He cries or screams. He watches the door (showing the so-called "orienting response"). He may even touch the closed door if he can crawl to it. Some researchers have suggested that the intensity of the infant's reaction to separation, particularly his crying, is an indication of the strength of the attachment.

Additional insight into the attachment behavior of infants who are separated from their mothers has been provided by researchers (Coates, Anderson, and Hartup, 1972) who observed infants of ten, fourteen, and eighteen months of age, first in the presence of the mother, then during a period of separation, and finally upon reunion with the mother. At all three ages, the infants cried most during the separation. After the separation they touched their mother, looked at her, and sought her physical proximity much more frequently than before—almost as if to reassure themselves of her return. Similar results have been obtained with apes (Spencer-Booth and Hinde, 1966). The increase in attachment behavior is considered to be an indication of separation anxiety.

The closer the infant's attachment, the stronger his separation anxiety. Institutionalized children who are deprived of a mothering figure do not exhibit separation anxiety at all, whereas Gandan infants, who are seldom separated from their mothers, manifest the anxiety as early as six months—about three months before most American babies do (Ainsworth, 1967).

To explain this, psychologists refer to the idea of discrepant (or unexpectedly different) schemata. At some stage in development the child incorporates his mother into his repertoire of schemata. Thus an African infant who is strapped to his mother's back all day will feel that the whole world depends on her coming and going. If she leaves without him, many of his schemata will be upset. Similarly, an American baby may incorporate his mother into his schemata for a room, an event, or a time of day. If mother always bathes him in the yellow-tiled bathroom, she cannot leave him there, even for a moment, without provoking a discrepant schemata and much crying.

Another comprehensive explanation for separation anxiety takes into account the actual differences the child experiences as a result of his mother's absence. A recent study (Escalona and Corman, 1971) concentrated on two children who, as it turned out, differed most interestingly in attachment and separation anxiety. The first subject, a little girl, had a very stressful relationship with her mother, yet showed great anxiety when separated from her. In her mother's presence there

Figure 6.4. Ghanaian mothers and children. Infants often learn to recognize their mothers faster when they go everywhere with them.

were "head-on collisions involving anger and stress for both, followed by loving reunions that soon led to excited, joyous play." When the mother left, the subject reacted with crying and other signs of displeasure; when her mother returned after a brief separation, she screamed and showed extreme anger at having been left. She followed her mother relentlessly and refused to play or interact socially with anything or anyone else. During periods of separation, the subject was left with a grandmother who was "less accommodating and attentive" than the mother.

The researchers compared this little girl with a little boy of the same age and economic background. The boy became attached to his mother later than the little girl, and his separation anxiety was also later and less pronounced. When his mother left him, he was momentarily anxious but soon turned to playthings. Very often he was left with his father who, though not so intense or active a companion, was nevertheless quite similar to the mother. Like the little girl, he engaged in social actions of greater complexity when his mother was present. However, he was not averse to seeking social contacts with others when she was not available.

In comparing the experiences of these two children, the researchers concluded that the differences in separation anxiety were the result of actual differences that the child experienced in his or her interaction with the mother, not his or her interaction with others in her absence. The little girl, being dependent on her mother for extreme emotional stimulation, showed stronger separation anxiety than the little boy, who could relate easily to both parents. The researchers concluded that the strength of an attachment can be partly explained by the fact that more intense feelings—pleasurable and painful—are associated with the mother. Separation anxiety can thus be explained as a protest against the loss of that stimulation which makes life worthwhile. Anxiety will be greatest when the child has no alternative sources of stimulation.

Long-term separation

The fear of separation characteristic of infants recurs again and again throughout childhood, during periods of insecurity and family upset, in fiction and in fantasy. The dramatic art of children often reveals separation anxieties. One film critic warns that children are universally terrified when Dumbo and his mother are separated in the Disney film. Being left, lost, or abandoned is a recurring fear of childhood.

To some children, it really happens. The effects have been well documented by John Bowlby, a psychologist who has made a lifetime study of separation and attachment. Bowlby concluded that a child left in an institution typically responds with protest, then despair, and finally detachment. He describes (1973) the behavior of children during the first days of one separation study:

> When the moment came for the parent(s) to depart, crying or screaming was the rule. One child tried to follow her parents, demanding urgently where they were

POSTPARTUM SEPARATION

Separation anxiety first occurs in infants of nine to twelve months. But researchers have long been interested in the possible effects of extended separations that occur earlier. There is much evidence that early separation in rhesus monkeys causes severe disturbance. And we have seen that maternal behavior in goats, sheep, and other species is greatly inhibited by separation during the period immediately after birth. It seems that the newborn infant is uniquely attractive to his mother and to other females of his species as well. The mother is more strongly disposed to care for her infant right after giving birth than she will be at any other time.

This seems to be the result of a special relationship between the infant and older members of the species. The newborn or infant is, of course, helpless. It must be fed and protected, not only against the environment, but also against older, stronger members of the group. In many species of animals, including man's closest relatives, the monkeys and apes, the infant has a distinctive "cute" appearance. If the animal has a coat of fur, the infant's coat often has a distinctive color.

All these features serve to convey a message to older animals: "I am a baby—protect me." The message is remarkably effective. In almost every primate species that has been studied, infants seem to be strongly attractive to adult and juvenile animals. The infant is treated with tolerance and solicitude even by individuals that are normally rather belligerent or aggressive. In some species the infant is so attractive that it is common for others besides the mother to take an active interest in caring for it.

What then are the effects of a separation during the postpartum ("after-birth") period? Such a separation occurs among humans when an infant is born prematurely and is placed in an incubator. Under most circumstances, the infant and mother can have only visual contact. Physical contact and a feeding relationship between mother and child may be postponed for as long as two or three months. One study tentatively suggests that early separation of mother and infant may disrupt the mother's later maternal and marital behavior (Leifer, Leiderman, Barnett, and Williams, 1972). In this study, mothers of premature infants were divided into two experimental groups. Members of the first group were allowed some contact with their infants through the portholes of the incubators. Members of the second group had no physical contact with their infants. Although there was no immediate difference in attachment behavior during the baby's first month at home, long-range differences appeared. The separated mothers showed a higher incidence of divorce, with two in this group eventually choosing to relinquish custody of the child. A broader observation was that both groups of mothers smiled at their infants and held them close less frequently than did mothers of full-term infants, who had been allowed to hold and feed their infants shortly after birth. The mother-child bond is a two-way street. It seems clear that separation immediately after birth makes it harder for the mother to grow into her part of the relationship.

going, and finally had to be pushed back into the room by her mother. Another threw himself on the floor and refused to be comforted. Altogether eight of the children were crying loudly soon after their parents' departure. Bedtime was also an occasion for tears. The two who had not cried earlier screamed when put in a cot and could not be consoled. Some of the others whose initial crying had ceased broke into renewed sobs at bedtime. One little girl, who arrived in the evening and was put straight to bed, insisted on keeping her coat on, clung desperately to her doll, and cried at a frightening pitch. Again and again, having nodded off from sheer fatigue, she awoke screaming for Mummy.

At the very early age we are discussing here, the child of course has no way of knowing whether the separation will be long or short. If separation continues the child may regress for a while to earlier patterns of behavior; Bowlby noted that a breakdown in sphincter control was usual. If the child is returned to her parents after days or weeks of separation, she will usually show some signs of detachment, treating her mother like a stranger. After a few hours or days the detachment usually gives way to other forms of behavior. But if a child is subjected to repeated or very prolonged separation during the first three years, the detachment may persist, in one form or another, for many years.

It seems that the effects of permanent separation are especially serious in the

Figure 6.5. Stranger anxiety. This little girl may grudgingly let Mother speak to a neighbor, but only if the neighbor soon goes away.

second six months of life—that is, immediately after the first specific attachment has been made. One investigator found that infants transferred to foster homes after the age of seven months showed severe emotional disturbances or traumas (Yarrow, 1964). The child cannot withstand, or understand, the breaking up of the relationship that is the largest part of his world.

Fear of Strangers

A second anxiety that is a direct result of the infant's first attachment is stranger anxiety, which appears at approximately eight months in American infants. Once the infant becomes specifically attached to the mother or mothering figure, he can be easily upset by the approach of an unfamiliar adult, especially if his mother is not present. The infant fixes his eyes on the stranger and stares, unmoving, for a short time; then he is likely to cry, scream, and show other signs of distress. If his mother is present, he will cling to her in panic.

Stranger anxiety is not a reaction to strangers as such, but rather a reaction to a discrepant schema. The baby has incorporated the schema of his mother's face and perhaps his father's face as well. He will be frightened by faces that fail to conform to his schemata, whether they are strange faces or merely his mother's face with unaccustomed dark glasses, his father in a hat. It is the discrepancy that triggers the infant's reaction. Interestingly enough, a stranger is not nearly so frightening when she turns her back (Zegans and Zegans, 1972).

Stranger anxiety is generally greatest when the mother–infant attachment is intense (Schaffer and Emerson, 1964). It is virtually nonexistent in institutionalized

children. Fear of strangers also seems to be influenced by the position of the child in the family and by the extent of his contact with persons outside the home. In one study (Collard, 1968), firstborn children and widely spaced children showed the most intense fear of strangers. Among the firstborns, children from isolated rural areas showed greater fear than children from urban centers.

In specific instances, the infant's reaction depends on momentary feelings of insecurity. The mother's presence makes the infant more secure in most exploratory behavior, including the exploration of new faces. Thus a mask constituting a discrepant facial schema will provoke crying and other signs of fright when it is worn by a strange experimenter. The same mask, worn by the mothering figure, is more likely to elicit laughter and smiles (Sroufe and Wunsch, 1972). Indeed, laughter is, like fear, a reaction to a discrepant schema; which reaction occurs depends on the child's developmental status as well as his feeling of security at the moment. Only after the child has incorporated the schema for crawling will he laugh at the incongruity of his mother crawling along the floor (Sroufe and Wunsch, 1972) or scream at the sight of a drunken man crawling in the street.

In our culture, stranger anxiety disappears toward the end of the first year, as the child comes in contact with a growing number of relatives, houseguests, and babysitters. The schema for the face becomes generalized to the extent that most faces fit comfortably within it. (Even so, a large birthmark may provoke fear, and a Santa Claus, in beardless times, causes much screaming.) The child continually develops his schemata as a means of dealing with new experiences in his world. However, stranger anxiety may not ever disappear entirely. With maturity, it may be that ". . . the delineation of the stranger comes to mean not so much an unfamiliar figure as the person who is different from one's cultural group" (Zegans and Zegans, 1972). As infants we are not afraid of other infants, and as adults we tend to prefer people very much like ourselves.

SOCIALIZATION

Toward the end of the first year, the mother–child relationship has begun to change. The baby is able to move about the house, crawling, creeping, and finally walking. He is able to follow his mother but is just as likely to creep out of her sight. The baby now has a will of his own and can go wherever his curiosity leads him. His social opportunities are increased as he recognizes an ever-growing number of faces. Even if he has not said his first "ma-ma," he babbles a great deal, and it is clear that there are words he understands.

One of those words is *no.* He hears it whenever he touches certain things. Usually he will not understand the reason for it because he hears it applied to widely different objects: the lamp cord, his sister's doll, and his own feces. Although the *no* may be arbitrary or unfair from the child's point of view, even so he must learn to stop whatever he is doing when he hears it. This learning is part of **socialization.**

Socialization is a very broad term for the process that guides the growth of our social personalities; it allows us to become reasonably acceptable and effective members of society. Attachment is a key factor in socialization, but not the whole of it. Through socialization we acquire the discipline, the skills and knowledge, and the tastes and ambitions that allow us to participate in the life of the family and, later, in the life of the larger group around us. It is not merely a matter of learning to avoid doing the things we are told not to do; it also involves learning to take on the responsibilities that are expected of us by our parents and others in authority.

In many important ways socialization continues well into the adult years. But the crucial first steps are taken before the infant is a year old. At this point he learns that he is no longer going to be allowed to play, cry, sleep, and eat purely according to his own wishes but that he is also going to have to take account of the demands of the outside world, particularly of his parents.

Different parents expect different kinds of behavior from their children. But at some point in the second or third year of life, the baby is supposed to stop wetting and soiling himself. At about the same time, everyone will try to teach him elementary table behavior, in the hope that he will also stop messing and throwing his food. He will be expected to kiss his parents good night, to wave bye-bye as relatives come and go, to be nice to toddler visitors, to keep his clothes on and his voice down. All these lessons are part of early socialization.

Some psychologists and philosophers have seen the process of socialization, or at least the part of it that requires obedience, as very painful and difficult for the child. The infant is asked to forego many of his most intense gratifications for the sake of a *no* that does not seem reasonable to him. However, other researchers have argued that obedience, like all other aspects of socialization, is a natural outgrowth of the mother–child attachment and can be accomplished without much pain or training. Researchers (Stayton, Hogan, and Ainsworth, 1971) point out that an infant with a responsive and cooperative mother tends to obey regardless of the mother's disciplinary technique. The affectional tie itself seems to foster a willingness to comply with parental signs and to imitate the behavior of parents and brothers and sisters. In one study (Stayton, Hogan, and Ainsworth, 1971), the brighter infants gave evidence at the age of twelve months of having internalized some of their mothers' prohibitions. They voluntarily arrested actions for which they had previously been reprimanded. Many a small child has been heard to tell himself "no-no" as he approaches a forbidden object.

However, socialization does not proceed smoothly in every household. A stressful mother–child relationship produces angry reactions to discipline. One nine month old girl

> . . . learned to indicate refusal on her part through the headshaking gesture soon followed by the words "no-no" . . . She obeyed prohibitions, but not without protest. Having desisted from the forbidden act she turned on her mother and loudly jabbered at her in unmistakable protest, as it were, "talking back." On the occasions when scolding and/or spanking followed she responded with a stream of angry jargon, addressing mother thus from across the room. (Escalona and Corman, 1971)

This little girl did not easily conform to her mother's wishes. She quite early developed a conscience that told her when she did wrong, but her extreme and ambiguous feelings often led her to rebel against that conscience and indulge in what her mother felt was socially inappropriate behavior.

If a mother has been consistently loving and respectful, the child in his behavior seeks naturally to renew her love. Socialization is thus motivated by the child's desire to please and his tendency to imitate. If the relationship has not been characterized by love and respect, the child may find his satisfaction—and his independence—in thwarting his parent.

Parents are not always to blame, however, if they have difficulty in socializing their child. Even the most conscientious and affectionate caregivers find some babies easier to love than others. An infant has a temperament of his own, and sometimes it fits in awkwardly with the temperament and daily routine of the parent.

Toilet Training

One of the earliest accomplishments in the baby's socialization is his becoming toilet trained. Most American children are expected to be toilet trained between the ages of one and a half to two years.

Ever since the famous psychoanalyst Sigmund Freud emphasized the significance of this step in development, psychologists have been interested in it. A comprehensive study (Sears, Maccoby, and Levin, 1957) reported that toilet training was completed at an average of eighteen months of age (with nighttime bladder accidents until about the age of two or later). A later study (Heinstein, 1966) found that the average age for completion of bowel training was twenty-two months. Today's children seem to be trained even later, perhaps because doctors advise it, parents' attitudes have relaxed, and families are smaller.

A child must reach a certain developmental level before he is physically able to control his anal and urethral sphincters, the muscles of elimination. In bowel training, the child must learn to defecate over a toilet—and otherwise restrain himself. To do this he must be able to relax his anal sphincter at will and first to signal his parents that he is ready to go to the bathroom. Bladder control, which comes later, requires similar abilities.

Since success in toilet training depends on maturation, we would expect that an eighteen month old child would learn much faster than a nine month old, and in fact this is true. Postponing toilet training until the age of two greatly reduces bed-wetting, soiling, and constipation in late childhood (Brazelton, 1962)—problems that are sometimes associated with early or coercive training. However, a child may voluntarily learn much earlier if, for example, he has older siblings to observe, or if he feels particularly sensitive to being wet.

In toilet training as in other areas of socialization, it is usually the mother–child relationship that has the most influence on success. Strict, coercive training methods are much more likely to trigger emotional upset than milder methods. But even in cases of strict training, warmth and affection on the part of the mother reduce the incidence of disturbances by more than half (Sears, Maccoby, and Levin, 1957). Early and overanxious training puts the child at a disadvantage and leads to increased "accidents," increased punishment, and undue emphasis on toilet matters.

Researchers recognize that the toilet training experience is difficult to isolate from other socialization experiences. It appears that mothers who are strict and early toilet trainers are also likely to restrict their children in "messing" activities—eating, finger painting, sand play, and bath splashing. Such mothers are also more likely to punish children, physically or otherwise, when standards of neatness or decorum are not met. It may be more useful to think in terms of *general* permissiveness or restrictiveness than to concentrate on a single experience such as toilet training. Personality theorists beginning with Freud have associated severe toilet training with an obsession for cleanliness and order, extreme thriftiness (or stinginess), punctuality, and neatness of dress. Significantly, these are among the explicit virtues of the restrictive mother.

Autonomy

The age at which the child learns to control his processes of elimination is also the age at which he begins to exercise his will. According to Erikson, the crisis of trust versus mistrust is soon followed by a new crisis of autonomy versus shame—the crisis that finds expression in the experience of toilet training.

We have **autonomy** when we are in a position to make our own choices. The baby exercises autonomy when he gains some control over his own bowels and bladder. Both to the baby and his parents, this is an important milestone. The baby's feces and urine are the first thing he produces in this world, and his feces in particular are likely to strike him as an outstanding accomplishment.

The control of the bowels and bladder comes to the child gradually. So does the pleasure of autonomy. The child finds that he can choose to "hold on" or "let go" and that there are rewards and sensations associated with each (Erikson, 1968). In elimination and in other ways as well, the baby is beginning to bring his body under his own control.

At this very time, however, the child finds that his mother is encouraging him—or commanding him—to control his bowels, not only for his own pleasure but because she wants him to. In many cases the mother–child relationship is very good, and the child does not feel that he has lost his autonomy. He can still make choices: he can choose of his own free will to please his mother and at the same time demonstrate his new abilities. Although it takes a while for his control to mature, his progress is steady and conflict with his parents is slight.

In other cases the mother imposes severe or early toilet training as part of a generally restrictive relationship. Like all children, he would like to prove to himself that he is equal to the task, but in doing so he would be conforming to his mother's wishes. Perhaps he would rather thwart his mother. If so, he may rebel by refusing to exercise the required control over his movements. Unfortunately, he defeats his own purposes with this tactic, for he denies himself the growing sense of autonomy that accompanies control. The child is faced with what Erikson (1968) calls "a double rebellion and a double defeat." He cannot be sure of himself.

The defeated child does have some options. He can attempt to assert his autonomy and control by eliminating willfully in situations not to his mother's liking. He can refuse to defecate when locked in the bathroom for that purpose. But the child's resolution weakens, and his control is not at first so developed as to allow him to be consistent in action, even if he is firm of purpose. With his sloppy record, he cannot help but doubt himself. Nor is he immune to feelings of shame even when his "accidents" are on purpose. Thus, doubt, shame, and "hateful self-insistence" may be the eventual results of severely restrictive toilet training (Erikson, 1968).

Although the toilet training experience is at the center of the struggle for autonomy, many other kinds of experience figure in it. For example, when the child shows a desire to begin dressing himself or using his spoon, unwanted adult

ERIKSON'S CRISES IN PSYCHOLOGICAL DEVELOPMENT

Basic Trust verses Basic Mistrust (first year of life)

Experiences and sensations that give the infant a sense of familiarity and inner certainty provide him with a sense of self. He feels that the world is benevolent or, at least, reliable, and he likewise trusts himself and his own capacities. He has established *basic trust.*

If the individual develops *basic mistrust* instead, in later life he may tend to behave irrationally, or to withdraw into schizoid or depressive states.

Autonomy versus Shame and Doubt (second year of life)

During the second year of life the infant develops muscular control; he moves about and begins toilet training. He needs firmness now, as a protection against the potential anarchy of his own impulses. The sense of self-control (autonomy) learned at this stage leads to a lasting sense of good will and personal pride.

A failure to achieve well-guided autonomy can lead, later, to compulsive neurosis, a pervasive sense of *shame* before the world, and compulsive *doubt* of the self and others.

Initiative versus Guilt (the preschool years)

Industry versus Inferiority (middle childhood)

Identity versus Role Confusion (adolescence)

Intimacy versus Isolation (young adulthood)

Generativity versus Stagnation (prime of life)

Ego Integrity versus Despair (old age)

help will reduce his sense of autonomy and fill him with self-doubt. Harsh criticism of his first efforts will force on him a memorable shame. If he has undressed himself for the first time—all by himself—he wants to be greeted with pleasure even if he appears before a house full of guests. If he has single-handedly completed his first meal, he does not want to be put to shame for the state of his T-shirt. The child, to develop autonomy, must learn that he can make choices and that those choices will not always lead to failure. This is a lesson to be learned in all areas of childhood endeavor and to be reaffirmed throughout adult life.

Sex Roles

The child raising controversies of yesterday focused in large part on techniques of toilet training and feeding. Today's mothers are likely to be more confused about an area of socialization that used to be taken for granted, the teaching of appropriate sex roles and behaviors. Parents wonder if a little girl should be socialized to behave like a little girl, according to stereotype and custom. Or is the role of women changing so quickly as to make early sex training a downright disadvantage? And what of the "aggressive" or "masculine" qualities that have always been condoned in little boys? Modern sociological literature questions the assumptions that there really are "feminine" and "masculine" behaviors that should be taught to children at an early age.

If the conclusions of a study published in 1969 (Goldberg and Lewis) indicate present attitudes, a child is still supposed to look and act like a girl or a boy. It is a terrible social blunder, the investigators found, to identify the sex of an infant incorrectly in front of the infant's mother. However, differences in appearance between boys and girls are not striking at the two year old level; most of them must be conveyed artificially, by dress or hair style. Behavioral differences, some of them at least, might be biological, and others, perhaps most or even all, might be the result of socialization.

Today it is no longer generally supposed that all distinctly feminine and masculine behavior is biological. Yet in every animal species, the female behaves differently from the male, and these differences can be seen in instinctual patterns that by definition are inherited, not learned. Nest building is a good example of instinctual feminine behavior in most birds. Similar distinctions are found in primates. Harlow (1962a) observed that young male monkeys engaged in much more rough-and-tumble play than females. Moreover, subsequent research has shown that when a pregnant monkey is given injections of male hormone immediately before she gives birth, her female babies will be more masculine in play and in other respects (Young, Goy, and Phoenix, 1964). Might such sex-related behaviors be inherited in humans?

Particularly in the case of little girls, observers have taken a certain pleasure in the thought that a child has somehow inherited the appropriate behaviors, along with a sense of her future sexual and reproductive role. Thus the poet Yeats was moved to write:

> When I watch my child, who is not yet three years old, I can see so many signs of knowledge from beyond her own mind: why else should she be so excited when a little boy passes outside the window, and take so little interest in a girl; why should she put a cloak about her, and look over her shoulder to see it trailing upon the stairs, as she will someday trail a dress; and why, above all, as she lay against her mother's side, and felt the unborn child moving within, did she murmur, "Baby, baby"? ("The Trembling of the Veil," 1922)

The modern psychologist would react to this passage with a great deal of skepticism—noting for example that boy children raised by their parents as girls will display many overtly feminine characteristics. For sex-appropriate behavior the psychologist is likely to offer two explanations. First, the child may learn through parental reward or reinforcement. Feminine acts please the father of a little girl and evoke his smile, his praise, his cuddling. These acts may be repeated not because the child is biologically disposed to perform them, but because she is rewarded

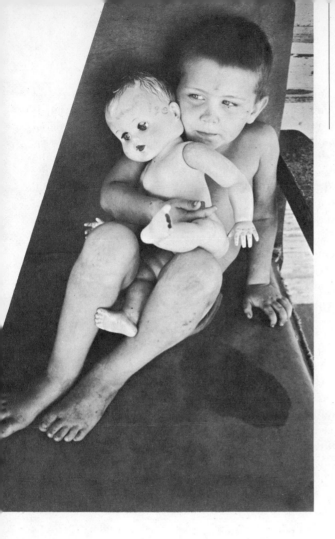

Figure 6.6. A boy can be as strongly attached to his doll as a girl can.

for doing so. A second explanation is found in the process of identification. The child adopts the parent of her own sex as her behavior model and proceeds to imitate him or her, becoming "masculine" or "feminine" insofar as the parent is. When behavior is shaped either by parental rewards or by identification, we can say that socialization is taking place.

An impressive amount of research has attempted to distinguish sex-related behavior that is inherited from that which results from socialization. One finds such studies in publications ranging from *Genetic Psychological Monographs* to *Ms.* magazine. In an extensive review of the psychological literature, researchers (Maccoby and Jacklin, 1971) comment on the inconsistency of the findings. The researchers, both women, note the possibility that "some of the presumed characteristics of the two sexes are more located in the eye of the beholder than they are in the behavior of the subjects." Nevertheless, one difference seems uncontested: males are more aggressive than females. This difference is observed in all cultures and can be seen as early in life as behavior can be observed.

Other sex-related behavior seems to be conveyed through the process of socialization. The process begins at birth with the pink or blue announcements and gifts. More important than these visible symbols is the mother's style of interaction with her infant. Mothers are more likely to breast-feed girls. Moreover, there is evidence that mothers of girls spend more time touching their infants and interacting with them visually and vocally (Goldberg and Lewis, 1969). And the little girls reciprocate this attention: "When the children were six months old, mothers touched, talked to, and handled their daughters more than their sons, and when they were thirteen months old, girls touched and talked to their mothers more than boys did." This study found that girls appeared to be more dependent than boys in a free play situation. For example, they were more reluctant than boys to leave their mothers' laps. Placed behind a frustrating barrier, girls were likely to cry and ask for help, whereas boys actively tried to remove the barrier. The differences in behavior appear to be the result of differential socialization by the mother.

In another study (Coates, Anderson, and Hartup, 1972), children were observed before, after, and during a separation from their mother; no sex differences were noted. Girl infants displayed no more distress at the mother's absence and no more need for proximity when she returned. Although females are supposed to be less exploratory than males and more in need of social interaction, one observer (Wenar, 1972) found no sex-related differences in a group of one year olds observed in their own home. Infants of *both* sexes chose, to a significant degree, to explore the environment rather than interact with the mother. Although there is some question as to whether most girl children display dependency behavior, there is little question that it is the product of socialization.

Another difference often observed among children is the tendency of little boys to be more physically active than girls. Boy children are biologically more muscular. Perhaps more important, however, is the fact that parents encourage their male children to be rough and boisterous but expect girls to be quiet and delicate in movement. Thus parents offer reinforcement when their sons swing hammers and bash toy lawn mowers about, and they are equally pleased when daughters talk patiently to dolls and stuffed animals. The style of play is influenced not only by this differential reinforcement, but by imitation. The boy who swings a toy lawn mower emulates his father's strength; the girl who swings a toy broom will probably not be seized with a sense of physical power, but will take pleasure in being helpful. As early as thirteen months, observers (Goldberg and Lewis, 1969) found differences in play style, with girls choosing toys that require fine movements and boys choosing toys that called for gross muscular coordination.

Girls also spend more time with toys that have faces, perhaps a reflection of the fact that girls as infants spend more time looking at facial stimuli. Especially potent in socialization is doll play, which begins in earnest some time after the second birthday. The little girl is overtly encouraged to display maternal behavior, and her boy playmates are recruited in nursery school as "fathers." The opportunities for the acquisition of sex-related behaviors increase as the child grows older.

Managing Emotions

Parents rather easily attribute complex emotions to their young infants. Attachment quickly becomes "love," the search for human stimulation may be termed "friendliness," and the cry for food or diaper change is sometimes seen as "crankiness" or "selfishness." In actuality, the emotional range of the infant is much more limited. Probably he can enjoy a state of simple contentment that cannot be reproduced in adult consciousness. His major problems are centered in his physical needs and his need for stimulation. Nevertheless, the infant does experience at least two emotional states that are socially important. He experiences fear and anger at people and things. Learning to manage these emotions in an acceptable way is an important goal of socialization.

Fears

We have seen that the two common fears of infancy are the fear of strangers and a more general anxiety about separation from or loss of the mother. But infants are subject to numerous other fears. The fear of falling, for example, has been demonstrated in visual cliff experiments discussed in Chapter 4. Other strong stimuli, such as unexpected noises, bright lights, and noisy mechanical toys, may also cause frantic crying. Even a mother, if she moves too abruptly or speaks too loudly, can frighten her child (Benjamin, 1963).

As the infant gains cognitive skills, she is, paradoxically, afraid of more situations. She learns to associate a particular person with a pain or disturbance previously experienced. If she was left with an aunt during her mother's absence, the sight of the aunt may provoke terrified crying. A bad experience with an animal will also be remembered at this stage. On being scratched by a cat, the infant may withdraw in fright from all animals. At a later stage, the child can differentiate the dangers of one animal from those of another; she may be afraid only of large angry cats, and not of kittens, dogs, and ponies.

The infant's fears are a useful index to her development. As we have seen, her fear of strangers appears to be a manifestation of the first specific attachment. Similarly her fear of the dark, if it occurs, is an association of darkness with bedtime and the loss of stimulation. Fear of a particular person implies recognition of that person. What the infant fears depends in part on her previous experiences, but also on her cognitive development.

Aggression

The tendency toward aggressive behavior seems to be part of man's biological inheritance. As noted, aggressive behavior is more readily evoked in males. In infancy it is not fully developed, but consists largely of tantrums.

Despite the seeming universality of aggressive behavior, individuals and societies differ in the extent and kind of aggression they display. The differences are partly a result of socialization. For example, the American infant is told not to hurt siblings, friends, and household animals. If he does so intentionally, he

AGGRESSION

Aggression is when "the other guy started it." We deplore the aggression of a child who bullies others and spoils their play, but if a child doesn't stand up for his rights we say he is not aggressive enough. In his case a little aggression would be a good thing.

Apparently the word *aggression* can mean many things, some of them reprehensible, others necessary or even admirable. There is, to be sure, a difference between instrumental aggression and hostile aggression, but we also have to recognize that *aggression* is really a catch-all term for a wide range of feelings and actions that may have little in common. Many recent books on animal behavior, for example, try to explain human aggression by studying monkeys and apes, wolves, rats, and even birds. In most of the species studied, researchers found a certain amount of "aggression" in competing for territory, mates, food, and for nesting, mating, or sleeping space.

There have been many attempts to understand and even remedy the problem of human aggression on the basis of animal studies, but animal aggression, unlike human aggression, is almost exclusively instrumental rather than hostile, unless the group is under severe stress. Furthermore, aggression in man is more complicated than in any other species. It can take many forms, and it can arise in any situation as a result of any combination of causes. Synonyms for *aggressive* include *militant, assertive, bold,* and *enterprising.* Judging from these definitions, aggression may sometimes seem justified.

Among young children, the aggressor is usually the one who gave the first shove, but as we grow older we realize that some offenses are unintentional, or at least understandable. We recognize that in some instances we ourselves may have unwittingly provoked someone else's aggression. When our country is attacked by another country, however, we brand the enemy as an aggressor and feel justified in retaliating with a force that is out of all proportion to the original offense.

is likely to be punished. For a child to attack a parent is a family disaster. In some societies, children are not so strongly socialized to control their angry and aggressive behavior. The Yanomamö Indians, who live along the border of Venezuela and Brazil, encourage their male children to express physically any anger felt toward their parents (Chagnon, 1968). The young child learns that if he beats his father in the face, he will be praised for displaying a fierceness much admired among his people. Understandably, Yanomamö boys attack their parents much more readily than their American age-mates. Though it may not be possible or even desirable to eliminate aggression, the socialization process can influence the readiness with which it is displayed. Socialization can also determine the appropriate objects for aggression and the means of expressing it. Thus, an American child will be taught to express his anger with words as soon as he is able. And he will learn that there are some people toward whom he must never show anger.

During the first two years of life, aggressive behavior is generally expressed as anger in the form of the temper tantrum. Sometimes the tantrum is a by-product of other socialization processes—very strict toilet training, for example, or other adult pressures that go against the child's abilities or temperament. A slow-starting child who is rushed from one activity to another may react with tantrums. And every mother knows what happens when a tired baby is subjected to too much stimulation. In such instances the child is simply unable to take the pressure, and so he sits right down and has himself a tantrum.

Another major cause of infant tantrums is loss of attention, sometimes coupled with infantile feelings of jealousy. Some children routinely throw tantrums when it becomes clear that their parents will be spending the evening elsewhere, with others. A more typical provocation is the birthday party or other social event. The two year old who always has his mother's attention watches in disbelief as other mothers and babies are fussed over. The extreme stimulation of noise, cake, and candles, compounded by the distance of his mother, may bring on crying, perhaps even a tantrum. Unfortunately, a mother in these circumstances is likely to be more embarrassed than sympathetic. Again, the tantrum results from disregard of the baby's capacity—in this case his capacity for enduring large, stimulating groups without the assurance of his mother's company.

The temper tantrum usually causes great alarm among parents. By adult standards, it is an impressive display. The child screams, kicks, and throws himself about in a wild fashion. He may even engage in self-hurting behavior—pulling his hair, biting his fingers, holding his breath, or banging his head on the floor. Parents can hardly ignore the outburst, especially since it so often happens in polite company. Yet most parents are fearful that giving the child what he wants or smothering him with immediate affection will only encourage further outbursts, with further concessions, in the future. Indeed this seems to be the case.

A famous longitudinal study (Goodenough, 1931) found that mothers generally do give in as a way of ending temper outbursts. Mothers reported that they could most effectively quiet the child by giving him what he desired, by eliminating whatever was frustrating him, or by simply diverting his attention with new toys

Figure 6.7. One of the ingredients of success in a display of temper is the infant's stamina. If he can scream longer than his mother can stand it, he will probably get what he wants.

and activities. Also effective were ignoring the child or putting him in a room by himself. However, these strategies are likely to cause confusion and ambiguity in modern parents. They know that giving in may cause the child to use anger and aggression as a means of achieving his ends in life. Yet they feel—perhaps unlike their own parents—that anger should not be bottled up or denied. Teaching the child appropriate expression of anger and control of aggression is one of the most difficult feats of socialization.

This study concluded that the control of anger in children is best achieved when the child's behavior is viewed with "serenity and tolerance." It is important to set reasonable standards for achievement and to recognize the child's needs, as well as the parents', when departures from schedule are made.

Such consideration should reduce outbursts. Should one occur, the mother can best help the child by exercising her own self-control. The child in the throes of a tantrum is quite possibly afraid of his own violent energies. If his mother too goes into a panic, this only adds to his fears. But if his mother remains calm and self-assured, he will feel that it is safe to express anger. He knows that if he goes too far, his mother will stop him—and knowing this, he can stop himself.

As the child grows older, the parents' own example becomes critical. The most aggressive behavior is found in children who have observed frequent and violent outbursts in their parents. The child who is often spanked will quickly see the point of physical aggression. This is not to say that he will necessarily be full of the hostile impulses that provoke aggression. It appears that parental inconsistency, rather than spanking as such, leads to angry and aggressive behavior in children. According to some observers (Sears, Maccoby, and Levin, 1957), children are most likely to be aggressive when their parents disapprove of aggression but nevertheless use physical aggression as a punishment—for example, by spanking a child because he has hit another child. When parents are generally permissive, yet resort to physical punishment, this inconsistency will likewise produce aggression in children. Socialization of aggressive behavior does not succeed when parents are arbitrary in their own actions and attitudes regarding physical punishment.

APPROACHES TO CHILD REARING

Child rearing practices usually do not undergo much change from one generation to the next. In most cases, a new mother imitates her own mother—intuitively, under the sway of childhood memories, or explicitly, under the supervision of grandmother herself. The tendency to mother as one was mothered is apparently quite strong. Even children who were physically abused or neglected by their parents revert to the same pattern with their own children (Steele and Pollack, 1968).

Nevertheless, some child rearing attitudes do change from one generation to the next, in part as a result of larger social changes. For example, it is not unusual for a new mother to be far more tolerant than grandmother of certain "messing" activities, such as emptying wastebaskets or slinging mud. Today's mother may also be less anxious about toilet training and masturbation; on the other hand, she will probably be more easily frightened by tantrums and other emotional upsets. Her viewpoint is determined not only by her own childhood experiences but by her familiarity with the current psychological literature and the baby "experts." Her needs as a woman and mother will of necessity reflect the numerous social changes that have occurred since she was a child. In some areas the changes are quite significant. For example, the attraction of a career outside the home has never been so high—nor the availability of domestic help so low—as it is today. Faced with new challenges and new "experts," the emerging generation of mothers develops its own style of child raising.

Changing Views

In the United States, the earliest child rearing philosophies were based on religion and morality. Colonial children were taught from infancy that reverence for their parents was analogous to reverence to God. The emphasis was on obedience, but the time was not so harsh as we might suppose. The Reverend Cotton Mather, having stated that "my word must be law" concludes that "I would never come to give a child a blow; except in case of obstinacy or some gross enormity. To be chased for a while out of my presence I would make to be looked upon as the sorest punishment in the family" (Calhoun, 1960). The goal of child rearing for Mather and other colonial authorities was to produce a God-fearing child with "a mighty desire of being useful in the world." Parental example, particularly of the religious sort, was more important than disciplinary method.

In colonial America, discipline was a cooperative effort in morality. The child was to contribute his good behavior lest he go to hell. But the parent too was

---

BABY BOOKS

More people have written—and perhaps even read—baby books in the last twenty-five years than ever before. Some of these books try to give practical, concrete solutions to specific problems of child care, and others develop general theories about parent–child relationships. Some deal with the needs and problems of children chiefly from the parents' point of view, whereas others, particularly a number in the recent crop of books on the subject, are more child-centered, attempting to show why a child feels and reacts a certain way. The exponents of the child-centered approach maintain that only by learning to discover the underlying meanings of a child's words and the motivations for his actions can a parent alleviate the root pressures and problems that cause the child to act in an undesirable way.

Undoubtedly the most popular of all recent experts has been Benjamin Spock. His *Baby and Child Care,* first published in 1945, has sold about twenty-five million copies and continues to be a leading baby book. Dr. Spock, a pediatrician, is concerned with the physical aspects of child care—how to make a formula, how to recognize the symptoms of chicken pox, and so on—as well as with the psychological aspects of raising children. In contrast to many of the books written by child psycholo-

gists, *Baby and Child Care* concentrates as much on preventing problems as on solving them after they occur. Spock advocates a relaxed but confident approach to child care. Parents are advised to give practical attention not only to all the child's needs but to their own as well, so that a relationship of mutual pleasure and trust is established. Spock believes that parental confidence is more important in child rearing than a specific theory or approach and that "good-hearted parents who aren't afraid to be firm when it is necessary can get good results with either moderate strictness or moderate permissiveness."

Several books appeared during the 1960s that emphasize the need for adults to look beyond the symptoms of a child's problems to find the underlying cause of the difficulty. Bruno Bettelheim's *Dialogues with Mothers* (1962) stresses the need for parents to ask themselves "If I were a child, why would *I* do this?" in order to get at the real reason a child acts in a certain way. Another authority, Haim Ginott, emphasizes respect between parents and their children, honesty in communication, and the recognition of hostile as well as benevolent feelings. His book *Between Parent and Child* (1965) attempts to show that children's "messages are often in a code that requires deciphering." If through patient, non-

under strictures of conscience, for his sins were to be visited upon his children (who might thus suffer in the next world for their parent's misbehavior).

Today, in middle-class America, the goals of child rearing are mostly psychological rather than religious. The child is to be happy, well adjusted, and productive in the world. Few parents are concerned with hell, but most show a comparable dread of mental illness and social delinquency. As in colonial days, the child is presumed to be punished for the sins of his fathers; popular belief contends that

critical conversation with a child, a parent can discover the child's underlying concerns, he will then be able to allay the anxieties that cause the child to "misbehave."

Lee Salk is considered by a number of his colleagues to be the leading expert in child care for the new generation of mothers. Like Dr. Spock, Dr. Salk, who is a psychologist, is particularly concerned with *preventing* emotional disturbance in children and discusses in his book *How to Raise a Human Being* (1969), which he co-authored with Rita Kramer, how the right kinds of stimulation and attention to children's needs at each stage of their development can prevent problems from occurring later. Like Bettelheim and Ginott, Salk is also very concerned with the problems of communication between adults and their children and the need to fathom the hidden meanings in a child's conversation, as the title of his most recent book, *What Every Child Would Like his Parents to Know,* indicates.

Several provocative new books go farther in their approach to child rearing than any of those already mentioned. Graham Blaine's *Are Parents Bad for Children?* (1973) essentially answers "yes" to the question in its title. Blaine traces the problems of today's teenagers to parental neglect or parental overinvolvement, but at the same time exonerates the parents from blame for these conditions, placing it instead on all of society. Since society has caused this predicament, Blaine reasons, the community should take some, if not most, of the responsibility of child rearing. Richard Farson's highly controversial book, *Birthrights* (1974), also maintains that adults—parents, teachers, judges, counselors—create the problems that handicap a child emotionally, but he is also sympathetic to them, understanding how frustrating the responsibility of raising children can be. According to Farson, "the major barrier to overcome is the oppressive condition of childhood itself," and he proposes economic, sexual, political, behavioral, and educational self-determination for children. By allowing them to make their own decisions about what they wish to learn, choose to eat, and so on, we will free them from the arbitrary, vacillating, and frequently humiliating regulation which is presently imposed upon them by adults.

These last two books make interesting reading indeed, but it hardly seems likely that Americans will turn over child raising authority to the state or the kids any time in the near future, and it is quite probable that Dr. Spock's book will continue to be a bestseller for some time to come.

emotional disturbance is more often than not the effect of destructive parental behavior. Today's parents turn to the psychologist rather than the minister, to the child care manual rather than the Bible. If we worry more about our children's behavior than we did before, perhaps it is because we do not have to worry so much about their bare survival.

The first psychological movement to have a strong effect on child rearing in this country was behaviorism, founded by J. B. Watson in the 1920s. An aggressive, controversial figure, Watson believed that the goal of the psychologist was to control and predict behavior through the manipulation of environmental stimuli. In other words, he believed that infants, as well as others, could be conditioned to behave in preplanned ways. Everything depended on learning and nothing on heredity. Watson's famous boast makes clear his position, even as it exaggerates it:

> Give me a dozen healthy infants, well formed, and my own special world to bring them up in, and I'll guarantee to take any one of them at random and train him to be any type of specialist I might select—a doctor, lawyer, artist, merchant, chief, and even a beggarman and thief, regardless of his talents, penchants, tendencies, abilities, vocation and race of his ancestors.

Since nobody was in a position to give Watson his "own special world to bring them up in," Watson developed some principles for use in the ordinary American home. He recommended that parents avoid emotional display and rely upon less threatening forms of reinforcement. "Never hug and kiss them," he wrote, "never let them sit on your lap. . . . Give them a pat on the head if they have made an extraordinary good job of a difficult task" (Watson, 1930). Watson's behaviorism, as well as other historical influences, can be seen in the child rearing attitudes of the time. Children were thought to need regular feeding and sleeping schedules if they were to grow up with any measure of self-control. They were toilet trained at the earliest possible age and expected to be neat, clean, and well-mannered thereafter. At a time when every man knew his place, children were prohibited from interrupting their elders with tales or questions. In short, the child was expected to show that he was well on the way to adult behavior. In the upper classes this meant learning a gentleman's habits; in the lower classes it meant learning a trade.

Watson's viewpoint has not entirely disappeared even today. A major force in modern psychology is B. F. Skinner, a behaviorist who believes that successful child rearing is accomplished through operant conditioning, the consistent rewarding of desirable behavior. Skinner's rational application of learning theory is not designed to produce a "model child" in the old-fashioned sense, but rather a creative and socially valuable individual. Still, few parents consciously condition their children in the manner Skinner suggests, and almost none choose to raise their infant in the controlled environment of the Skinner "box," even though attractive models are available.

The behaviorists' viewpoint has been effectively opposed by a liberal train of thought that follows loosely from a second great school in psychology—the school of Sigmund Freud. Freud was a Viennese psychiatrist who was not initially concerned with child behavior. His patients were mostly adult neurotics, and much of his clinical writing is concerned with the causes of adult disturbances, both emotional and physical. Invariably Freud found that he could neither understand nor treat the neurotic ailment unless he could locate its origin in early childhood experience. He found that disturbances were very often caused by overly restrictive or punitive treatment on the part of parents. For example, certain malfunctions of the intestinal track can be traced to harsh toilet training; certain neurotic dependency patterns are associated with restrictive mothering. Modern parents may not be familiar with all the ramifications of Freudian theory, but they do know that it predicts dire consequences for too much parental strictness. Parents are now anxious lest they inhibit, rather than spoil, the child.

Another important recent influence on child rearing has come from psychologists and anthropologists whose cross-cultural studies have shown the limitations of universal theories of behavior. Anthropologist Margaret Mead (1928) showed that the sexual stresses felt by most American adolescents did not affect children in Samoa. Later, psychologist Karen Horney (1937) observed that the neurotic personality type she had treated in England differed from the one she encountered in the United States. A number of studies showed that the problems experienced by individuals in one culture are often the result of the particular child raising and socialization customs of that culture. Mead's *Coming of Age in Samoa* voiced a common theme in suggesting that anxieties, in this case pubertal anxieties, were caused by our own restrictive attitudes, rather than by any natural tendencies of man. Psychologists like Horney and Erikson and anthropologists like Mead and Bronislav Malinowski have had a liberalizing effect on American child rearing.

Attention

Among the most confusing questions in infant care has always been the question of what constitutes spoiling. Needless to say, the answer depends on one's overall concept of child raising. To Watson and his followers, spoiling occurred when a mother fed and fondled her child on demand. The child was supposed to be taught that crying will not result in his being picked up or played with whenever he likes. In 1972, however, a researcher (Ainsworth) concluded that this kind of "spoiling" on the part of the parents really prevents the child from acting spoiled. It was found that infants whose needs for physical contact were regularly met did not protest when they were put down. Infants whose cries were regularly attended cried less, not more, than infants who were ignored. Contrary to Watson's thinking, the fussers and criers tended to be infants who were not given enough attention.

In other words, it does not appear to be possible to spoil an infant, if "spoiling" means having his immediate needs met. Babies thrive on being fed, having their diapers changed, and being cuddled and talked to. A few minutes of human attention is worth more than all the toys on the market; giving a baby some extra

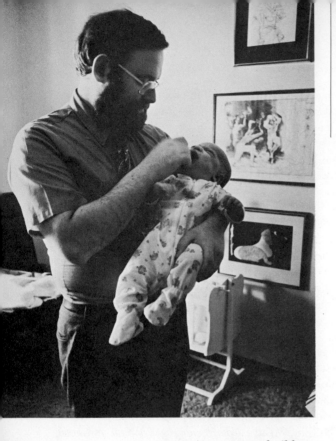

Figure 6.8. A father and mother can share the many hours of feeding, holding, and talking that will meet their infant's need for attention.

attention seems to build trust and advance cognitive learning—particularly language learning. It must not be forgotten, however, that infants need rest too.

Concern with spoiling may arise when the baby comes to demand certain kinds of stimulation. If he is held almost constantly during Grandmother's visit, then he will certainly object when the visit ends and he is once more relegated to the playpen. His mother may imagine he has been spoiled, but it is natural for an infant to protest a loss of stimulation. His behavior suggests only that he is experiencing a temporary discomfort, as he does when he is wet or hungry. Grandmother's spoiling may even be beneficial. There is reason to believe that the baby might develop faster if he experienced more or less constant physical contact during waking hours. African infants who do experience such contact are notably precocious in learning to talk (Lusk and Lewis, 1972).

Temporary upsets over loss of stimulation give parents of infants no real cause for concern over spoiling, but this is not the case with older children whose every wish is satisfied. Some people assume that the pattern of spoiling begins in infancy, in maternal responsiveness. However, there are real psychological differences between an infant and a child, even an eighteen month old child. As Erikson points out, the first task of infancy is to establish trust, and the second is to gain autonomy. Trust can only develop when the mother meets most of the child's needs on a regular basis. Autonomy, on the other hand, requires that the child begin to satisfy some of his own needs, his need for exploration, for manipulation of toys, and so on. Sometimes autonomy is threatened by spoiling.

The overindulgent mother may bring everything to the child, putting new and better toys in his hands before he has had the chance to choose among the old. When the infant wants something, or wants something done, mother gets or does it for him, instead of helping him figure out how to do it himself. Spoiling, for the toddler, often amounts to a simple disregard for his developing autonomy. Because the child does not learn to use his initiative, or even to "make do," he has only one way of showing his power—by making demands on others. His needs are met, but inappropriately. He has indeed been spoiled.

It is this pattern, observable not only in children but in adults, that discourages some parents from meeting their infant's every need. The difference is obvious. The infant is in the process of developing a sense of trust—not autonomy. A mother can only make him more trusting if she "spoils" him. It is not until he begins to be able to make some of his own choices and satisfy some of his own needs that spoiling becomes an issue.

Discipline

People who work or live with children have always been interested in the process by which the child learns to conform to the wishes and demands of adults. Modern researchers speak of socialization, parents of discipline. The two are not entirely equivalent. Usually we use the word *discipline* to refer to the means by which a child is made to obey. Socialization is a broader concept, implying not only obedience but adoption by the child of some of the attitudes and beliefs of his elders. When the baby is told not to touch a glass tray, this is an instance of discipline—a command plain and simple, and one to which neither the parent nor the infant attaches much social importance. However, in complying with the "No, don't touch," the baby is at the same time learning a more general social rule: to obey his parents and other adults. This rule is part of the broader process of socialization.

Learning theory suggests that the child learns best when rules are applied consistently. He quickly learns that he is supposed to obey adults, for this rule is never varied. Children may sometimes feel confused as to which adult they are to obey in a given situation—mother or father, teacher or parent—but they always expect an adult to be in control. Even in children's play, the roles are structured: "You're the baby and I'm the Mommy, and you have to do what I want!"

What then of children who "always" disobey? They too have learned the broad social rule that children obey adults. But for many of them, this is the only rule that never changes. Take the case of Gary:

Eighteen-month-old Gary, playing with pots and pans, is one day given great approval since his activity keeps him busy for two hours as his mother completes a task, while three days later he is scolded and spanked for the same behavior because his mother had just finished arranging the pots and pans and did not wish them disturbed. Six-year-old Gary is encouraged to eat his dinner watching television because it is so difficult to drag him away and, besides, if his attention is

engaged he eats more since he is not mindful of the food. The same Gary, two weeks later, is scolded roundly for setting himself down in front of the television set at dinner time because mother has suddenly decided that it is not proper to eat in front of the television. (Thomas, Chess, and Birch, 1968)

In Gary's case, discipline is inconsistent. Yet Gary's required social role *is* consistent: he is always supposed to obey. Naturally he doesn't. Without any standards or models of behavior, Gary is likely to follow his own preference a good bit of the time. Although his parents may regret that he gets his own way so often, they fail to realize that doing so does not necessarily make Gary happy. Like all children, he believes that the world is, and should be, run by adults (if only for the sake of children). Misbehavior, even when reasonable under the circumstances, will make a young child feel quilty and insecure.

For discipline to be successful, parents must be consistent in their behavior and demands. In infancy this is usually not so difficult. Many of the commands involve matters of safety: few parents are inconsistent when it comes to allowing a child to put his hand on an electric burner. Safety rules seem to be learned more readily, with less stress, than other rules—probably because parents do not hesitate to impose them.

Though safety rules are positively accepted in infancy, other less justifiable forms of discipline may cause physical or emotional upsets. Some parents punish a child for crying—a practice that does little to establish trust. Others punish the infant for failing to conform to eating or sleeping schedules. Disciplinary conflicts are frequent when child and parent are not temperamentally well matched—for

© 1959 United Feature Syndicate, Inc.

example, when the child is highly active and distractible and his mother persistent and regular. Since nearly all children enjoy messing, a fastidious mother will also have more than her share of disciplinary troubles.

As the child develops a sense of autonomy, he will occasionally misbehave as a means of asserting his independence. Misbehavior may take the form of aggression, stubbornness, or casual disregard of parental rules. Common forms of misbehavior include refusal to go to bed, refusal to eat, and refusal to produce bowel movements at the right time. Parents differ greatly in punishment procedures. Some temporarily withdraw affection; others take away possessions and, later, privileges; still others resort to a swat on the backside. While there are advantages and disadvantages to each approach, the important thing again seems to be consistency. For example, if affection is withdrawn, the child must understand why—and he must know what he can do to regain his standing.

Punishment is not successful if it does not give consideration to the child's developing autonomy. For example, one cannot deprive a child of his oldest, proudest possession without depriving him of some sense of self as well. Recognition of cognitive limitation is also important. Infants have no concept of sharing and no concept of cheating. Punishing a very young child for being selfish or for cheating will simply result in angry confusion. Young children react very strongly to such verbal abuse. A child who is continually told that he is selfish, dirty, or lazy will in all probability accept the description rather than the disciplinary recommendation that is implied by it. In accepting the verbal stigma, the child shows a deep tendency to identify with the parent—even at cost to himself. A common sight in the nursery is that of a little girl chastising her doll with the words "*Bad* baby, *bad* baby."

CHILD ABUSE

A problem that seems to be increasing in our society is child abuse, the willful physical abuse of children by one or more parent. In many cases, "abuse" is a very mild term to describe the injuries inflicted on the child; all too often, newspaper reports describe cases of children who have been bound, beaten, stabbed, and burned by their parents. An attorney for the National Center for the Prevention and Treatment of Child Abuse and Neglect reports that death from such treatment "is not particularly unusual" (Fraser, 1974). The Center estimates that at least 72,000 children, and possibly as many as 150,000, are seriously abused in the United States each year.

Child abuse is difficult to study. The victim, the "battered child," is usually under twelve months of age—too young to perceive his situation, let alone describe it. Even if he is older, he may be reluctant to blame the abusing parent.

Despite the difficulties, there has been some research on the causes of child abuse and the characteristics of child-abusing parents. One sad fact is inescapable: "As infants and children, all of the [abusing] parents were deprived both of basic mothering and of the deep sense of being cared for and cared about from the beginning of their lives" (Spinetta and Rigler, 1972). One study (Fontana, 1973) suggests that parents who abuse their children have in common a great difficulty in developing trust, a difficulty that is linked to their own isolation.

Most abusing parents have been found to be unrealistic and demanding of their infants. Researchers have noted the tendency to assume that the child is capable of providing adult love and assurance (Melnick and Hurley, 1969). Perhaps it would be more accurate to say that the abusing parent, deprived of adult care during his formative years, has no conception of the qualitative difference between child and adult attachments. It is as if the parent is seeking in the infant the love and consideration she never received from her own parents. The infant instead turns out to be a helpless, squalling thing—another child dependent on what cannot be depended on.

Child abuse seems to occur in all classes of society, but most frequently in families that are subject to severe social and economic stresses. Divorce, the absence of the father, and the lack of community support are all characteristics of families that produce a battered child. Of course, not all stressful families practice child abuse. The emotional structure of the parent is a deciding factor. Abusing parents tend to be immature, unable to control anger and hostility or to cope with ordinary difficulties of life. However, some exhibit cold and compulsive behavior, and still others are moody, passive, and dependent (Merrill, 1962). Few abusing parents have any understanding of child rearing. In fact, the parent will generally defend the right to use physical force as a disciplinary measure, even to the point of injuring the child (Wasserman, 1967). Whereas abusing parents were once presumed to be severely disturbed, current research suggests that most simply lack impulse control.

ACTION ON CHILD ABUSE

Recent years have seen increased recognition of child abuse as a major problem. In 1974 the federal government provided $85 million for local child protection services. In New York City, where some 19,000 cases of child abuse were reported in 1973, a Special Services for Children division of the municipal government is responsible for investigating charges of child abuse and providing child protective services. These services include counseling, home aid, homemaking services, and, as a last resort, placement of the child in an institution or foster home.

Laws in twenty-two states now require teachers to report suspected cases of child abuse, and all states have laws making physicians and certain other people responsible for reporting such cases. In several communities, twenty-four-hour crisis intervention centers or services are available, providing counseling or even nursery care.

A number of hospitals are also developing programs to counsel potential child abusers. Hopefully, by providing parents with good child care models and giving them training, it will be possible to avoid the situations that give rise to child abuse and neglect.

Solutions to the problem of child abuse are not immediately apparent. Better medical care and firmer legal prosecution do not keep the child from being hurt in the first place. Alleviation of economic stresses through social welfare programs and reduction of unwanted children through birth control have been suggested, and so has the establishment of national and community health services that would permit intervention by society when the situation in a family seems to place the child at risk (Gil, 1969).

CULTURE AND UPBRINGING

Every parent raises his child with the understanding that the child will at some point be delivered over to society at large. In Western cultures, this means that he will go to school, join his local peer group, and eventually enter adult institutions such as the factory, office, church, and political party. But in other cultures children must take other directions and therefore receive different training. In the Yanomamö tribe, for example, children are trained to be self-assertive and physically aggressive, and in others, like the Hopi Indians, they are expected to merge their ambitions with those of the group. Even within a single culture, differences are evident. A Jewish American child who attends a Yeshiva study group is taught to argue with his teachers, as argument is a traditional way to understanding. To an Italian American child in a Catholic school, arguing with the teacher is usually considered disrespectful. Ideally the child's home training will have prepared him to display behavior appropriate to the culture and subculture to which he belongs. Indeed it appears that differences between cultures are not only reflected in different approaches to child rearing, but sometimes caused by them.

Class Differences

In some societies child rearing practices vary widely from one social class to another. For example, in nineteenth-century England, upper-class children were mothered by nannies, taught by governesses, and seen by their parents only under polite circumstances. During the same period, poorer children were raised in close quarters by their own mothers and sent out to work as soon as they could get a job. Today, among the Wolof of Senegal, the differences in life-style are just as great. A child born into an uneducated village family will grow up in a small stone house without a refrigerator or indoor water supply. Most of the family's activities will take place

Figure 6.9. Country babies may be brought up differently in some ways from their city cousins.

CROSS-CULTURAL STUDY

In cross-cultural study, as in other areas of child psychology, the research focus has shifted from feeding and toilet behaviors to the investigation of mother–infant attachment.

Of particular interest are studies that attempt to show how attachments and other culturally influenced behavior can affect the rate of development. Here again, Gandan infants have been much studied because of their constant physical contact with the mother. One observer (Gebér, 1958, 1960) found that the Gandan infant is typically quite advanced in motor skills, language, and social behavior during the first year of life. A comparative study (Gebér, 1960) showed that "Westernized" infants from the same area were not so precocious, apparently because they experienced less interaction with the mother. A more recent study of the Wolof of Senegal (Lusk and Lewis, 1972) found that the Wolof infant, like the Gandan, receives a great deal of stimulation from his mother and other ever-present caregivers.

African infants do not continue in accelerated development past the second year if they remain in the traditional home setting, but attending a nursery school will maintain their fast rate of development. Nursery school also brings "Westernized" infants up to the same level (Gebér, 1958, 1960; Lusk and Lewis, 1972). The study of development in traditional African settings will doubtless be the subject of continued research, motivated by our need to determine the different effects of maternal stimulation.

outside, with the child carried about by the mother, siblings, and other relatives. A child born into a wealthier, more educated Wolof family will grow up with twentieth-century conveniences like a car, refrigerator, and indoor plumbing. As an infant he will spend most of his time in a crib (Lusk and Lewis, 1972).

Considerable research has been devoted to identifying child rearing differences among lower, middle, and upper-middle socioeconomic groups in the United States. Frequently an attempt is made to explain class-related behavior on the basis of early training. The results have been interesting, if contradictory.

An early comprehensive study was conducted in Chicago (Davis and Havighurst, 1947). It established a number of generalizations that remained more or less unchallenged for over a decade. The data showed that lower-class mothers breast-fed their babies more often, weaned them later, toilet trained them later, and spanked them more often than did middle-class mothers. The typical middle-class mother used a bottle and started toilet training earlier. She was more likely to use praise and other rewards as a means of discipline.

Later studies have questioned these generalizations. One extensive survey (Sears, Maccoby, and Levin, 1957) found more permissiveness among the middle class. The researchers, working in Boston, did not discover meaningful differences in feeding practices. However, the findings did support the Chicago data in some instances. Again, physical punishment was more prevalent in the lower class, and verbal measures, such as the threat of withdrawal of love, were more common in middle-class families.

The overall differences in the findings of the two surveys may indicate a regional difference, a change in child rearing styles during the intervening years, or perhaps an insensitivity in the research method, which in both cases was the interview. Some subsequent research has suggested that such differences as exist are relatively insignificant in that they apply to very limited aspects of child rearing and are not consistent from one study to another (Littman, Moore, and Pierce-Jones, 1957).

The feeding and disciplinary practices that occupied some of the early researchers in class differences are no longer at the center of interest. In the 1970s, more attention has been given to the quality of attachment between mother and infant. Thus some of the more recent research has attempted to find class differences in attachment behaviors. Researchers are especially interested in the effect of any such difference on cognitive growth—and on consequent learning in the public school, where class differences are sometimes reflected in grades. It appears that infants of the lower and middle classes differ importantly in only one kind of attachment behavior: middle-class infants are more sensitive to vocal stimulation and tend to vocalize more in the presence of their mothers (Messer and Lewis, 1972).

Child Rearing in Other Cultures

The study of child development is international in its subjects and in many of its assumptions. Piaget's studies were based on observations of Swiss children, and several of the attachment studies cited in this chapter were conducted with British children. But do these findings apply equally well to children in other cultures, to American and Eskimo and Zulu children? In an attempt to answer this question, researchers in child development have carried out many studies of cultural differences and their bases in different patterns of child care.

To date, however, no one has clearly shown that any particular feeding or toilet training method will have a predictable effect in every culture that practices it. This is partly because any given child rearing practice is closely integrated with other practices. In one culture, for example, permissive feeding might be part of an approach that also includes permissive toilet training and easy tolerance of childhood sexuality and aggression. But in another culture the same degree of permissiveness in feeding might be associated with the opposite attitudes toward toilet training and sexuality. In such a variety of settings it is very difficult to tell just which practice is causing what effect.

Cross-cultural studies of breast feeding have shown that it is unrestricted in most preliterate (nonreading) and traditional societies (Newton, 1972). In many cultures the infant even sleeps with his mother so that he may be fed and comforted during the night. The Mundugumor of New Guinea, however, nurse their children standing up and push them away abruptly as soon as the feeding can be terminated

(Mead, 1949). The Marquesans of the South Pacific nurse their children irregularly and with many misgivings, because they feel that lengthy nursing causes misbehavior later in childhood (Whiting and Child, 1953).

Breast feeding of all varieties seems to decline as a society becomes more sophisticated (Jelliffe, 1962). Here the role of technology is obvious: only with advanced knowledge of nutrition, sterilization, and so on, can a culture provide a safe substitute for breast milk.

Studies of play behavior promise to reveal some interesting cultural differences in children. In one recent study (Finley and Layne, 1971), the play behavior of children from Cambridge, Massachusetts, was compared with that of Mayan children from the Yucatan Peninsula. The investigators concluded that the American subjects were more active and manipulative in their approach to toys, whereas the Mayan children were passive, socially oriented, and more visual in their explorations. Studies such as this may help researchers distinguish cultural from biological factors in behavior. If it is suggested that boys are more manipulative than girls, for example, the Mayan results will have to be accounted for.

Preliterate cultures are not the only subjects of cross-cultural study. Urie Bronfenbrenner, in his survey (1970) of child rearing in Russia, has attempted to describe "the making of a new Soviet man." He found that Russian infants are held in their caregivers' arms substantially more than American children. The Russian child also receives more kissing and cuddling and is much more likely to be breast-fed. Bronfenbrenner notes, however, that the infant does not have as much freedom of movement as American infants and is not allowed to stray far from adult eyes even when he is much older.

From birth, the Russian child is introduced to a variety of mothering figures in addition to his own mother. He is quite comfortable with strangers as he grows up. Of particular interest is Bronfenbrenner's description of the socialization process that comes into full play as the child enters nursery school. Parental discipline is accomplished through withdrawal of love. Among peers, as at school, there is a strong and ideological need for conformity in good behavior.

Child rearing practices in China are of particular interest because China, with a population of over 800 million, is the largest nation in the world, and child rearing innovations there constitute the largest "experiment" ever conducted. But unlike the Soviet system of child care, which is highly centralized, there is much diversity in China. The Chinese believe in self-reliance and in suiting training and education to the specific needs of the country's different regions.

Much of Chinese life, both urban and rural, is organized around the commune, which one observer (Sidel, 1972) characterizes as a "planned, self-contained community where you . . . create a system of interdependence in which nearly all of one's needs are met within the commune." The daycare needs of working mothers and the educational needs of infants and children are met with nurseries, kindergartens, and primary and middle schools.

At about two months of age, an infant is taken to work by his mother. She nurses him twice a day, but the rest of the time he stays in a "nursing room" until about the age of one and a half. Then, especially in the cities, he will usually go to a nursery school. The nursing room may have from twenty-seven to sixty babies, ranging in age from two to eighteen months. The children are supervised by several women (the observer found fourteen in the sixty-child nursing room) drawn from the factory staff; the children call them "Auntie." At about a year to a year and a half, communal toilet training is begun, and all children seem to learn toilet training without difficulty.

The multiple or shared mothering found in the Soviet system also seems to be common in China. The caregivers are permanent figures in the infant's world, and all of them seem to be warm and giving; in fact they are chosen for those qualities, rather than on the basis of special training or credentials.

In the nursery school, children are trained to become accustomed to mass activity. There are short lectures, "military" training, singing, and a certain amount of free play; the more active children are not restrained, but are encouraged to help the teacher. The observer reports that out of several hundred children she had seen, only three or four misbehaved. These were firmly but gently calmed by their elders; she never saw an adult become angry at a child.

Out of its particular situation and needs, China has clearly created a system of child rearing fundamentally different from our own. Family life, however, is still very important in China, and although children seen by the observer were calm, they were also alert, active, and social.

Figure 6.10. In India, infants are often cared for by their older brothers and sisters.

References

Ainsworth, M. D. The development of infant–mother interaction among the Ganda. In B. Foss (Ed.), *Determinant of infant behavior.* Vol. II. New York: Wiley, 1963.

Ainsworth, M. D. *Infancy in Uganda: infant care and the growth of love.* Baltimore: John Hopkins University Press, 1967.

Ainsworth, M. D., Bell, S. M., and Stayton, D. J. Individual difference in the development of some attachment behaviors. *Merrill-Palmer Quarterly,* 1972, *18,* 123–143.

Bell, R. Q. A reinterpretation of the direction of effects in studies of socialization. *Psychology Review,* 1968, *75,* 81–95.

Benjamin, J. D. Further comments on some developmental aspects of anxiety. In H. S. Gaskill (Ed.), *Counterpoint.* New York: International University Press, 1963.

Bowlby, John. *Attachment and loss: separation.* Vol. II. New York: Basic Books, 1973.

Brazelton, T. B. A child-oriented approach to toilet training. *Pediatrics,* 1962, *29,* 121–128.

Bronfenbrenner, U. *Two worlds of childhood: U.S. and U.S.S.R.* New York: Basic Books, 1970.

Bronfenbrenner, U. Socialization and social class through time and space. In Maccoby, E. E. et al. *Readings in social psychology.* New York: Holt, 1958.

Calhoun, A. C. *A social history of the American family* (3 volumes). New York: Barnes & Noble, 1960.

Chagnon, N. A. *Yanomamö, the fierce people.* New York: Holt, 1968.

Coates, B., Anderson, E. P., and Hartup, W. W. Interrelations in the attachment behavior of human infants. *Developmental Psychology,* 1972, *6,* No. 2, 218–230.

Collard, R. R. Social and play responses of first born and later born infants in an unfamiliar situation. *Child Development,* 1968, *39,* 325–334.

Davis, W. A., and Havighurst, R. J. *Father of the man.* Boston: Houghton Mifflin, 1947.

Erikson, E. *Identity, youth and crisis.* New York: Norton, 1968.

Escalona, S. K., and Corman, H. H. The impact of mother's presence upon behavior in the first year. *Human Development,* 1971, *14,* 2–15.

Finley, G. E., and Layne, Otis, Jr. Play behavior in young children: a cross-cultural study. *The Journal of Genetic Psychology,* 1971, *19,* 203–210.

Fontana, V. J. *Somewhere a child is crying.* New York: Macmillan, 1973.

Fraser, Brian G. The tragedy of child abuse. *Compact,* 1974, *8*(2), 10–12.

Freedman, D. G. The effects of kinesthetic stimulation on weight gain and smiling in premature infants. Presented at the annual meeting of the American Orthopsychiatric Association, San Francisco, 1966.

Gebér, M. The psychomotor development of African children in their first year and the influence of mother behavior. *Journal of Social Psychology,* 1958, *47,* 185–195.

Gebér, M. Problemes posés par le développement du jeune enfant Africain en fonction de son milieu. *Travail Hum,* 1960, *23,* 97–111.

Gil, D. G. Physical abuse of children: Findings and implications of a nationwide survey. *Pediatrics,* 1969, *44,* (5, Supplement) 857–864.

Goldberg, S., and Lewis, M. Play behavior in the year-old infant: early sex differences. *Child Development,* 1969, *40,* 21–31.

Goldfarb, W. Effects of psychological deprivation in infancy and subsequent stimulation. *American Journal of Psychiatry,* 1945a, *102,* 18–33.

Goldfarb, W. Psychological privation in infancy and subsequent adjustment. *American Journal of Orthopsychiatry,* 1945b, *15,* 247–255.

Goodenough, F. L. *Anger in young children.* Minneapolis: University of Minnesota Press, 1931.

Harlow, H. F. The heterosexual affectional system in monkeys. *American Psychologist,* 1962a, *17,* 1–9.

Harlow, H. Social deprivation in monkeys. *Scientific American,* 1962b, *207,* Nov. 136–146.

Harlow, H., and Harlow, M. H. Learning to love. *American Scientist,* 1966, *54*(3), 244–272.

Harlow, H. F., and Zimmerman, R. R. Affectional responses in the infant monkey. *Science,* 1959, *130,* 421–431.

Heinstein, M. *Child rearing in California*. Berkeley: Bureau of Maternal and Child Health, State Department of Public Health, 1966.

Horney, K. *The neurotic personality of our time*. New York: Norton, 1937.

Jelliffe, D. B. Culture, social changes and infant feeding: current trends in tropical regions. *American Journal of Clinical Nutrition*, 1962, *10*, 19–45.

Laing, R. D. *The Divided Self*. Chicago: Quadrangle Books, 1960.

Leifer, A. D., Leiderman, P. H., Barnett, C. R., and Williams, J. A. Effects of mother–infant separation on maternal attachment behavior. *Child Development*, 1972, *43*, 123–148.

Littman, R. A., Moore, R. C. A., and Pierce-Jones. Social class differences in child rearing: A third community for comparison with Chicago and Newton. *American Sociological Review*, 1957, *22*, 694–704.

Lusk, D., and Lewis, M. Mother–infant interaction and infant development among the Wolot in Senegal. *Human Development*, 1972, *15*, 58–69.

Maccoby, E. E., and Jacklin, C. N. Sex differences and their implication for sex roles. Address delivered at American Psychological Association Meeting, Washington, D.C., 1971.

Mead, M. *Coming of age in Samoa*. New York: William Morrow, 1928.

Mead, M. *Male and female: A study of the sexes in a changing world*. New York: William Morrow, 1949.

Melnick, B., and Hurley, J. R. Distinctive personality attributes of child-abusing mothers, *Journal of Consulting & Clinical Psychology*, 1969, *33*, 746–749.

Merrill, E. J. Physical abuse of children: An agency study. In De Francis, V. (Ed.) *Protecting the battered child*. Denver, Colo.: American Humane Association, 1962.

Messer, S. B., and Lewis, M. Social class and sex differences in the attachment and play behavior of the year-old infant. *Merrill-Palmer Quarterly*, 1972, *18*, 296–306.

Murphy, L. B. Infants' play and cognitive development. *Play and development*. New York: Norton, 1972.

Newton, N. Battle between breast and bottle. *Psychology Today*, *6*, July 1972, 68–70.

Provence, S., and Lipton, R. C. *Infants in institutions: A comparison of their development with family-reared infants during the first year of life*. New York: International Universities Press, 1962.

Rheingold, H. L. The effect of environmental stimulation upon social and exploratory behavior in the human infant. In B. M. Foss (Ed.), *Determinant of infant behavior*. Vol. I. London: Menthuen, 1969.

Rheingold, H. L. The modification of social responsiveness in institutional babies. *Monograph of the Society for Research in Child Development*, 1956, *21*, 2, Serial No. 63.

Rosenblatt, J. S. The development of maternal responsiveness in the rat. *American Journal of Orthopsychiatry*, 1969, *39*, 36–56.

Rowell, T. *Social behaviour of monkeys*. Baltimore: Penguin, 1972.

Schaffer, H., and Emerson, P. E. The development of social attachments in infancy. *Monographs of the Society for Research in Child Development*, 1964, *29*, 3, Serial No. 94.

Sears, R. R., Maccoby, E. E., and Levin, H. *Patterns of child rearing*. Evanston, Ill.: Row, Peterson, 1957.

Sidel, R. *Women and child care in China: A first hand report*. New York: Hill and Wang, 1972.

Skeels, H. M. Adult status of children with contrasting early life experience. *Monographs of Society of Research in Child Development*, 1966, *31*, 1–65.

Spencer-Booth. Y., and Hinde, R. A. The effects of separating rhesus monkey infants from their mothers for six days. *Journal of Child Psychology and Psychiatry*, 1966, *7*, 179–197.

Spinetta, J., and Rigler, D. The child abusing parent: a psychological review. *Psychological Bulletin*, 1972, *77*(4), 296–304.

Spitz, R. A. Hospitalization: an inquiry into the genesis of psychiatric conditions of early childhood. In A. Freud et al. (Eds.), *The psychoanalytic study of the child*. New York: International University Press, 1945.

Sroufe, L. A., and Wunsch, J. P. The development of laughter in the first year of life. *Child Development*, 1972, *43*, 1326–1344.

Stayton, D. J., Hogan, R., and Ainsworth, M. Infant obedience and maternal behavior: The origins of socialization reconsidered. *Child Development*, 1971, *42*, 1057–1069.

Steele, B. F., and Pollack, C. B. A psychiatric study of parents who abuse infants and small children. In R. E. Helfer and C. H. Kempe (Eds.), *The battered child*. Chicago: University of Chicago Press, 1968.

Thomas, A., Chess, S., and Birch, H. G. Temperament and behavior disorders in children. New York: New York University Press, 1968.

Wasserman, S. The abused parent of an abused child. *Children*, 1967, *14*, 175–179.

Watson, J. B. *Behaviorism*. New York: Norton, 1930.

Wenar, C. Executive competence and spontaneous social behavior in one-year-olds. *Child Development*, 1972, *43*, 256–260.

Whiting, J. M., and Child, I. L. *Child training and personality: A cross-cultural study*. New Haven: Yale University Press, 1953.

Yarrow, L. J. Separation from parents during early childhood. In M. L. Hoffman and L. W. Hoffman (Eds.), *Review of child development research*. Vol. 1. New York: Russell Sage Foundation, 1964.

Yarrow, M. R., Campbell, J. D., and Burton, R. V. *Child rearing: An inquiry into research method*. Jossey-Bass, 1968.

Yeats, W. B. The trembling of the veil, 1922. In *The Autobiography of William Butler Yeats*. New York: Macmillan, 1953.

Young, W. C., Goy, R. W., and Phoenix, C. H. Hormones and sexual behavior. *Science*, 1964, *143*, 212–218.

Zegans, S., and Zegans, L. S. Fear of strangers in children and the orienting reaction. *Behavioral Science*, 1972, *17*, 407–419.

SUMMARY

1 The infant's attitude toward himself and the world around him is derived from the care and attention he receives. His attachments before the age of six months are indiscriminate; then he forms a primary attachment to his mother or mothering figure. The quality of this special, first social relationship is a crucial factor in the child's development.

2 As with other species, human attachment takes place at about the same time that the infant becomes mobile and just before he develops a fear of strange objects or persons. It is not sufficient for the formation of an attachment relationship to merely meet the infant's gross physical needs. Physical contact, smiling, feeding, and a positive orientation toward these activities are all necessary. Studies of children raised in institutions and foster homes indicate that the most damaging element of the experience may be the lack of stimulation and attention that a mothering figure would ordinarily provide.

3 The mother–infant relationship is also the source of the first major anxieties that the child experiences. Separation anxiety—anxiety at being separated from the mother—is directly proportional to the intensity of the infant's primary attachment.

4 When the infant develops a will of his own and the ability to get around, the process of socialization begins. Through this process the individual learns that the world does not respond to him alone, but that he will have to conform to many demands. Toilet training is one aspect of socialization that is acquired deliberately, but other important aspects are acquired more subtly. The child's socialization in sex roles, for example, and the management of emotions, fears, and aggression are heavily dependent on the attitudes and examples offered by his parents.

5 A child masters disciplinary rules best when they are applied consistently. Confusion and frustration can result from conflicting demands or a mismatch of the child's temperament and that of his parents.

6 Cross-cultural studies have shown that cultural differences are reflected in a wide variety of approaches to child rearing. The Soviet Union and China, for example, have systems of multiple or shared mothering. These unfamiliar methods of child rearing offer us a new perspective on our own cultural norms.

FURTHER READINGS

Bronfenbrenner, U. *Two worlds of childhood: U.S. and U.S.S.R.* New York: Russell Sage Foundation, 1970.

Bronfenbrenner contrasts patterns of maternal care in the U.S. and the U.S.S.R. His findings show that the care infants and preschool children receive in the daycare centers in Russia is well adapted to their needs. Training in individualism and competition starts early in life in the U.S. and its effects soon become apparent.

Davis, W. A. and Havighurst, R. J. *Father of the man: How your child gets his personality.* Boston: Houghton Mifflin, 1947.

A classic discussion of child development and child rearing with an emphasis on class differences. Includes an appendix on social class differences in child rearing practices. The approach is personal with interesting examples from case histories.

Kagan, J. *Change and continuity in infancy.* New York: Wiley, 1971.

Kagan conducted longitudinal research on a large sample of children, who were studied from the age of four months to four years. The author hypothesized that there are continuities in the behavior of an individual child over time if the observed behavior can be related to an underlying personality trait. Differences of sex and social class in cognitive and behavioral development were also studied.

Montessori, M. *The secret of childhood.* B. Carter (trans.), New York: Longmans, Green, and Co., 1936.

Sensitive account of the newborn and early childhood by the founder of an important educational philosophy. The Montessori method emphasizes the necessity of treating the child with dignity and respecting his individuality. A spiritual as well as scientific approach.

Rabin, A. I. *Growing up in the kibbutz.* New York: Springer, 1965.

This study compares the growth and personalities of children brought up in the kibbutz in Israel with American family-reared children. The subjects are infants from the ages of ten months to seventeen and a half months.

Ribble, M. A. *The rights of infants: Early psychological needs and their satisfaction.* New York: Columbia University Press, 1965.

This is a book devoted to the defense of babies as human beings in miniature whose dignity and needs must be respected. Dr. Ribble describes normal infant behaviors and suggests reasonable responses. There are case histories of the results of the absence of adequate mothering.

Part 3

THE PRESCHOOL YEARS

Eating was not only an exploration and an act of conquest—an acquired taste in the real sense of the phrase—but also my most solemn duty: "A spoonful for Mama, and another for grandmama. . . . If you don't eat anything, you won't grow up into a big girl." I would be stood up against the doorframe in the hall and a pencilled line would be drawn level with the top of my head; the new line would then be compared with an earlier one: I had grown two or three centimetres; they would congratulate me, and I would swell with pride. But sometimes I felt frightened. The sunlight would be playing on the polished floor and the white-enamelled furniture. I would look at Mama's armchair and think: "I won't be able to sit on her knee any more if I go on growing up." Suddenly the future existed; it would turn me into another being, someone who would still be, and yet no longer seem, myself. I had forebodings of all the separations, the refusals, the desertions to come, and of the long succession of my various deaths. "A spoonful for grandpapa. . . ." I went on eating, all the same, and I was proud that I was growing; I had no wish to remain a baby all my life. I must have been intensely aware of this conflict to be able to remember in such minute detail a certain book from which Louise used to read me the story of Charlotte. One morning Charlotte found on her bedside chair a huge egg, almost as big as herself, made of pink sugar. This egg fascinated me, too. It was both stomach and cradle, and yet you could eat it. Refusing all other food, Charlotte grew smaller day by day; she became minute: she was nearly drowned in a saucepan, the cook accidentally threw her away into the dustbin, and she was carried off by a rat. She was rescued; Charlotte, now chastened and scared, stuffed herself so greedily she began to swell and swell until she was like a gigantic bladder of lard; her mama took this monstrous balloon-child to the doctor's. I gloated, but with a new restraint, over the pictures illustrating the diet the doctor had prescribed: a cup of chocolate, a nicely coddled new-laid egg, and a lightly grilled chop. Charlotte returned to normal size and I came out of the adventure safe and sound after having been reduced to a foetus and then blown up to matronly dimensions.

I kept on growing and I realized that my fate was sealed: I was condemned to be an outcast from childhood. I sought refuge in my own reflection. Every morning Louise would curl my hair and I would gaze with satisfaction at my face framed with ringlets: dark hair and blue eyes did not often, so they had told me, go together, and I had already learned to appreciate the value of the unusual. I was pleased with myself, and I sought to please. My parents' friends encouraged my vanity: they politely flattered me and spoiled me, I would stroke the ladies' furs and their satin-sheathed bosoms; I admired even more the gentlemen with their moustaches, their smell of tobacco, their deep voices, their strong arms that could lift me nearly up to the ceiling. I was particularly anxious to arouse the interests of the men: I tried to attract their attention by fidgeting and playing the ingénue, seizing any look or word that would snatch me out of my childhood limbo and give me some permanent status in their grown-up world. . . .

One morning there was a thunderstorm; I was playing with Aunt Lili in the dining-room when the house was struck by lightning; it was a serious accident, which filled me with pride: every time something happened to me, I had the feeling that I was at last *someone*. I enjoyed an even more subtle satisfaction. On the wall of the outside water closets clematis was growing; one morning, Aunt Alice called me to her in her dry, squeaky voice; a flower was lying on the ground; she accused me of having picked it. Picking flowers in the garden was a crime whose gravity I was well aware of; but I hadn't done it, and I denied the accusation. Aunt Alice didn't believe me. Aunt Lili defended me with vigour. She was the representative of my parents, and my only judge. Aunt Alice, with her speckled old face, belonged to the race of wicked fairies who persecute little children; I witnessed with great complacency the struggle waged for my benefit by the forces of good against the forces of error and injustice. In Paris my parents and grandparents indignantly took up arms in my defence, and I was able to savour the triumph of virtue.

Sheltered, petted, and constantly entertained by the endless novelty of life, I was a madly gay little girl. Nevertheless, there must have been something wrong somewhere: I had fits of rage during which my face turned purple and I would fall to the ground in convulsions. I am three and a half years old, and we are lunching on the sunny terrace of a big hotel . . .; I am given a red plum and I begin to peel it. "No," says Mama; and I throw myself howling on the ground. I go howling all along the boulevard . . . because Louise has dragged me away from the square . . . where I was making sand-pies. At such moments, neither Mama's black looks nor Louise's stern voice, nor even Papa's special interventions could make any impression upon me. I used to howl so loudly, and so long, that . . . I was sometimes looked upon as a child martyr by benevolent and misinformed nursemaids and mothers. 'Poor little thing!' cried one lady, offering me a sweet. All the thanks she got from me was a kick in the shins.

—Simone de Beauvoir
Memories of a Dutiful Daughter

7
Physical and Perceptual Development

You can almost tell when a child emerges from infancy just by watching her walk. Instead of seeming ready to fall at any moment, she gets around with great confidence. Sometimes, in fact, she throws caution to the winds, runs everywhere, climbs everything. Her social relations, meanwhile, begin to extend beyond the family circle, and though she can still be painfully shy, on occasion she can be surprisingly bold.

In the preschool period—roughly from age two to age five—the child makes enormous progress. She learns to talk so that not just her parents but anyone can understand her and to say nearly anything she has in mind. She asks questions about what she sees, hears, and smells, and even about what she only remembers or imagines. She begins to play cooperatively with other children. Her attention span constantly lengthens until, by the time she is five or six, she will be ready to start kindergarten or first grade.

The child's physical development is the foundation of this progress. Her increasing size and strength enable her more and more to find her way without adult protection and guidance, while the development of her central nervous system prepares her for formal education.

PHYSICAL GROWTH

At age three, the average boy is a little over three feet tall and weighs over thirty pounds; by age five, he has grown to about forty-four inches and forty-three pounds. There are individual variations, but girls tend to be slightly shorter and lighter than boys. A child who is big for his age at the beginning of the preschool years will probably still be big for his age at the end of the period. There is also a fairly strong correlation between the height of the preschool child and the height he will attain as an adult, though there are individual exceptions: it is not uncommon for a child who is small at four or five to develop into a larger than average adult.

Boys and girls develop at about the same pace during the preschool years and through childhood until puberty. Girls usually reach half their adult height shortly before they are two years old. Most boys do not reach their halfway point until they are almost two and a half, but boys generally have more height to attain as an adult. One of the most significant developmental differences between preschool boys and girls is that boys have more muscle and girls more fatty tissue. In both sexes the infant fatty tissue is gradually replaced, but girls tend to retain it longer than boys (Breckenridge and Murphy, 1969).

Body proportions change dramatically in the preschool period. The trunk and legs grow rapidly, but cranial growth is not so fast as in infancy. As a result, by age six a child's legs equal about half his body length, a ratio that will remain constant for the rest of his life. In other words, the average six year old already has the body shape of the adult he will become.

In the preschool child's growing skeleton, cartilage turns into bone and existing bones grow larger and harder. By age three, most children have a complete set of temporary teeth (also called milk teeth or deciduous teeth). The soft or liquid foods of infancy are left behind in favor of meat, fruits, and vegetables. The child leaves the high chair and joins the family at the table.

Muscular development accounts for most of the weight gained during the preschool years by both boys and girls. Because the large muscles develop more rapidly than the small ones, motor abilities progress from broad to precise. A two year old can, for example, build a tower of six or seven blocks and kick a large ball, but he cannot do many things a five year old can, such as cut with scissors, catch a small ball, copy letters, or hop on one foot. With time and practice, the smaller muscles mature and the child performs increasingly complex motions requiring more and more precise coordination. The small muscles do not reach full maturity, however, until adolescence.

While the skeleton and muscles of the preschool child are developing, so is the nervous system—the all-important central control. By age five, the brain has reached 75 percent of its adult weight, and only a year later, 90 percent. It is also during the preschool years that *myelinization*—a sheathing of the nerve fibers in the brain with a white material called myelin—is completed. This sheathing permits speedy transmission of nerve impulses. Myelinization is usually complete before a child begins his formal education.

DEPRIVATION DWARFISM

Jonathan is three years old and in the hospital. Looking into his crib we see a very small, thin child—you might think he was just over one year—legs sprawled like an infant, sucking his thumb, and staring blankly ahead with listless, sad eyes. We might think that he is suffering from a disease or malnutrition, but in fact Jonathan is a victim of *deprivation dwarfism.* But what has he been deprived of? His parents are middle-class Americans, and he has been fed and sheltered like other middle-class children. He has no serious illness; he was not born with any physical defect. He has been deprived of only one thing, love. His parents didn't want a child, and when he was born they didn't hold him, talk to him, smile at him, or play with him. An adult may *say* "I'm dying of loneliness," but an infant can really do it.

Researchers (Gardner, 1972) have been studying the relation between deprivation dwarfism and physiological development in children. They suggest that being deprived of affection almost always leads to emotional and physical disturbance in the child. The disturbance is registered at first in the higher, more developed brain centers. These brain centers send messages to a more "primitive" part of the brain, the hypothalamus, which in turn regulates the pituitary gland, the "master gland" of the endocrine system. The pituitary is responsible for regulating the release of somatotrophin, the growth hormone that stimulates cells to reproduce. When children suffer from emotional deprivation they produce much less growth hormone. The result is a boy like Jonathan.

The relation between sleeping patterns and the release of growth hormone is also being studied. The findings, so far, support the hormone theory. Most growth hormone is released into the bloodstream during a stage of sleep when the higher brain centers are the least active. Victims of deprivation dwarfism have very irregular sleeping patterns. It seems possible that because of their emotional situation these children never reach this particular stage of sleep, for when they do return to normal growth, they also develop normal sleeping patterns (Shaywitz et al., 1971).

Deprivation dwarfism is an extreme example of how emotional environment can affect a child's physical growth. It can be isolated and studied by researchers because the affliction is so severe and its symptoms are so obvious. Some children, however, may exhibit symptoms of emotional deprivation that are less obvious. They may be small and weak, even though they are not dwarfs, or they may often be sick. Parents often think that these children simply have a "poor constitution;" it may not occur to them to look for a better explanation or for possible emotional causes. But emotional environment seems to have a great effect on a child's physical development. There is evidence that even in adolescence, emotional deprivation can affect physical well-being; a common problem among older children is malnutrition resulting from a loss of appetite.

A positive, affectionate, loving environment is not just a luxury for a child. We should realize that a basically loving environment is as important for a child's physical development as food and shelter.

Figure 7.1. Climbing, swinging, running, swimming—the preschool child is naturally attracted to all free movements because they help him develop the various muscles of his body.

The slow brain-wave patterns of infants gradually change to a faster rhythm and reach a peak of frequency during the preschool years. These faster brain-wave patterns are often accompanied by a tendency to the outbursts of temper for which preschool children are notorious. In fact, investigators have observed a definite relationship between tantrums and increases in brain-wave frequency.

Many other physiological changes occur during the preschool years. Breathing becomes slower and deeper; the heart beats more slowly and more steadily; and blood pressure increases. Thus, by age five, most children are physically prepared for the intense learning that will be demanded of them in middle childhood.

Poverty, Diet, and Disease

In normal, healthy children, the genetic potential is helped toward fulfillment by healthful, invigorating environmental conditions. The quality of a child's nutrition and health care strongly influences his development.

Unfortunately, a majority of children in the world today receive neither proper nutrition nor adequate medical attention. They do not get enough protein for building body cells, or enough vitamins and minerals for structural development, or enough carbohydrates for energy. The children of poverty-stricken areas in Africa, India, Pakistan, and South America are short and slight compared to other children (Meredith, 1968). When people are poor, they are usually malnourished. Chronic malnutrition—usually beginning before birth—can produce permanent

"Boy—I'm just no good in the morning until I've had my milk!"

LAND OF PLENTY?

Orchards heavy with fruit, tables laden with the riches of a bountiful harvest, amber waves of grain—the American dream has always included all kinds of good things to eat. The bounty of our fertile land covers millions of acres and fills thousands of miles of store shelves. Nutritional abundance is an American tradition.

It is true that most Americans have more than enough to eat. But most of us, including most of our children, are not really well fed. We drink less milk, for example, than our parents did. We eat fewer whole-grain products, fresh fruits, and vegetables, and what we do eat is often inferior in quality.

Our eating habits have changed significantly since World War II, mostly as a result of what is done to our food in the processing plants, on its way from the farmer to the grocer. Changing food from its natural, raw state is nothing new, of course; human beings have been processing what they eat since the discovery of fire. But in recent decades the food industry has added more and more substances to what we eat, and only a few of these additives have any nutritional value. At the same time, many new "foods" appear in the stores that have no food value at all. Although we are full, and many of us are too fat, we are not giving our bodies the essential nutrients they need. This nutritional deficiency is especially critical for someone who is still growing.

Food additives are used for many reasons. Less than ten percent of all food additives have any value for our bodies; all the rest are put in to make the product look better, taste better, or last longer, or to make it cheaper to get on the market. At least 661 million pounds of these substances are added to foods in the United States. The average American consumes more then three pounds of them a year.

Regulation of food additives is the responsibility of the Food and Drug Administration, but the law in this area is difficult to formulate and even harder to apply; many nutritionists believe there is no real regulation of the food industry. As a result, many scientists are worried about the additives in our diet; special subjects of concern are the cumulative effects of chemicals that are taken for long periods of time, the possible dangers of combining certain additives in the body, and especially what these substances may do to children. Infants and preschoolers in particular have lower tolerances than adults for many additives. One study (Feingold, 1973) indicates that the artificial dyes and flavorings found in almost all processed foods cause hyperactivity in children.

What can parents do about this? Most of us know pitifully little about what foods, in what combinations, are best for us. However, a hearty helping of common sense can help parents in many of their decisions. Relatively natural foods such as fresh meat and eggs, milk, and whole grains are generally going to be better for our children than synthetic or heavily processed foods; no special training is needed to know that. Foods with relatively few additives should be preferred.

Part of our responsibility to our children is to teach them to eat what is good for them. And there is good evidence for believing that they will probably like it better.

physical deformities and mental incapacity. Furthermore, poorly fed children, even when their growth is not stunted, are more susceptible to infections of the eyes, ears, and respiratory system and are less able to combat their illnesses. They are less alert mentally and less active physically.

Illness early in life is a particularly serious problem among the poor in the United States. Although each generation in general has produced larger, healthier babies than the generation before it, millions of children continue to suffer from respiratory illness, bad teeth, and other such conditions related to nutritional deficiencies. A recent survey (Schaefer and Johnson, 1969) showed that among children under six years old, 12 to 16 percent suffer from vitamin C deficiency and about 30 percent from vitamin A deficiency. One third of all American children have anemia severe enough to require medical attention.

Malnutrition can result from the consumption of "junk foods" that provide only "empty calories"—that is, refined carbohydrates. In a consumer culture it is difficult to keep a child from eating presweetened cereals, french fries, candy bars, and soft drinks. Day after day the child sees this kind of food recommended on television by his favorite cartoon characters and TV personalities. Yet when junk foods make up a large part of the diet, the result may be nutritional deficiencies, often accompanied by obesity. It is not uncommon for a child today to be both overweight and undernourished.

Physique and Personality

Many investigators have tried to establish a link between physique and personality. How convenient it would be if we could confidently describe someone's personality merely by classifying his body type! So far, however, researchers have usually been frustrated by the tendency of actual people to be exceptions to the rules. Nevertheless, the ingenuity of these researchers has provided some provocative ways of thinking about the relationship of physique to personality. For example, some theorists (Bayley and Bayer, 1946) have proposed a pattern of *androgyny*—the varying distribution of the characteristics of both sexes in one person. They believed that "male" and "female" personality traits could be correlated with certain physical characteristics, such as the amount of fat and muscle tissue in the person's body.

This scheme overlaps in many ways with the more widely known system of *somatotyping* proposed by the psychologist W. H. Sheldon (1940). According to this system, body types can be grouped into three broad categories: the soft and rounded *endomorph*, the well-muscled *mesomorph*, and the thin and frail *ectomorph*. Each of these somatotypes is supposedly correlated with certain personality traits—the friendly, easy-going endomorph; the bold, self-assertive mesomorph; and the shy, socially restrained ectomorph. Certainly these patterns can sometimes be found. President William Howard Taft, probably the roundest man who ever sat in the White House, was noted for his geniality; Muhammud Ali is very well muscled and is equally bold and self-assertive. But how do we fit ectomorphs such as Mick

Jagger or Ralph Nader into this scheme? Or the "endomorph" whose body type is a result of anxiety and overeating? Perhaps the answer is that somatotyping simply reflects social stereotypes: if you have a body like Santa Claus, you had better act jolly, because people expect it. In any case, few people clearly belong in any one of the three categories. What personality could be predicted for a person who is a mesomorph above the waist and an ectomorph below?

Even if physical *type* cannot be related to personality, however, physical *development* may have much influence on personality formation. The better-developed child often becomes a leader because of his greater strength and skills, while the less-developed child may tend to become shy and withdrawn. It seems, therefore, that social factors influence children of certain body types to develop certain personality characteristics.

Locomotion and Manipulation

As her body matures, the child discovers that she can do many new things—run, jump, climb, balance herself. The preschool years are marked by great advances in strength, speed, and coordination.

As the child discovers with delight that she can lift and move objects that defeated all her earlier efforts, her new muscular ability contributes much to her growing sense of self-confidence. There seems to be little difference in strength between boys and girls until around age six, and the lead that boys take from then on does not become pronounced until adolescence. Before adolescence, most of the difference is probably a result of cultural attitudes: in our society, most boys are encouraged to develop their physical strength and most girls are not.

Speed becomes increasingly important for the preschool child during his play. Can he beat his brother to the other end of the supermarket aisle? Can he build a tower of blocks faster than his friend? Can he be the first to get to the top of the jungle gym? Because speed is largely a function of reaction time, the child's success in such races depends on the speed of his responses. The sharpening of these responses is an important function of speed-oriented play.

Coordination

More complex than either strength or speed is coordination—the channeling of strength and speed into smooth, rhythmic, accurate movements. Consider these two actions: throwing a stone into a lake and throwing a ball to a person several yards away. Coordination—voluntary muscular control—makes the difference between them. The ability to judge time and distance and to relate them to muscular functions does not come easily to the preschool child, as it requires control of the fine muscles.

The motor behavior of a three year old shows his increased control over his body. He delights in running, with sudden starts and stops. He turns corners rapidly and jumps up and down with ease. His coordination has developed to the point that he can stack as many as ten blocks before they tumble in a heap.

Figure 7.2. Locomotion.

At age four, the child can skip and jump forward, as well as run and jump straight up and down. He probably cannot yet throw a ball with much strength or accuracy, but he can swing his arms freely without any exaggerated movements of his torso.

By the time he is five or six, the child is capable of increasingly complex feats such as climbing, balancing, and throwing. His coordination has matured to the point where his skills are recognized by other children, and his social life begins to involve rivalry and cooperation.

There is nothing automatic about this process, however. One study (Guttentag, 1972) raises questions about the influences of a child's culture on his motor development. In a comparison of the spontaneous movements of black four year olds with white four year olds, the researcher found that the black children showed a significantly greater number and variety of movements than the white children. These differences could be caused by genetic factors, but cultural orientation may also play a part. A child who is encouraged to move about freely will learn to develop greater mobility than a child who is not rewarded for such behavior. It is possible that black parents do, in general, encourage such movement more than white parents.

Manipulating Materials

As a child becomes more capable of performing complex tasks, she becomes more interested in the world. She studies shells at the beach and stones in the park, and examines pictures and machines that she had barely noticed before. She suddenly seems to be thinking about things; she asks questions and listens carefully to the answers.

Many of the child's efforts to learn about the world involve the manipulation of raw materials. The preschool child is eager to play with almost anything. She finds excitement not only in paints, construction paper, and clay, but also in pipe cleaners, drinking straws, paper bags, toothpicks, and rubber bands. As her coordination develops, she becomes increasingly skillful in handling these materials. The three year old who can finger-paint and fold paper grows into a five year old who can paint with a brush and cut with scissors. When a child discovers that she can cut things out and paste them together in new combinations, converting raw materials into constructions that she really designs, rather than merely assembles, she has reached a new level of maturity in her creative play.

No matter what materials the child manipulates, her mastery of them will develop in a similar sequence. Younger preschool children delight in investigating the materials themselves. Fingerpaints and modeling clay are sources of pure sensual pleasure as they are squished between the child's fingers; then they become interesting *things* to be manipulated in as many different ways as possible. The child explores the medium to become familiar with all of its potential for her play, discovering and practicing the physical skills required to work with each new

Figure 7.3. Mixing sand and gravel to make "cement."

material. Given paints and a brush at this stage, the child will lavish form and color in broad, abstract strokes across her paper. She shows little interest in pictorial representation or in precision, but as she gains skill, she moves fluidly through several different shapes in her work, discovering what the material can do and what she can do with it.

Gradually the preschool child develops a longer attention span and her physical coordination and skills increase so that she has more control over her play materials. She is able to take the time needed to build a tall block tower that will stand on its own. Her paintings become representational and eventually may contain elaborate details, involving patience and planning for their execution. Pencil drawings lend themselves to representation even in the earlier stages of the child's play, but as she becomes more skillful, her figures of people become more detailed and accurate in that, for example, the limbs are connected to the torso rather than to the head. The human face is by far the favorite subject of preschool drawings. The younger child carefully draws the eyes, nose, mouth, ears, and hair, but then he indicates the rest of the body almost as an afterthought, rapidly sketching the arms and legs as stiff lines and the hands and feet as circles. Only later do details of clothing and background begin to appear.

By age five, most children have progressed beyond the rudimentary stick figures of their earlier efforts. However, their drawings still reflect their distinctive view of the world. Heads tend to be disproportionately larger than bodies, and people tend to be larger than background objects.

The preschool period is a period of many exciting discoveries. As the child becomes more and more aware of his expanding motor capabilities, he is spurred on to new levels of creativity and, ultimately, social interaction. The skills the little boy develops as he competes during active play help determine his status in the eyes of others and, perhaps even more important, in his own eyes.

PERCEPTION

Perception is the individual's raw seeing, hearing, feeling, tasting, and smelling activity. It is his sensory input plus the initial categories and interpretations his mind automatically gives it. During the preschool years, perceptual awareness develops to the point where initial perceptions usually trigger a chain of complex mental processes aimed either at problem solving or at acquiring a fuller understanding of the situation. It is true that some perceptual awareness seems to be built into the human nervous system—depth perception, for example. But in the preschool years the child's perceptions become finer, sharper, and more reliable. He begins to understand more clearly what pleases him and what hurts him, and why; more important, he begins to see the world more nearly as an adult does, and this maturing perception makes him more and more a part of that world.

Attention

Attention is not an ability but a quality of mental life that can be focused or shifted to some extent by conscious effort. Usually, however, it is habitual or immediate—it turns to the objects that call it.

Each of us is constantly aware of the many sights, sounds, and smells of the environment. It is impossible to heed all of these things all the time, so we respond to certain of them more intensely than others, according to our own individual needs and interests. This selective response is called *attention*. There is probably no sharp difference between the attention of infants and that of preschoolers. Infants are much more aware of details of the world around them than many people suppose.

Part and whole

An important aspect of the development of attention is the perception of an object both in its entirety and in its component parts. Imagine a small girl whose mother takes her to a department store in a large suburban shopping center. As the girl stops for a moment to look up at a display of toys, her mother might disappear for a moment around a corner. What happens then? For a two or three year old, the experience might be terrifying—in the many-aisled store, with piped-in music and hundreds of strange people shopping, she may feel herself completely lost. She looks for Mommy, but all the women look alike to her at a distance. She may run from one shopper to another, growing more and more panicky. When she finally does find Mommy, it may be several hours before the fright wears off.

For a five year old, getting lost in the same place may be only slightly alarming, or even enjoyable. This may be partly because she has been through it before—she knows her way around. But more important, she knows how to look for Mommy. She knows that Mommy is a tallish woman with short brown hair and a green overcoat, so she does not run to women who look somewhat different. She may remember what she and Mommy were shopping for and go to the part of the store where they are most likely to find each other. She will probably also be able to recognize her mother (and other people as well) not only by their features and clothing, but also by their characteristic gestures or ways of walking. What makes the difference is the older girl's ability to see both parts and wholes. She has learned to recognize the details of the things and people that are important to her and to use them to find her way around in a confusing situation. She now has the ability to focus on details and, at the same time, to see how they fit into the overall situation.

There are two basic theories that try to explain how this ability develops. Some theorists suggest that we first make sense of a whole person, place, or thing, and only later pick up the finer details. Other theorists see the process the other way around. According to them, we learn to recognize parts or qualities of things first, and later we add up these bits so that we can recognize the larger wholes. In any case, the process is aided in the preschool period by the learning of concepts that bring the details together into a meaningful picture. For example, a certain picture might be described by a three year old as "lots of books in rows," whereas a five year old might say, "That's a library." The sight of a group of hard-hatted men operating huge machines and swinging steel beams on a city street might be meaningless to a three year old, but at age five he might say knowingly, "The men are putting up a building."

Younger children characterize what they can of an object, preferably the whole if they recognize it, and if not, then an outstanding part. The ability to attend to both the whole and the parts at the same time develops with age. The development of language, which gives the child concepts of collective wholes, such as libraries, also plays a critical role not only in the reporting of perception, but in the original perception itself (Flavell, 1963).

Shape and color

An object may be attended to in a number of ways: a part may be seen as more outstanding than the whole, for example, or the shape as more important than the color. Researchers have conducted many studies on children's preferences between shape and color. In one classic study (Brian and Goodenough, 1929), a child was shown two objects alike in shape and color and was asked to complete the set by choosing between two other objects, one like the originals in shape but not color, and the other like the originals in color but not shape. For example, the original objects may be red circles and the choice objects yellow circles and red squares.

Early studies of this sort indicate that preschool children strongly preferred shape over color. In the case mentioned, for instance, most children chose yellow circles over the red squares. Recent research, however, has emphasized the influence of instruction and experience on shape and color preference. For example, in one matching experiment (Modreski and Goss, 1972), four year olds were found to prefer shape to color. Some of the children were then trained in naming colors. When the matching experiment was repeated, the trained children named colors more often than the others, though the overall preference for shape seemed to persist among them all.

Attention span

We all know people—children and adults—who can grasp very easily the essence of a situation or problem, but whose attention wanders as soon as the initial novelty wears off. The length of time we can focus our attention on a given object or task is called our **attention span**. Attention is sustained longer as perceptual abilities grow and concepts and skills develop.

Three characteristics of an object or event seem to determine whether a child will give it sustained attention. The first is rapid change. A flashing light, for example, will hold her attention longer than a steady light. The second is novelty. The child trying pistacchio ice cream for the first time will pay special attention to its taste and color because they are different (but not too different) from the ice cream she is used to. The third characteristic, which seems to become important after the child is about nine to twelve months old, is harder to describe: basically, it is that the child will give increasing attention to a relatively familiar object, like a cartoon, that suggests ideas for her to play with. Here the object elicits sustained attention because it causes the child to use her mind actively, and the activity may be pleasurable in itself.

Children may be capable of quite sustained attention at a very early age. A one year old may play at a single task for fifteen minutes or longer. But attention span increases greatly during the preschool years. A young preschooler usually does not spend much time at a single activity, which often causes problems for the psychologists who would like to test his emotional and intellectual development. But by the time the child has been in school a short time, his attention span has increased remarkably. This change seems to be linked to development in other areas—general intelligence, improved memory and analytical skills, the ability to ignore distractions, and probably most important, increased motivation. It is the motivation to spend a long time on a single task that enables a child to do well at anything he may turn his hand to, from reading to doing somersaults. The development of an adult attention span is obviously an important part of becoming ready for the demands of the later childhood years.

Discrimination

You are given a one-pound weight and a two-pound weight and asked to distinguish between them. You would find it quite easy to decide which weight had the extra pound. Now you are given two other weights, one twenty pounds, the other twenty-one pounds. In this case, you would find it difficult to detect the extra pound.

This aspect of perceptual development is called **discrimination**. Children learn to discriminate among objects—that is, to tell the difference between one and another—through their own observations and experiences. For example, it makes little difference to a child whether a glass on the table is on his right or his left; all he cares about is whether he can reach it and whether it has milk in it. Thus, he may learn to discriminate between near and far, and full and empty, more quickly than he learns to discriminate between left and right.

Daily life requires the ability to make many other distinctions, most of which must be learned by experience. A child burned by a stove may at first stay away from the stove whether it is hot or cold; later he must learn that it was the heat, not the stove, that burned him. There are also discriminations to be made in the social sphere. At age three, a child may not grasp the difference between "mine" and "yours," but sooner or later guidance from others—maybe in the form of playground quarrels—will pound the message home.

Figure 7.4. Where's that marble? In order to find it, you must discriminate its color, shape, and texture—all obscured or modified by being in the grass—from that of other objects.

Because their experience is more limited, younger children generally require more clues than older children do to recognize objects and tell them apart. A three year old, for example, may require a great deal of detail to recognize a picture that a six year old can readily identify from a sketch or outline. Research suggests that it is only from about the fourth year on that children learn to distinguish pictures on the basis of form, size, orientation, or even color (Inhelder and Piaget, 1964).

Long before he can discriminate among graphic symbols, the infant learns to differentiate between facial expressions. His mother's pleasure or anger, for example, are evident to him from the way she smiles or the way she creases her brow. There is some evidence (Pick et al., 1972) that we learn very early in life to see a downward curving line as representing a frowning mouth and to see an upward curving line as representing a smile.

Discrimination involves the ability to recognize the distinctive features of similar but nonidentical things. One researcher (Gibson, 1963) has studied the development of this ability through the use of letterlike forms, or graphemes, a standard tool for studying perceptual development in children. By varying the distinctive features of each grapheme, she hoped to learn more about the development of discrimination in young children. Working with a group of 160 children aged four to eight, she showed each child a set of twelve standard figures one at a time. Then the child was shown a set of variations on the standard figures. The variations involved the curving of straight lines; the rotating, tilting, or reversing of the figures; and the closing or breaking of contours. The children were asked to choose the variant that exactly matched the standard. (In many cases no exact match was possible.) The number and the kinds of errors the children made were then counted and analyzed according to age group.

The experiment showed which errors are most characteristic of children of each age. Errors in closure (for example, confusing "O" and "C") were rare even among the youngest subjects tested. On the other hand, errors involving the slanting of previously unslanted lines were common even among the oldest subjects tested.

Marked differences were observed between the responses of four and five year old subjects. The older children were consistently more successful in distinguishing certain transformations: line-to-curve (the change from "U" to "V"), rotation ("M" to "W"), and reversal ("d" to "b"). A broad range of individual differences was observed with all age groups, but it seems clear that, in general, different types of perceptual abilities tend to appear only at particular ages, partly as a result of inner development and partly as a function of experience.

Recognizing the native alphabet

Because the ability to recognize the letters of our own alphabet and tell one letter from another is the basis of reading, it is a very important kind of discrimination ability. Most children begin to learn their own alphabet late in the preschool years, at about five or five and a half. That, of course, is the age when most children start school.

Figure 7.5. Recognition of the letters will come when the brain is sufficiently mature, but it helps to have lived with them before.

PLAYING WITH DOLLS

Suzie is spending a quiet afternoon at home with her dolls. Suddenly she throws little girl doll at mother doll, knocks father doll off the chair, and drowns brother doll in the sink. Suzie has expressed aggression with play.

At the preschool age, children who find it difficult to verbalize their emotions can project anger, frustration, or aggression through play activities. For this reason psychologists often use dolls and play furniture to test personality and study child development. Children arrange the toy furniture, give the dolls names, and tell stories about life in the dollhouse. While the child plays and talks to the dolls, the psychologist encourages and questions him. As the child becomes less aware of reality and more absorbed in his fantasy world, his activities reveal his emotional preoccupations. Test results show that, except in cases of excessive timidity or abnormal aggression, the behavior traits and attitudes revealed in doll play correspond with the way the child behaves in real life (Millar, 1968). Children raised in permissive homes, for example, play more with dolls representing adults. Characteristically, doll play is widely imaginative since make-believe allows the child to do what would normally be unacceptable.

It is still uncertain whether doll play purges emotions or whether it encourages aggressive habits. In boring surroundings it stimulates and excites children. It gives the child a chance to explore feelings, invent new situations, and understand puzzling events. Doll play can also be a social event, providing the child with the opportunity to associate with others his age.

Interestingly, dolls belonged to the adult world before becoming children's toys. In Europe, dolls were originally wooden statuettes of empresses. In Japan, wooden or clay images of the emperor and empress were bought for each daughter. On a special feast day of the dolls, the girl made offerings of sake and dried rice to the effigies. She took her dolls with her when she married and later gave them to her children. Each boy in a family also received a set of dolls; he would display his effigies of heroes and commanders on the feast day for flags.

Thus, boys and girls have enjoyed doll play down through the ages, despite the common belief that only girls look after dolls. It seems that the doll's proportionately small size in relation to the adult figure appeals to all children—dolls can be dismembered, dragged by the hair, or pushed to the bottom of the toybox.

But why do children play with dolls at all? As long ago as 1896, the psychologist G. S. Hall found that children do not treat dolls as if they were real babies, although doll play is often very emotional; he concluded that children like doll play because it is imaginative. It allows them to experiment with the things and relationships around them through the medium of fantasy. According to Piaget, make-believe play declines when the child becomes capable of thinking logically and of coping socially and emotionally. But we never really outgrow fantasy. Though its overt expression disappears, fantasy continues to find expression in daydreams.

It would be a mistake, however, to think that going to school is the only way the child learns the alphabet. Before she attends school, she has already learned a great deal about the alphabet from magazines, books, signs, and television. At first the letters look like so many interchangeable shapes. Then, rather suddenly, the letters begin to form a pattern—the child begins to discriminate the elements of her own language. She goes to school and learns to read; but more than that, she goes to school *because she is ready* to read.

Researchers (Keislar, Hsieh, and Bhasin, 1972) have shown that this is true in many societies besides our own. They reasoned that if an important part of alphabet learning occurred informally, before formal schooling began, then children who were nearing school age should be able to distinguish between letters (and even words) written in their own alphabet better than letters and words written in a different, unfamiliar alphabet. They tested 153 children, boys and girls, in Formosa, India, and the United States. The children, all preschoolers, were divided into three age groups and tested to see how well they discriminated characters in Chinese, Hindi, and Roman alphabets (English is written in the Roman alphabet).

The results of the study were fairly consistent from one society to the next. The two younger age groups could not discriminate reliably between characters printed in any language; the American children, for example, could not tell a "b" from a "w" any better than they could tell two Chinese characters apart. The oldest group, however, aged five to five and a half, did significantly better. The Indian children did best in Hindi, the Chinese children did best in Chinese, and the Americans did best in the Roman alphabet, even though none of these children had been taught to read in school.

How can we explain this? Part of the answer is that the growing preschooler develops a new discriminatory ability that allows him to tell one letter from another. To that extent, learning to read depends on such internal developments as maturation of the brain. A lot of it is social, however. Some children who watch "Sesame Street" on television can identify letters when they are only three years old. If you have ever watched Bert and Ernie and the other muppets, you know how delightful preschool education can be, no matter what age you are. It is also important that the child be encouraged and guided in learning the written language at home. A little girl who is surrounded by books and magazines, as well as television and toys, will learn from them. As she becomes more interested in the written language, her parents will often respond by teaching her letters and words. By the time she enters school, she has pretrained herself in recognition of the written language. Experience may be as important as age in taking the first step toward reading.

Studying Perception in Children

A major problem in the study of perceptual development in preschool children is the lag between a child's perception and his performance—that is, he perceives more than he can show. Can researchers adequately compensate for his performance limitations in designing tests? How do we really know what a child perceives? At age three, for example, the average child can draw a circle, but he cannot draw a square until age four, or a triangle until age five. This does not mean, however, that the three year old cannot tell a triangle from a circle.

Obviously researchers must be extremely cautious about using a child's drawings as an index of his perceptions. More generally, they must make the level of motor development achieved by the child an important consideration in devising tests. Although certain known motor capabilities generally characterize each age group, failure to allow for individual variation could lead the researcher to false conclusions.

It is also important to realize that features of the outer world that are obvious and important to a grownup may be far from obvious to a child. If a child draws a glass of water, he will usually draw a line showing the surface of the water parallel to the bottom of the glass, even if the glass is tilted. He may know that water in a glass has a level surface, but for him that fact may not be particularly important. A child with a coloring book may use his crayons with total disregard for the colors of real objects, but we should not suppose that he believes apples are blue and kittens green. A child's response to a test situation may reflect his perceptual priorities—the kind of differences he considers to be relevant—as much as his actual perceptions.

The difference—in this case an actual lag—between perception and performance was further explored in a recent study (Odum and Lemond, 1972). Children of various age groups were shown a variety of familiar facial expressions, including fear, joy, anger, disgust, and surprise. Subjects were asked to identify these expressions and then to recreate them. In most cases, the children could identify expressions far more easily than they could reproduce them. The lag between perception and performance did not seem to be significantly reduced with increasing age; performance improved considerably, but discrimination of expressions improved even more.

References

Bayley, N., and Bayer, L. M. The assessment of somatic androgyny. *American Journal of Physical Anthropology*, 1946, *4*, 433.

Breckenridge, M. E., and Murphy, M. N. *Growth and development of the young child*. Philadelphia: Saunders, 1969.

Brian, C. R., and Goodenough, F. L. The relative potency of color and form perception at various ages. *Journal of Experimental Psychology*, 1929, *12*, 197–213.

Feingold, B. Testimony before the Senate Select Committee on Nutrition and Human Needs, April 30, May 1–2, 1973. *Congressional Record*, October 30, 1973, p. S19736.

Flavell, J. H. *The developmental psychology of Jean Piaget*. New York, D. Van Nostrand, 1963.

Gardner, L. I. Deprivation dwarfism. *Scientific American*, 1972, *227*(1).

Gibson, E. J. Development of perception: Discrimination of depth compared with discrimination of graphic symbols. In J. C. Wright and J. Kagan (Eds.), Basic cognitive process in children. *Monograph of Social Research in Child Development*, 1963, *28* (2), 5–32.

Guttentag, Marcia. Negro-white differences in children's movement. *Perceptual and Motor Skills.* 1972, *35*, 435–436.

Inhelder, B., and Piaget, T. *The early growth of logic in the child.* New York: Harper, 1964.

Keislar, E. R., Hsieh, and Bhasin, C. An intercultural study: Discrimination and informal experience. *Reading Teacher,* Nov. 1972.

Meredith, H. V. Body size of contemporary groups of pre-school children studied in different parts of the world. *Child Development*, 1968, *39*, 335–369.

Millar, S. The psychology of play. London: Penguin, 1968.

Modreski, R., and Goss, A. E. Young children's names for and matches to form-color stimuli. *Journal of Genetic Psychology*, 1972, *121*, 283–293.

Odum, R. D., and Lemond, C. M. Developmental differences in the perception and production of facial expressions. *Child Development.* 1972, *43.* 359–369.

Pick, A. D., Hales, J. J., Christy, M. D., Frankel, G. W., and Glick, J. H. The effect of a human facial context on the discrimination and recognition of curved lines. *Psychonomic Science,* 1972, *27*(4). 239–242.

Schaefer, A. E., and Johnson, O. C. Are we well fed? The searches for an answer. *Nutrition Today,* 1969, *4*(1), 2–11.

Shaywitz, B. A., Finkelstein, J., Hellman, L., and Weitzman, E. D. Growth hormone in newborn infants during sleep-wake periods. *Pediatrics*, 1971, *48*(1), 103–109.

Sheldon, W. H. *The varieties of human physique.* New York: Harper, 1940.

SUMMARY

1   The preschool child not only grows in height and weight, but his body proportions begin to approximate the adult form and his nervous system matures. By age five the brain is 75 percent of its adult weight; myelinization of the nerve fibers is completed, permitting speedy transmission of nerve impulses.

2   Proper nutrition and health care are crucial to normal development. Children need proteins for building body cells, vitamins and minerals for structural development, and carbohydrates for energy. Poverty-stricken children often lack adequate nutrients and medical care and, as a result, may not develop to their full intellectual and physical potential. American children at all economic levels consume "junk foods" that endanger their development by filling them up without providing essential nutrients.

3   Theories that propose a link between body type and personality have proved unconvincing. However, physical development may influence personality; the better-developed child may become a leader, while the less-developed child may become timid and withdrawn.

4   Great advances in strength, speed, and coordination occur in the preschool years. The child also becomes increasingly skillful in handling tools and materials. At first he uses blocks, clay, and other materials to experiment with the medium rather than to make representational objects. Later, his longer attention span and improved skills result in more planning and precision. The child acquires status among playmates and a good self-image through the development of skills.

5   In young preschool children, the ability to perceive both the parts and the whole of an object at the same time is somewhat limited; the older preschooler learns to focus on details and fit them into the overall situation. He also makes use of unifying concepts, for which language is critical.

6

The improvement of attention is part of the child's perceptual development. Better memory and analytical skill, a growing ability to ignore distractions, and increased motivation all contribute to lengthening the attention span.

7

Preschool children learn to differentiate between objects through observation and experience. This process is sharpened as they develop the ability to recognize distinctive features in similar but nonidentical things. Learning to tell the letters of the alphabet apart depends on maturation of the brain and exposure to the alphabet at home and on television.

FURTHER READINGS

Chukovsky, K. *From two to five.* Berkeley: University of Calif., 1968.

    Observations by a Soviet poet and writer of children's books on the development of thought processes and the acquisition of language. Chukovsky says young children need fairy tales and that they use fantasy to come to terms with the real world. Also, that children have a natural creativity in language use that can be stifled or encouraged, depending on the response of adults.

McWilliams, M. *Nutrition for the growing years.* New York: Wiley, 1967.

    A nutritionist discusses suitable diets for each stage of development and explains why eating patterns change. The book has an interesting chapter on how to teach nutrition to nursery school children, at the same time teaching them something about color and form. Height and weight tables are included.

Smith, L. *The children's doctor.* Englewood Cliffs, N.J.: Prentice-Hall, 1969.

    Smith is a medical doctor who has had a popular television series. In this book he offers pediatric advice based on the patterns of development. The book emphasizes that children cannot learn until their neuromuscular mechanism is mature enough and clearly shows the relationship of physical development to activities and skills. An entire chapter is devoted to the hypermotor child.

Sparkman, B., and Carmichael, A. *Blueprint for a brighter child.* New York: McGraw-Hill, 1973.

    A small but explicit book that describes child development and tells how to bring out intelligence. Among other things, the authors tell why some toys are better than others for making children think and suggest simple games to teach the preschooler basic mathematical and verbal skills. They pioneered a preschool program in the South.

8
Cognition and Language

By age two, the child already understands a lot about what is going on around him. He knows his family and a large number of other people, and he usually knows what to expect from all of them. He has begun to understand and use language, and his memory may be surprisingly good. For example, two year old Joshua had a much older brother, who rarely visited the family and was practically a stranger to Joshua. The brother arrived for a visit one night after Joshua was asleep and then went to sleep himself, leaving in the hallway a guitar which he had brought with him on a visit six months before. When Joshua woke up the next morning, he delighted everyone (except his brother, who was still in bed) by pointing to the instrument case standing by the door and announcing: "Pete's guitar!"

Most children Joshua's age are alert to things around them, but they are only beginning to *organize* their perceptions. Over the next few years they will become reasoning and reasonable beings as they learn to think *about* events and people, time and space. Joshua, proudly announcing his discovery in two words, stands at the threshold of these developments; in this chapter we will look at some of the ways his intellectual world is about to change.

COGNITIVE DEVELOPMENT

Jean Piaget regards intelligence as a biological adaptation—as a system by means of which the individual maintains a balance between his own needs and the demands of the environment. When Piaget began his work, most psychologists subscribed to the view that a complete explanation of cognitive development could be found in the environment and the organism's responses to it. Piaget, on the other hand, emphasizes the ways the child develops from within—the constant patterns of growth and change in a variety of environments.

Unlike many earlier researchers, Piaget was not especially concerned with the content of thought or the variations of individual development. He did not study why one child is more clever than another or what the subject matter of a child's thoughts may be. Instead, he focused on the processes he thought were common to all children.

He found, for one thing, that children learn very early to recognize things and at the same time to make a variety of distinct sounds. But at first these two operations are unrelated. It is only with time and experience that the child begins to establish connections between sound and thing in order to ask for a toy. In other cases as well, the child has a tendency to integrate psychological structures into higher and more complex systems—a process Piaget calls *organization.*

All cognitive growth, according to Piaget, takes place by means of two processes: organization, which integrates one psychological structure with another, and *adaptation,* which modifies psychological structures to suit the environment. As we saw in Chapter 5, adaptation consists of assimilation and accommodation, two complementary processes that are present in every act of cognition. An individual assimilates each new experience to what he already knows, and at the same time he accommodates what he knows to take the new experience into account.

Assimilation and accommodation are the same at all ages, though the matters they deal with may become more "intellectual" as the child matures. A preschool child who hears thunder for the first time may think that someone has slammed a door loudly in the next room. His previous experience with loud noises forms his perceptions: the new experience has been assimilated to the preexisting psychological structure.

On second thought, however, the child may realize that the thunder was too loud to have been caused by someone in the house. Probably he will hear the thunder again and then begin to readjust all his ideas of loud noises and where they come from. Now, instead of fitting the new experience into the old categories, he revises his preconceptions in order to accommodate the new experience.

Piaget recognizes that many changes in our cognitive life occur little by little and that they occur sooner in some people's lives than in others'. Nevertheless, he believes that we do achieve certain capabilities at more or less definite times, (though we have long been building up to them) and that we then stay at that stage until we are ready to move up to the next. Although different people advance to the next stage at different times in their lives, Piaget maintains that the sequence of stages is the same for everybody. The period from birth to about two years old is, as we have seen, the sensorimotor period. From age two until age seven, the child's cognition is what Piaget calls "preoperational."

Preoperational Thought

The **preoperational** period of cognitive development, which can be subdivided into a *preconceptual* stage (roughly two to four years of age) and an *intuitive* stage (roughly four to seven), begins with the first appearance of symbolic representation. Symbolic representation is the substitution of a mental image, word, or object for something that is not immediately present.

The symbolic representation that characterizes preoperational thought differs from the sensorimotor intelligence of infancy in several fundamental ways. First, representational thought is faster and more flexible. Unlike sensorimotor intelligence, which can link actions and perceptions one at a time but cannot achieve a cohesive overview, representational thought can grasp many events at once and consequently can consider past, present, and future in a single effort. For example, a child may enjoy sailing a toy boat. Representational thought allows him to think about sailing it in the bathtub, in a mud puddle, or in a pond. He can consider which of these his mother will allow and where he would be most likely to meet his friends. Representational thought helps him to decide where he wants to sail his boat on this particular occasion.

Second, representational thought is not limited to goals of concrete action. The child at this stage is capable of reflection and of reexamining his knowledge; he can contemplate as well as act. The young sailor can remember that the last time he sailed a boat in a mud puddle it got stuck, and then when he sailed it

PIAGET'S PERIODS OF COGNITIVE DEVELOPMENT

Sensorimotor Period (birth to 24 months)

Preoperational Period (2 to 7 years)

Coordinates schemata, engages in symbolic thinking, and makes novel responses. However, cognition has four limitations:
1. Centration: focuses attention on one aspect of a situation and disregards the others. Unable to take two dimensions into account at the same time (e.g. size and number) and thus unable to understand the relation between them.
2. Inconsistent in conservation of continuous qualities, such as length, quantity, weight, and volume.
3. Focuses on static aspects of reality. Cannot follow or fully understand dynamic features.
4. Thought is irreversible. Cannot understand how something may change and then return to its original condition.

Concrete Operational Period (7 to 11 years)

Formal Operational Period (11 years on)

Figure 8.1. Whatever the play house represents to the boys—a castle to be stormed or a burning building to be saved—they have shared the idea and are playing it out.

in the pond, he lost it.

Third, representational thought enables the child to deal intellectually with numbers and such qualities as size. By thinking with symbols, he can extend his scope beyond himself and the concrete objects he encounters every day. The young sailor's boat may have one mast and one sail, and although he may never have seen a boat with more, his understanding of number enables him to conceive of a boat with three—or, in principle, six or twelve—masts and any number of sails per mast.

Finally, representational thought can be codified and, most important, socialized; that is, we can translate our thoughts into forms that can be communicated to other individuals. Whereas sensorimotor intelligence is private and unshareable, the child at the preoperational stage can sail his boat with a friend, and the two of them can imagine together that one is the captain and the other the first mate. The enriched intelligence and imagination of the preoperational stage can make even private play into a representation of shared social experience.

The development of preoperational thought is a slow and gradual process. According to Piaget, the origin of representation is imitation. For example, a child may at first turn his torso in imitation of a closing door, but gradually his imitations become more subtle and internalized. He may begin to close his fist, for example, instead of turning his body to imitate the door. Still later, his fingers twitch as a remnant of his previous imitation. Finally, the imitation becomes completely internalized. The representational function has matured when imitation takes the form of a purely mental image.

Characteristics of Preoperational Thought

Although the changes that announce preconceptual thought are of immense importance in cognitive development, the thinking of the preschool child is far from mature. One of Piaget's central themes in describing the preoperational stage is the egocentric quality of the preschool child's thought and behavior. Anyone who has ever attempted to carry on a logical discussion with a young child knows how frustrating it can be. It does not generally occur to the preschool child to adjust her thoughts or her expressions of those thoughts in such a way that they may be logical to anyone other than herself. Because she finds no need to reexamine her own logic, she is generally incapable of thinking about her own thought processes. Most adults make a strong effort to understand what children are trying to say, so egocentrism does not begin to decline until increased social interaction with other children forces the child to acknowledge her mutually dependent relationship with other thinking beings.

A related feature of preoperational thought is called centration. **Centration** is the child's tendency to center her attention on a single feature of an object or situation. Because of her inability to balance the various features involved, the preschool child frequently errs in her judgments. For example, she may insist that a tall thin container holds more water than a short wide one even when she sees the contents of one transferred to the other. Here she is centering on the height of the liquid.

Furthermore, preoperational thought is usually static. The preschool child is concerned more with states than with transformations, so she may be incapable of taking the in-between steps into account. She can focus on the beginning and the end of a process—for example, the changing of a ball of clay into a long, thin snake—but find it extremely difficult to conceptualize the intermediate stages of the transformation.

Preoperational thought also tends to be irreversible. The preschool child cannot retrace her steps to reexamine a conclusion she has already formed. She tends to behave as though thoughts are as irreversible in her mind as physical events are in time. A child at this stage of development finds it extremely difficult to understand how liquid transferred from a tall thin container to a short wide one and then back again can regain its original appearance. She cannot readily conceive of the possibility that anything may return unchanged to a previous condition.

These, then, are the characteristic features of preoperational thought: it is egocentric, static, and irreversible. None of these features is unique to the preoperational stage; sometimes our thought may show one or more of them even

Egocentrism

If we say that Charlotte is "egocentric," what does it mean? That she is only interested in herself, has little concern for others, and tends to be selfish? But what if Charlotte is about three or four? She is still egocentric, but at her age we don't expect her to act otherwise.

Then what do we mean by **egocentrism** in a child? When Charlotte talks to you she seems to expect you to know everything she knows. If you join her in a game, she has her own rules and follows only them. If your ideas conflict with Charlotte's, she doesn't pay them any attention. She plays by a very rigid "moral" code: if you break one of her toys by mistake, you can't expect her to forgive you just because it was an accident.

Piaget refers to this kind of thinking as "egocentric." There is an egocentric stage at which the child is interested primarily in herself, though not out of conceit or selfishness. She has just discovered the idea of "self" but not "others." Egocentrism, as it appears in normal child development, is an integral part of growing up.

Piaget focuses on two major aspects of egocentrism: language and moral judgment. The egocentric child uses language mainly for practice and for communication with herself. When we adults speak with people, we automatically consider how much they already know of what we are talking about. The egocentric child cannot do this because she is not yet able to take another's point of view.

According to Piaget, young children can behave morally only by learning and following rules. The child's conception of the rules comes from an authority figure, a parent, whom the child believes is all-knowing and infallible. The child thus sees the rules as sacred and inflexible.

Piaget also found that children in the egocentric stage are much more concerned with the material outcome of an event than with the intention of the actor. The child, he says, is unable to put himself in the place of the actor, to empathize with another's feelings. Therefore real morality is not possible, because without this empathy the child can have no real system of ethics.

There is some evidence, based on more recent studies, that the egocentric child is not necessarily as rigid as Piaget supposed. The studies show that younger children often talk and listen to each other carefully and sympathetically. Young children also play together in cooperation with each other, and may consider intention in making moral judgments. Piaget's discovery of childhood egocentrism has led later researchers, using more sensitive and sophisticated analytical methods, to study the same question. This new research will probably redefine the concept of egocentrism in child development.

much later in life. During the preschool years, however, these features are interdependent and mutually reinforcing. Taken together, they make preoperational thought distinctive.

Reasoning

Efforts at reasoning may take a number of different forms during the preschool period. The most fundamental type is "reasoning" based on memory of past events. A child who is bathed every day after dinner may observe her mother filling the bathtub at that time and think: "Mommy is filling the tub, so it must be time for my bath." Actually, this is an observation based on memory and not a logical reasoning process. It might be supposed that the girl's thought is based on deductive reasoning: Mommy's filling the tub at this hour has always been followed by a bath before, so filling the tub again today will again be followed by a bath. It is more likely, however, that the girl recognizes a simple situation that she remembers from before and that her thought is automatic rather than reasoned out.

A second type of "reasoning"—or more accurately, nonreasoning—characteristic of the preschool period is the adoption of personal preference as evidence for matters of fact. Michael may want to play outside even though there is a violent storm. His mother's objection that he will get wet makes no impression on him; he may actually believe that because he wants to go out he will not get wet. In an adult we would call this wishful thinking, but in the preschooler it is natural. He has not yet realized that facts can be quite independent of his strongest desires.

Figure 8.2. The cause of her mirth may not actually be in the book. In any case, *he* doesn't see it.

Preschoolers' reasoning is limited in other ways. In 1965 the East Coast was struck by a massive power failure that blacked out most of the Northeast for a day and a half. At the exact moment the power failed, a boy of about five ran his tricycle into an electric pole in upstate New York. According to newspaper accounts, the boy saw the lights go out all over town and believed his collision was the cause. He ran home fully expecting to be punished for having broken the power system. This illustrates that although preschoolers have begun to develop a grasp of cause and effect relations, it is still a shaky grasp. They do not yet know how to fit chance and coincidence into the system.

In our society, adult reasoning is based on two logical processes: we reason from general rules to particular facts, or we start with the particular facts and use them to formulate general rules. These processes are called *deduction* and *induction,* respectively. It is typical of preschoolers that they resort to a third, invalid logic called *transduction.* Like the boy who thought he caused the blackout, the preschooler may assume two particular events are connected just because they occur together. If a child's father comes home from work every day as night begins to fall, the child may assume that one causes the other; he may even try to make Daddy come through the door by turning on the lights.

As he grows older, the preschool child grows more flexible in his reasoning. His thoughts become less centered and more reversible. Slowly, he develops the ability to balance one feature of an event with another and to understand the various transformations that are involved. When the child can consistently apply these elements of logical thinking to his reasoning process, the stage of preoperational thought has come to an end.

CONCEPTS

Although the preschool child has left the infantile period far behind, he has a picture of the world that is widely different from the one he will have just a few years later. To understand the child's world in this period, it is necessary to learn how he understands—and in what ways he fails to understand—the basic concepts of time, space, quantity, and relation.

Time

The concept of time is difficult for the preschool child. Having had little past that he can remember, he has only a scanty basis for conceptualizing notions of past, present, and future. Generally, children seem to exhibit a clearer understanding of "yesterday" and "today" than of "tomorrow."

The concept of time is closely related to the notions of motion and speed. Because the child has had little experience in dealing with distance and velocity, he tends to confuse time with space. A four year old boy is taken for two drives lasting about the same time but to different destinations and is told that on the second trip he went farther than on the first. He may then suppose that the second trip lasted longer.

If on a third trip the car stops frequently for gas or food, the boy may be convinced that this trip was the longest, although there was no real difference in elapsed time. Here we can see that his centration on stopping points is very important to his estimation of time; his inability to decentrate prevents him from taking certain elements into account, such as the speed of the car.

Most preschool children are incapable of adding successive intervals of time. Given that durations A, B, and C are equal, for example, the child cannot deduce that $A + B = B + C$. Again, it is the inability to concentrate on two aspects of a problem simultaneously that limits the child in his comprehension of this fundamental principle of logic. In their estimates of the passage of time, children seem to be more concerned with ending points than with starting points.

Space

As adults, we are very much concerned with spatial orientation: indeed, we use a great variety of words to describe relations in space. *Up* and *down, left* and *right, under* and *over, here* and *there, in* and *out* help us to achieve a clear conception of how things are situated in space.

A young child does not start with all these linguistic aids to help him understand space. He learns to deal with and name spatial phenomena as they affect him personally. The word *left* and *right,* for example, are meaningless to him until he is taught to raise his right hand or turn to the left.

Many aspects of time and space are closely interrelated. For example, the elements of starting and stopping—the beginning point and the end point—are common to both phenomena. Many of the child's misconceptions about time have close counterparts in his efforts to deal with space. The tendency to centrate, the irreversibility of thought processes, and the inability to concentrate on transformational states all make it extremely difficult for children to make mature judgments concerning the measurement of space.

Drawing by Garrett Price; © 1955
The New Yorker Magazine, Inc.

Quantity

Adult perception of quantity generally rests on two fundamental concepts: *conservation* and *one-to-one correspondence*. These concepts are not usually used consciously, but they account for our ability to make sense of a world where it is often important to make accurate estimates of quantity under conditions that may be confusing or misleading.

In preschool children these concepts are still poorly developed. The tests used by Piaget to investigate them often involved presenting children with two identical beakers filled with identical amounts of water, or asking children to examine or handle identical balls of clay. Then, as the child watched, the shape of the water or clay was changed; the water might be poured from a short, wide beaker into a tall, narrow one, or the clay might be molded into a narrow sausage shape. When the child consistently recognizes that the changes in form do not change the amount of water or clay involved, he has learned to conserve quantity.

At the age of about four, children are usually quite unable to conserve quantity. In the experiments with water, for example, the four year old will usually concentrate on the height of the water in the beaker; being unable to decentrate, he will not understand that the quantity of water has remained constant. By the age of five or six the ability to conserve has begun to develop, and it is well established by about age seven. It is interesting to notice that conservation of different properties develops at different ages. At age six, Sara may have a sure grasp of conservation of quantity; at the same time she will almost certainly not be able to conserve continuous weight or volume, because these concepts do not develop until several years later.

Another aspect of quantity is number, and this is where the concept of one-to-one correspondence is important. Given a number of objects, an adult can construct a second set with the same number simply by counting. If the given set contains six members, for example, we simply take six other objects to create the second set. Even if we were unable to count, however, we could still create a second set by matching up the new objects with the originals one by one.

As adults, we take it for granted that quantities are not altered by physical arrangement. Ten pennies remain ten pennies whether they are in a line, in a circle, or in a pocket. Neither this concept—referred to as conservation of number—nor that of one-to-one correspondence is at all obvious to the preschool child, who is unable to compensate for the effect of density on length. Later in her development she may consider either length *or* density, but it is not until the end of the preoperational stage that she can consider both factors simultaneously and then divorce these spatial elements from her conception of number. Preschool children may attend to number rather than length, however, when the quantities involved are extremely small.

The ability to count does not necessarily indicate a mature concept of quantity. Children may count equal numbers and still deny numerical equality. In Figure 8.3, for example, a child who can count may insist that the top row contains more pennies than the bottom row even though she agrees that each contains five.

Figure 8.3. Which row has more pennies? The top row—as seen by preschoolers.

Relation

The ability to conceive of relations is one that begins to develop in infancy. The infant can discriminate between objects and, to some degree, differentiate levels of intensity. For example, he perceives that one sound is louder than another or that one object is larger than another.

As we might expect, the preschool child has difficulty in dealing with relations that involve more than two elements. If he is handed two beanbags, he may be able to say that the green one, for example, is heavier than the yellow one. He can make such absolute distinctions rather easily. But if we now give him a red beanbag that is even lighter than the yellow one, he may be unable to tell us which of the first two was the heavier. He centers on the immediate experience and becomes uncertain about the relationship he learned just a moment ago.

Piaget devised a number of experiments designed to test children's grasp of order among objects. One study involved the ordering of a series of different-sized sticks. The child was given ten sticks and told to arrange them in ascending order—that is, to put the smallest stick first, the next smallest second, and so forth.

The youngest group tested (ages four to five) offered a variety of unsuccessful solutions to the problem. Some created an entirely random arrangement. Others began correctly and then continued at random. An interesting approach attempted by some children was to select any stick at random to start and then to line up the sticks in such a way that the top of each stick extended slightly above the top of the preceding stick, but without regard to the bottoms.

This solution—focusing on the tops of the sticks and ignoring the bottoms— exemplifies the inability of young children to center on more than one aspect of a situation at the same time. Although five and six year olds were considerably more successful, they too experienced much difficulty, proceeding in a manner that might best be characterized as trial and error. It is not until after the preschool years that children consistently exhibit the ability to devise a logical plan of action in order to solve such problems.

Classification

One of the most important operations to develop during the preschool years is that of classification. The ability to organize objects and ideas into useful categories is a fundamental prerequisite for mature reasoning.

Classes have four fundamental properties. First, classes are *mutually exclusive*. No figure, for example, can belong both to the class of circles and the class of squares. Second, a class can be determined by its *intension*—that is, by the common characteristic shared by all its members. Third, a class can be determined by its *extension*—that is, by the list of all its members. And fourth, intension must define extension; we should be able to name the members of a class if we know the characteristic that they have in common.

In order to test the preschool child's ability to classify, experimenters present the child with an assortment of objects and then request that he group the ones that go together. Young children rarely complete this task in a consistent way.

Some of them create entirely random "classes." For example, they group red circles with blue triangles and green squares. Others begin to form classes on one principle and then abandon it in favor of some other principle. For example, a child may assemble a red triangle, a green triangle, and a blue triangle and then switch over to a blue circle, a blue square, and then, perhaps, to a red square. Although he perceives similarity of attributes, he is not yet able to concentrate throughout on a single attribute. Children also have difficulty in applying the notions of "all" and "some" which are necessary for purposes of classification.

As the preschool years near their end, children begin to group objects successfully and to exhibit the ability to subdivide groups into constitutent components as well; however, the five or six year old who accomplishes this task may still fail to fully understand the true nature of classification. Some concepts, such as color, are established early, but the development of mature conceptual capabilities is not complete until after the preschool period.

MENTAL IMAGERY

Piaget considered the problem of the child's mental imagery to be central to the entire study of cognition and language. Mental imagerv was commonly viewed as bundles of sensations which were linked through associations. Piaget rejected this accepted view. Accordingly, what he attempted to do was demonstrate that the ability to form mental images is the essential first step in the development of mature thought.

The study of mental imagery is difficult because images, by their very nature, are private. They can only be externalized in a simulated form. The most direct means of examining mental imagery is through language—that is, by allowing the subject to describe his own images verbally. Unfortunately, it is difficult enough for most of us to describe the objects we have before our eyes, let alone the images we have in our minds. This difficulty is magnified many times in the case of children because of their limited ability to talk.

A second approach to the study of mental imagery is the analysis of drawings. This method shares some of the drawbacks of the linguistic approach. Few children—indeed, few adults—can draw well. In addition, the kind of drawing needed to depict a mental image requires a good memory. But memory is not well developed during the preschool years, and a child cannot reproduce an image that he can no longer remember.

A third approach involves the child's selection of a drawing from a collection assembled by the experimenter. This method bypasses the limitations of a child's artistic skills and helps overcome the problem of memory retention; however, the drawings from which the child must choose may be no more than rough approximations of his own actual images. The omission or addition of certain details to the original image may lead to a faulty interpretation on the part of the experimenter.

Clearly, none of these approaches alone is adequate to indicate accurately the nature of mental images. In combination, however, these techniques have been used effectively to study the development of mental imagery in preschool children.

Imagery in the Preschooler

During early infancy, a child responds almost exclusively to events that occur in the present and to objects that are within his sensory range at the moment. Around the age of eighteen months, she begins to have mental images. As we have seen, these images originate as imitative actions that grow increasingly internalized. The child becomes able to represent to herself past events and objects that are not before her at the moment. This ability is a prerequisite for symbolic thought.

The first images that children are able to produce are essentially static; they recreate an object or a scene whose elements are constant and unchanging. Young children find it relatively easy to form a mental picture of situations that do not involve movement or transition.

A far more difficult image for young children is the imagery of movement, or kinetic imagery. In one experiment which was designed to test the development of kinetic imagery, some children were shown a pair of stacked blocks. The top block was subsequently displaced in such a way as to overhang the bottom block. After a while the top block was returned to its original position. The children were then asked to draw the blocks as they had appeared in their displaced position. They were also shown an assortment of drawings and asked to select from these drawings the one which correctly pictured the blocks when they were displaced.

As a control, the children were also asked to draw the displaced blocks while looking at them.

This experiment demonstrated that preschool children cannot form a clear mental image of a situation that involves movement. The pictures drawn and selected by the children suggested a general awareness of movement, but no distinct image of its exact nature. The child forms a general impression of the situation although he is incapable of analyzing specific details.

During the preschool years, and in fact up to about age seven, the child's imagery is extremely static, and it therefore imposes sharp limits on his impressions and thinking. His imagery is distorted from an adult point of view because of his inability to decentrate, to understand the dynamic aspects of the environment, or to link his isolated observations into a meaningful picture of the world around him.

LANGUAGE

One of the most fascinating aspects of human development is the acquisition of language. Psychologists and linguists—and psycholinguists, whose studies include aspects of both fields—have devoted a great deal of attention to examining the relative importance of heredity, environment, and training in the development of language. How is the essentially nonverbal infant transformed into an active member of the adult language community in the span of a few years?

The study of language development in the twentieth century has been characterized by several shifts in emphasis. The diary studies conducted in the early part of the century, in which the linguist or psychologist recorded the development of his own children, were rejected as unavoidably biased. Instead, psychologists began to study patterns of language development in a wide cross-section of children. Their studies concentrated on such matters as the frequency with which certain words occur, the parts of speech used, and the average sentence length typical of a sampling of children's utterances at various ages.

Eventually it became apparent, however, that these studies tended to create a static picture of language development. In stressing certain milestones of development—for example, that children produce their first sentences between the ages of two and three—early researchers tended to overlook the transformational elements of language development. The transition from two-word utterances to three-word sentences, for example, is characterized not only by a difference in sentence length but by significant changes in the child's understanding of syntax and grammatical rules as well. In the 1950s, researchers began to work with smaller groups of children in order to discover not what *form* language takes but what children *know* about language at various stages of development. This approach was subsequently replaced by the effort to formulate a rule system that accounts for the child's structuring and use of language.

ALL THE COLORS OF THE RAINBOW

When we learn to name the colors of the rainbow—or the colors in our crayon box—we discover at the same time that they are distinct hues. What makes this a discovery is that we have to sharpen our perception to see, for the first time, the difference between similar colors such as yellow and orange, or violet and blue. We never perceived them as different until we made the effort to tell them apart.

For some of us, learning the colors seems effortless. We learn the names of all the colors without ever stopping to ask ourselves whether the color we are looking at is blue or green. Others of us set out consciously to distinguish among the colors and get their names straight. The names are easy to remember, but actually seeing the individual hue for the first time is a matter of perceiving for oneself what one has never perceived before.

No one can convey the perception to you. Someone can put the color in front of you and show you matching and contrasting hues, but in the last analysis you must perceive it for yourself. And when you do, the discovery that there *is* such a color as orange can be quite exciting. First you see it in your coloring book, then in your T-shirt, then in pumpkins and other natural objects where the color is not so pure. The discovery is made again and again, and it is exciting every time.

In principle, almost everyone is capable of perceiving all the colors of the spectrum, from red to violet. The colors are everywhere in the world, and our eyes and brains are equipped to "read" them. We know that many animals besides man have excellent color vision and that they can distinguish between similar objects of different colors. Not all human cultures, however, divide the spectrum into the same colors as we do. In the Greek language, for example, there is no single word for blue; two distinct words are used for two different shades of blue. In Japanese, on the other hand, a single word is used to refer to the two colors we call blue and green. And a very different way of seeing the world was found in Southern Italy sixty years ago; according to an English traveler (Douglas, 1915), Calabrian peasants called all objects either black or white.

Recently, the emphasis has shifted from the description of language development to its explanation. Psycholinguists are attempting not only to define the grammatical rules by which early speech is governed, but to examine the relation of those rules to the child's understanding of language meaning and functions. In this way, the study of language is more closely integrated into the study of cognitive development as a whole.

Word Meaning

By the age of eighteen months, most children are speaking in "sentences" of one and two words. Psycholinguistic research indicates that the meanings that children assign to their early utterances often bear little resemblance to conventional word usage. A statement such as "dog find," for example, may mean "help me find the dog," "look what the dog found," "the dog found my toy," or some other notion. To understand it, parents need clues from the child's previous use of words and the present context.

A recent study examined the relationship between word order and the ability of young children to understand simple commands (Wetstone and Friedlander, 1973). Experimenters discovered that very young children generally respond to commands such as "Give to ball the Mommy" as readily as they do to "Give the ball to Mommy." Older children, with a better understanding of language, find it harder to understand the scrambled sentence. The young children apparently respond to familiar verbal clues, not to details of syntax and grammatical structure. They utilize the parts of a sentence they understand and ignore the rest.

Developmental psychologists have been especially interested in the acquisition of terms of comparison and relation. This is important because it is only when children have mastered such terms that researchers can ask them questions to learn how they perceive relationships.

Children appear to use and understand comparative terms such as *more, big,* and *long* before they are able to grasp their opposites, *less, little,* and *short.* Researchers (Donaldson and Balfour, 1968) who have studied three and four year olds have found that they have a clear understanding of the concepts "more" and "same" but that these children have not yet learned how to use the words which signify those concepts. For instance, when a child said "more," he consistently meant "more." However, when he said "less," he also meant "more." When a three year old described two things as "different," he might well mean that they were the same.

It is clear, then, that we cannot analyze children's word meanings according to most conventional adult standards. Until children learn these adult standards, they impose their own meanings on words on the basis of private and individual rules. Therefore, our understanding of these rules ultimately depends less on cataloging individual statements than on studying the relationship between language and thought.

Grammar

It is true that few adults have a clear understanding of the formal rules of grammar; yet, whether or not we know a gerund from a participle, most of us are able to speak in essentially well formed sentences that can be readily understood by other English-speaking people. Preschool children seem to achieve a fundamental mastery of the rules of language prior to any formal training. How do children who are as young as three or four acquire an understanding of grammatical speech?

In analyzing the structure of a child's utterances, we should not assume that he will either use adult grammar or none at all. It seems, in fact, that his grammar is based on rules of his own making.

The child's first sentences, as we saw in Chapter 5, have only two words. Some of them take the form of pivot word plus x word, but others do not have a pivot structure. One typical sentence structure among young children appears to take the form of noun plus noun. Consider, for example, the sentences "cup glass" (I see a cup and a glass), "party hat" (This is a party hat), "Kathryn sock" (This is Kathryn's sock), "sweater chair" (The sweater is on the chair), and "Kathryn ball" (Kathryn will throw the ball). These five sentences represent five distinct semantic relationships—conjunction, attribution, possession, location, and subject-object. Unlike adult statements, the meaning of these utterances cannot be deduced out of context. "Kathryn ball," for example, could mean "Kathryn wants the ball," "Kathryn lost the ball," or "the ball belongs to Kathryn" (Slobin, 1971).

Sentences composed of three or more words require more grammar than a two-word sentence, and this is difficult for the preschool child. Certain grammatical transformations that are required in order to form questions and negations, for example, are very common sources of confusion for children at this age. The child who can successfully transform the statement "He can leave" into the question "Why can he leave?" may then try to express the negative question with "Why he can't leave?"

When children make attempts to correct their own grammar on the basis of observed rules, the phenomenon of overregularization frequently results. The child who has already learned to say "he went" and "he came," for example, may suddenly begin to say "he goed" and "he comed" instead. He tries to make these words conform to known patterns because he wants to regularize and perfect his speech.

Toward Communication

From his observations of children at play, Piaget concluded that during the pre-operational stage, speech serves two distinct functions. It may be noncommunicative—*egocentric*, in Piaget's phrase—or it may be communicative. Egocentric speech is an essentially private exercise, but it shades gradually into communicative, social speech.

Piaget described three basic manifestations of egocentric speech: repetition (in which a child repeats someone else's words), monologue (in which a child speaks aloud at length to no one), and the collective monologue (in which children speak aloud at length in the presence of others without making an effort to be understood). Egocentric speech functions both as a form of play and as language practice. Besides enjoying his own speech patterns, the child who talks aloud to himself may believe that his words are somehow related to their referents in reality. He may, for example, say "I move the table" as he attempts to do so in the belief that speaking the words will help him to perform the task.

Even speech that is intended to convey information to others is limited, at first, by the child's basic egocentrism: he does not try very hard to make his speech intelligible to others. In telling a story, for example, he uses pronouns without specifying their referents. "She can't come in my room," he may say, and never say who. Also, he juxtaposes bits and pieces of information without interrelating them. In the early preschool years, children find it difficult to see the world through the eyes of others, and thus they do not realize that a particular effort is necessary to make their speech really communicative. Because adults often make a special effort to understand a child's speech, there may be little pressure on the child to adjust his language to meet the needs of others until other children begin to challenge his egocentrism with their own.

"*It says 'No cats.'*"

Drawing by Chon Day; © 1960
The New Yorker Magazine, Inc.

Figure 8.4. As he draws, the child may be talking to himself, telling himself what he is doing, what the figure means, something his father said last week, or a fantasy that just occurred to him.

Piaget conceives of cognitive development as broadly following a path from the nonsocial, nonverbal thought of the infant to the socially expressed thought of the school-age child with the egocentric stage of the preschool child in between. Piaget argues that social pressures demand the development of more effective modes of communication and force the child to convert much of his private thought into language, thus drawing him out of his egocentrism.

The Russian psychologist L. S. Vygotsky agrees with Piaget that egocentric speech is not successful as communication, but he rejects Piaget's belief that children *intend* their egocentric speech to be uncommunicative. Vygotsky's own studies of children at play revealed a close relationship between their egocentric speech and their nonverbal activities. He describes the case of the child who, in the process of drawing a streetcar, broke the point of his pencil. "It's broken," he said aloud and, taking up the watercolors, began to draw a *broken* streetcar as he continued to speak aloud about the change.

At first, Vygotsky observed, egocentric speech marks the end result or turning point in an activity, then it is gradually shifted toward the middle, and finally to the beginning of the activity. When it comes at the beginning it has a directing, planning function (Vygotsky, 1962). Vygotsky relates this phenomenon to the normal developmental pattern in which a child first creates a drawing and then names it, then some months or years later names his drawing when it is halfway finished, and finally decides his intentions before beginning.

On the basis of these observations, Vygotsky has come to believe that the egocentric speech of the preoperational stage differs only in form from the more developed speech of older children. Egocentric speech, he suggests, should not be considered a fundamentally distinct type of language use but a transition from vocal to inner speech. When older children, after solving a problem silently, are asked to describe their thoughts, they generally reveal the same process that the preschool child expresses aloud. In Vygotsky's view, inner speech serves the same function in adults as egocentric speech does in children.

Vygotsky argues that the child's speech is intended to communicate right from the start. As the child turns inward, some of his speech becomes noncommunicative, or egocentric. In effect, the child begins to think aloud. Gradually he begins to employ his power of inner speech to serve the function previously served by his vocalized egocentric speech.

Language and Environment

Each of us learns language not only in a particular society, or "speech community," but in a particular region, neighborhood, town, and family. Exactly what we learn, and when and how well we learn it, depends on many things: Are we rich or poor? Black or white? Do we live in Maine, California, or Texas? Is Daddy a farmer, a teacher, or a construction worker? The way we learn our language will depend to some extent on the answers to questions like these.

Studies indicate that economic, social, and cultural factors play a significant role in language ability during the preschool years. The speech of children from middle-class families tends to be more complex, fluent, and grammatical than that of children of lower socioeconomic status. Generally, middle-class children speak more frequently, use more complex sentence forms, and hesitate less in speaking. Lower-class children tend to use pronouns where middle-class children use nouns; this makes the language of the lower-class children less flexible and more closely tied to its context.

Sociocultural status seems to influence not only sentence structure, but the types of words children learn as well. Middle-class children seem to master action words better than lower-class children do (Jeruchimowicz et al., 1971). This is probably less because they have a better understanding of action concepts than because they are given more opportunity and encouragement to learn and use abstract terminology.

However, studies that judge children's language abilities on the basis of their command of standard English may lead to the unjustified conclusion that children

BLACK ENGLISH

Recently, some linguists and educators have reached the conclusion that black children have been treated unfairly, especially by the educational system, because of their use of language.

The idea of Black English, as it is called, has become a highly controversial issue during the last few years. Most white Americans are convinced that the distinctive speech pattern of black Americans is a sloppy, "illiterate" rendition of Standard English, and that it should be remedied by education. A growing number of linguists, however, are suggesting that Black English is a distinct dialect with its own rules of pronunciation and grammar.

The roots of Black English can be traced back to the days of the American slave trade. It was not uncommon at that time for slave traders to separate Africans who spoke the same language. In order to communicate with one another, the Africans were forced to develop a commonly understood language based on that of their captors.

In succeeding generations, a small number of blacks began to learn the structure of Standard English. The great majority, however, were in no position to receive any formal training in their owners' language. Instead, they developed a new language by grafting English words onto the structure of their native languages and pidgin dialects. In the twentieth century, increased exposure to Standard English, improved educational opportunities, experiences in the armed forces, and urbanization contributed to the development of the dialect that was to emerge as Black English.

One major difference between Black English and Standard English involves pronunciation. Words like *find, found,* and *fond* may be pronounced almost exactly alike, the vowels being very similar in Black English. The pronunciation of *that* as *dat, mouth* as *mouf,* and *help* as *hep,* are examples of consonant changes characteristic of Black English.

The most significant difference between Black and Standard English, however, involves the rules of grammar. It would appear that Black English does not involve the random dropping of suffixes and tense distinctions, as grammarians once assumed; rather, Black English is based on a systematic grammar that adheres consistently to its own rules. Each of the statements *I done go, I done gone, I been done gone,* and *I done been gone,* for example, expresses a specific state of affairs.

The function of speech in the black community also differs significantly from its function in the white community. The black speaker is much more conscious of his style and fluency.

The child who has grown up hearing his parents, friends, and neighbors speaking Black English may have difficulty adapting to the demands of his teachers. Educators have become increasingly aware that the apparent learning difficulties of many black students may actually be rooted in a language problem. Some linguists have gone so far as to suggest that ghetto children be taught to read Black English first.

At this point, the future of Black English is uncertain. Undoubtedly, it will continue to be spoken for some time. Perhaps the traditional dialect of the black community will be used as a teaching aid that may serve to reduce the antagonism that presently exists between some teachers and their black students.

of minority groups are deficient in language skills. What some studies may fail to take into account is that the language of a minority may be different without being inferior.

At the same time, a child from a low-income neighborhood may speak like her parents and friends and still have an excellent understanding of standard English. In recent studies focusing on language comprehension rather than language production, it has been discovered that, on their own terms, low-income children often have much greater language skill than they used to be given credit for.

INTELLIGENCE AND ITS MEASUREMENT

Probably because a child can talk and reason in the preschool period, IQ tests given at this time are more reliable—more likely to yield similar scores from one time to the next—than tests given in infancy. IQ is still more variable, however, than it will be after the child is age six. Some individuals vary more widely in IQ tests than others. The preschoolers that seem to have the most constant IQs are those with subnormal intelligence.

The most widely used intelligence test given to preschool children is the Stanford-Binet test. It consists of a series of subtests that range from very easy to very difficult. A typical item for two year olds, for example, is the building of a block tower; three year olds are asked to identify the parts of the body, and four year olds to identify certain pictures and extract information from them. The child takes the subtests one after another in order of increasing difficulty, and the most difficult one he can pass indicates his mental age.

The directions for taking the Stanford-Binet test are given orally, and the tasks required depend increasingly on vocabulary. It would be possible, therefore, for a child to fail a subtest merely because he could not understand the directions or express his thoughts, not because the substance of the test was beyond him. Furthermore, the language used in the Stanford-Binet test comes from middle-class usage, and the test has long been recognized to have a middle-class bias. This means that it is less reliable in testing the intelligence of children who are not from the middle class.

Another difficulty with the Stanford-Binet test is that it is designed to measure a general level of intelligence, not the particular elements or aspects that comprise intelligence. Conceivably, therefore, a child could be brilliant in some ways and yet get an average score on the test. In view of all of these limitations, psychologists have recently placed less importance on IQ.

What are some of the factors that influence the development of intelligence? A recent study (Scott and Smith, 1972) indicates that maternal IQ and educational background are not directly relevant factors but that certain circumstances of family life are of tremendous importance. Children from families that not only emphasize language development and academic achievement, but also provide materials in the home for general learning, are usually more intelligent than children from families that do not do these things.

Figure 8.5. What can a gerbil teach a child? A great deal, perhaps, that is difficult to test for. It also attracts him to the preschool center, where he can learn a great deal from the surroundings.

PRESCHOOLS AND DAY CARE

In the past, the preschool years were looked upon by many people as merely a time for children to "enjoy being children" before taking on the burden of formal education. Although no one today would deny that it is important for children to enjoy themselves, parents also recognize that a great deal of personal and social development can be achieved through proper guidance during the preschool years. As the immense growth potential of the preschool child has come to be recognized, more and more attention has been paid to the channeling of preschool energy into constructive and creative directions, and the advisability of universal preschool education is being discussed.

What Did You Do At School Today?

Despite the increasing popularity of preschool education, there is little general agreement on its proper goals and functions. Should the program concentrate on emotional development, teaching the child to be independent and self-reliant? Should the stress be on academic subjects, preparing the child to learn reading and arithmetic when he begins his formal education? Should the emphasis be on socialization, teaching the child to cooperate and interact with others? Or perhaps the school should be no more than a well-organized daycare center, providing proper guidance for children as they learn from each other in the course of free play.

There are no easy answers to these questions. The ideal preschool program attempts to provide for all of the child's complex needs, encouraging social co-operation and personal autonomy while fostering intellectual growth. In reality, few programs are broad enough to incorporate all the roles that theorists have proposed for them. In most programs, emphasis has been on providing space, materials, and companionship for the preschooler and encouraging him to play under professional supervision.

Supervised play can be an important tool of education. Painting and working with clay may be the best way for the preschool child to learn about the relationships among color, shape, and line. Children who assemble puzzles or play with blocks may discover more about function, design, logic, and mathematics than they could learn from systematic instruction in those subjects. Doing often proves to be a better teacher than telling.

The development of language, especially, is stimulated by every aspect of social interaction. In sociodramatic play, playmates pool their vocabularies, learning new and unusual words as they are demanded in the context of a game. Observers at one nursery school counted forty-three technical terms used by children playing "hospital" (Lindberg, 1971). Dramatization, singing, and the recitation of poetry teach children to use language in ways that will benefit them immeasurably in their later efforts at reading and writing.

A child can learn a great deal through drilling and rote instruction. This approach may seem tedious to an adult instructor, but most children delight in it, provided the circumstances and timing are right.

Programs for the Low-Income Child

Traditionally, preschool education was largely restricted to the children of the affluent, as they were the only ones who could afford to hire teachers, pay for equipment, and establish institutions to care for their young children. In the 1960s, however, new public undertakings in the United States, especially those associated with the War on Poverty, led to increased federal support of education, and funds were provided to develop preschool programs such as Project Head Start. The purpose of these programs was to provide children from low-income groups, particularly urban blacks and the rural poor, with access to an enriched early environment. It was felt that such early intervention in the children's education might offset the disadvantages they faced and enable them to begin formal schooling on an equal footing with children from other socioeconomic classes.

Obviously, an activity that takes up only a few hours of the child's day will ultimately be of little value if the rest of the day is spent under negative and counterconstructive circumstances. For this reason, federal programs have attempted to reach out to the family and the community as well as the child—or to invite the community to reach out to the program. Ideally, local programs are intended to be extensions of the community rather than institutions urged on them from the outside. Although the broad goals of the program have been outlined by the U.S. government, Head Start guidelines stressed "the individualization of each program in terms of the community's perception of its needs and resources" (Klein, 1971).

Programs intended to educate low-income children are not always welcomed by educators. Some critics argue that no matter how much the community may participate in the operation of programs, the structure and goals of preschool programs are ultimately determined by professional psychologists and educators under the influence of government fund-dispensing officers. They object to "the usually implicit, sometimes explicit assumption that all we need to do is modify the environment of poor black people to make it more like the environment of middle-class whites and the world will be made whole" (Kessen, 1970). Such assumptions, the critics believe, undermine the goals of preschool programs.

Effective community participation requires that the community itself become conscious of its needs and goals and that the community be actively involved in the educational programs. Ideally, community leaders would welcome guidance from professionals. But it may be preferable to leave supervision and control of the program in the hands of the community so as to avoid confrontations of the sort that closed down many programs in recent years.

In most cases, preschool programs for low-income children have met with the enthusiasm and cooperation of parents and community. This success is partly a reflection of the functioning of the programs as social services. Children enrolled in preschool programs are assured health and nutritional care in addition to educational benefits. The program also serves a baby-sitting function, making life somewhat easier for the working mother who would not otherwise be in a position to provide adequate day care for her young child. Through neighborhood preschool programs, parents may also achieve a feeling of community cooperation and pride that may have been missing earlier. Most importantly, however, Americans believe strongly in education. Most parents assume that preschool education will provide their children with the skills they need to succeed in school and, ultimately, in life.

References

Donaldson, M., and Balfour, G. Less is more: A study of language comprehension in children. *British Journal of Psychology*, 1968, *59*, 461–472.

Douglas, N. *Old Calabria*. M. Secker, 1915.

Jeruchimowicz, R., Costello, J., and Bagur, J. S. Knowledge of action and object words: A comparison of lower- and middle-class Negro preschoolers. *Child Development*, 1971, *42*, 455–464.

Kessen, W. Early learning and compensatory education. In Korten, F., Cook, S., and Lacy, J. *Psychology and the problems of society*. Washington, D.C.: American Psychological Association, 1970.

Klein, J. Head-start: National focus on young children. *National Elementary Principal*, 1971, *51*, 98–103.

Lindberg, L. The function of play in early childhood education. *National Elementary Principal*, 1971, *51*, 68–71.

Piaget, J. *Judgment and reasoning in the child*. New York: Harcourt Brace Jovanovich, 1926.

Scott, R., and Smith, J. Ethnic and demographic variables and achievement scores of preschool children. *Psychology in Schools*, 1972, *9*, 174–182.

Slobin, D. I. *Psycholinguistics*. Glenview, Ill.: Scott, Foresman, 1971.

Vygotsky, L. S. *Thought and language*. Cambridge: M.I.T. Press, 1962.

Wetstone, H., and Friedlander, B. The effect of word order on young children's responses to simple questions and commands. *Child Development*, 1973, *44*, 734–740.

SUMMARY

1 Piaget believes that in the preoperational period of cognitive development, which extends from about two to seven years, the child goes through a preconceptual stage and then an intuitive stage. During this period he makes great strides in using symbolic representation. Representation begins in imitation and gradually becomes purely mental.

2 The child in the preoperational stage has limited reasoning powers. His thinking is egocentric, static, and irreversible. Errors in judgment result from centration. He often reasons through transduction and has an imperfect understanding of time, space, quantity, and relation.

3 Piaget observed that until the child understands the concepts of conservation and one-to-one correspondence, he cannot understand that a quantity has remained constant when it is presented to him in a changed form. Because young children have difficulty centering on more than one aspect of a situation at the same time, they have difficulty in understanding relationships.

4 Psycholinguists are attempting to discover the grammatical rules that the child uses as he first learns to talk. Piaget believes that the child does not intend to communicate with the egocentric speech characteristic of the preschool period, whereas Vygotsky thinks that it is meant to communicate but fails to do so.

5 Although the Stanford-Binet IQ test is the most widely used intelligence test, it relies heavily on the understanding and use of language, and it tests for general intelligence rather than particular intellectual abilities. Moreover, socioeconomic factors and individual motivation affect test scores. Psychologists are therefore placing less importance on IQ.

6 Professionals disagree over whether the prekindergarten school should emphasize academic instruction, socialization, or supervisory care. Government-sponsored preschool programs for low-income children have been criticized for attempting to impose middle-class values. However, many communities have recognized the benefits of preschool programs.

FURTHER READINGS

Evans, R. I. *Jean Piaget, the man and his ideas.* New York: Dutton, 1973.
> This is largely a dialogue between Piaget and the author, including a discussion of intelligence testing and the application of Piaget's ideas to education. It carries a summary of theories and a glossary of Piaget's terms, and additional commentary by the author and others.

Ferguson, C. A., and Slobin, D. I., *Studies of child language development.* New York: Holt, Rinehart and Winston, Inc., 1973.
> This collection of readings about language development studies in various cultures is in two parts. One is concerned with the child's development of competence in using the characteristic sounds of his native language and the other, with the acquisition of grammar.

Matterson, E. *Play and playthings for the preschool child.* Baltimore: Penguin, 1967.
> This is a practical guide to the selection, arrangement, and use of many kinds of play materials in the nursery school environment. It is also a source of insights into preschool behavior. "All children destroy before they create," the author writes, suggesting that young children like to reduce a thing to its component parts as a way of understanding it.

Maynard, F. *Guiding children to a more creative life.* New York: Doubleday, 1973.
> This book offers a philosophy and programs to develop creativity. The author defines the ingredients of creativity as fluency, flexibility, redefinition, and elaboration. Extensive lists of related books for the teacher and parent are included, as are specific suggestions for evaluating books and records for children.

Reissman, F. *The culturally deprived child.* New York: Harper, 1962.
> Reissman pioneered in studying the effects of poverty and discrimination on the minds of children. The attention attracted by his findings had much to do with the later establishment of Head Start programs to provide low-income preschool children with cultural enrichment.

Sharp, E. *The I. Q. cult.* New York: Coward, McCann and Geoghegan, 1972.
> This book sharply criticizes IQ tests. The author centers on the work of Piaget as the likely source of new kinds of culture-free tests of mental development. She writes about the research of Pinard, who is a follower of Piaget and is experimenting with such tests at the University of Montreal's Institute of Psychology.

9
Personality and Society

Many of us have learned (perhaps later than we would like to admit) that intelligence and competence are far from being all we need in life. The varying feelings we have throughout the day, our usual attitudes toward ourselves, our families, and society as a whole—all this is fully as important as our IQ, our verbal skills, and our physical prowess. After all, these feelings and attitudes determine the way we use our abilities. A sense of self-worth and confidence can help a child meet the challenges of growing up with eagerness and thus contribute to his success. Too much self-doubt, on the other hand, can discourage him from making new contacts with other people and entering situations that require him to develop new abilities.

The development of personality begins at or before birth, but the preschool years are the time when certain emotional patterns are set. We become conscious of our personal identity; infantile dependency is replaced by new patterns of social relations; aggression becomes more focused and is channeled into socially acceptable forms. Moral development becomes possible as the preschooler learns to understand the feelings and needs of others. Social relations become richer as fantasy, play, and humor develop within the family; the patterns of trust or fear, compassion or selfishness that are learned at home are gradually extended to the outer world. Our relations with everyone we meet will be colored for many years by the attitudes and expectations we develop before we are six.

EMOTIONAL DEVELOPMENT

The preschool years are a time of dramatic and sometimes painful change. No longer indulged because of his helplessness, the preschooler finds that his growing awareness and abilities bring with them demands and responsibilities. It becomes important to deal with some surprising new problems: Who am I? Am I a boy or a girl, and what difference does it make? Who can be trusted, and who cannot? When can I show anger, and when must I control it? What should I be afraid of, and how should I manage fear?

These problems are met by the preschooler for the first time, but he does not settle them. People keep on dealing with them all their lives, and though the circumstances and relationships change as we mature, the patterns of meeting these problems that are laid down in the preschool years tend to abide. They form the core of that hard to define something that we call "personality."

Identity

Before we can begin to develop relationships with others, each of us must first establish some notion of his own identity. For most adults, the outlines of a personal identity are fairly well established: the person is what his job, interests, ideas, and relations to family and friends make him. The preschool child, however, lacks many of these determinants, and as his egocentric view of the world ceases to work, he realizes for the first time that he needs them. People no longer go out of their way to see things from his point of view; he must learn to look at things in a way that will make sense not only to himself but to those around him.

The child's first reference point for self-identification may be her own name. Early in infancy, the little girl learns that she is Rhonda and that her name is a very special part of herself. Her awareness of the relationship between herself and the sound that refers to her does not depend on her ability to speak or understand language. Before she has acquired any language skills, Rhonda has established some sense of her own identity.

Among the earliest and most important sources of self-identification is gender. Just as recognition of her name is strongly reinforced, she is continually reminded that she is not a boy but a girl. By the age of two or three, almost all children are able to identify their own gender. Although Rhonda learns to apply the label "girl" to herself, however, she may not yet have learned in any clear way the physical and social meanings of being a girl (Kohlberg, 1966). At this age she may understand that some of the children she meets are also girls, but it may take another year or two before she can infallibly recognize the gender of others.

A child's notion of gender is rarely based on the genital differences or other biological characteristics. She determines it instead by means of clothing, speech, and hair style. If the trend toward similarity in men's and women's fashions gains ground, preschoolers may either attach less importance to gender, or they may take longer to notice the difference.

Figure 9.1 In the past, gender identification often included the idea that girls do not play as strenuously as boys. This little girl does not seem to have heard of the idea, and is probably healthier for it.

It may seem curious that we speak of "gender" rather than "sex," but there is a very good reason: sex is biological, whereas gender is social. Gender depends on how the individual is viewed by himself or herself and by others. As we saw in Chapter 6, gender identification is expressed in behavior that is, at least in part, learned rather than inherited. Much of the behavior that is associated with being "feminine," for example, is socialized behavior, so that gender identity may be determined more by the expectations of one's parents and one's culture than by biological sex.

Inasmuch as gender seems to depend on superficial characteristics, the preschool child may believe it can be altered merely by changing external features—if a boy dresses and behaves like a girl, he becomes one. Many children also believe that gender can change with age; a four year old boy may say he wants to grow up "to be a Mommy." It is not until the age of five or six that most children are convinced that sexual identity is not determined just by behavior and appearance.

Once a child has learned to distinguish between males and females, he begins to learn the various roles and attributes that are associated with gender. A boy learns to "act like a boy" and a girl learns to "act like a girl." Recently, many people have begun to question the wisdom or justice of teaching children that boys and girls are fundamentally different. Some social and emotional problems are

"My mother and father aren't home."

undoubtedly associated with an overemphasis on sexual stereotypes, but a realistic awareness of sex roles as they exist in society is still a vital aspect of the child's development of a self-image. It has been a major concern of developmental psychology, therefore, to study the mechanisms by which children establish their sexual orientation.

One approach to the development of sexual attitudes is to explain them by social expectations and social reinforcement—that is, to show how we are rewarded for conformity to sexual norms and punished for deviance. Although the reinforcement of cultural normality certainly plays an important role in the shaping of sexual attitudes, it does not fully explain sex typing. Moreover, simple reinforcement does not account for the great number of people, young and old, who deviate from the prescribed norms.

An alternative approach to the origins of sexual identity, and one that at first seems to explain more, is to suppose that children identify certain sex roles with their parents. According to this theory a boy would normally pattern his behavior after his father's behavior, and a girl would act like her mother. This theory was tested (Kohlberg, 1966) by asking children to describe the differences they saw between men and women. Men were almost always described as powerful and aggressive. Women were almost always described as passive and nurturing. The striking fact was that children whose parents did not fit the pattern said the same thing as children whose parents did fit it. Children tended to see sexual roles according to the same stereotypes regardless of whether the mother worked or stayed at home, and regardless of whether or not there was a father in the house. There are probably as many kinds of paternal and maternal behavior as there are parents, and yet children seem to ignore these differences when they form notions of what men and women are like.

On what basis, then, do children form their notions of sex roles? To a great extent, the child's concept of sex stereotypes is based on his own observations of adult society both in real life and on television and movies. It is made clear to children at an early age that men assume the aggressive roles in our culture. Women are cast as housewives and schoolteachers; men play the roles of soldier, policeman, athlete, and politician. Furthermore, children tend to equate physical size and strength with power and social prestige. Because he is usually larger and stronger, Daddy is assumed to be smarter and to wield more authority than Mommy.

The child is an active participant in the formation of his concept of sex roles. He does not merely imitate, but explores and thinks in his own way. As one researcher (Kohlberg, 1966) put it:

> Both research results and clinical observation indicate that much of the young child's thinking about sex roles is radically different from the adult's. His physical concepts of anatomical differences, birth, sexual relations, etc., are quite different, as are his concepts of the social attributes and values of males and females. . . . The child's sex-role concepts are the result of the child's active structuring of his own experience; they are not passive products of social training.

There is no doubt, however, that preschoolers build up their sex role identification partly by taking the example of a model; boys tend to model themselves after men (usually their fathers) and girls after women (usually their mothers). To a great extent, the child's choice of a model is a function of his or her own egocentricity. In the early preschool years, a boy will choose to play with a boy rather than a girl because he finds the boy more like himself, and at this egocentric stage, this pleases and attracts him. Apparently children prefer to play with (and to model themselves after) members of their own sex largely because of a narcissistic enjoyment of seeing themselves reflected in others.

In some respects, the search for a suitable sex-role model is more complicated for girls than it is for boys. Whether or not a father figure is present, a boy may

FAMILY AND COMMUNITY

Anthropologists have found that in cultures throughout the world the family takes many forms. The smallest, simplest unit is the *nuclear family,* a mother a father, and their children. In earlier times in the United States, the nuclear family was a smaller, subordinate element of a larger *extended* family, which might include grandparents, aunts and uncles, and cousins.

What effect does this have on the way we grow up? Many people believe that the small nuclear family is just right for twentieth-century America, for it develops a free, independent spirit. Others, pointing to the rebelliousness of our youth, the apparent breakdown of many of our institutions, and the isolation and alienation felt by many of us, believe society would be better if the American family were larger. Certainly American children are encouraged to think in terms of living "on their own"—the image we use is of a fledgling bird leaving the nest. Many Americans have never met some of their uncles and aunts, and many have only a very distant relationship with their grandparents.

But there are exceptions to this pattern—not only the rural and urban communes that became widely known in the 1960s and 1970s, but a great number of religious communities like those of the Amish, the Mennonites, and the Hutterites. Among these, the Hutterites, a German-speaking sect that had its origin in the sixteenth-century Protestant Reformation, are fairly typical. Living on communally owned land in some 170 closed self-sustaining and independent communities in the Dakotas and Alberta, the Hutterites need no help from the outside, or even communication with it. Incursions from outside are actively resisted because the Hutterites teach their young an ethic that is in almost complete opposition to the notions of personal independence that most other American children learn. The Hutterite goals are utopian and demanding. They are not goals that an individual, or a family, can reach alone. For that reason the Hutterite family is more strongly bound to the colony than most American family members are bound to each other. Marriage to outsiders is not just uncommon, it is unheard of. And child rearing is not left to an isolated pair of parents, it is a structured community activity.

Between infancy and the school years the Hutterite child is expected to be "good": to sleep when he is put to bed, to share food and playthings, to avoid quarrels (or at least to make up immediately after a quarrel), to keep out of older people's way. Perhaps most important, he is trained never to reject any member of the colony. During this period he is disciplined often, but the sense of being loved and valued is never lost.

By the time the child is ready for kindergarten, at age three, he has already begun to learn what will be the central rule of his life: that the colony's welfare is more important than that of the individual. He also has learned that there are no strangers in the colony.

In this self-contained world, there is almost no such thing as loneliness. The Hutterite family subordinates its personal needs to those of the community and its future. During his life the Hutterite is involved intimately with his whole society; and the whole community takes responsibility for shaping each member.

Figure 9.2. Little girls usually have ample opportunity to model themselves after women who play traditional female roles. It is less likely that the children will have a successful businesswoman as a model. Thus, most girls learn that women are people who look pretty and take care of babies, a role that more and more adult women are finding too narrow.

readily model himself after some strong and socially prestigious male image. A young girl, on the other hand, may encounter some difficulty in finding a suitably dynamic female model in a male-dominated culture. If she cannot be powerful like her father, she must settle for being "nice" and nurturant like her mother. As we have seen, the assumption of these sex roles generally occurs despite the actual circumstances of the child's own family situation.

Dependency

None of us is an entirely independent individual. To some degree, everyone relies on others for information, support, and emotional comfort. Our **dependency** varies with the extent to which we rely on others. As adults, we recognize that dependency is a give-and-take process. We are glad to receive nurturance, but we recognize that sometimes we must nurture others in return. The young child's dependent behavior is not nearly so reciprocal. He expects to be nurtured but he is unaware of the necessity of giving something in return.

Dependent behavior in children takes the forms of affection seeking and instrumental help seeking. *Affection-seeking* dependency can be seen in the child's demand "Look at me!" He is extremely pleased to be noticed and praised. *Instrumental help seeking*, on the other hand, involves dependency in performing some new or difficult task. A little girl building a sand castle at the beach may ask for help from her mother even though she could do it herself. In this kind of situation, the child's need for dependency is satisfied in two ways: she gets "practical" help in her play, and at the same time the adult's willingness to help reassures the child that Mommy cares for her.

To study the emotional dependence of children, one researcher (Harris, 1968) examined the extent to which children look to adults for behavioral cues. Two experimenters, a man and a woman, offered children three to five years old their choice of two toys that were identical except for color. Hidden observers recorded the frequency with which the children looked at the experimenter rather than at the toy before choosing. It was assumed that looking at the experimenter was, for the child, a means of seeking support. It was also assumed, tentatively, that the children regarded the experimenters (young men and women who were relatively strange to the children) as, in some sense, stand-ins for their own parents. The process was repeated sixteen times for each subject, with four different sets of toys.

The researcher concluded that children rely heavily on cues from adults in making choices, especially in the younger age group. She also found that boys tended to look at the female more than at the male experimenters, and the girls looked more often at the men. On the whole, however, the children tended to look at women more than men. Does this mean that mothers tend to provide children with stronger support for their dependency needs? Do boys tend to seek support from their mothers more than from their fathers, and is the opposite true for girls? As yet there are no answers to these questions, but they indicate some of the complexities involved in dependent behavior.

Dependency and Self-Image

The preschooler's concept of himself is difficult to understand and even harder to analyze because his language skills are not very strong and his view of the world is still largely egocentric. He may, therefore, have a complex and subtle system of views and perceptions but be unable to express them. It has become clear, however, that the child's independence and self-confidence, not only in the preschool years but in later life, have much to do with how his parents deal with his early dependency.

Generally speaking, all parents discourage dependent behavior. As parents, we try to protect our children from danger and frustration while simultaneously trying to prepare them to face danger and frustration on their own. The greatest challenge of parenthood is to strike a proper balance between under- and over-protectiveness.

Despite popular notions to the contrary, studies suggest that children who are regularly punished for dependent behavior or are punished for ordinary offenses by being deprived of love or attention tend to grow up to be more dependent than children whose early dependent behavior is indulged. In other words, children who are not offered the nurturance they need when young may continue to seek it as

Figure 9.3. At this daycare center, children receive the nurturance they need while their mothers are away from home.

they grow older. Often the child turns to the nursery teacher or to other children if he does not find sufficient nurturance at home.

Overly protective parents who encourage dependency and offer assistance where it is not needed may also be harming their children. In later life the children may be slow to learn how to help themselves and may rely excessively on other people for help just as their undernurtured playmates do. One investigator (Baumrind, 1971) found that the children of parents who were warm and understanding, but at the same time demanding and authoritative, tended to be self-confident, outgoing, purposeful, and self-controlled in a nursery-school test. On the other hand, the children of indulgent, permissive parents—parents who encouraged dependency and failed to let the child know, clearly and consistently, what was expected of him—tended to be aimless in their behavior and to lack self-reliance. Clearly, some degree of self-discipline and self-reliance must be demanded of the child. Parents must make the effort to find some middle ground in discouraging dependent behavior in order to allow their children to develop a mature and independent self-image.

As a child matures, he begins to depend less on his parents and more on other adults and children. In an experiment designed to test the relationship between fear and attachment, a researcher (Schwartz, 1968) exposed children to frightening objects either in the presence of their mothers or in the presence of an adult stranger. Contrary to expectations, most of the preschool children tested expressed less anxiety in the presence of the stranger than in the presence of their own mothers. It is possible that the children felt freer to express their feelings in the presence of their mothers and were more inhibited by the stranger; nevertheless, this study did suggest that in the later preschool years, the child depends less exclusively upon his mother for support.

Initiative Versus Guilt

In his now classic work *Childhood and society* (1963), psychoanalyst Erik Erikson theorized that the preschool child experiences a developmental crisis as he becomes less dependent, a conflict between what Erikson terms *initiative* and *guilt*. As the child grows physically and as his intellectual capabilities mature, he develops an increasing sense of his own power—his ability to make things happen. He becomes more and more able to control his physical environment as he gains mastery over his own body; he begins to understand that other people have different motivations and perceptions than he does; and he delights in his own ability to figure things out. This growth supports what Erikson calls initiative.

There is in every child at every stage a new miracle of vigorous unfolding, which constitutes a new hope and a new responsibility for all. Such is the sense and the pervading quality of initiative. The criteria for all these senses and qualities are the same; a crisis, more or less beset with fumbling and fear, is resolved, in that the child suddenly seems to "grow together" both in his person and in his body. He appears "more himself," more loving, relaxed and brighter in his judgment, more activated and activating. He is in free possession of a surplus of energy which permits him to forget failures quickly and to approach what seems desirable (even if it also seems uncertain and even dangerous) with undiminished and more accurate direction (Erikson, 1963).

At this developmental stage the child is ready and eager to learn and work cooperatively with others to achieve his goals. He learns to plan realistically, and he is willing to accept the guidance of teachers and other adults. It is at this stage, according to Erikson, that the child's energy is directed "toward the possible and the tangible, which permits the dreams of early childhood to be attached to the goals of an active adult life."

The danger of this stage is that the child's newfound energy will lead him to act, or to wish to act, in ways that will make him feel guilty. Along with this great sense of power comes an increasing awareness of the requirements that limit behavior. Donald feels angry at his little sister and realizes that he would like to push her out of the high chair, an act that he knows he is able to do. But he also realizes that pushing his sister would bring punishment from his mother. He cannot always do what he wants.

Both the adults and the other children in Donald's world require him to develop self-control and some responsibility for what he does. As the child grows in the ability to observe himself, he is expected to control himself—and he becomes able to punish himself with guilt if he fails to fulfill that expectation. On the one hand, the child is experiencing himself as more powerful that ever before; on the other hand, he is beginning to realize that he must control his own behavior and that he will feel guilty if he fails in control.

> The child indulges in fantasies of being a giant and a tiger, but in his dreams he runs in terror for dear life. . . . Here the most fateful split and transformation in the emotional powerhouse occurs, a split between potential human glory and potential total destruction. For here the child becomes forever divided in himself. The instinct fragments which before had enhanced the growth of his infantile body and mind now become divided into an infantile set which perpetuates the exuberance of growth potentials, and a parental set which supports and increases self-observation, self-guidance, and self-punishment (Erikson, 1963).

If this crisis is handled well, the child learns to function in ways that will allow him to use his initiative constructively. He will take pleasure in his own increasing power and become more able to cooperate with and accept help from others. He will find ways in which he can use his energy and capabilities in a strong, solid way that will allow him to get some of what he wants without violating his developing sense of right behavior.

Less happily, the child may be unable to find the balance between initiative and guilt. His own desire for control and mastery may become conflicted with

ERIKSON'S CRISES IN PSYCHOSOCIAL DEVELOPMENT

Basic Trust versus Basic Mistrust (first year of life)

Autonomy versus Shame and Doubt (second year of life)

Initiative versus Guilt (the preschool years)

During the preschool years the child has a boundless supply of energy, which permits him to learn all kinds of activities and ideas quickly and avidly. He concentrates on successes rather than failures, and does things for the simple pleasure of activity. Autonomy becomes more focused and effective. The child becomes "more himself"; in his social life he is, in Erikson's words, "on the make."

The danger in this period is that the child's exuberant and aggressive explorations and conquests may lead him into frustration. His new physical and mental strength encourages ambitions that may turn out to be beyond his abilities—inevitably, he sometimes fails or is defeated. Unless he can come to terms with these disappointments he may be overwhelmed by resignation, guilt, and anxiety.

Perhaps the best way to help the child at this age is to encourage him to play constructively, to do some chores around the house, or to help care for younger children. In this way the conflict between initiative and guilt may be resolved by the establishment of a constructive moral sense; it can set the individual on the road to goals that are not only possible for him, but also deeply satisfying. If the conflict remains unresolved, in adult life the individual may be inhibited or impotent (socially as well as sexually), or he may overreact by compulsive "showing off."

Industry versus Inferiority (middle childhood)

Identity versus Role Confusion (adolescence)

Intimacy versus Isolation (young adulthood)

Generativity versus Stagnation (prime of life)

Ego Integrity versus Despair (old age)

his wish for the acceptance and support of others or with the dictates of his developing conscience. This conflict may lead him to overcontrol himself, to close off his energy to satisfy the requirements of obedience or to avoid guilt. He may become resentful of those who require control of him or even resentful of his sense of inner control. If the conflict is not resolved, the child may grow into an adult who feels that the only way he can get what he wants is at the cost of doing something that he believes is wrong—or, alternatively, that the only way he can do what is right is to deny himself the things that he wants.

Aggression

In recent years there has been a very active and noisy debate about the nature and origin of aggression in human behavior. In our society, aggression is not necessarily an undesirable form of behavior. A person who is unable to act aggressively even when it is necessary may be ineffective and frustrated. Each of us, child and adult alike, must act to promote his self-interest, and when this can only be done at the expense of someone else, it may be called aggression. But as we saw in Chapter 6, this aggression can be purely instrumental or it can be hostile.

Theories of aggression

Freud and his followers were among the first to attempt a psychological explanation of hostile aggression. The psychoanalytic approach assumes that aggression is an instinctual human impulse. The Freudian view explains much of human behavior on the basis of sexual drives that we make ourselves ignore—that is, we *repress* them. Although in the course of growing up we succeed in repressing these drives, they remain very much alive. The conflict between these instinctual drives and our norms of behavior leads to frustration, and this frustration finds an outlet in occasional bursts of hostile aggression. Thus, for the Freudians, frustration is the immediate cause of aggression, but there is always a basic sexual conflict underlying the frustration.

A somewhat simpler explanation is offered by the frustration theory of aggression. This resembles the Freudian theory except that the element of sexuality is left out. According to this view, hostility is simply a function of frustration: the more frustrated a child feels, the more hostility there will be in his behavior. If this view is correct, a four year old girl who is constantly taunted and teased by an older brother against whom she is helpless will build up a tremendous amount of hostility. If she in turn has a younger brother, we may confidently predict he is in trouble if he cannot run fast.

The frustration theory of aggression concludes that punishment is generally ineffective as a long-term deterrent to aggressive behavior. For one thing, the child who is punished by his father may see the father's behavior as another form of aggression. Far from having a corrective result, the punishment may serve as a model for further aggression on the part of the boy. Furthermore, the child who anticipates punishment for aggressive behavior that he feels is justified may have his frustration intensified through self-inhibition. Ultimately, it is argued, the inhibition of aggression leads to the heightening of frustration and, consequently, to an intensification of aggressive behavior. Frustration theories of aggression argue that frustration and misdirected aggression can be minimized by the displacement of aggression into healthy outlets. That is, destructive behavior may be averted, and a child may behave less aggressively, if he releases energy through physical activity and even through the vicarious aggression shown on television and movies.

Another theory of aggression is the instinct learning approach. Not entirely unlike the Freudians, adherents of this position argue that aggression stems from instinct; like any animal species, humans are occasionally hostile. The instinct learning theorists suggest that although instinct gives us a predisposition toward aggressive behavior, early experience—"training" in aggression—is necessary before we will actually behave aggressively. This theory, unlike the frustration theories, tries to account for both instrumental and hostile aggression; both kinds

Figure 9.4. Yelling is one way of expressing aggression—probably a better way, as this little girl seems to have learned, than hurling raisins off the table.

are seen as a form of learned behavior that is developed through practice and reinforcement. This theory stresses imitation as a source of aggressive behavior. Because its adherents argue that children learn aggression by observing the aggressive behavior of others, they differ strongly from the frustration-aggression theorists in one important way: they believe that exposure to violence in the environment or in books, movies, and television can make a child engage in such behavior himself some day. It is impossible to decide among these theories until further research provides conclusive new data. In the meantime, however, we can learn how aggression works and how to deal with it.

Aggression in preschool children

Most research on the aggressive behavior of preschool children has been based either on observations made under test conditions in nursery schools and daycare centers or on the (frequently biased) reports of mothers. A child's pattern of aggression at home may differ significantly from his behavior under laboratory conditions. Nevertheless, it is possible to make a number of useful generalizations about aggression in the preschool child.

During infancy, aggressive behavior usually takes the form of temper tantrums.

They may be a reaction to physical discomfort, such as a chafing diaper or gas in the stomach, or to emotional states, such as frustration, overstimulation, or loss of attention. As the child matures, his behavior is increasingly influenced by interaction with other children and adults. Most aggression during the preschool period is triggered by the social conflicts that arise in the course of cooperative play; yet, despite the increase in provocation, overtly aggressive behavior generally decreases with age. In most cases, however, the decline of physical aggression is accompanied by an increase in verbal aggression. Hitting may be replaced by name-calling, and children learn to be as sensitive to names as to sticks and stones.

The preschool child is not always clear about the distinction between accidental

"Jane, I promise. I'll be a good daddy."

and intentional aggression. He may retaliate in the same way against a child who bumps into him by accident as to one who pushes him on purpose. Before he can learn to accept the accidental knocks and bumps of normal play without wanting to react aggressively, he must learn to understand the difference between intentional and unintentional injuries. This may be harder for the preschooler than we might think, since his egocentric mode of thinking is not well suited to making such distinctions.

The decline of physical aggression during the preschool years may be a reflection of the change in parental disciplinary techniques during these years. Generally, parents start to deal with aggression in a more authoritative manner. In the belief that infants cannot understand verbal prohibitions, parents may ignore outbursts, try to divert the child's attention, or use force to quell aggression; but as the child grows older, he is scolded, threatened, or deprived of privileges as a punishment for misbehavior. The increased use of verbal controls by parents as children grow older may serve as a model for the child's choice of verbal rather than physical aggression in the preschool years.

The sex of a young child is a major factor in his or her pattern of aggressive behavior. In almost all studies, boys have been reported to be more aggressive than girls. This should not be surprising in light of the strong cultural stereotypes we discussed earlier.

The possibility is currently being investigated that aggression may be caused biochemically. Researchers have observed that female rats injected with the male hormone testosterone display more of the aggressive behavior that is characteristic of the male rat. It is of course impossible simply to generalize from these experiments to human behavior, and in any case aggression in human beings is not just a result of body chemistry but is also the outcome of many complicated psychological and social factors.

The relationship between aggressive behavior and socioeconomic status is also unclear. At one time, psychologists assumed that lower-class parents were less repressive of aggression than middle- and upper-class parents and that, consequently, lower-class children were provided with outlets to relieve their aggressive impulses while middle- and upper-class children grew anxious and frustrated as a result of their inhibitions. It seems likely, however, that this theory reflects the middle-class bias of the researchers. Many mutually contradictory studies have left the relation between aggression and socioeconomic status unclear. Ultimately, individual differences may prove to be of greater importance in human behavior than generalized distinctions based on social structure.

Is the pattern of aggression displayed during the preschool years relevant to future behavioral development? Long-range studies indicate that it is, especially for boys. Researchers (Kagan and Moss, 1962) have found that patterns of aggressive behavior in children three to six years old gave surprisingly good indications of the kinds of behavior the children would show as adolescents and, to some extent, as adults. Children who were dominant, competitive, and indirectly aggressive to their peers tended to be especially competitive as adults. Childhood aggressiveness, then, may not be a transient phase. On the contrary, it may last, although in a different form, throughout the individual's entire lifetime.

Fear and Anxiety

As children, we all had fears and anxieties which we probably have forgotten now. In some form and degree, however, the fears of childhood remain with us. Generally, we are afraid of that which is unknown or incomprehensible to us. For young children, the category of things incomprehensible is an uncomfortably large one.

Because the infant perceives the whole world on an essentially sensorimotor level, his fears may be readily relieved by removing the immediate cause. As the child grows older, he encounters many new and frightening situations, and he is no longer easily comforted. Now he comes to rely more heavily on nurturance and comfort from his mother and other trusted adults. A critical characteristic of the maturing process is the expanding ability and need to find comfort socially, in one's parents and peers, and ultimately in oneself.

Social stress is a primary source of fear for the preschool child. Not knowing how to act in a new social situation, the child is easily frightened by exposure to unfamiliar people and places. Shyness and silent withdrawal are common responses. This may not be serious if it occurs only occasionally, but the child may need support and encouragement from her parents in such situations. Without it, shyness may develop to the point where the child is seriously hampered in her social relationships by a fear of the unfamiliar that can remain for many years.

Fears may also be learned through conditioning and reinforcement. A child may acquire fears through exposure to frightening films or television shows. For example, she may be afraid to get a haircut after seeing a film in which the barber is portrayed as a killer. More directly, a child may acquire fears on the basis of her own experience. Having once been stung by a bee, the child may run in terror from any buzzing insect. Other common "irrational" fears among preschoolers are fear of the dark, fear of being washed down the drain in the bathtub, and fear of being flushed down the toilet.

Some of the child's most terrifying fears originate in her own imagination. From year to year the preschooler develops a more and more powerful capacity to conjure up vivid scenes and situations. She uses her imagination to entertain ideas that she would not enact in reality and to vent her aggressions privately, but she also uses it to invent fearsome perils. At bedtime, a shadow on the ceiling may become a ravening beast; a dark corner may conceal nameless horrors. It is important for parents to take these fears seriously because they are very real to the child even if their causes are not. Parents may best deal with them by encouraging children to express their feelings and ideas freely, without being made to feel foolish or guilty. Then the parents may offer comfort and support.

Ultimately, fear is a highly individualized response. One child's nightmare may be another child's joke. In general, children gradually become less expressive of their fears, and their responses to frightening objects become more constructive as they grow older. Eventually, every child develops ways to overcome irrational fears and to manage those that have some basis in fact.

MORAL DEVELOPMENT

One of our most important character traits is the ability to tell right from wrong. *Moral development, conscience,* and *ethics* are all terms we use to name the process through which we learn to deal fairly with others. The preschool child's training and experience gradually teach him which actions are considered acceptable by other people and which are not. He learns that doing certain things, or even wanting to do them, may lead to punishment.

Ethical behavior, however, consists of more than avoiding punishment by behaving properly. In a fuller sense it means understanding that the needs of others are as valid as our own. If you find a stranger's wallet and return it because you think you may have been seen picking it up, you are behaving cautiously. If you return it out of consideration for the owner, you are acting ethically. This distinction, obvious enough to adults, is seen only gradually by the preschooler.

Piaget believes that moral development, like all phases of human growth, occurs in a series of stages. In view of the egocentricity of the preschool child, Piaget doubts that children below the age of seven are capable of empathizing with others to the degree required for truly ethical behavior. He suggests that preschool children cannot be taught ethics but can only be trained to behave properly.

Later research (Borke, 1971) has taken issue with Piaget's interpretation of the behavior of preschool children as entirely egocentric:

> Observations of young children interacting suggest that preschool youngsters are not only aware that other people have feelings but also actively try to understand the feelings they observe. The 2½ year old who holds out a toy to a crying child certainly appears to be demonstrating an awareness that the other youngster is experiencing unhappy feelings.

This study suggests that from three years of age, children may be aware that other people have feelings and that these feelings vary according to the situation in which the person finds himself. The researcher notes, however, that children are able to recognize happiness and fear in others more readily than they can recognize sadness or anger. No difference was observed between boys and girls, but older children demonstrated much more empathetic capability than younger ones. This general trend for social sensitivity to increase with age supports Piaget's thesis that egocentricity declines gradually toward the end of preschool years, even if children begin to show some capacity for empathy a few years sooner than he thought.

Figure 9.5. Because they enjoy their tea and cake, these children understand that Lassie will enjoy hers too.

It is the child's increasing social awareness that largely accounts for the early manifestations of sympathy, conscience, and generosity during the preschool period. As he becomes more conscious of the needs and concerns of others, he begins to desire the satisfaction of their needs as well as his own, and his behavior shows a growing capacity for sharing and compassion. In an experiment designed to study generosity in children, researchers (Rutherford and Mussen, 1968) observed that generosity is closely linked to other moral characteristics such as cooperation, altruism, lack of interpersonal aggression, and sympathy. They further suggested that these aspects of moral development are closely linked to the child's perception of the same-sex parent as warm, affectionate, and nurturant.

The proposition that preschoolers are capable of a higher order of moral behavior than Piaget thought has also been suggested by studies of the child's conception of social justice. In an experiment designed to study leniency toward cheating, researchers (Ross and Ross, 1968) tested the attitudes of preschool children both before and after they were allowed to cheat successfully at a given task. They found that children who cheated became more tolerant of cheating in others, while those who did not cheat became more severely critical of cheaters. Apparently, even at a very early age, learning to obey the rules involves expecting others to obey them as well.

It appears that children have a fairly conventional notion of social justice by the end of the preschool period. A recent study (Irwin and Moore, 1971) suggests that young children understand that returning a stolen toy is more meaningful than merely apologizing for having stolen it. They were not only able to make the fundamental distinction between right and wrong, but they also recognized that in order to right a wrong it may not be enough just to say "I'm sorry."

Although these studies take Piaget's work as their starting point, they challenge his description of the preschooler as an amoral being who behaves properly only in response to adult authority. On the contrary, they have found that preschoolers are well on the way to internalizing and understanding basic moral considerations.

SOCIAL RELATIONS

Other people influence the child's development from the moment of conception, but it is a long time before he knows it. For several months in infancy he does not even suppose that other people—or any of the objects he sees around him, moving or stationary—exist when they are out of his sight. And it is a year or two later before he realizes that other people are persons like himself: that they do things because *they* want to, that they have feelings and occupations of their own. They continue to influence him all the while, of course, but as he gradually becomes aware of their autonomy, he begins to react to them in new ways. He learns to recognize social influence for what it is, and to understand that it can be mutual.

Play and Fantasy

As a child establishes relationships, he imagines them a hundred different ways in fantasy. One of the most pleasant activities engaged in by children and adults alike is the creation of fantasies. It is rarely the time-wasting pastime it was once believed to be; indeed, it can provide a useful stage for feelings and ideas that the individual could not carry out in real life. Through fantasy, children can explore their ever-expanding social world privately. In most cases, fantasy is a reaction to real events and not a withdrawal from them. Children may find in fantasy the solution to problems that had previously defeated them in reality.

Fantasy often involves a substitution in which one object or situation is used to stand for another. For example, a little girl may alleviate her frustration at being unjustly punished by having her Mommy doll apologize to her Baby doll. Toys used in this way are incorporated into the fantasy, which thus becomes more real and satisfying to the child.

Much of a child's early play is simple imitation and simulation; that is, she pretends to do things that she has thought of or seen others do. At first, the acting may involve incidents of little dramatic content; she simply pretends to drink a glass of water, for example, or closes her eyes and lies still in imitation of sleep. As her experience and imagination expand, however, and her fantasies grow more complex, her playacting will become more and more dramatic. Eventually she may stage complete episodes in the medium of dramatic play.

Several sex differences have been observed in the pattern of fantasies reported by children. Generally boys' fantasies involve more action and aggression and incorporate a greater number of objects, judging at least from their own reports.

SOCIAL PLAY

According to Piaget, preschool children are egocentric—that is, they are not yet sensitive to other people's feelings and ideas. Young children can play only in parallel with others, alongside them, but not cooperatively. Each child has his own reasons and rules. The presence of another child is not important to the preschooler or his game (Piaget, 1951).

More, recent observation and research, however, suggest that Piaget might have constructed his developmental timetable too rigidly to fit the facts. A number of experimental studies indicate that cooperative, sympathetic behavior is not necessarily an exception (which it would be, according to Piaget) but is actually quite common. It has been demonstrated that even by the age of two years, a child's play is highly influenced by the actions of another child (Maudry & Nekula, 1939).

Cooperative play is distinguished from parallel play mainly by the amount of influence a play partner has on a child's activities. Between the ages of two and five, young children tend to play by acting out fantasies. They may want to pretend they are grownups, animals, storybook or television characters. When these fantasies overlap, the children will play cooperatively (Isaacs, 1946). Cooperation may break down if the individual fantasies conflict with one another. Both children may want to be the hero and neither the villain: then play gives way to quarreling. Between the ages of three and four, quarreling becomes common.

Although mothers may find this difficult to accept, quarreling and competitive behavior are indications of growing social awareness. The children

mutually influence their activities and show that they are beginning to understand each other's feelings. If one child threatens to hit another, it is clear that he intends to frighten his playmate and is able to do so because he can "put himself in the other's shoes;" while two year old children often ignore each other, by age five playmates may be in open competition with each other in games. This competition is often reflected in the conversations of five year olds. If one child says his father is as strong as a bear, the next child's father is as strong as an elephant and the next child's father is as strong as a dinosaur. Cooperative play involving sex and bodily functions is also common in preschool children; such games as "playing doctor" give children an opportunity for mutual exploration of sexual organs and their functions.

Children play most cooperatively, and their behavior is most social and sympathetic, when they are familiar with their situation and their playmates. Brothers and sisters pay more attention to each other and play together at earlier ages more frequently than most experimental studies indicate (Millar, 1968).

Social background and experience have a strong influence on when a child will begin to play cooperatively. Piaget based his theory of play on observations of Swiss children in a nursery school where solitary activities were encouraged much more than in the average American setting. The substance of Piaget's insights into child development still seems valid, but there is a great deal of evidence that children are capable of social, sympathetic behavior earlier than he supposed.

The fantasies described by girls, on the other hand, are more detailed and passive and are more often concerned with human relations. But these patterns conform suspiciously to culturally reinforced notions of masculinity and femininity. A girl who has a fantasy involving violence or aggression may be afraid she will be criticized if she expresses such thoughts. A recent study (Cramer and Bryson, 1973) suggests that preschool girls and boys do not differ much in the content of their fantasies, although later, in the early school years, girls do begin to fantasize less about aggression.

Humor

As the preschooler develops a rich fantasy life, he also begins to develop a sense of humor. Several theories have been proposed to explain the origin of humor. The most important is Freud's, which was first published in 1916. The core of his theory is that the pleasure we take in humor is based on its ability to relieve us of psychic strain. Thus a threatening or serious situation may suddenly turn comic if we adjust our mental approach so that it seems trivial or ludicrous. The stress disappears, and our laughter expresses our relief.

For a preschooler who is undergoing a great deal of frustration and anxiety, fantasy and humor can be important releases. Of course, in many cases, laughter is much more than just a mechanism that serves to relieve stress, but it can perform the valuable function of a safety valve during the difficult preschool years.

Because children's thinking does not follow the logic of adult thought, their jokes do not always make adults laugh. Humor is generally based on incongruity; that is, we laugh at things that turn out differently from what we expected, or that do not fit into a framework of normality. But a child has very much his own sense of what is normal. He may laugh at a minor verbal or visual imperfection and find no humor whatever in a more striking incongruity.

What does the preschool child laugh at? Studies suggest that young children laugh most in response to ongoing physical activities: tickling, teasing, romping. Preschoolers are also more likely to laugh if they realize the situation they are in is socially unacceptable. Preschool children are fond of telling long and rambling jokes—sometimes memorized and sometimes improvised—which usually fail to end in any sort of recognizable punch line. Young children take delight in the physical humor of facial expressions and pratfalls, gradually developing a more sophisticated appreciation of verbal humor as they mature. Eventually, the child's attempts at word play begin to approach a level of cleverness bordering on wit.

Children often find humor in word play. They delight not only in hearing and reciting riddles and nursery rhymes but in listening to and singing songs as well. Early in the preschool period, children develop the ability to make up simple songs that often give useful insights into their thoughts and feelings at the time. Humorous ideas may also be expressed through dance. Most children are quick to respond to rhythm and music, using their bodies freely for self-expression without the inhibitions felt by many adults, and often portraying imaginative creatures.

Imaginary companions

Preschool children also commonly adopt imaginary companions. Such companions may assume any form—human or animal, male or female—and may bear any relationship to the child. The companion, for example, may be an amiable friend, or he may be an outlet for the child's aggression and hostility. It has been observed that girls are generally more apt to have imaginary playmates than boys and that creative and outgoing children are more apt to have them—or at least talk about them—than more introverted children. The imaginary companion is also more prevalent among firstborn and only children.

The imaginary companion usually disappears as the child becomes more involved with real playmates. In the absence of other children, however, the imaginary companion may serve a valuable function for the young child:

> One of the many crucial components in socialization and personality development is social interaction with siblings and peers. In the absence of such interactions [later] social interaction with age-mates may be greatly reduced. Some of the necessary developmental experiences can be provided through the vehicle of an imaginary companion. With this companion, the child can practice and develop social and language skills which might otherwise develop more slowly. (Manosevitz et al., 1973)

The creation of imaginary companions is a dramatic illustration of the importance of play and fantasy for the preschool child's development of the skills required in interpersonal relationships.

Peer Relationships

The child's first interpersonal relations are generally restricted to parents and brothers and sisters, and so his earliest concept of social interaction is patterned after what he sees at home. As he begins to generalize these concepts to people outside the immediate family group, the child reflects his perceptions of his own family situation through his social behavior. If he finds close contact with his family to be rewarding, he tends to seek out warmth and comfort from others as he grows older. The child who feels he is denied parental affection, on the other hand, may learn to avoid personal interactions, preferring instead to cultivate his independence and self-reliance.

The preschool child's increasing ability to interact with other children is reflected in his changing pattern of play. Shortly after infancy, children begin to engage in parallel play—that is, they play in the presence of other children, often using the same materials, but without any intentional sharing or personal interaction. Then gradually they begin to participate in cooperative play: they share playthings, organize games, make friends. Cooperative play reflects the child's growing capacity to accept and respond to ideas and actions that are not originally his own. It is as much the result of a healthy self-esteem as of normal maturation.

Around the age of four, most children begin to combine fantasy and play in a more complex form of imaginative imitation called *sociodramatic play*. Sociodramatic play is similar to dramatic play except that it involves the cooperative playacting of several children at the same time. In playacting with others, the child both acts and reacts, his imagination roaming freely in response to the cues given by the other actors. With older children, sociodramatic play may continue for days.

Sociodramatic play is broader and richer than the private and parallel play that precedes it. In pairs or in larger groups, children begin to combine isolated activities into relatively integrated fantasy situations. A chair and a radio may be transformed through the miracle of imagination into a spaceship as a group of children enact a trip to the moon. By sharing their private fantasies, children teach each other things that no adult would ever think of teaching them. Through sociodramatic play, children learn to interact with others and to lay the foundations of interpersonal relationships.

Figure 9.6. From parallel play to cooperative play. At first the child engages in his own play privately, though another child may be present. Later, two children can play together, especially in an unstructured "game" such as exploring materials. Finally several children play cooperatively, agreeing on the rules of such games as "store."

Increased social interaction brings with it more opportunity for quarrels and disagreements and usually brings out verbal aggression as well. It is during the preschool years that children begin to develop competitive responses. The desire to do better than others is absent in infants and appears to develop gradually as the child ages. In our culture competitiveness is strongly reinforced even in the early preschool years. The child who is passive or submissive—especially if he is a boy—is told to assert himself and to stand up for his rights. Theoretically, of course, it is possible to be assertive without being unpleasant about it, but preschoolers find it hard to see much difference between competitiveness and hostile aggression.

This can raise a problem for parents who are reluctant to punish their child for hostile behavior unless they are sure he will understand the reason for punishment. If they wait until he can see why certain kinds of aggressive behavior are

wrong, then they can correct him through example or explanation. Before that time, however, the child may be unwilling or even unable to curb his hostile impulses without firm adult intervention. Obviously the parents must help the child learn to strike a reasonable balance between assertiveness and passivity, but how they deal with a particular situation depends on many factors, including the child's age, birth order, and the social environment.

Perhaps the most significant advance the preschool child makes in his relationship to his peers is the establishment of personal one-to-one friendships. The three year old acquires various playmates, but at this early age his egocentricity prevents him from seeing much importance in the differences between them. Soon, however, he begins to have preferences: one may be too passive to have much fun with; another may be a bully. The children who are the most fun to play with are soon singled out as special friends, though the relationship may not be sustained or consistent yet because very young preschoolers respond strongly to feelings that change from moment to moment.

IMAGINATIVE PLAY

The childhood of the Brontë children, early in the Victorian era, gives us a classic example of how important imaginative play can be in a child's development. Many of us are familiar with the writings of Emily Brontë, author of *Wuthering Heights,* and her older sister Charlotte, author of *Jane Eyre* and other novels. Few realize, however, that the two sisters, along with their brother Branwell and their younger sister Ann, spent years of their childhood in a self-designed world of fantasy.

The Brontë children were raised in Haworth, Yorkshire, England, by their father, a clergyman, and their aunt, Miss Elizabeth Branwell. Except for an extremely brief stay at a nearby boarding school, Charlotte and Emily received all their education from their aunt and father. In the rough moors around Haworth, discouraged from mingling with the local children, the Brontës were isolated not only by geography but by the social prejudices of their father. Yet the Brontë children attained a higher level of creativity than any of their more worldly neighbors.

What the young Brontës lacked in travel and experience they more than made up in curiosity and imagination. The Reverend Patrick Brontë and his sister-in-law were very private people who did not want their own privacy to be infringed and therefore did not invade the privacy of the children. Left to themselves, Charlotte, Ann, Branwell, and Emily eagerly pursued romance and adventure wherever it could be found.

One day in June, 1826, the Rev. Brontë returned from Leeds with a present for his nine year old son. Young Branwell was delighted with his new box of wooden soldiers and was eager to share his gift with his three sisters. The girls proved to be no less excited than their brother. Charlotte, the oldest, immediately claimed the noblest soldiers of the lot, announcing that he was to be none other than the much admired Duke of Wellington. Her sisters immediately followed suit, each choosing a soldier and assigning it a name. It was left to Branwell to choose the soldier to be known as Buonaparte.

The preschool child usually chooses friends he perceives as being similar to himself. For this reason, a child's close friends are usually of the same sex and age as the child himself. The establishment of personal friendships marks an important step in the child's awareness of other people as distinct and unique individuals.

CHILDHOOD PSYCHOSIS

During the preschool years the child normally begins to develop a sense of his own identity and the world around him. He begins to speak more clearly and to form more or less healthy attachments to others. But some children follow a very different path. Their relationships with others may be severely impaired, even nonexistent; they may have almost no sense of self-identity; they may be unable to learn to talk or understand others; they may be unable to tolerate any change

Before long, the young Brontës were imagining and acting out elaborate military campaigns for the armies of Wellington and Buonaparte. As the children tired of battle strategies, their soldiers took on new identities and new names. The Young Men, as the soldiers were called, began to assume the roles of writers, artists, and statesman; yet, as they shifted from one social role to another, each of the Young Men retained his personality.

By the summer of 1827, the Young Men's Play had given way to the game of Our Fellows in which each of the soldiers represented the head man of his own private island. Emily's head man, Clown, stood four miles tall, but the poor fellow was dwarfed by Charlotte's Hay Man, Branwell's Boaster, and Ann's Hunter, each of whom stood a proud ten miles high!

After a few months, this game was replaced by the Play of the Islanders. At first, each child chose a real island and listed real people to populate it. By the following June, however, Charlotte had relocated the islanders to the Is-land of Dreams, an island on which stood a palace of white marble containing the magnificent Hall of the Fountain. Winding his way cautiously through a series of dark underground passages, secret doors, and concealed stairways, an explorer might ultimately arrive at some mysterious cell or even a dungeon filled with instruments of torture.

And so it went, through adventures in Africa to the establishment of the "Glass Town Confederacy." As a later writer put it, the Brontë children were able to use imagination as "an Aladdin's lamp through whose magic power they transcended time and distance, walked with kings, and swayed the destiny of a mighty empire" (Ratchford, 1941). From 1829 to 1845 the Brontë children faithfully recorded the detailed adventures of their imaginary characters in their imaginary worlds. That effort undoubtedly helped to develop and shape the creativity of the two girls who would later produce some of the most renowned literature of the nineteenth century.

BRUNO BETTELHEIM

Every society, ancient or modern, tribal or urban, has had to deal with the problem of mental illness. One man who has devoted a great deal of energy to helping the mentally ill is Dr. Bruno Bettelheim. Born in Vienna in 1903, he is the author of numerous books on psychology and psychiatry and teaches both subjects at the University of Chicago. He has been concerned with the problems of infantile autism and childhood schizophrenia.

Dr. Bettelheim's interest in the problem of mental illness stems in part from his personal experiences in two Nazi concentration camps, Dachau and Buchenwald. Essentially, he views the mental patient as an individual who is trapped within his own inner prison. In the conventional mental institution, the patient's feelings of helplessness and confinement are intensified, not reduced. In the hope of finding a humane and effective treatment of mental illness, he helped to create the Orthogenic School of the University of Chicago.

The Orthogenic School was established as a therapeutic community that would help the disturbed individual rejoin the outside world. There are no bars on the windows and no locks on the doors. The child enters the school only after inspecting the premises and deciding for himself whether or not he wishes to go.

A fundamental flaw in the conventional mental institution is the clear-cut hierarchy that gives staff members almost absolute power over the patients.

At the Orthogenic School, every effort is made to erase fear and mistrust. Therapists are available twenty-four hours a day and meet daily with other staff members to discuss their feelings about the patients and the institution. Every member of the community is encouraged to participate in making decisions.

The aim of therapy is to restore to the patient a justifiable feeling of self esteem. At the Orthogenic School, the patient acquires a sense of his own importance.

Children—like all of us—tend to behave in accordance with the expectations of others. A child who is expected to lie or cheat, for example, is more likely to do so than a child of whom honesty is expected. This is especially true for the mentally ill. The Orthogenic School strives to display maximum trust and confidence in its patients.

Perhaps the most distressing feature of the typical mental institution is its almost complete lack of privacy. Because Dr. Bettelheim is concerned with building up the patient's self-respect, bedrooms, bathrooms, and recreation areas at the school are not only spacious and colorful, but offer patients privacy. Individuality is encouraged, not repressed.

All of this is fine in theory, of course, but does it work? The answer seems to be a very definite yes. More than 85 percent of those who have completed treatment at the school have been restored to full social activity. Former patients of the Orthogenic School have gone on to become social workers, nurses, bankers, businessmen, commercial pilots, construction workers, jornalists, and teachers.

The work of Dr. Bettelheim and his associates indicates that progress in the treatment of childhood psychoses depends on the creation of humane therapeutic institutions.

in the world around them. When these symptoms (or a number of others) appear in severe form, psychologists describe the condition as a schizophrenic syndrome, or more generally, **childhood psychosis.**

This condition, or rather set of conditions, is hard to define with any precision. The psychoses are a broad group of disorders, and their exact clinical dimensions have never been determined. The symptoms of severe emotional disturbance, however, are all too obvious. A visit to the children's ward of a city or state hospital is a frightening experience that can leave the observer shaken. Children of different ages lie motionless on the floor or sit huddled against the wall, staring vacantly before them, oblivious to their surroundings. Some crouch tightly in a corner, eyes squeezed shut, while others spin through the room, whirling for hours in what seems like a grotesque parody of normal childhood play. What is it that could possibly lead to such tragedy?

The answer, unfortunately, is that no one really knows. Some have suggested that the major cause is the parents' failure to give the child the attention he needs, physically or emotionally. Other researchers have tried to trace childhood psychosis to metabolic or biochemical malfunctions, to brain damage, or even to genetic causes. There is some evidence to support all of these theories, but so far each theory has been able to account for some cases but not others. Many years of research will be necessary before it will be possible to pinpoint the specific environmental, psychological, or physiological causes of psychosis. In the meantime, the emphasis must be on diagnosis and therapy.

In a review of the literature on childhood psychosis, a researcher (Goldfarb, 1970) singled out nine signs of severe emotional disturbance. We have already noted some: severe impairment of emotional relationships, an apparent unawareness of personal identity, inability to learn or to use language, and an abnormal resistance to changes in the environment. The other signs listed in the review are obsessive preoccupation with particular objects; abnormal perception of stimuli; acute and excessive anxiety, especially in situations that should not be frightening; distorted patterns of movement, such as rigid immobility or hyperactivity; and a history of serious mental retardation.

No single one of these signs is necessarily a sign of emotional disturbance. When clinicians use them as psychotic symptoms, what they look for is a pattern in which a number of the signs appear together and in severe form. "Unawareness of personal identity," for example, does not mean simply an occasional lapse back into self-forgetfulness; as used in this sense it might refer to the child's abnormal behavior toward himself, examining parts of his body as though they belonged to someone else or even mutilating himself.

Psychosis often takes the form of schizophrenia or autism, two disorders that are themselves not clearly defined. **Schizophrenia** is a rather general term for disturbances that have a detachment from reality at their core; the symptoms may include regression to an earlier stage of development, bizarre behavior, apathy, and destructive rages. **Autism** is a near-total withdrawal that occurs when the child can achieve a feeling of safety only by shutting out the world. In a mild

Figure 9.7. At a child care center, a boy imitates the things he has seen his mother do. Opportunities to play in constructive ways help a child develop self-esteem.

case, the autistic child can avoid contact or interaction with others; he rarely looks at people, and when he does, his gaze does not indicate normal attention. More severe symptoms are extreme isolation, refusal to hear or speak to others, virtually no interest in people (although the child may be fascinated by an object), and obsessive insistence that nothing be changed, apparently in an effort to produce a state of perpetual monotony. The autistic child may show some of these symptoms from the earliest days of life.

Treatment of the pyschotic child is usually geared toward minimizing symptoms in order to help the child live as normal a life as possible. Therapy, often centered around structured or unstructured play, is designed to teach the child to express his feelings freely and, by building his self-respect, ultimately to improve his social functioning. Obviously, therapy will be of little ultimate value without the cooperation of the child's parents, so working with the family is an important part of treating the child. Institutionalization is a drastic step which is avoided under all but the most extreme circumstances.

The outlook for psychotic children has improved over the years, but it remains bleak. In some cases, therapy has succeeded in improving social behavior, but it is rarely able to reverse fundamental deficiencies in intellect, perception, and language. As they continue to explore the possible origins and treatments of childhood psychoses, psychologists are discovering that every instance of emotional disorder in children is a unique case and that each one requires unique diagnosis and treatment.

References

Baumrind, D. Current patterns of parental authority. *Developmental Psychology Monographs*, 1971, *4*, 99–103.

Borke, H. Interpersonal perception of young children. *Developmental Psychology*, 1971, *5*, 263–269.

Cramer, P., and Bryson, J. The development of sex-related fantasy patterns. *Developmental Psychology*, 1973, *8*, 131–134.

Erikson, E. H. *Childhood and society*. New York: W. W. Norton, 1963.

Goldfarb, W. Childhood psychosis. In *Carmichael's manual of child psychosis*, Paul H. Mussen (Ed.), New York: Wiley, 1970.

Harris, L. Looks by preschoolers at the experimenter in a choice-of-toys game: Effects of experimenter and age of child. *Journal of Experimental Child Psychology*, 1968, *6*, 493–500.

Hostetler, J. A., and Huntington, G. E. *The Hutterites in North America*. New York: Holt, Rinehart and Winston, 1967.

Irwin, D., and Moore, S. The young child's understanding of social justice. *Developmental Psychology*, 1971, *5*, 406–410.

Isaacs, S. *Social development in young children*. London: Routledge, 1946.

Kagan, J., and Moss, H. A. *Birth to maturity*. New York: Wiley, 1962.

Kohlberg, L. A Cognitive-developmental analysis of children's sex-role concepts and attitudes. In *The development of sex differences*. E. F. Maccoby (Ed.), Stanford: Stanford Univ. Press, 1966.

Manosevitz, M., Prentice, N. M., and Wilson, F. Individual and family correlates of imaginary companions in preschool children. *Developmental Psychology*, 1973, *8*, 72–79.

Maudry, M., and Nekula, N. Social relations between children of the same age during the first two years of life. *Journal of Genetic Psychology*, 1939.

Millar, S. *The psychology of play*. London: Penguin, 1968.

Piaget, J. *Play, dreams and imitation in childhood.* London: Heinemann, 1951.

Ratchford, F. *The Brontë's web of childhood.* New York: Harper & Row, 1941.

Ross, D., and Ross, S. Leniency toward cheating in preschool children. *Journal of Educational Psychology*, 1968, *60*, 483–487.

Rutherford, E., and Mussen, P. Generosity in nursery school boys. *Child Development*, 1968, *39*, 755–765.

Schwartz, J. C. Fear and attachment in young children. *Merrill Palmer Quarterly*, 1968, *14*, 313–322.

SUMMARY

1 Basic patterns of emotional and social behavior are set in the preschool years. They begin with the establishment of gender identity. Gender is largely determined by how the child is viewed by society and by himself. The development of a self-image involves a realistic awareness of sex roles in society.

2 One explanation for sex roles is that they are formed by society's rewards for conformity and punishment for deviance. To a great extent a child is influenced by the sex stereotypes he observes in life and in television and the movies, which show men as strong and aggressive and women as passive and nurturing. The egocentricity of preschoolers leads them to prefer the company and to follow the example of people similar to themselves, especially in sex.

3 Dependent behavior takes the form of seeking affection, attention, and help in doing things. Studies suggest that children whose early dependency is indulged tend to grow into less dependent people than those for whom deprivation of love or attention is used for punishment. However, overprotective parents may prevent the child from becoming self-reliant. As a child matures, he begins to depend less on his parents and more on other adults and children.

4 Erikson theorized that the preschool child experiences a developmental crisis of initiative versus guilt. The child takes initiative as he becomes aware of his own powers; initiative may lead to guilt when his thoughts or actions place him in a position that he recognizes as "bad."

5 Freudian theory explains aggression as an instinctual human impluse, arising out of sexual frustration. A similar view, the frustration theory, sees frustration without the sexual element as the source of aggression. The instinct learning theory holds that aggression stems from instinct but that early training or imitation is necessary for it to result in overt behavior.

6 Physically aggressive behavior generally decreases with age, with verbal aggression replacing physical aggression. Studies show that boys are more aggressive than girls and that patterns of aggression evident in the preschool years may continue in later life.

7

Social stress is one source of fear in the preschool child, and the child's own imagination is another. Most children develop ways to overcome irrational fears and to manage those that have a rational basis.

8

Piaget suggests that preschool children, because they are egocentric, cannot understand moral values; other investigators have found that preschoolers do become aware of the feelings of others. The development of generosity and cooperation are closely linked to the child's perception of warmth and affection in the parent of the same sex. The child's concept of social justice is influenced by his own obedience to the rules.

9

Fantasy is used by the child to deal with feelings and ideas that he cannot express in real life. Like a sense of humor, it helps relieve him of frustration and anxiety. Young children laugh most at physical humor and gradually find humor in words. They often adopt imaginary playmates.

10

How the child relates to his peers usually depends on his interfamily relationships. The preschool child's increasing interaction with other children is seen in his greater participation in cooperative play. At about age four, children begin sociodramatic play. One-to-one personal relationships develop, usually with children of the same sex.

11

Whether the cause of childhood psychosis is environmental, biochemical, or genetic is difficult to determine, but it is recognizable by a pattern involving several symptoms. Therapy for it is very difficult.

FURTHER READINGS

Church, J. *Understanding your child from birth to three.* New York: Random House, 1973.

    This child psychologist has some interesting things to say about language acquisition in a book that covers the broad areas of early development. For example, he believes that children from bilingual families in the United States should be taught in the native tongue, with English as a second language. He suggests a number of ways for parents to aid the development of fluency, "a liberating gift."

Hymes, J. J. *The child under six.* Englewood Cliffs, N.J.: Prentice-Hall, 1968.

    On the premise that if you know why the preschooler does something, there is less chance of trouble, this child development specialist often shows us the world from the preschool child's view. Hymes offers advice from observations of children in many kinds of situations, and his enjoyment of them shows in the writing.

LeShan, E. J. *How to survive parenthood.* New York: Random House, 1965.

    Just because traits such as jealousy and aggression are considered "normal" behavior by psychologists is no reason for parents not to step in when such feelings make children behave in antisocial ways, this child psychologist advises. The book consists of down-to-earth discussions about dealing with children.

Wing, L. *Autistic children.* New York: Brunner, Mazael, 1972.

    A British physician who has studied autistic children writes that autistic behavior almost always begins from birth and becomes most obvious from ages two to five. Distortions of perception create complex emotional and behavioral problems that call for expert handling. She suggests ways to help integrate autistic children into society.

Part 4
MIDDLE CHILDHOOD

We played robber now and then about a
month, and then I resigned. All the boys did.
We hadn't robbed nobody, hadn't killed any
people, but only just pretended. We used to
hop out of the woods and go charging down
on hog-drivers and women in carts taking
garden stuff to market, but we never hived
any of them. Tom Sawyer called the hogs
"ingots," and he called the turnips and stuff
"julery," and we would go to the cave and
powwow over what we had done, and how
many people we had killed and marked. But
I couldn't see no profit in it. One time Tom
sent a boy to run about town with a blazing
stick, which he called a slogan (which was
the sign for the Gang to get together), and
then he said he had got secret news by his
spies that next day a whole parcel of Spanish merchants and rich A-rabs was going to
camp in Cave Hollow with two hundred elephants, and six hundred camels, and over a
thousand "sumter" mules, all loaded down
with di'monds, and they didn't have only a
guard of four hundred soldiers, and so we
would lay in ambuscade, as he called it, and
kill the lot and scoop the things. He said we
must slick up our swords and guns, and get
ready. He never could go after even a
turnip-cart but he must have the swords and
guns all scoured up for it, though they was
only lath and broomsticks, and you might
scour at them till you rotted, and then they
warn't worth a mouthful of ashes more than
what they was before. I didn't believe we
could lick such a crowd of Spaniards and
A-rabs, but I wanted to see the camels and
elephants, so I was on hand next day, Satur-
day, in the ambuscade; and when we got
the word we rushed out of the woods and
down the hill. But there warn't no Spaniards
and A-rabs, and there warn't no camels nor
no elephants. It warn't anything but a Sunday-school picnic, and only a primer class at

that. We busted it up, and chased the children up the hollow; but we never got anything but some doughnuts and jam, though Ben Rogers got a rag doll, and Joe Harper got a hymn-book and a tract; and then the teacher charged in, and made us drop everything and cut. I didn't see no di'monds, and I told Tom Sawyer so. He said there was loads of them there, anyway; and he said there was A-rabs there, too, and elephants and things. I said, why couldn't we see them, then? He said if I warn't so ignorant, but had read a book called *Don Quixote*, I would know without asking. He said it was all done by enchantment. He said there was hundreds of soldiers there, and elephants and treasure, and so on, but we had enemies which he called magicians, and they had turned the whole thing into an infant Sunday-school, just out of spite. I said, all right; then the thing for us to do was to go for the magicians. Tom Sawyer said I was a numskull.

"Why," said he, "a magician could call up a lot of genies, and they would hash you up like nothing before you could say Jack Robinson. They are as tall as a tree and as big around as a church."

"Well," I says, "s'pose we got some genies to help *us*—can't we lick the other crowd then?"

"How you going to get them?"

"I don't know. How do *they* get them?"

"Why, they rub an old tin lamp or an iron ring, and then the genies come tearing in, with the thunder and lightning a-ripping around and the smoke a-rolling, and everything they're told to do they up and do it. They don't think nothing of pulling a shot-tower up by the roots, and belting a Sunday-school superintendent over the head with it—or any other man."

"Who makes them tear around so?"

"Why, whoever rubs the lamp or the ring. They belong to whoever rubs the lamp or the ring, and they've got to do whatever he says. If he tells them to build a palace forty miles long out of di'monds, and fill it full of chewing-gum, or whatever you want, and fetch an emperor's daughter from China for you to marry, they've got to do it—and they've got to do it before sun-up next morning, too. And more: they've got to waltz that palace around over the country wherever you want it, you understand."

"Well," says I, "I think they are a pack of flatheads for not keeping the palace themselves 'stead of fooling them away like that. And what's more—if I was one of them I would see a man in Jericho before I would drop my business and come to him for the rubbing of an old tin lamp."

"How you talk, Huck Finn. Why, you'd *have* to come when he rubbed it, whether you wanted to or not."

"What! and I as high as a tree and as big as a church? All right, then; I *would* come; but I lay I'd make that man climb the highest tree there was in the country."

"Shucks, it ain't no use to talk to you, Huck Finn. You don't seem to know anything, somehow—perfect saphead."

I thought all this over for two or three days, and then I reckoned I would see if there was anything in it. I got an old tin lamp and an iron ring, and went out in the woods and rubbed and rubbed till I sweat like an Injun, calculating to build a palace and sell it; but it warn't no use, none of the genies come. So then I judged that all that stuff was only just one of Tom Sawyer's lies. I reckoned he believed in the A-rabs and the elephants, but as for me I think different. It had all the marks of a Sunday-school.

—Samuel L. Clemens
The Adventures of Huckleberry Finn

10
Growth and Personality

By the time a child starts grade school, she has formed a personality that no one—adults or other children—can mistake. Her personality is absolutely individual; it began to develop before she was born and will continue to change until she dies. But in the elementary-school child we sense—sometimes quite suddenly—that the child is a little *person*. She has characteristic ways of behaving that we recognize as distinctly her own and that we can predict to some extent if we know her well.

Each individual personality develops under the influence of countless major and minor factors. We can even say, in a broad sort of way, what these influences are. The strongest factor in the development of personality is undoubtedly the child's individual social history. Most of the child's learning is from her social experiences, and although these experiences are sometimes supervised by parents and teachers, more often they occur in spontaneous family or neighborhood settings. No two children have exactly the same social histories, even if they are twins who do everything together.

A second kind of factor that influences personality is the cultural. Through everything from music, television, and incidental remarks overheard but hardly understood by the child to deliberate modeling and training, the child is encouraged to embody the typical or ideal personality of her culture. Third, there is the particular situation—the elements of place and time that bring out some personality traits and leave others in reserve.

Finally, there are the factors involved in biological makeup: facial features, physique, growth rate, and temperament. Genetic heritage provides the potential for these traits. One way of thinking about genetic potential is to regard it as setting the outside limits toward which environmental factors can advance the child's development.

As one researcher (Mussen, 1973) has put it, these four types of factors are "interwoven—operating, interacting, and affecting personality development concurrently." Together they have formed a distinct personality for each child entering grade school, and together they will continue to form it as she grows.

PHYSICAL DEVELOPMENT

A child's growth rate and physique are not entirely the result of his genetic inheritance. They are also affected by his diet, by the health care he receives, and by the kinds of physical exercise he is encouraged to do. These influences then affect the child's personality through his growth rate and physique. Without mini-

---

PREVENTING HEART DISEASE WHEN IT STARTS—IN CHILDHOOD

The State of Arizona is now working with 10,000 families of preschool children in an effort to prevent heart disease when it really starts—in early childhood. The program, which focuses on diet, exercise, blood pressure, obesity, and cigarette smoking, will be expanded to 13,000 additional families next year, at a cost of $10 to $13 a family.

The program . . . is based on a cardiovascular intervention study that Dr. Glenn M. Friedman and his colleagues established in their private pediatric practice in Scottsdale, Ariz., three years ago.

Dr. Friedman's prescription includes a reduction in the amount of protein foods consumed each day to the level recommended by the National Academy of Sciences (the average American currently consumes twice the recommended daily allowance for protein). Dr. Friedman emphasizes a decrease in animal proteins, since all of these are high in cholesterol and saturated fats, the substances that promote . . . hardening of the arteries.

The pediatrician also encourages families to pry themselves and their children away from the television set and instead spend the time exercising. He favors activities like bicycle riding and swimming that can be enjoyed by the whole family and by the child for the rest of his life.

Dr. Friedman [points out] that cardiovascular disease, which kills

mizing the importance of social and cultural factors, researchers are recognizing more and more that a child's physical development has a strong influence on his personality. One researcher (Tanner, 1962) put it this way:

> All the skills, aptitudes, and emotions of the growing child are rooted in or conditioned by his bodily structure. Behind each stage of learning lies the development of essential cell assemblies in the brain; behind each social interaction lies a body image conditioned by the facts of size and early or late sexual maturation. . . . How fast a child grows and what type of body structure he has can exert a crucial influence on the development of his personality. The child's sense of identity is strongly linked to his physical appearance and ability.

Physical Appearance

The rate of growth in the elementary school years is not as spectacular as it is in infancy or adolescence, although some children do experience a small burst of growth between the ages of six and eight. As the child grows, his trunk tends to become slimmer, his chest broader, and his arms and legs longer and thinner. At the same time the size of his head gradually approaches the adult proportion of one-seventh to one-eighth of his total height. His permanent teeth appear, making the bottom part of the face look "heavier." Toward the end of middle childhood,

---

more than one million Americans a year—25 per cent of them before the age of 65—is like "an iceberg."

"The disease process and risk factors have their inception in the pediatric age group where there is presently no significant screening or intervention," he noted. "It is only when the problem emerges . . . with the onset of a coronary or a stroke that we seem to get concerned. By then, it is too late."

As Dr. Friedman summarized current prospects for the American infant, "There is a 50 percent chance or greater of him developing an increased blood cholesterol, a greater than 30 percent chance he will smoke, a 10 to 20 percent chance of being obese, and perhaps a 45 percent chance that he will become sedentary"—all of which gives him a better than 50 percent chance of . . . a coronary or stroke.

Noting that living patterns are established in childhood and that "the family lives together, eats together, exercises together, and perhaps even smokes together," Dr. Friedman concluded that a family-oriented prevention program is needed. He said that the 3,400 families his group has been following in Scottsdale, a middle-class community near Phoenix, has shown that parents are willing and able to follow his prescriptions. . . .

—Jane E. Brody in *The New York Times*, November 16, 1973

the youngster may look as though parts of his body are out of proportion, and indeed some parts do grow faster than others. The awkward appearance and movements that are temporary results of uneven and rapid growth may cause even the most normal child to feel sensitive or worried about his body.

Physique and personality

The body is a particularly important instrument of the school-age child's success. Size and body build are key factors in achievement at sports and other play activities, and a large portion of the child's prestige comes from his physical ability. Of course size has no direct influence on academic achievement, but it does seem to have some indirect effect. It has been shown, for example, that from the age of six on, physically large children average higher scores on tests of mental ability than do smaller children (Scottish Council, 1953; Tanner, 1962). This correlation of height and intelligence persists into adulthood but gradually diminishes (Tanner, 1966).

The relation between body build and personality has been summarized in these words:

> Small, poorly coordinated, and relatively weak children are inclined to be timid, fearful, passive and generally worried. In contrast, tall, strong, energetic, well-coordinated children of the same age are playful, self-expressive, talkative, productive, and creative (Mussen, 1973).

It should be emphasized that the personality traits described are not the immediate and direct result of the child's genetic endowment. That is, physical attributes do affect the child's aptitudes, interests, and, thus, personality formation. But, perhaps more important, his physical appearance affects how others react to him, and thus how he regards himself.

For example, adults and classmates tend to treat a small, thin child as though he were delicate, dependent, and incompetent. The child's limited ability at sports will further reinforce their opinion and his own of his competence. The result may be that he avoids sports and other forms of competition altogether, thereby perpetuating his physical frailty and the responses which it elicits. In time, he consequently develops the personality characteristics that people expect of him because of his size. On the other hand, adults and classmates will tend to react to the tall, muscular child as though he were competent; his own competence at games will foster his further success; and he will be encouraged to develop outgoing traits.

Maturation

The wide differences in size that can be seen in adolescence are not a major problem for school-age children. We grow fairly evenly through middle childhood, until by the age of eleven most boys have attained about 85 percent of their mature height. However, at this time the girls' adolescent spurt, which began two years before

Figure 10.1. As young horsewomen develop their skill they impress others with their competence and courage.

that of boys, will make many girls taller than the boys in the classroom. Though born lighter, girls will have become as heavy as the boys by the age of about eight, and heavier by the age of nine or ten. It is not until the age of about fourteen that the overall size of males exceeds that of females.

Many of the small, underdeveloped children in the classroom are only growing at an entirely normal but relatively slow rate of maturation. Some of them will keep their thin, lanky physiques as adults, but many others will grow up to be taller and stronger than their previously more robust peers. Unfortunately, later physical prowess may not be enough to reverse the psychological effects of early experiences. Longitudinal studies indicate that the late-maturing boy's relative unpopularity and low social status will probably have resulted in feelings of anxiety, inadequacy, and expectation of rejection by the group. According to certain studies (Jones, 1957; Mussen and Jones, 1958a and 1958b), early maturing boys are less neurotic and more sociable than late maturers, even as young adults.

Because of the normal variation in rate of maturation, it has been suggested that *developmental age* (defined as degree of physiological maturity), rather than chronological age, be used in assessing personality development (Tanner, 1962). This would involve the measurement of such factors as dental maturity, skeletal maturity (i.e., bone age), and the amount of water in the muscle cells. Also as we noted earlier in this chapter, the child's shape changes in middle childhood. A European investigator who has used these changes to determine developmental age has proposed that a child start school only after attaining a certain level of "form-change" and that he go on to the subsequent level at school only after attaining the next stage of form-change (Zeller, 1952). In other words, physiological maturity should receive greater emphasis than chronological age in determining the rate at which the child advances through his schooling. The value of this recommendation can be appreciated if we observe how children who are noticeably tall or short or obese are often mocked by their classmates.

Environment and Growth

Researchers have found a definite correlation between height and socioeconomic class in that children from upper-income homes grow taller and, in some countries, mature earlier. It is likely that variation in nutrition and in regular patterns of exercise and sleep account for a part of this difference. However, there is also strong evidence that a pattern of social mobility tends to push tall people upward and short people downward on the social scale (Scott, et al., 1956; Thompson, 1959), reinforcing the genetic pool of short individuals from low-income homes.

Physical growth can also be inhibited by severe psychological stress in the home. A study (Powell, Brasel, and Blizzard, 1967) of children originally thought to be dwarfed by disorders of the pituitary gland reported that the children's growth accelerated as soon as they came to the convalescent hospital, though no growth hormones were given them. At home, the children had been subjected to stress caused by marital discord, promiscuity, alcoholism, and physical abuse. Far from being starved, however, they gorged themselves at the table—and at garbage cans and the cat's dish. They stole food from the neighbors and drank water from the toilet bowl. This behavior disappeared in the hospital and the children rapidly caught up to their normal growth level. Psychological stress does not commonly result in dwarfism—the brothers and sisters of the children reported in this study were nearly normal in size—but even a low incidence of this pattern illustrates the potential effect of psychological factors on physical growth.

SELF-AWARENESS

As a cultural anthropologist has noted (Mead, 1934), the self consists of both the "I" (the one who acts) and the "me" (the one who is the object of an action). Between the ages of eight and twelve, then, we can say that the child starts to

"*This neighborhood sure has changed since I was a kid.*"

define "what makes me me." In the process, he may become more aware of his own emotions and exhibit them in new ways. For example, fears which had once been expressed primarily through actions (crying or running) may now be channeled into anxiety. The identity crisis which is experienced as a result of this new awareness is probably not as strong as that which may occur during adolescence, but it is as crucial to the child's development.

At the same time that the child begins to understand what makes him who he is, he also develops an understanding of what makes others who they are. Through the self-awareness that arises from his social interactions, he becomes more sensitive to his own attitudes about others—he may seek out those who are similar to him and shun those he perceives as different—and, likewise, he becomes more sensitive to attitudes that his peers and adults have toward him. He also becomes more aware of those forms of social behavior that win popularity and may adopt some of the traits that he perceives as approval-getting in others.

Self-Esteem

With his new self-awareness, the child invariably compares himself to his peers, and, at the same time, finds that they are comparing themselves to him. As a result, a kind of informal but fairly rigid "pecking order" is established in the schoolroom. The child's self-esteem is, essentially, his self-judgment of his own abilities, influence, and popularity. To a certain extent, it is a mirror image of the judgment of others. His degree of self-esteem will affect his behavior—either by limiting or extending the range of things he will attempt, whether in academic tasks, sports, or friendships. Low self-esteem tends to make the child less original and more imitative, whereas high self-esteem brings out initiative and independent judgment.

In comparing children of high and low self-esteem, one team of investigators (Taylor and Combs, 1952) found that better-adjusted children viewed themselves more matter-of-factly and showed greater self-acceptance than did less well-adjusted children. Another researcher (Coopersmith, 1967) similarly discovered that children with high self-esteem were able to devote more time to others and to external activities because they were less preoccupied with themselves. High self-esteem children asserted themselves even at the risk of disapproval, showed initiative, were confident of their own judgments and capabilities, and took leadership roles. On the other hand, low self-esteem children withdrew in their fear of disapproval, tended to be quiet and unobtrusive, did not participate in groups, and were filled with self-doubts about their own judgments and capabilities.

This same study notes a correlation between child rearing and self-esteem. Parents of children with high self-esteem usually possessed a high degree of self-esteem themselves, and further, they tended to be reasonable and fair in punishing their children. Parents of children with low self-esteem tended to have low self-esteem and tended to alternate erratically between harsh and permissive treatment.

Figure 10.2. The respect that boys show each other builds their individual self-esteem.

Sex-Role Development

By the time a child is of school age, he has already learned the concepts of "male" and "female" and has already begun to learn and display attitudes and behavior appropriate to his or her sex. Once the child has left the relatively closed family environment to enter the larger world of school, he will begin to broaden his knowledge of sex roles, adopting the stereotypes about masculinity and femininity that are dominant in his society and culture. Our own traditions teach, for example, that boys should be tough and aggressive, and girls polite and submissive; that athletic skill is a male trait, and cooking a female trait.

There is still some disagreement as to which sex differences are the product of sex hormones. Some evidence, largely from animal studies, suggests that prenatal hormones determine the differences in male and female aggression levels, and aggression is considered a crucial sex-typed behavior. Nevertheless, most psychologists agree that socialization is a more important factor than sex hormones in a child's acceptance of sex-typed behavior from middle childhood on. The child learns what the prevailing sex roles are, and he embodies them to win approval.

Strong evidence in favor of the socialization theory of sex roles has been provided by studies (Money, 1957, 1965a, 1965b) showing that regardless of his hormone makeup, a child is comfortable in, and behaves according to, the prescribed roles of the sex he was raised to think he belonged to. If by mistake a child of one sex is raised as a member of the other sex, by the age of three or four the need to conform to what has been learned as sex-appropriate behavior is so strong as to be nearly impossible to erase. For example, a boy raised as a girl wants to do "female" things and perceives his genitals as an embarrassment. In such cases, it appears more feasible to change the child's sex characteristics by surgery or hormone treatment than to change the child's psychological sense of sex identity.

However, later research indicates that sex identity is the result of a complicated interaction of nature and nurture, and that prenatal hormones are a major factor (Money and Ehrhardt, 1973). Cited were studies of girls who had accidentally received unusually large amounts of male hormones in the womb. Although these girls usually grew up to be normal and became wives and mothers, during childhood they displayed more aggression, preferred more rough play and utilitarian clothing, and tended to strive more to dominate the childhood pecking order than did girls with the usual amount of prenatal hormones. Nevertheless, the earlier findings about changing sex identity after age four were still considered applicable.

Available evidence on the subject was summarized by another study (Hutt, 1973) as tending toward the conclusion that behavior is "primarily a function of the early sexual differentiation of the brain, and secondarily . . . an effect of circulating hormone levels." One investigator found that even one month olds were reared differently according to sex (Escalona, 1974). When boy babies followed an object with their eyes, parents were observed to bring the object closer so that the child could comprehend it; whereas when girl babies followed the object, parents were observed to cuddle the child, distracting it from the object. In other words, boys were encouraged to master their environment (aggression) and girls encouraged not to.

Regardless of what the inborn differences may be, it is clear that sex-role stereotypes are learned. Although there are probably physical predispositions, a child learns sex roles by observation and continues to display them because they are reinforced by social approval. The child observes these roles not only in his parents but in other adults and in his peers as well.

Aggression

Numerous studies have found that teachers and peers of boys from five to fourteen rate boys as more aggressive, noisy, and negative than girls of the same age. Similarly, a range of studies (Bach, 1945; Bandura, 1961) has shown that after observing aggressive behavior, boys exhibit more physical aggression than girls, although both sexes are on par in terms of verbal aggression. The tendency for boys to be more aggressive than girls is also reflected in the caseloads of the courts and child guidance clinics, where about three times as many boys as girls are referred (Elkind, 1971). In playtime activities, boys are observed to engage in more rough-and-tumble play than girls. Girls who want to engage in rough play are

Figure 10.3. Soccer for boys, sack races for girls. As girls begin to participate in more robust games, the sack race may disappear forever.

discouraged, either on the grounds that it is "unladylike" or that girls would not be able to keep up with boys in rough activities.

It should be noted, however, that tomboy behavior, long considered merely a stage, has recently gained wider acceptance. Girls have been admitted to such male preserves as the Little League, although it required court action to bring this about. Researchers (Money and Ehrhardt, 1973) have noted that the norms of male and female aggressiveness form a continuum, and tomboy behavior should not in any way be considered abnormal. Whether tomboyism is a result of hormonal imbalance (normal, but high on the continuum) or whether it is the result of child rearing practices, it may actually be healthy in terms of a girl's muscular development. Some researchers have predicted that as rigid differentiation of male and female roles in terms of physical activity breaks down, aggression patterns in boys and girls will become more similar.

Dependency

By middle childhood girls tend to be less aggressive than boys, but they are not yet more passive (dependent). It is not until the teens and college that girls are judged by themselves and by observers to be more dependent than boys. Actually, evidence in this area is not clear-cut, although a number of studies support the claim that, after middle childhood, females show greater social passivity, dependency, and conformity than males (Lindzey and Goldberg, 1953).

Sexual latency

Following Freud, psychoanalysts have called middle childhood the period of *sexual latency*—a time of transition that follows the oedipal crisis and precedes the storm of puberty. Freud (1938) argued that at this time "libidinal drives" were sublimated, making this a relatively calm and nonsexual period during which children tend to prefer the company of members of their own sex.

> The influx of sexuality does not stop even in this latency period, but its energy is deflected either wholly or partially from sexual utilization and conducted to other aims. The historians of civilization seem to be unanimous in the opinion that such deflection of sexual motives from sexual aims to new aims, a process which merits the name of *sublimation,* has furnished powerful components for all cultural accomplishments. We will, therefore, add that the same process acts in the development of every individual, and that it begins to act in the sexual latency period.

In a sense Freud merely applied to the period of middle childhood the nineteenth-century notion that it was necessary to abstain from sex in order to accomplish physical and creative acts (a theory still held by many major football players). It was in middle childhood, Freud theorized, that it becomes necessary for the child to divert his sexual energies to "education." In this, we find the seeds of Erikson's theory of "initiative versus inferiority"—a theory that argues that during latency, a child's "whims" are converted to "productive" behaviors.

Erikson (1968) calls the latency period a "psychosexual moratorium in human development—a period of delay which allows the child to attend whatever 'school' his culture provides" before he becomes a mate and parent. In other words it is a temporary respite from sexual priorities so that the child can focus on gaining the skills necessary to carve out a social niche. However, many commentators have pointed out that there is no evidence that the child's curiosity about sex or his impulse to masturbate lessens during middle childhood.

Industry Versus Inferiority

The developmental crisis of middle childhood, according to Erik Erikson, is centered in the growing need for the child to use his abilities in ways that will be satisfying to him and acceptable to society. Erikson calls this crisis *industry versus inferiority*; it is an extension of the preschool conflict between initiative and guilt. In middle childhood the individual develops a strong sense of industry unless he is hampered by a sense of his own inferiority. It is at school that the child receives the "systematic instruction" in the ethic of technology that develops his sense of industry:

> The child must forget past hopes and wishes, while his exuberant imagination is tamed and harnessed to the laws of impersonal things—even the three Rs. . . . He now learns to win recognition by producing things. . . . He develops a sense of industry—i.e., he adjusts himself to the inorganic laws of the tool world. He can become an eager and absorbed unit of a productive situation. To bring a productive situation to completion is an aim which gradually supersedes the whims and wishes of play (Erikson, 1963).

During this period of development, the child learns the "fundamentals of technology"—in Western culture, the basic tools of literacy and mathematics that will make later specialization possible. Further, the child internalizes the production ethic, learning to value work and cooperation. It is his acceptance of these values, and his acquisition of skills at work and cooperation, that will make the child a productive member of his society:

> This is socially a most decisive stage: since industry involves doing things beside and with others, a first sense of division of labor and of differential opportunity, that is, a sense of the *technological* ethos of a culture, develops at this time (Erikson, 1963).

Ideally, the child will develop a sense of industry as one strong component of his personality. However, he faces two basic dangers: on the one hand, he may overreact and overvalue utilitarianism: "If he accepts work as his only obligation," Erikson says, "and 'what works' as his only criterion of worthwhileness, he may become the conformist and thoughtless slave of his technology and of those who are in a position to exploit it."

On the other hand—and this is the countertheme of this stage of childhood— the child may develop a sense of inferiority that impedes his ability to acquire the necessary sense of industry:

ERIKSON'S CRISES IN PSYCHOSOCIAL DEVELOPMENT

Basic Trust versus Basic Mistrust (first year of life)

Autonomy versus Shame and Doubt (second year of life)

Initiative versus Guilt (the preschool years)

Industry versus Inferiority (middle childhood)

Building on the previously developed trust, autonomy, and initiative, the child can achieve a sense of industry. In school he learns the basic tools of literacy and cooperation that will enable him to become a productive member of society, and a sense of achievement becomes important to him. He learns the satisfaction of persisting at a task until it is completed and of using his skills to perform according to his own and other's expectations. In a culture like ours where achievement is often measured in terms of doing better than someone else, he also learns to compete and to measure his productivity in relation to that of others.

The dangers of this period are twofold: on the one hand, the child may learn to value achievement in work above all else; he may alienate his peers by his excessively competitive behavior. On the other hand, he may feel unable to perform the tasks required of him and develop a sense of inferiority that prevents him from trying. Experiences of failure may lead to the child's feeling that he is inadequate, that he cannot be successful as a worker. In extreme cases, this sense of inferiority can affect the child's attitude toward work for life.

Identity versus Role Confusion (adolescence)

Intimacy versus Isolation (young adulthood)

Generativity versus Stagnation (prime of life)

Ego Integrity versus Despair (old age)

The child's danger, at this stage, lies in a sense of inadequacy and inferiority. If he despairs of his tools and skills or of his status among his tool partners, he may be discouraged from identification with them and with a section of the tool world. . . . The child despairs of his equipment in the tool world and in anatomy, and considers himself doomed to mediocrity or inadequacy (Erikson, 1963).

Such feelings, the result either of the child's not really being prepared for the school experience, or of problems encountered at school, may force the child to regress to behavior more appropriate to an earlier age:

To lose the hope of such "industrial" association may pull [the] child back to more isolated, less tool-conscious familial rivalry. . . . It is at this point that wider society becomes significant in its ways of admitting the child to an understanding of meaningful roles in its technology and economy (Erikson, 1963).

PERSONALITY PROBLEMS

Psychologically speaking, a normal child is one whose behavior is in harmony with his environment and with himself. But even a perfectly normal child experiences problems in growing up. Temporary personality problems may in fact be a sign

Figure 10.4. The school-age child is eager to master the use of tools and become a productive individual.

that the child is facing up to new situations he is encountering at home and at school. It is only when problem behavior becomes severe that a child can be said to be "disturbed" or neurotic. According to one estimate (Vaughan, 1961), only about 10 percent of all children have severe enough personality problems to require professional treatment. Often, a wise parent or teacher may be able to help the child identify his problem and learn to deal with it effectively.

When an otherwise healthy child suddenly begins to have fights, or refuses to go to school, the problem may or may not have a psychological basis. For example, the child who seems to get into a fight almost every night after school may be psychologically disturbed, or he may be defending himself against a bully. Thus, apparently neurotic behavior may in fact be quite normal. It is important for the adult to deal with each problem individually. The key, of course, is defining what is normal and what is abnormal in each case.

Fear and Anxiety

Fear is a natural response to real or imagined danger. School children find many things in their environment that they cannot understand or control, and that they may perceive as threatening. A precocious child may be afraid of things that his peers have not yet learned to see the danger in (Holmes, 1935), but some children develop unwarranted fears, such as the fear of dogs or fear of crossing the street.

What causes a child's particular fears? Psychologists, regardless of orientation, tend to agree that fears are learned. Sometimes a child's fear results from his experience of real dangers. Sometimes it is taught to him, unconsciously, by his parents or siblings. Sometimes, as in fear of storms, it results from the child's misunderstanding of situations.

Typically, during the elementary-school years, the child may develop a fear of supernatural dangers, of accidents, of school failure, or of ridicule. At this age, many children are afraid of storms, dogs, or crossing the street—all "dangers" that they do not know how to control. A child's experience will determine his fears: a child from a low-income home tends to fear the physical dangers associated with poverty, such as lack of food or shelter, while the middle-class child is more afraid of such threats as academic failure (Angelino, et al., 1956).

Anxiety, like fear, is a response to a felt danger, which may or may not be real. However, anxiety is usually not directed toward a specific object or situation. In fact, the anxious child often does not know exactly what is worrying him. Outwardly he may only seem nervous; his anxiety is mostly indirect or internal. Though the preschool child shows his anxiety by a generalized excitement, the elementary-school child may develop specific symptoms: insomnia, headaches, stomachaches, or tics, such as repeated blinking or yawning.

Anxiety in children is quite common. Many children are apprehensive in new situations but are able to deal with them after the initial anxiety. Sometimes the child's own fantasies about a situation scare him. But only the child with excessive or habitually chronic anxiety should be viewed as having a personality problem.

One major source of anxiety is conflict—that is, the struggle between two or more desires or emotions that cannot be satisfied. Psychologists distinguish three basic types of conflict. The boy who likes pie and cake equally but must choose only one dessert faces *approach-approach* conflict. In contrast, the girl who must go to a piano lesson she hates or stay home and get a spanking experiences *avoidance-avoidance* conflict. The most frequent and most difficult to deal with is *approach-avoidance* conflict, as in the case of the child who wants to ride on a merry-go-round but is afraid he will fall off.

The patient adult can help the child understand and come to terms with his conflict, thus lessening the child's anxiety and preparing him to make future decisions. The child who has serious anxiety problems is probably one who frequently finds himself in situations that allow no relief. For example, a child who lives with a tyrannical grandmother may have a strong desire to fight back and at the same time may fear standing up to her because she is stronger. The child may also want to hit her and at the same time think he is evil just for wanting to do so. Such a child may not learn to express either his fear or his anger directly and may develop some of the more extreme types of anxiety.

Phobias, Obsessions, and Compulsions

A child who says he dislikes lakes, streams, and swimming pools, and feels anxious whenever he sees one, can be said to fear water. But the child who is constantly anxious that he might drown and does not want to leave home because he fears this possibility has a **phobia.** Basically, a phobia is a severe and excessive fear aroused by a particular object or situation and characterized by an extreme desire to avoid the object.

Simple admonitions to be careful can lead to phobias. A child who is warned that he might drown in the creek may come to believe all water is dangerous. Phobias can also be absorbed from parents or peers who have said nothing about the subject. The child's father, for example, may fear dogs, or fear they may harm his child; and though he may try to hide it, the father will pass on this fear like a contagion. Though parents usually try to protect the child from what he fears, gradual exposure to the feared object is probably the most efficient way to cure any but the most persistent phobia. One experiment (Bandura, 1961) showed that children could be cured of a phobia of dogs merely by watching a child who was not afraid interact more and more closely with a dog. This experiment supports the hypothesis that many phobias are absorbed from models, whether they are parents, siblings, or peers.

School phobia upsets most parents and teachers more than any other because it can disrupt the whole pattern of a child's life. It is characterized by a refusal to go to school, anxiety at school and the thought of school, and usually by physical complaints, such as stomachaches or sore throats. These physical symptoms are caused by the child's anxiety, not by a virus. School phobia is equally common in boys and girls. Although it seems to be more frequent among higher socio-economic groups (Hersov, 1960), it is likely that when school phobia occurs in low-income groups it tends to be labeled truancy and treated in a more authoritarian manner (Milman, 1966). However, one researcher (Davidson, 1961) has pointed out a distinction: "while the truant runs away from school, the school phobic runs back to his home."

The onset of school phobia has been associated with experiences in the classroom, as in the case of a ten year old girl embarrassed by her early breast development and sensitive to the ridicule of her less-developed classmates. Many psychologists have felt that school phobia is a sign of family disturbance and that the mother is ambivalent about having her child leave her to attend school. However, a recent study (Kessler, 1972) points out that there is no real proof that the child's mother is to blame for school phobia. The study shows that school phobia does not run in families and that mothers whose children have entirely different psychological problems often have the same sort of inner conflict.

The best way to handle school phobia is usually to get the child back to the classroom as soon as possible, though not by coercive means. One way is for the mother to sit in the classroom with the child for as many days as it takes the phobia to disappear. This works in a large majority of cases, especially if the treatment is started as soon as school phobia appears.

An **obsession** is a persistant preoccupation—an idea a child cannot get out of his head. Most obsessions begin as phobias. A child with a dog phobia may find that taking great pains to avoid dogs still does not reduce his anxiety. He

---

THE PSYCHOLOGY OF FEAR

Research on fear began in the 1920s, when the psychologist John B. Watson conditioned an eleven month old boy, Albert, to feel terror at the sight of a white rat (Watson, 1920). Albert was a very cheerful child, and the only thing that would frighten him normally was a startling, loud noise that Watson made by clanging two steel bars together. By presenting the white rat and at the same time clanging the steel bars, Watson successfully conditioned the boy to fear the rat. Following the experiment, Albert also developed a fear of other furry objects, such as rabbits and dogs. Watson concluded that most human fears are learned this way—an otherwise neutral object, such as the white rat, will become frightening only if it is associated with a painful or frightening object.

A subsequent researcher (Miller, 1948) carried this idea even further. In a similar experiment, the researcher administered electric shocks to rats whenever they were in a white, lighted chamber. The rats learned to escape through a door to a safe, dark chamber—and they would dart through the door even when no shocks were administered, because they had been conditioned to fear the white compartment. Again, there seemed no doubt that the fear was learned.

But in a slightly altered replication of the experiment, the results were very different. If the rats were given shocks when they were in the dark chamber rather than the white one, they were very slow to learn to avoid the "dangerous" chamber. Some never learned the avoidance behavior at all; and if they did, it could be "unlearned" very quickly. These results seemed to support the theory that animals, including human beings, are genetically "programmed" to learn to fear certain things. Thus, the dark chamber might signify safety to a night-adapted animal such as the rat.

One psychologist (Seligman, 1972) points out that dark, dangerous animals and hostile strangers have always been with us. Most human phobias involve insects, animals, open spaces, heights, or strangers—all things that were truly threatening in earlier times.

Unpredictability probably also contributes to our fear of violence, for we are better able to cope with danger if we are prepared for it.

When the situation is uncontrollable, fear may become chronic. Many advantageous internal bodily changes occur when one is frightened on a short-term basis. Long periods of unrelieved fear, on the other hand, can do serious physical and psychological harm. Relief from fear is necessary if a person is to function and develop normally.

may begin to think about dogs all the time, worrying constantly that he will meet one, that it will attack him, and that he will not be able to escape.

Obsessions tend to be either precautionary or repugnant. The precautionary ones may involve cleanliness or health; the repugnant ones tend to involve such fantasies as hurting someone or doing something bad. The child's obsession is a kind of self-torture and usually helps him avoid his feelings of guilt.

When the child can no longer control his anxiety by merely thinking and instead begins to do something, his obsession becomes a **compulsion**. A child obsessed with neatness may straighten the objects in his room several times a day. It is an irrational action that the child feels compelled to perform over and over again. Compulsions often arise out of or coexist with obsessions. There are, similarly, precautionary and repugnant (or punishment) compulsions. For example, a child obsessed with cleanliness may develop the precautionary compulsion of wiping doorknobs free of germs several times a day.

Figure 10.5. This boy has an exceptional skill at copying. To interpret his attention to detail as "compulsive" might be a mistake.

Figure 10.6. A calm, understanding talk is often a good way to handle frustration.

Such ordinary daily activities as dressing and washing can become highly complicated compulsive rituals. In the early stages, such behavior will win the child approval, and it may take the parent or teacher a long time to realize that the child has lost control and cannot stop the repeated washing or haircombing.

But the adult should not be too quick to diagnose a compulsion as abnormal. Even normal children, particularly seven and eight year olds, exhibit some compulsive behavior. The common childhood game, "Step on the crack, break your mother's back," which involves compulsively avoiding sidewalk cracks, is one example of such behavior. Rules, ceremonies, and rituals are essential elements of all games, and children's games, particularly the ones they play when they are eight years old, usually involve many rules. Games become more flexible as the child reaches nine or ten; the child's guilt lessens and he learns to live more comfortably with his conscience.

How can you tell if a child's compulsion is normal or abnormal? As one researcher (Kessler, 1972) puts it, the "common compulsions are like games which the child enjoys playing by himself or with others, and he has no feeling of inner coercion. In the pathological form, the compulsion is unique to the child, and he derives no pleasure or social benefits from it."

Hysteria

Like the phobias, obsessions, and compulsions, **hysterical** symptoms develop in children who have strong anxiety responses. Hysterical symptoms tend to fall into two groups: the child may develop a tic, such as a constant clearing of his throat, or he may lose a function, as in deafness or muteness that is not caused by any physical reason. Cases of hysteria are believed to be far less frequent today than in former times when anxiety could not be expressed directly.

Tics usually involve the muscles of the face, neck, and head, as in repeated blinking, yawning, or shrugging of the shoulders. Studying 487 elementary school children, researchers (Lapouse and Monk, 1968) found that 12 percent of the children had unusual movements, twitching, or jerking. Another study (MacFarlane, et al., 1954) found that tics and mannerisms peak in girls at six years old and in boys at seven. Tics can be a great annoyance. Usually they are cured by simply ignoring them, but sometimes they require professional treatment.

Frustration and Aggression

Psychologists, beginning with Freud, have stressed the effect of early childhood frustrations on later life. But frustrations are part of our daily existence and affect people of every age level. In a competitive society, the loser—whether in a simple game or in competition for a parent's love—feels frustration. Youth itself is a source of frustration; so many privileges are withheld "until you get older."

A child who persists in a task in spite of failure or in spite of not attaining success is said to have a high frustration tolerance. The child who gives up easily and who may exhibit aggressive behavior or emotional outbursts in the face of frustration is said to have a low frustration tolerance.

Aggression is a common response to frustration. Essentially, it is the expression of the child's anger in the face of frustration, and is one of the most noted behavior problems in the classroom. It may range from talking back to kicking toys and even vandalism. Because aggression upsets others, it has been given more attention than withdrawal reactions, which many psychologists feel pose a more serious problem for the child himself.

Aggression may be directed toward the object or person that causes the frustration, or it may be directed against some other target. One analysis of aggression (Rosenzweig, 1944) divides it into three categories: *extrapunitive* aggression is directed against the frustrating objects or other objects in the child's environment; *intropunitive* aggression is directed against the child himself; and *impunitive* aggression attempts to avoid the situation by some other behavior.

A frustrated child who cannot act out his aggression directly on the cause of his frustration often *displaces* his aggression—that is, he directs his aggression against some other person or object. The child who bullies a younger child, for example, may have been frustrated by his father or another child who is stronger than he is. A typical case is that of a boy who bit and pinched his parents to get attention but was forced by punishment to stop. The same behavior then appeared at school. When, after counseling, parents began to give the child more attention, the school biting problem disappeared.

Behaving in a manner more suitable to a younger age is called *regression*. The five year old who reverts to wetting his pants, just like his baby brother, may be attempting to reclaim the parental affection he sees lavished on the baby. His regression is evidence that he cannot think of another way of gaining the attention that he has lost and is jealous of. Obviously, then, regression is one way a child deals with the tensions of frustration, but it is not the most desirable way, since it temporarily prevents him from learning more mature methods of coping with the problem.

Regression may occur from time to time in even a normal child, but he can be helped to understand the problem that frustrates him and will suggest a better way for the child to cope with it.

Delinquency

Children who are habitually late, truant, or unable to get along with others, who lack interest in schoolwork or resist authority, may be exhibiting *predelinquent behavior*—behavior that, in the experience of a psychologist, usually precedes actual lawbreaking. But even normal children occasionally exhibit such behavior, so it is not wise to jump to conclusions. Tests like the Delinquency Proneness Scale and the Haggerty-Olson-Wickman Behavior Rating Scales can be helpful in analyzing problems (Garrison, et al., 1967). In middle childhood, delinquency may take the form of stealing, vandalism, setting fires, sadistic behavior, truancy, rebellious behavior, or running away from home.

The predelinquent or delinquent child is "expressing through action some feelings or concerns that he cannot talk about or find other ways to resolve" (Weiner and Elkind, 1972). Although most psychologists still believe that delinquent behavior requires treatment of the individual offender, increasingly they point out that society may be as much at fault as the delinquent:

> One way of looking at a great deal of delinquency is to consider it as an attempt to relieve oppression or as a kind of social activism or dissent. In violating the law, the delinquent is often directly or indirectly clamoring for change within his family unit or within his society. (Halleck, 1972)

Delinquency, in other words, is not considered just a psychological problem. Rather than punishing the delinquent, parents, teachers, and friends can encourage him to continue to defend himself against the real oppressions in his life, yet bring him to understand and control his responses to internal conflicts—conflicts that cause him to see more oppression than is really there.

Sociopathic Personality

One distressing childhood personality problem—sociopathic or psychopathic personality—can be hard to detect, and when noted, very difficult to treat. Unlike the ordinary delinquent, the sociopath may undertake an act of violence without any real motive, or may overreact to a small slight. For example, a child who is not allowed to watch his favorite television show may set fire to the house. Although many psychiatrists have supposed that the sociopath has a criminal nature, today most believe that sociopathy is simply a severe failure in socialization.

The child sociopath's relationships are self-serving and superficial because the child is too absorbed in his own fantasies and desires to care about anyone else. Unlike most delinquents who worry about the welfare of the gang, the sociopath really does not care about his fellows. He may persuade them to undertake crimes they would never imagine themselves and then leave them in the lurch.

The sociopath often persuades others—peers, parents, and teachers—into doing what he wants. He often has an attractive personality and can be very convincing because he is acting out fantasies that seem more real to him than ordinary reality. But he does not make a very efficient schemer because he lacks a sense of reality. He is so absorbed in the moment that he cannot foresee the consequences of his acts; his judgments are poor and he usually does not learn by experience. Typically, the child sociopath is a frequent liar, cannot be relied on, and never feels guilty for what he does.

Some psychologists feel that the sociopathic personality appears in children with an inborn predisposition. Brain damage, or a biological imbalance, or possibly some part of the child's genetic endowment might cause the condition. Many other psychologists, however, feel that the child's parents are at fault. Typically, these children have fathers who are successful, stern, remote, busy, and frightening and mothers who, on the other hand, are frivolous and indulgent. Basically, the two parents have conflicting attitudes toward life and toward the child, though both usually care a great deal about appearances and want the child to reflect well on them. The parents may therefore take a great deal of trouble raising the child but express little real love for him (Greenacre, 1945). The child is confused and angered by the inconsistent discipline he gets from his parents and by what he senses is their rejection of him. The child's seeming lack of conscience has resulted because being good has never gotten him what he wanted: acceptance by his parents.

What can be done for the child sociopath? The parent or teacher should not attempt to treat the child himself, but call in professional help. The disorder is difficult to treat, but in many cases professional care has brought good results (Kaplan, 1971).

References

Angelino, H., Dollins, J., and Mech, E. V. Trends in the "fears and worries" of school children as related to socio-economic status and age. *Journal of Genetic Psychology,* 1956, *89,* 263–276.

Bach, G. Young children's play fantasies. *Psychological Monographs,* 1945, *59* (2).

Bandura, A., et al. Transmission of aggression through imitation of aggressive models. *Journal Abnormal Social Psychology,* 1961, *63,* 575–582.

Coopersmith, S. *The antecedents of self-esteem.* San Francisco: W. H. Freeman, 1967.

Davidson, S. School phobia as a manifestation of family disturbance. *Journal of Child Psychology and Psychiatry,* 1961, *1,* 270–278.

Elkind, D. *A sympathetic understanding of the child six to sixteen.* Boston: Allyn and Bacon, 1971.

Erikson, E. H. *Childhood and society.* New York: W. W. Norton, 1963.

Erikson, E. H. *Identity: Youth and crisis.* New York: W. W. Norton, 1968.

Escalona, S. "Activity and passivity: Influences of maternal style on early ego development," *The William Menacker Lecture.* New York: Presented to the New York University Program on Post-Doctoral Study and Research in Psychology and the Psychoananlytic Society, January 5, 1974.

Freud, S. *The basic writings of Sigmund Freud.* New York: Random House, 1938.

Garrison, C., Kingston, A. J., and Bernard, H. W. *The psychology of childhood.* New York: Scribner's, 1967.

Greenacre, P. Conscience in the psychopath. *American Journal of Orthopsychiatry,* 1945, *15,* 495.

Halleck, S. L. Delinquency. In Wolman, B. (Ed.), *Manual of Child Psychopathology.* New York: McGraw-Hill, 1972.

Hersov, L. A. Refusal to go to school. *Journal of Child Psychology and Psychiatry,* 1960, *1,* 137–146.

Holmes, F. B. An experimental study of the fears of young children. *Child Development Monographs,* No. 20, Pt. 3. New York: Teachers College, Columbia University, 1935.

Hutt, C. Sex differences in human development. In B. S. Smith (Ed.), *Readings in Child Psychology.* New York: Meredith, 1973.

Jones, M. C. The later career of boys who were early- or late-maturing. *Child Development,* 1957, *28,* 113–128.

Kaplan, L. *Education and mental health.* New York: Harper, 1971.

Kessler, J. W. Neurosis in childhood. In B. B. Wolman (Ed.), *Manual of child psychopathology.* New York: McGraw-Hill, 1972.

Lapouse, R., and Monk, M. A. An epidemiologic study of behavior characteristics in children. In Quay, H., *Children's behavior disorders*. Princeton: Van Nostrand, 1968.

Lindzey, G., and Goldberg, M. Motivational differences between males and females. *Journal of Personality*, 1953, *22*, 101–117.

MacFarlane, J. W., Allen, L., and Honzik, M. P. *A developmental study of the behavior problems of normal children*. Berkeley: University of California Press, 1954.

Mead, G. H. *Mind, self, and society: From the standpoint of a social behaviorist*. Morris, C. W. (Ed.). Chicago: University of Chicago Press, 1934.

Miller, N. E. Studies of fear as an acquirable drive: Fear as a motivation and fear-reduction as reinforcement in the learning of new responses. *Journal of Experimental Psychology*, 1948, *38*, 89–101.

Milman, D. H. School phobia: Clinical experience. *New York State Journal of Medicine*, 1966, *66*, 1887–1891.

Money, J. Influence of hormones on sexual behavior. *Annual Review of Medicine*, 1965a, *16*, 67–82.

Money, J. Psychosexual differentiation. In J. Money (Ed.), *Sex researcher, new developments*. New York: Holt, 1965b, 3–23.

Money, J., and Ehrhardt, A. A. *Man and woman, boy and girl*. Baltimore: Johns Hopkins University Press, 1973.

Money, J., et al. Imprinting and the establishment of gender role. *A. M. A. Archives Neurological Psychiatry*, 1957, *77*, 333–336.

Mussen, P. *The psychological development of the child*. Englewood Cliffs, N.J.: Prentice-Hall, 1973.

Mussen, P. H., and Jones, M. C. The behavior-inferred motivations of late- and early-maturing boys. *Child Development*, 1958a, *29*, 61–67.

Mussen, P. H., and Jones, M. C. Self-conceptions, motivations, and impersonal attitudes of late- and early-maturing boys. *Child Development*, 1958b, *28*, 243–256.

Powell, G. F., Brasel, J. A., and Blizzard, R. M. Emotional deprivation and growth retardation simulating idiopathic hypopituitarism. *New England Journal of Medicine*, 1967, *276*, 1271–1278.

Rosenzweig, S. An outline of frustration theory. In Hunt, J. (Ed.), *Personality and behavior disorders*. New York: Ronald Press, 1944.

Scott, E. M., et al. A psychological investigation of primigravidae. *Journal of Obstetrical Gynecology*, British Empire, 1956, *63*, 338–343.

Scottish Council for Research in Education. *Social implications of the 1947 Scottish Mental Survey*. London: University Press, 1953.

Seligman, M., and Haber, J. *Biological boundaries of learning*. New York: Appleton Century Crofts, 1972.

Tanner, J. M. *Growth at adolescence*. Oxford: Blackwell Scientific Publications, 1962.

Tanner, J. M. Galtonian eugenics and the study of growth. *Eugenics Review*, 1966, *58*, 122–135.

Taylor, C., and Combs, A. Self-acceptance and adjustment. *Journal of Consulting Psychology*, 1952, *16*, 89–91.

Thompson, A. M. Maternal stature and reproductive efficiency. *Eugenics Review*, 1959, *51*, 157–162.

Vaughan, W. T., Jr. Children in crisis. *Mental Hygiene*, 1961, *45*, 354–359.

Watson, J. B., and Rayner, R. Conditioned emotional reactions. *Journal of Experimental Psychology*, 1920, *3*, 1–14.

Weiner, I., and Elkind, D. *Child development: A core approach*. New York: Wiley, 1972.

Zeller, W. *Konstitution und Entwicklung*. Göttingen: Psychologisch Rundschau, 1952.

SUMMARY

1   Growth rate and physical characteristics affect the child's aptitudes, interests, popularity, and personality development. Self-awareness increases in middle childhood, accompanied by greater sensitivity to the attitudes of peers and adults.

2   Most psychologists believe that socialization is a more important factor than hormones in a child's adoption of sex-typed behavior. Freud described middle childhood as a period of sexual latency, in which the child could focus on the development of skills.

3   Erikson theorized that in middle childhood the individual undergoes the crisis of *industry versus inferiority*. In this crisis, the child will develop a strong sense of industry unless he is hampered by a sense of his own inferiority.

4   Fears are learned, whether they are warranted or not, and may result from experience or teaching. Conflict is a major source of anxiety. The three basic types of conflict are *approach-approach, avoidance-avoidance, and approach-avoidance.*

5   Phobias can result from the child's own experience, or they can be transmitted by models such as parents, siblings, and peers. Phobias may lead to obsessions, and obsessions may lead to compulsions. Normal children exhibit some compulsive behavior. Abnormal compulsion involves a loss of control and can involve highly complicated rituals. Hysterical symptoms arising out of strong anxieties may take the form of repeated physical responses, such as facial tics or apparent illness.

6   Children who persist in difficult tasks are said to have a high frustration tolerance; those who give up easily, a low frustration tolerance. Aggression is a common response to frustration, and it may be directed against the cause of the frustration or some other target. Regression is another means of dealing with frustration.

7   Predelinquent behavior may take the form of habitual lateness, truancy, or belligerence. Middle-childhood delinquency may take such forms as stealing, vandalism, and setting fires. Most psychologists feel that delinquency is both a societal and an individual problem.

FURTHER READINGS

Bettelheim, B. *Dialogues with mothers*. New York: Free Press of Glencoe, 1962.

> In Bettelheim's opinion, theories do not have much practical value when parents run into trouble with children. He recommends a careful investigation into each troublesome circumstance to find out why children react as they do. The quality of daily interactions between parent and child is an all-important influence on personality development, he writes.

Briggs, D. *Your child's self-esteem*. Garden City, N.Y.: Doubleday, 1970.

> Briggs writes that a negative self-concept is the root cause of misbehavior, and that "the key to inner peace and happiness is high self-esteem, for it lies behind successful involvement with others."

Gruenberg, S. M. *Parents' guide to everyday problems of boys and girls*. New York: Random House, 1958.

> A guide to dealing with children from the ages of five to twelve, not recent but still useful. In her chapter on character and responsibility, Gruenberg discusses such traits as honesty, attitude toward work, sex, and money, and includes a chapter on the handicapped child.

Lederman, J. *Anger and the rocking chair: Gestalt awareness with children*. New York: McGraw-Hill, 1969.

> A personal account of Gestalt methods used with "disturbed" children in an elementary-school classroom. This readable book is intended to teach or suggest to others ways of giving troubled children a sense of themselves. Photographs by Lillian R. Cutler depict classroom situations.

Lundin, R. W. *Personality: a behavioral analysis*. New York: Macmillan, 1969.

> A study of behavior, emphasizing the role of learning. Lundin cites experimental and clinical studies in his explanation of normal, neurotic, and psychotic behavior.

Von Hilsheimer, G. *How to live with your special child*. Washington, D.C.: Acropolis, 1970.

> An off-beat book by an innovative educator who believes there are better ways of teaching self-control than by inhibiting behavior. Von Hilsheimer has things to say about diet and sleep for children, the importance of touching exercises, training for perception integration, and redirecting the impulses of young troublemakers.

11
Learning and Cognition

There comes a time with a grade school child when you suddenly notice that she talks just like an adult. By then she is also probably reading everything in sight, and so you may conclude that the development of her mind is basically complete—all she needs now is more information. Indeed, the contents of her mind will increase dramatically in the next few months and years, but there will also be some changes of a more fundamental nature. Her ability to think in abstract terms, for example, will make important advances. She will also come to perceive some highly complex aspects of the environment that had eluded her before, and she will become more efficient at remembering what she learns.

Partly as a result of this cognitive development, she will soon be much better able to see the world from the viewpoint of others—an ability that will enable her to participate more successfully in social situations. She will also grow more effective as a problem solver, both in daily life and in schoolwork.

PROBLEM SOLVING

We begin to do things on purpose early in infancy, and this can be regarded as solving problems in that most deliberate actions have to overcome some resistance or obstacle. We do not begin to solve problems in a thoughtful way, however, until we can imagine a possible solution without putting it instantly into effect. Most of us acquire this ability at about two years of age, and then we improve rapidly; by the time we are in elementary school we can apply some ingenious solutions to the problems we face. Several of our mental abilities have developed in ways that make each step of solving a problem much easier. In order to examine the different ways in which our problem solving abilities improve, psychologists have identified a number of separate steps that we usually take toward the solution of any problem. The main steps are perception, memory, and applying hypotheses.

In perception, the first step, the child perceives an "event"—that is, he becomes aware of a situation that involves some kind of problem to solve. His perceptions provide him with different kinds of information: the way different objects in the situation look, for example, and the way they are related to one another. In the next step, memory, the child draws forth data from his memory that will help him to deal with the new situation. For example, he may try to remember past experiences that were in some way similar to the present one and might, therefore, offer clues to solving his new problem. Finally, the child considers the different ways in which the problem might be solved, chooses among them, and then acts upon his choice.

Whatever the outcome of this process—whether the problem is solved to the child's satisfaction or requires new thought and appraisal—the child will store away some amount of information that he has derived from his experience, and he will then use this information in future situations. As the child grows, his problems will undoubtedly multiply; even play activity will involve more numerous and difficult problems and decisions. But as he progresses through middle childhood, his ability to solve these problems will increase.

Perception

Whether the child at school age has a greater capacity to perceive than the preschool child is a matter of some dispute. But there is no question that he is a better problem solver, and it is partly because he has devised new ways to organize and retain learning.

Through the preschool period the child learns to focus his attention on more and more elements of a situation with a single "take." By the time he is in grade school, he is capable of learning and classifying a considerable amount of information. The most significant perceptual advances have come through the acquisition of new words and concepts, which increase his capacity for thinking. For example, he does not need to look at two objects to know that one and one make two; instead, he understands the concepts of one and two and the concept of addition.

Memory

Human memory works very much like the memory unit of a computer, except that some information in the human memory may be irretrievable (although most psychologists believe it can never be deleted). Sometimes we wish to hold information only momentarily, for temporary use; for example, we may remember a telephone number only for the length of time needed to dial it. On such occasions, our memory is deliberately short. The information is entered into a temporary storage unit of the mind known as *short-term memory*. Though "memorized," this information will be unavailable to us for use in the future—not because it has been deleted, but simply because it has not been filed away into the proper area of the mind. The area that stores information for permanent use is called *long-term memory*; the ability to retrieve information from this storage area is known as *recall*.

In the middle years of childhood, we become more capable of recalling information from long-term memory. Moreover, a child at this age is capable of making a conscious (or unconscious) effort to retain short-term memories long enough for them to be transferred into the long-term reserve. The ten year old child has a much better recall than the child of four because he can shift information into long-term memory and has more efficient devices for retrieval.

The older child's greater facility with classification gives him a distinct edge over the younger child in remembering information (Rossi, 1966). Classification of information is a basic skill for independent thinking and problem solving, and

Figure 11.1 Learning with a computer capitalizes on the affinity between computer operations and human mental functioning. Here students answer arithmetic problems given by the computer.

it relies on both short-term and long-term memory. In an experiment with memorization strategies (Neimark et al., 1971), children from first to sixth grades were shown sets of pictures related to four categories: animals, furniture, clothing, and transportation. But the children were not told that all the pictures belonged to these classes. They were given three minutes to look at the pictures displayed at random on a table and to arrange them in any way that would help them remember the pictured objects. Children in the first to third grades, with the exception of a few third graders, showed no inclination to classify the pictures, but an increasing tendency to arrange pictures by category was found among children in grades four through six.

Applying Hypotheses

The final step in solving a problem is the assessment of possible solutions (hypotheses) and the application of one or more of them to the problem situation. As the child grows older, the greater amount of information she has about many things will tell her when additional information is needed in order to reach a correct answer. She can also apply more than one rule in solving a problem. The teacher says to Mary, "If I give you ten apples and you give one to Jane and one to Tommy, how many apples will you have left?" Mary applies two rules: first, one plus one equals two; and second, two from ten equals eight. So she answers: "I still have eight apples."

If Mary's hearing had been faulty and she thought the teacher said two instead of ten, she would have given a wrong answer. If she had heard correctly but recalled the problem incorrectly, she still would have given a wrong answer. She needs correct perceptions and correct recollections before she can arrive at correct solutions or reasonable alternatives for decision making.

Figure 11.2 Putting on skates can be a real problem. If the child does not remember how the laces should go or gives in to a hasty impulse, his shoe will soon come loose.

Some children make more errors than others even when they have good perceptions and recall, simply because they do not take the time to think a problem through. This is why impulsive children tend to make more mistakes than reflective children. They are quick to give an answer without sufficiently considering the problem. The reflective child gives herself more time to think about the problem and its solution before answering. Reflective children are generally anxious to achieve high scores, but reflectiveness may also have something to do with temperament. Although it is possible to train children to think before offering hypotheses, the tendency to be either impulsive or reflective generally appears to be consistent in people over the years.

READING DISORDERS

Among the total elementary school population in the United States an estimated 15 to 20 percent of the children are retarded readers; they read at the level expected for students a grade or more below their own (Bond and Tinker, 1973). There are several factors that may cause reading disorders in young children, including slow maturation; low intelligence; physical conditions such as fatigue, malnutrition, or chronic illness; undetected problems in hearing or vision; and psychological and social problems. A child may not speak English at home, and this may be what is making it hard for him to learn to read. Finally, if none of these factors seems to be causing the reading difficulty, the student who is retarded in reading may have a learning disability: a minor neurological malfunction that affects his perception, cognition, or memory.

Usually a reading disorder is caused by several factors, not just one. Many tests have been developed to diagnose reading disorders, most of them designed to discover only one or two of the possible causes. Thus, teachers and psychologists use several tests to identify a pattern of causes.

Causes of Reading Disorders

Reading problems due to late maturation are usually temporary. A child of normal intelligence, for example, may start off as a slow reader simply because his neurological development has not caught up with his mental age; when it does, the child will be able to read at his grade level.

Today's teachers are aware that difficulty in learning to read may make the child feel that he is a born loser and that such a self-concept will be a source of problems throughout his life. Early reading difficulties are themselves a source of later reading retardation because they create frustration and a sense of inadequacy that hamper a child's further efforts to learn. A large percentage of high school dropouts, for example, have had severe reading disabilities that have contributed to repeated academic failures and a sense of hopelessness. Their negative feelings about themselves, their abilities, and their prospects are confirmed in the job world, where there is no place for the uneducated except at the bottom of the economic ladder. The dropout rate is one of the reasons why schools have increased their efforts to diagnose reading disorders in the early grades and develop effective remedial programs.

In the past, teachers unfortunately tended to look upon all reading retardation as evidence of feeble mindedness, but today schools have facilities for testing children for intelligence, so the teacher is able to determine with some degree of confidence whether the reading problem is actually related to low intelligence. However, even in the case of less intelligent children, other disabling factors may be involved in reading retardation.

The observant teacher often finds clues to the causes of reading difficulties in the behavior of her students. Noticing that a child brings his book too close to his face when he reads and loses his place frequently, a teacher may guess that this student has poor eyesight and recommend an eye examination. If she has observed that he does not seem to hear unless he is looking directly at her, she may suspect that the child's poor classroom performance is related to a hearing problem. Hyperactive or highly impulsive behavior may suggest that the child's learning problems are due to an endocrine disturbance.

Reading difficulties may also be related to emotional disturbances, though it is often difficult to determine whether a reading problem is the cause or the result of such disturbances. A child's confusion, fear of competition, and low opinion of herself may act as blocks to learning. If Judy's mother calls her stupid each time she does something wrong at home, she will come to school with a self-concept of stupidity that will be evident in her classroom performance. Judy's belief that she is incapable of doing anything right may become a self-fulfilling prophecy unless she receives help from an understanding teacher.

Low-income children show a disproportionately large number of reading difficulties. A child from a low-income family often lives in an overcrowded and tension-filled environment where not only his emotional but also his physiological needs are rarely satisfied. He may be so malnourished and deprived of sleep that he does not have the energy to concentrate in school.

Where both parents have to work at tiring, mind-deadening jobs to support the family, they seldom have the energy to read stories to their children or even to talk with them. This is unfortunate, because these are means by which children develop perception and memory. Watching television is helpful, but the picture screen does not take the place of an interested, communicative parent. Thus, unless the low-income child has been exposed to preschool training in a child care center, he often begins elementary school untrained to listen. His understanding also may be severely hampered by his limited vocabulary of subcultural words or by the fact that the only language spoken at home is a foreign one.

Expectation and limitation are factors in the child's attitude toward learning to read. A disadvantaged child's lack of motivation may reflect the feelings of parents whose lack of academic and job opportunities has robbed them of hope for a better life. In contrast, a middle-class child's enthusiasm may reflect the attitudes of educated parents who encourage and expect their child to succeed scholastically. Moreover, when a child sees his parents reading books and periodicals, his desire to imitate them may provide an added incentive for him to learn to read.

There are a number of children from all backgrounds who cannot read, or read with great difficulty, and none of the above factors is the major cause of the disorder. These children have a learning disability. Identification and study of learning disabilities is very recent. We know very little about what they are, what causes them, or how to teach these children. However, a great deal of research is being done in this area, and it is becoming possible to teach children with learning disabilities to read.

Diagnosis and Remedies

Judy, David, and Michael are in the same third grade class. Their teacher has noticed that all three appear to have difficulties in reading. She gives the whole class the Stanford Achievement Test, a standardized test that compares each student with all other students in the same grade, and finds that Judy, David, and Michael read on the level of the first graders. This indicates severe reading retardation, but it does not tell her the reasons for the problem.

Where should she look next? She gathers information about each of the children and looks for patterns. Judy and David are nine years old, but Michael is only eight. He entered the first grade when he was five. While Judy and David have above-average IQ scores, Michael's is below average. The teacher calls Michael's parents and discovers they do not speak English. At this point the teacher has made a thorough *general diagnosis,* and she has enough information to plan

Figure 11.3. This student is attending a school that specializes in bilingual education. Many "reading problems" turn out to be merely the difficulties that arise from speaking one language at home and another at school.

and carry out a remedial program for Michael. She could test him in more detail, but there is really no need for it. Since Michael's age and IQ are lower than the average student in his class, he cannot be expected to have developed the skills necessary for reading at the third grade level, nor is it likely that he could suddenly catch up with the class. His IQ score suggests that he may have difficulty in mastering the nuances of spoken English, and so learning to read will be even harder. The teacher's remedial program for Michael might be based on the regular developmental reading program, starting at Michael's present level. However, she would pace the program to Michael's abilities and maturational readiness. She would also stress language skills, listening and speaking, and sound discrimination.

Now, why are Judy and David having problems? The teacher moves to the next level of diagnosis, *analytical reading diagnosis*. She may use one or more of several specific reading tests.

In testing Judy, the teacher finds that she can read words she knows even when she is only allowed to look at the word, but Judy will not attempt to sound the word out no matter how much time she is allowed to look at it. This finding indicates that Judy has a *sight vocabulary*, a number of words she has memorized and can recognize. However, Judy is unable to use *phonics*—to sound out words from their spelling. Beginning readers are usually taught both a sight vocabulary and phonics.

The teacher now knows that Judy's major disability in reading is probably that she does not use phonics. The next question is why. Has she simply never picked up the skill of using phonics, or does she have a problem relating sounds to letters? The teacher gives Judy further tests to determine whether she can hear the different sounds in similar words, and whether she can blend sounds she has heard separately into words.

It turns out that Judy can do all these things very well. As a final test, the teacher shows Judy some nonsense words made up of common sounds, and she is unable to pronounce them even if she can see the separate parts of the words. For example, one word on the test is "trock." Judy cannot even begin to pronounce it, so the teacher shows her only "tr." Judy is still unable to pronounce the sound even though she has just read the word "train" after seeing it for only half a second.

At this point the teacher decides that she can prepare a remedial plan for Judy with no further testing. Judy simply does not know how to use phonetics. Perhaps she was in a reading program that did not teach phonetics or was absent from school when they were introduced. The teacher plans a remedial program for Judy that focuses on a structured, developmental approach to phonics. At the same time, the teacher encourages Judy to enlargen her sight vocabulary.

David's performance on the reading test is different from Judy's. He is very nervous and does not always pay attention to the teacher's instructions. When he is unable to do a task, he becomes very upset. He can read some words when he is allowed all the time he wants, but when he is only allowed half a second he freezes and is unable to respond. David has particular trouble blending sounds into words and hearing differences in the sounds of similar words. He is, however, able to pronounce some of the nonsense words that Judy had so much trouble with. The teacher concludes that David has some limited knowledge of phonics and some sight vocabulary, but that his response to the test calls for closer examination. She carries the diagnosis to the third and most complicated level, *case-study diagnosis.*

At this level she needs the help of specialists in different fields. David is sent to a speech therapist to have his hearing tested. The therapist finds that David's ability to hear sounds is normal, but his abilities in blending and discriminating sounds are lower than what would be expected of a child his age. This is an indication of general neurological immaturity, so David is sent to a neurologist. He finds that David is neurologically immature and suggests that it is probably a temporary problem. The neurologist warns, however, that David should be watched closely for signs of development. If they do not appear within a year, a learning disability might be present.

David is also sent to a clinical social worker who interviews David and his parents. His parents are terribly concerned that David do well in school, and they pressure him to do better. They have been disappointed that he is not doing well and have decided that he is lazy or stupid. David has felt guilty, angry, and confused. He has come to hate school and reading because he fails. His parents' and his own attitudes make him hate himself for his failure.

Now the teacher can construct a remedial program for David. Her program is designed to match David's maturational level, for certain levels of neurological maturity are prerequisites for developing reading skills. By matching her expectancies with David's capabilities, the teacher hopes to provide David with goals he can meet. Reading will no longer be frustrating and degrading, and David will be able to succeed and see his progress. The teacher includes exercises, particularly in auditory discrimination, that might accelerate David's maturation in specific areas that are particularly important to reading. David's ability in phonics and his sight word vocabulary are areas of relative strength that the teacher will use to help him with his weaknesses.

This is normal writing.

Figure 11.4. Mirror writing. For some children, the "backwards" version is more natural to write than the "forwards" version.

LEARNING DISABILITIES TEST

Seven year old Luis was having trouble in school. His family spoke Spanish at home—was this all that was holding him back? His home in many ways was not a happy place—was his learning problem mainly emotional, then? His teacher suspected there might be more to it than that, and arranged to have Luis tested by a specialist using one of the standard tests for learning disabilities.

The specialist used the Illinois Test of Psycholinguistic Abilities, which consists of several subtests. Overall, Luis's performance on the test showed that he had a psycholinguistic age of only five years and one month. At visual and motor tasks, however, he was much better than at hearing and speaking. On a test measuring his memory of visual objects displayed in a certain order, his score was equal to that of an average eleven year old.

The visual and motor tasks Luis did so well were all at what the specialist called the *automatic* level—the most basic level of mental functioning, where performance is measured by such tasks as finding hidden objects in a picture, memorizing, and putting sounds together to make a word. His abilities at the *representational* level were not as high as they should have been, con-sidering his automatic abilities and his age. This is the level at which reasoning and application become important, and he should be able to see the relations between objects, understand questions based on relations, and express himself using gestures and words.

Luis's scores on the listening and speaking subtests also showed a wide difference between his abilities at the automatic and the representational levels. Again, his highest score was in memory, an automatic ability. On the average, Luis's scores for listening and speaking at the representational level were about the same as a two year old's.

To see if Luis had any difficulty in hearing, the specialist gave him an informal hearing test, and it did seem that he could not always distinguish between two similar sounds, whether they were in English or Spanish. As a result, the specialist was not sure that Luis's scores in listening and speaking were valid measures of his abilities. He was probably more skilled than the test indicated, though definitely not as skilled as he should have been.

Despite this uncertainty about the validity of the test results in one area, the specialist concluded that Luis did have a psycholinguistic disability that

LEARNING DISABILITIES

For many years, teachers and diagnosticians were baffled by children who could not read although none of the usual causes of reading retardation was present. Often these children were considered mentally retarded, even though they were able to do some things very well. Sometimes they were simply termed "unteachable." Then in 1937, psychologist Samuel Orton discovered that some children tended to reserve or rotate letters of the alphabet. For example, they would confuse "b"

was not directly related to his bilingual background. However, she suggested further tests. She recommended that Luis's hearing be tested by a bilingual speech therapist and that he take some specific tests that would show why his abilities at the representational level were so much lower than at the automatic level.

The specialist suggested that even before the further tests were given, Luis should enter a special program in English as a second language, and that the teacher in the program should use pictures and written words to capitalize on Luis's strong visual memory. From the records she noticed that he was being taught reading by a method depending primarily on sounds, and not doing very well at it. She contacted his teacher—the one who had referred Luis to her in the first place—and suggested that he might do better if he were taught the written words by sight, as he would probably be very good at memorizing what words look like.

In this subtest, the specialist shows the boy a picture of an object and asks him to demonstrate its use without saying what it is. Here the boy demonstrates the use of a telephone.

with "d" and "p" with "q." He found other children whose writing at first appeared to be nonsense but in reality was *mirror writing:* it was quite normal when read in a mirror (Figure 11.4).

Most important, however, Orton found that most children who tended to reverse letters or write mirror style have an unusual neurological trait concerning the dominance of one side of the brain over the other. The right side of our brain controls most of the left side of our bodies; the left side of our brain controls the right side of our bodies; and most of us are either right-sided or left-sided. A right-sided person not only uses his right hand best, but his right eye leads his left eye and he favors his right foot. If a person has *cross-dominance*, however, he might use his right hand best, but his left eye leads his right eye. Some people do not have any *fixed dominance* at all—that is, there is an equal chance that they may use either side (Orton, 1937). There is some controversy now over the role of dominance patterns in learning disorders, but all psychologists agree that Orton made an important contribution by connecting learning disorders to neurological patterns. It is now generally accepted that learning disabilities are caused by one kind of neurological malfunction or another, though we cannot yet pinpoint the source of each type of malfunction because the nervous system is so complex.

There are a great many different learning disabilities. Some children, for example, cannot organize what they see. Some cannot remember what they hear; others cannot make associations between letters and sounds, or apply such simple concepts as "same" and "different"; and of course some read and write backwards. There are also many theories, diagnostic techniques, and programs currently being used to help children with learning disabilities. Most of these theories are based on the idea that children must go through specific developmental stages to gain certain abilities, and learning-disabled children have not gone through the proper sequence because of some neurological problem. One program (Kephart, 1960) follows the development stages generally laid out by Piaget. It includes physical exercises, such as hopping, skipping, and walking on boards; perceptual exercises, such as matching similar objects and putting objects into categories; and the integration of physical and perceptual exercises, such as puzzles and matching designs on pegboards. Another program (Fernald, 1943) teaches children to read through feeling and hearing a word as well as seeing it in writing. The child traces the word before he writes it on his own so that the integration of all the things he feels and perceives is fixed before he actually produces the word. Later he reads the word he has written, and it is always a word of his own choice.

Users of all these techniques report good results with children who have learning disabilities, but there is no objective evidence that any one technique is better than another. It is possible that the improvement is not brought about by the technique but the children improve for other reasons.

The study of reading disorders and learning disabilities is a relatively new field and advances are being made at a rapid pace. However, many children with learning disabilities suddenly improve and the psychologist cannot tell why. It is known that many adults have slight disorders but get along perfectly well; usually they are not even aware that they have a problem. Apparently they have learned to compensate, and many children with disorders will learn to compensate in the same way.

It is, of course, important for parents, teachers, and physicians to be aware of the possible problems in learning and to be concerned if there is evidence of one. Too much concern, however, can do the child more harm than good. One professor in the field warns his class not to get upset when they find they have a learning disability or a reading disorder, because by the end of the course every student will have found that he has some minimal problem.

STAGES OF COGNITION

In Jean Piaget's theory of cognitive development, the period from roughly two to seven years is called the preoperational period. It is followed by the **period of concrete operations,** which extends to approximately the age of eleven. In order to understand "concrete operations," one must comprehend the meaning of the term *operation* in the theory.

According to Piaget, an operation is a process that changes its object. The change may be the result of a physical action, as is typical of the sensorimotor period, of a thought about an action, as in the period of concrete operations, or a manipulation of ideas—that is, thoughts about thoughts, as in the stage of formal operations. To be capable of thoughts about possible actions, a person must be able to go beyond what can be immediately perceived and take steps to change (in thought) what is presented to one's senses by the environment. Thus, for example, the child who imagines a train ride is beginning to go beyond what is immediately present to his senses. He is making the first beginnings toward mentally manipulating the environment.

In the preoperational phase, however, the child's thinking is still limited in a number of ways. We saw in Chapter 8 that although he can go beyond what his senses perceive, he usually cannot reverse a mental operation. This was illustrated by the experiment in which children were asked to arrange a bunch of sticks in order of size, smallest to largest. Preoperational children could not do this task. Slightly older children, almost at the concrete operational stage, succeeded, but only by trial and error. After the age of seven years, however, the children used

PIAGET'S PERIODS OF COGNITIVE DEVELOPMENT

Sensorimotor Period (birth to 24 months)

Preoperational Period (2 to 7 years)

Concrete Operational Period (7 to 11 years)

Classifies concrete objects by category and begins to understand the relations among categories. Does not, however, think of the categories as abstract or formal entities; they are still just groups of concrete objects.

1. Decentration: becomes able to focus attention on more than one aspect of a situation at a time.
2. Consistently conserves such qualities as length, quantity, weight, and volume.
3. Begins to grasp changes in objects or situations throughout the entire dynamic sequence, not just the static beginning and end points.
4. Thinking becomes reversible. Able to conceive that the effects of some action or transformation may be reversed by a subsequent action.

Formal Operational Period (11 years on)

Figure 11.5. Although the level of the liquid is higher in the narrow container, a child at the stage of concrete operations soon realizes that its volume is the same as it is in the wide container.

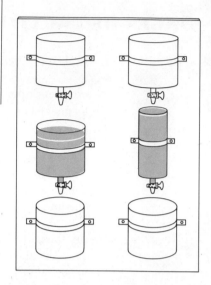

a systematic approach. They first found the smallest stick, then looked through the pile for the next smallest, and so on. What these children were able to do, and the less advanced children were not, was to reverse the direction of their thinking: they looked for the stick that was *bigger* than the previous one but *smaller* than the remaining ones (Piaget, 1970).

Another limitation in the preoperational child is his lack of awareness of the principle of conservation of physical qualities. For example, when a volume of water is poured from a tall, narrow beaker to a wide beaker, it reaches a lower level in the wide beaker, but the child in the concrete operational stage is not fooled. He realizes that the volume of water remains the same—is conserved—even though the shape of the container has been changed (Figure 11.5).

Decentration

What is important to realize here is that both reversibility and conservation—aspects of thinking that make their appearance with the attainment of the concrete operational stage—involve the child's ability to shift the focus of his attention from one part of the situation to another. With the stick problem, he can say that Stick A is smaller than Stick B, and, therefore, Stick B is bigger than Stick A. He can switch from "smaller than" to "bigger than" and back, and he can see that these relationships are reciprocal. In the conservation of volume problem, he can shift his attention from focusing on height alone to focusing on both height and width in relation to each other. Piaget calls this ability to shift the center of one's attention *decentration.*

This ability to decenter from the immediate situation begins before the period of concrete operations, but as the child progresses, it becomes more and more general and is applied to increasingly complex problems. In the area of conservation, for example, the child first masters conservation of number. Twelve beads remain twelve beads whether they are placed in a straight line, a circle, or a heap. The child is able to decenter from the configuration of the beads and to see that their number remains constant. Conservation of weight—the realization that equal weights remain equal despite changes in appearance such as shape and volume—is a more complex sort of judgment. It does not appear until two or three years after the beginning of the concrete operational stage. Conservation of volume does not appear until even later, and problems involving transformation of the physical state of objects (for example, the dissolving of sugar in water) make their appearance last. Decentration also figures significantly in relationships of part to whole. The concrete operational child can, for example, see that ten blue beads and five red beads make fifteen beads and that there are more beads altogether than there are beads of either color. The child includes both kinds of beads in the class of beads and can reason simultaneously about the class and each of its subgroups. The preoperational child, on the other hand, would have trouble saying that there are more beads than there are blue beads because he could not easily decenter from

Figure 11.6. Measuring ingredients to fill a recipe is a good lesson in conservation of volume and weight.

Drawings made by normal six and seven year olds (this page) and by disturbed children of about the same age (opposite page). Notice the differences in their renderings of proportions and of hands and arms in the drawings at the top of the two pages. The drawing at the lower right shows the child artist's vision of himself being tortured in various ways.

the fact that there are more blue than red. Not only does he lack a firm grasp of the concept of class, but his thinking is not reversible: he applied the term *more* to the blue beads the first time, and he continues to do so.

Another way in which the thought of the child in the concrete operational stage differs from that of the child in the preoperational stage is in the former's ability to grasp a sequence of actions or events all at once. He can have an overall mental picture of a sequence of events, such as an inning of a baseball game, that involves past, present, and future; and he can describe this sequence of events without having to perform them. The preoperational child, by contrast, has trouble describing sequences. He needs to act them out because he is quite centered in the present.

A concrete operational child is also better able to understand how physical objects can go through a series of changes. One experiment (Inhelder, Bovet, and Sinclair, 1967) has demonstrated this fact quite clearly. Children were shown transparent jars of different shapes that were arranged on top of each other and emptied through spouts in their bottoms. The children observed the liquid fall from one jar to the next until it reached the bottom jars, which were identical in shape to the top jars but different from the jars in between. It was found that from this display a vast majority of the preoperational children did not learn anything about conservation of volume, whereas, in general, concrete operational children did. The experiment demonstrated that the preoperational children could not coordinate a series of perceptions—in this case, the liquid in each jar. In other words, they could not decenter from a static condition to a process.

One crucial implication of centration and decentration is its relation to the child's egocentricity. According to Piaget's theory, the sensorimotor child and the preoperational child tend to view everything in the world in relation to themselves—that is, in relation to their momentary state (including felt needs and interests). They cannot decenter from themselves in order to take the viewpoint of other people, as concrete operational children can.

Taking the viewpoint of others is closely related to the comprehension and use of social-relational terms. For the child to understand that he is his brother's brother, for example, or his mother's son, he must grasp the nature of reciprocal relationships. This, in turn, implies the mastery of reversibility in thinking, which is a characteristic of concrete operational thought. Obviously, the development of the ability to decenter from oneself and take the role of others has important consequences for the child's ability to understand the feelings of others and function socially. Hence, cognitive growth is closely tied to the development of social behavior and morality.

Structure and Environment

Piaget's theory is neither a purely biological theory, in the sense that it sees all growth and action as the outcome of instinctual needs (thirst, hunger, sex), nor a pure learning theory, like the various forms of behaviorism. Rather, the Piagetian model explains the growth of cognitive structures as the result of the child's interaction with the environment. The kinds of cognitive structures that human beings can develop are determined both by the human being's biological nature (both his instinctual needs and the nature of his body, which conditions the kinds of actions he can take) and the nature of his environment.

The development of intelligence is not totally predetermined by heredity, because human beings are very malleable. However, the development of cognitive intelligence does not depend entirely on the environment either, because what a person perceives depends on the cognitive structures he already has that can be used to incorporate this perception.

For example, an only child may experience some difficulty in playing games and learning to follow rules at school because he did not have an opportunity to participate in situations involving rules at home. On the other hand, the only child might develop certain creative abilities to a high degree because he was more inclined to engage in fantasy play with imaginary playmates early in his life.

MORAL DEVELOPMENT

Piaget has conducted extensive studies of the attitudes children have toward rules. He found that, from about the age of five, children begin to feel that obedience, duty, and rule keeping are of great importance. He also noted that a sense of personal judgment and choice—that is, a sense of justice—develops as children mature (Piaget, 1965).

At the earliest stage that Piaget tested—children from ages two to about five—there is little concern for rules. A child in this age group who is involved in playing a game of marbles, for example, has slight interest in "winning" the game, but is more concerned with exploring by himself the muscular control he can achieve by manipulating the marbles themselves in various ways. At the approach of the fifth year, Piaget's children began observing the rules of the game as played by older children, trying to imitate the older children's behavior but without a sense of commitment or cooperative agreement on how the game should be played.

From about the age of five to nine or ten, the child tends to regard the rules as sacred and unchangeable, the only guidelines to proper and acceptable behavior. During this period he perceives the world in terms of *moral realism,* in which the rules are considered to come from the same authoritative sources as natural laws. Just as a child of this age comes to understand that touching a hot oven will burn him or that scattering toys around the house will make Mommy and Daddy angry, so he comes to regard any variation in the rules of the game of marbles as a serious violation of good behavior. The child at this age thinks only of the consequences of breaking a rule: pain or punishment.

One six year old boy told Piaget that the idea of the marbles game and its rules "just came into peoples' hands," and that "Daddies show little boys how

KOHLBERG'S LEVELS OF MORAL DEVELOPMENT

Level I: Preconventional Morality (Early Middle Childhood)[a]

At this level, the child makes moral judgments solely on the basis of anticipated punishment and reward—a good or right act is one that is rewarded.

Stage 1 morality focuses on the power and possessions of those in authority and on the necessity for the weak to please the strong in order to avoid punishment. You do what you do in order to avoid displeasing those who have power over you.

Stage 2 morality focuses on the pleasure motive: you do what you do in order to get what you want from others. There is a sense of fair exchange based on purely pragmatic values and of noninterference in the affairs or values of others. Reciprocity is practical—you do for me, and I'll do for you.

Level II: Conventional Morality (Late Middle Childhood)[b]

At this level, right behavior is that which is accepted, approved, and praised by other people who are seen by the child as being in positions of authority. The child seeks to avoid guilt by behaving in ways that will be approved by the social conventions of his culture.

Stage 3 morality focuses on maintaining the approval of those immediately involved in judging the child's behavior. Justice at this stage is seen as reciprocity or equality between individuals.

Stage 4 morality has been called "law and order" morality; this is the stage at which the focus is on obeying the rules for their own sake. Justice is seen as the reciprocity between each individual and the social system. Societal order is very important in making judgments at this stage.

Level III: Postconventional Morality (Adolescence)

[a] Kohlberg found that about 95 percent of all moral judgments made by seven year olds are at this level.

[b] Kohlberg found that about 40 percent of all moral judgments made by ten year olds are at this level.

to play." When pressed to acknowledge that the rules might be changed, the boy admitted it, but said he did not know how to change them. To the six year old a game had to be played in a certain way. Asked why, he replied, "Because God didn't teach them [any other way]." The likelihood of punishment resulting from the detection of a lie by an adult is often what constitutes its seriousness. In the eyes of a child at this stage, a mistake that brings punishment is worse than a harmless lie that goes undetected.

Between the ages of five and ten, role-taking—the ability to consider another person's point of view—becomes an increasingly important factor in the child's moral growth. In a recent study (Ambron and Irwin, 1974), two Piagetian dimensions of moral judgment—intentionality (the motive of an individual) and restitution (punishment that provides for restoration of damage)—were correlated with three dimensions of role taking. These were perceptual (the ability to take the visual perspective of another), cognitive (the ability to take into account another person's knowledge), and affective (the ability to relate to another's emotions). Kindergarten children and second graders were used as subjects. The study clearly indicated developmental differences between five year olds and seven year olds. The seven year olds not only got higher scores on cognitive and affective role taking than the five year olds, but they also were better able to consider the motives of others in questions of moral judgment.

The development of these role-taking skills and of reciprocal understanding becomes even more evident in the next few years. Piaget found that by the age of about ten, the child's moral development begins to enter a more mature phase, in which the reverence for rules yields to a "morality of cooperation"—that is, a growing awareness that both oneself and others have reciprocal needs and rights. The older child learns that there is a difference between a natural rule, such as the fact that one will be burned by touching a hot iron, and a moral rule, which can be altered.

At this stage, children modify the rules of a game of marbles in many ways, provided that all the players agree on the changes. The child is developing a sense of justice, with which he is able to appreciate the viewpoints and wishes of others and to realize that they can also understand and value his. At first, deviation from the accepted rules may be regarded as not playing fair. But once everyone in the group agrees on what is "fair," a new rule is established. When Piaget asked an eleven year old, "Did your father play the way you showed me, or differently?" he received the answer, "Oh, I don't know. It may have been a different game. It changes. It still changes quite often."

By the age of twelve, Piaget's subjects were generally adjusted to the idea that any game rules would be fair if all the players accepted them. When asked which form of the game would be the truest one, a twelve year old insisted that the best-known one would be truest and fairest—in other words, the one most currently subject to the morality of cooperation. This represents a long step up from obedience to fixed laws and outside authority. As one researcher (Longstreth, 1968) expressed it:

> The younger child believes that all instances of disobedience should be, and are, automatically punished . . . while the older child believes that such transgressions are not always wrong, nor are they always punished. . . . Again, the younger child believes that a transgression requires punishment, with no necessary relationship between the misdeed and its consequences . . . while the older child believes the punishment should be related to the nature of the crime . . . if there is to be any punishment at all.

The study of moral judgment in children was initiated by Piaget more than thirty years ago. Since then, many investigators have explored the reasoning a person uses when she is confronted with a hypothetical moral conflict. The individual's responses are examined with regard to the meaning that a situation has for her and the relation of her choice to that meaning (Rothman, 1971). Lawrence Kohlberg has been one of the most active and influential of these investigators, and his study (1963) of development of moral thought in children can be compared with that of Piaget.

Kohlberg came to the conclusion that a moral sense is not acquired simply through the acceptance of society's rules as taught by precept, punishment, or identification with respected figures. Instead, he found that it involves an internal, personal series of changes in social attitudes. He diagramed this series of successive changes in three levels, each with its own characteristics. Each level must be achieved and assimilated before the child can progress to the next level. When the moral reasoning characteristic of one level proves inadequate for coping with the problems of the individual, she begins to strive toward the next level.

In much the same way that Piaget used stories to elicit a response from his subjects, Kohlberg established a set of increasingly complex moral dilemmas. Each dilemma presented a situation in which acts of obedience to rules or authority were contrasted with human needs or the welfare of others. Each child was asked to make a choice between performing the act of obedience or the act sympathetic to the needs of others. He was then asked a series of questions intended to clarify the reasoning that led to his choice.

At Level I, Kohlberg interviewed a group of children aged four, five, and seven, using doll figures to act out the moral dilemma. Each dilemma consisted of a story in which disobedience to a rule or an adult resulted in either a reward or a punishment. One such story involved a boy who was told by his mother to stay in the house and watch the baby while she went to the store. As soon as the mother left, the boy ran outside and played. The mother, upon returning, gave the disobedient boy some candy. Kohlberg's four year olds tended to disregard the boy's disobedience because the act brought a reward. The seven year olds, however, expressed feelings of conflict because they sensed an injustice in rewarding evil—they could conceive of the reward being offered but in general felt that disobedience would necessarily lead to punishment, and that, therefore, the story was unrealistic. Kohlberg finds in this a correspondence to the moral realism of Piaget's younger children.

As an example of the child's developing morality of cooperation, Kohlberg cites a boy of ten who, asked "Why should someone be a good son?" said "Be good to your father and he'll be good to you." The conflict in thinking that arises at this level of moral development is illustrated by one child's reaction to the following story. Joe was promised by his father that if he earned fifty dollars by himself he could go to camp. Later, however, Joe's father wanted the money and asked Joe to give it to him. Joe lied, saying he had only earned ten dollars. He gave his father the ten dollars and kept the rest for himself. Joe then told his younger brother what he had done.

The question asked about this story was, "Should the younger brother tell his father what Joe did?" A ten year old answered, "In one way it would be right to tell on his brother or his father might get mad and spank him. In another way

Figure 11.7. These "Tiger Cubs" at a Jordanian training camp take pride in acting like little soldiers.

it would be right to keep quiet or his brother might beat him up." The ten year old was not consistent in choosing obedience to authority over allegiance to a brother's needs, but he was consistent in viewing punishment as the inevitable outcome of whatever choice the younger brother might make.

At Level II of moral development, Kohlberg found a tendency to accept a stereotyped view of what makes a good person. This was not the "goody-goody" behavior that is meant only to win the approval of others and escape blame, but rather the emergence of an admiration for those who perform a role properly and who like and help other people. There was also an awareness of the need for authority to make society function in a just manner. Kohlberg asked a thirteen year old boy what he thought about President Eisenhower. The boy's comment was, "President Eisenhower has done a good job and worked so hard he got a heart attack and put himself in the grave, just about, to help the people."

Another boy, asked what he would think if he were Joe's younger brother in the dilemma described above, said, "If my father finds out later, he won't trust me. My brother wouldn't either, but I wouldn't have a *conscience* that he [my brother] didn't."

Kohlberg interprets this statement as equating "conscience" with an avoidance of disapproval by authorities but not by peers. Later, the same boy stated, "I try to do things for my parents, they've always done things for you. I try to do everything my mother says, I try to please her. Like she wants me to be a doctor and I want to, too, and she's helping me get up there." In this instance, the boy is not expressing fear of disapproval by his superiors but an identification of his own wishes with theirs and an effort to anticipate their desires.

References

Ambron, S. R., and Irwin, D. M. Roletaking and moral judgment in 5- and 7-year olds. *Developmental Psychology*, 1974 (in press).

Bond, G., and Tinker, M. *Reading difficulties.* New York: Appleton-Century-Crofts, 1973.

Bruner, J. S. *The process of education.* Cambridge, Mass.: Harvard University Press, 1960.

Fernald, G. *Remedial techniques in basic school subjects.* New York: McGraw-Hill, 1943.

Flavell, J. H. Concept development. *Handbook of child psychology.* New York: Wiley, 1970.

Inhelder, B., Bovet, M., and Sinclair, H. Developpement et apprentissage [Development and learning] Schweizer-ische Zeitschrift für Psychologie und ihoe Anwendungen, 1967, *26*, 1–23.

Kagan, J., Klein, R. E., Haith, M. M., and Morrison, I. J. Memory and meaning in two cultures. *Child Development,* 1973, *44*, 221–223.

Kass, C. E. Some psychological correlates of severe reading disability (dyslexia). In D. J. Sivers et al. (Eds.), *Selected studies on the Illinois test of psycholinguistic abilities.* Madison, Wisc.: Photo Press, 1963.

Kephart, N. *The slow learner in the classroom.* Columbus, Ohio: Charles E. Merrill, 1960.

Kohlberg, L. The development of children's orientations towards a moral order; I. sequence in the development of moral thought. *Vita Humana,* 1963, *6*, 11–33.

Kohlberg, L. Development of moral character and moral ideology. In M. L. Hoffman and L. Hoffman (Eds.), *Review of child development research.* New York: Russell Sage Foundation, 1964, *1*, 383.

Longstreth, L. E. *Psychological development of the child.* New York: Ronald Press, 1968.

Lore, R. K. Some factors influencing the child's exploration of visual stimuli. Unpublished doctoral dissertation. University of Tennessee, 1965.

Neimark, E., Slotnik, N., and Ulrich, T. Development of memorization strategies. *Developmental psychology,* 1971, *5*, 427–432.

Orton, S. *Reading, writing, and speech problems in children.* New York: Norton, 1937.

Piaget, J. *The moral judgment of the child.* New York: Free Press, 1965.

Piaget, J. *Genetic epistemology.* New York: Norton, 1970.

Rossi, E. Development of classification behavior. *Child Development,* 1966, *37*, 137–142.

Rothman, G. R. An experimental analysis of the relationship between level of moral judgment and behavioral choice. Unpublished doctoral dissertation. Columbia University, 1971.

SUMMARY

1 In middle childhood, problem-solving ability improves primarily through an increase in the capacity to remember. The child becomes more capable of recalling information from long-term memory and of deliberately retaining short-term memories long enough to transfer them into long-term reserve. Also, he remembers more information by being able to classify it. In applying hypotheses, impulsive children make more mistakes than reflective children.

2 Many possible factors may cause children to be retarded readers. Often a teacher can identify the cause of an individual child's reading problem by means of a general diagnosis. Causes that are not revealed by a general diagnosis can be pinpointed with special reading tests, and once the cause is found, the teacher can start a remedial program.

3 Learning disabilities, unlike most of the conditions that result in retarded reading and other difficulties in school, are caused by neurological malfunctions. Special techniques to help children with learning disabilities have had encouraging results. To a slight extent, almost everyone, including adults, has some learning disability or other, but most people manage to compensate for them.

4 At about age seven, most children enter what Piaget calls the period of concrete operations. At this level of cognitive development they learn to apply the principles of reversibility and conservation and are able to decenter from the immediate situation and from themselves.

5 Piaget found that young children tend to regard rules as inviolable, but as their moral understanding develops they realize that rules can be made up and changed if everyone concerned agrees to it. They become more adept at taking the viewpoint of others.

6 Kohlberg has established a series of stages that most children pass through as they improve their moral understanding. An individual prefers the highest stage he can comprehend because it is broader and more consistent than the one below it, but he might not be able as yet to apply it to every moral dilemma that he confronts.

FURTHER READINGS

Dechant, E. V. *Improving the teaching of reading*. Englewood Cliffs, N. J.: Prentice-Hall, 1974.
Second edition of a comprehensive book on reading development, causes of reading disabilities, and remedial approaches.

Englemann, S. *Preventing failure in the primary grades*. New York: Simon & Schuster, 1969.
A child's mind closes to learning when school is a confusing place where he experiences failure. Englemann offers a program to help children who have failed to learn basic reading and arithmetic skills.

Larrick, N. A. *Parent's guide to children's education*. New York: Trident, 1963.
Despite the title, this book is as much for teacher as for parent. Believing that home and school teaching go hand in hand, Larrick discusses influences on the motivation to learn and teaching children to observe and evaluate. The book has separate sections on teaching language arts, arithmetic, and science.

Lidz, T. *The person*. New York: Basic Books, 1968.
Lidz discusses many of the crucial issues of middle childhood, including the development of a sense of responsibility, relations with the opposite sex, and development of moral judgment.

12
Home, Peers, and School

DEPOSIT LITTER
=IN=
BASKETS

Nathan can hardly wait for summer. He has already found some boards to use for a roof on the tree hut, and Mr. and Mrs. Cooper—the parents of his best friend, Steve—have promised to take him canoeing with them in July. Of course he and Steve will sleep out again this year. One night last year they stayed awake and counted twenty-six shooting stars!

As the Coopers have evidently recognized, Nathan and Steve are inseparable. This deathless friendship is something new in their development: during the first few years of elementary school, both boys had several playmates and got along with them well enough, but now they seem to have chosen each other as blood brothers. It is the first time anyone has meant almost as much to either boy as he means to himself.

Nathan and Steve are practically members of each other's families now, and what they find in their alternate homes is likely to be quite congenial to them. Although they would not be capable of such deep friendship if they were still largely egocentric—unable to see things from each other's viewpoint, to feel each other's moods—Nathan nevertheless chose Steve from all the boys in the neighborhood, and Steve chose Nathan, because they liked each other better than anyone else. And the main features of their characters came straight from their homes.

THE HOME

If Nathan finds Steve confident and trusting, it is probably because the Coopers are warm, affectionate people—not only toward Steve but toward each other as well. Unfortunately, the opposite is also likely to hold true: when parents are hostile to their child much of the time, he begins to feel and act as if he were among enemies everywhere. He grows afraid to approach others in hope of finding a friend. Soon he stops trying to gain love and tries only for what he knows how to get—hostile attention. He actually works at being mean and annoying to his parents and siblings, and to his peers and teachers as well. He develops what psychologist Harry Stack Sullivan (1953) called a *malevolent* character—that is, he deliberately wishes harm. In middle childhood, as the approval of teachers and peers becomes more important to him than ever before, his malevolence can lead him into a vicious circle of isolation and rejection.

By contrast, a child who feels loved at home is not afraid to seek the esteem of teachers and playmates. He feels equal to the tasks that he must perform in order to win the approval of others. He develops a sense of industry in school and a capability for cooperation with peers.

One particularly notable feature of the child's character that is closely related to warmth or hostility in the home is the extent of his internal control over how he acts. Lack of internal control over behavior has been closely associated with parental rejection and punitiveness (Bronfenbrenner, 1961). A strong correlation has also been found between aggression on the part of the child and parental rejection and punitiveness (McCord, McCord, and Howard, 1961).

An extreme example of the effects of parental rejection can be found in this description of an aggressive boy:

> Andy . . . lived in various boarding homes, having little or no contact with his own mother for long intervals of time. When he was six, his mother was killed in an automobile accident, and his father, who had in the interim married again, took him to live with him. His stepmother was a cold, unfeeling woman, overprotective of three half-siblings while confronting Andy with obvious rejection. She loaded him with household chores, criticized and nagged him. He, in turn, released all his hostility against his siblings. At times he was sadistic and tried to burn them with a wood-burning set . . . (Redl and Wineman, 1951).

There are a number of possible explanations for why severe punitiveness on the part of parents leads to a lack of control in the child. One logical explanation is that the child, feeling that everyone in his life is potentially hostile, supposes that hostility is the normal—probably the only—way to get along in the world. Another theory (Bandura and Walters, 1963) is that children tend to imitate their parents. Thus, if a parent shows direct physical aggression in punishing a child, the child will tend to adopt this aggressive behavior when dealing with peers or siblings. It is also possible that physical punishment and verbal abuse may make the child sensitive to occasions for punishment, without teaching him what to do and what not to do in the absence of the punishing parent (Aronfreed, 1968).

Withdrawal of parental affection, on the other hand, produces an internal feeling of anxiety in the child, even when the parent is not physically present. Thus, the child is motivated to change his behavior to reduce his anxiety and win back the parent's love. If the child feels unloved by his parents in the first place, however, a withdrawal of their affection will be nothing new to him. Thus, it will not be likely to teach him to control his behavior.

One observer (Ginott, 1972) has pointed out that when a parent punishes or reprimands a child, the reprimand may be either helpful or harmful, depending on the parent's attitude. He can condemn the transgression but still preserve and communicate his basic acceptance of the child, or he can attack the child's self-esteem in a hostile fashion. If the parent attacks the child's person as well as his act, he may provoke a defiant response but not the desired change in behavior, as the following scene illustrates:

> During dinner, Len, 10, was eating noisily with his mouth open. His father yelled, "Leave the table. You eat like a pig. Do you know what a pig is?" "Yes," cried Len, "the son of a swine." (Ginott, 1972)

In less obvious cases, hostility takes an indirect form and arises in complicated ways. Erikson (1968) has described a typical situation in which a mother complains to the child about the father. The mother may indicate that it is the father's fault that she is inadequate as a woman. (Or vice-versa, a father may let the child know that he feels emasculated by the mother.) Underneath the expressed complaint is the hidden complaint that the child is failing to make a good parent out of her (or him). Particularly in middle-class homes, anger at or disappointment with the child may be repressed by the parent but nevertheless demonstrated in subtle ways, as when parents use the child in an attempt to fulfill their own lost hope for themselves.

Autonomy and Control

The emotional climate of the home also influences the degree of **autonomy** accorded the child—that is, what sorts of matters she is allowed to decide for herself. Parents can react to the child's growing ability to manage by herself by giving her all the freedom she needs, or they can stifle her with too much control. By the age of eight years, for example, most children are able to decide for themselves what they should wear; they eat well and have considerable ability with personal hygiene and grooming (Gesell, 1949). They may need occasional advice or reminders, but generally they are able to look out for themselves in these respects. If a child is babied by her parents, however, she may not learn to do these things as rapidly as other children do; and if the parents insist on keeping a close watch over her and never allow her to try things for herself and make mistakes, she may fail to develop a sense of independence and personal responsibility. The child who is never trusted will not become worthy of trust.

Parents may care very deeply for their child and still avoid protecting and controlling her too much. They can impose certain definite requirements and leave it up to the child to fulfill the requirements. When they follow this approach the child has a good chance to develop internal controls over her behavior, but if they are overprotective and overindulgent—if they never let the child struggle for anything but always give her whatever she wants—she may have little reason to

THE SINGLE PARENT

Once upon a time, at least in story-books, every child had two parents who were married to each other, loved each other, and stayed together while the children grew to adulthood. In America today, however, more and more children are growing up, at least during part of their childhood, with only one parent.

Census reports from 1973 give the dimensions of the increase in families headed by one parent. Among black families in the United States, 35 percent are single-parent families. Almost 10 percent of all white families fall into the same category, as do about 17 percent of families of Spanish background. A growing percentage of the mothers, about 13 percent, have never been married. In all there are about 6.5 million single-parent families in the United States (*New York Times,* 1974) and the number is growing. It is clear that alternatives to the two-parent family are becoming more widespread.

Children in America today may live in a family in which one of the parents is the second or third spouse of the other, and in this situation the step-parent often brings his or her own children from a previous marriage into the new family. The women's liberation movement has encouraged both women and men who have never been married to assume parental responsibilities. Some children live in families in which the adults are a homosexual couple, and still others live in communal groups where several adults of both sexes make a home together with all of their children. Each of these arrangements has the potential to provide a loving environment in which children can grow; each can also be devastating.

So can the ordinary variety of divorce. But then living in a home with two parents who hate each other can be even more damaging to children; most authorities agree that parents should not stay married only for the sake of children (Dodson, 1974). If divorce seems the best solution, there are several steps that parents can take to make the change less painful for their children. The children should be reassured that they are not being abandoned, that both their mother and their father will continue to love and care for them although living apart. The reasons for the divorce need not be explained (and could hardly be comprehended by a small child in any case), but the child needs to be told that he is not responsible for the dissolution of the marriage. It is not unusual for many children to assume unconscious guilt for the marital difficulties of their parents.

In most cases, the father leaves home after a divorce, and the mother is awarded custody of the children. A father can help his child to feel loved if he explains that he is sending the

believe that what she does makes a difference in the world. She may never blame herself for hurting a playmate or cheating in school (Bronfenbrenner, 1961).

In grade school we often see children who find it impossible to share with others or to participate in activities except on their own terms. If they cannot be the leader, or if they lose in a game, they become furious, accuse other children

mother money to help pay for the things the child needs and if he keeps in close contact through telephoning and regular visits. Many counselors warn the divorced parent to avoid the temptation to overindulge the child during these visits (Dodson, 1974). Because divorce is becoming more and more common, the child will probably have at least one peer friend whose parents are also divorced, and this makes things seem more normal. It is not unusual for divorced parents to work out an amenable relationship that is more satisfactory for the children than their marriage had been. In short, divorce need not be an unrelieved trauma.

Unconventional parenthood outside of marriage presents different problems. Women who become pregnant outside of marriage and decide to bear and keep their children often are motivated by their own unresolved psychological problems (Klein, 1973); if this is the case, they are likely to find that parenthood only complicates their problems. A pregnancy that results from a need for love, a desire to be punished, or competitive feeling with one's mother can only lead to disaster for both the new mother and her child. At the same time, there are single women who are psychologically mature and can handle the many problems of parenthood outside of marriage; these women obviously have as good a chance of being good mothers as do married women.

Most communal family situations, whether they include homosexual parents, heterosexual parents, or both, can offer a child the security of an extended family at a time when the strains on the nuclear family are growing more and more severe. Having several adults available for child care and as role models relieves some of the pressure on the single parent. The extended family also provides more opportunities for strong peer-group identification if there are other children of about the same age (Klein, 1973). Like the nuclear family, however, the communal family is not guaranteed to remain intact, and the potential advantages of such a situation therefore must be weighed against its potential instability.

Single-parent families raise many important problems. Will the child have adequate models for sex-role identification? Will he have opportunities to understand the role of the opposite sex in adult relationships? Can one person assume all of the responsibilities of parenthood without feeling resentful? Mature single parents are finding ways to meet these problems. They point out that the two-parent nuclear family has been a failure for many children; and they believe that alternatives can be developed in which both the parent and the child will find room for their fullest growth.

of cheating, and go away sulking. Such children are often those whose parents give in to their every demand, do everything for them, and give them preferential treatment over other siblings in their family.

Figure 12.1. Bicycling through the streets of New York every day making deliveries, this boy demonstrates the high degree of competence and responsibility that can be expected of school-age children.

One-Parent Homes

The absence of a parent always has important consequences for the child's social adjustment. However, a lot depends on why the parent is missing. If the home is broken because of marital discord, the child may feel isolated and rejected. Sometimes he tries to win the esteem that he does not get at home from peers in a delinquent gang, but more often the remaining parent's esteem is sufficient. In many cases the parents part in a friendly way, and the child is able to maintain contact with them both.

Several studies have shown, however, that the children who have lost a parent are more likely to experience difficulties than those who have not. One study, for example (Brown, 1961), found that children who lost either a mother or a father between the ages of five and fourteen had a much greater chance of becoming depressive later in life than those who had both parents. An explanation for such correlations has been proposed by John Bowlby (1967) in an article on childhood mourning. According to Bowlby, a child is less capable of dealing with the loss of a parent than an older person might be. Normally, whenever we experience the loss of a loved one, we go through a mourning period in which we try to recover the lost person and feel angry at the lost person for leaving us. Then finally the mourning process runs its course, and we face up to the reality of the loss. Children, however, may not go through the whole process because the feelings are too severe. Instead, they either repress the feelings or displace them onto other objects. Later in life they may show very little feeling about anything or anyone, or may be generally angry and hostile.

Siblings

Brothers and sisters are the child's first peers. The child learns much from his interactions with his siblings and from observation of his parents' responses to his siblings' behavior. Often he generalizes this information to his relationships with teachers and schoolmates.

In many families, especially in large ones, siblings are classified by the family into distinct types. One child in the family, according to researchers (Bossard and Boll, 1960), is identified as the responsible child, "the one that is looked up to, the one that assumes direction or supervision of the other siblings, or renders service to them." The researchers have also found seven other types frequently reported by siblings themselves. The responsible child is usually the firstborn sibling; the second-born is often labeled the popular or social one. The eldest having claimed the position of power and responsibility, the second-born often tries to gain recognition through likability. Another type is the social butterfly who tries to gain recognition outside the family. This sibling may be third, fourth, or fifth in birth order. The fourth type (but not necessarily the fourth-born) is the serious sort who tries to gain recognition through doing well in school. The fifth type is the asocial or even stubbornly antisocial one who withdraws from competition in the family.

SIBLINGS AND PERSONALITY

The most famous theories of personality formation, including Freud's, start with the parent–child relationship; countless research projects have been carried out to investigate the ways in which mothers and fathers influence the personality of their children. But what about the child's brothers and sisters? They are the child's first peers; he lives with them during his most formative years; and in large families he gets more attention from them than from his parents.

Recent research in Germany (Toman, 1969) has attempted to study the influence of siblings by identifying the child's position in the family according to sex and seniority. A boy, for example, may be an older brother of brothers, an older brother of sisters, a younger brother of brothers, or a younger brother of sisters. Similarly, a girl may be an older or younger sister of brothers or sisters. Thus, there are eight possible positions that an individual may take in a family, and the German study strongly suggests that there is a typical personality according to each position.

For example, the study claims—not very surprisingly—that the older brother of brothers tends to be a leader. He gets along well with other men, particularly if they are younger brothers themselves, but has difficulty accepting women as people. As a father he insists upon order and discipline, and in politics he favors strong leadership. The younger brother of sisters, on the other hand, is not so well liked by other men, but women are attracted to him—in fact, he can usually find some women who will wait on him hand and foot. As a father he is inattentive, especially if his child is a boy, and he has little concern for politics.

An older sister of brothers, the German study tells us, is a good sport; men like her even though she has a practical turn of mind. She may want a large family, and her children will come to her with their problems. In politics she believes in moderation and conciliation. The younger sister of sisters, by contrast, is anything but practical. She seeks adventure and change.

This child may spend a lot of time away from home and refuse to participate in family activities but, unlike the social butterfly, he does not necessarily seek recognition outside the family. The sixth type of sibling also withdraws from the family but in a different way: instead of absenting himself physically, he simply avoids the responsibilities that all the others accept. He will be reluctant to clean up around the house and at times will not even hear when requests are made of him. The seventh type is the one who is chronically ill, has physical defects, or is a hypochondriac. Often he learns to utilize his physical problems as a means of getting favor or attention. Finally, there is the spoiled sibling who is generally the youngest and is babied and catered to by everyone, including the parents.

The major problem for the child of any type seems to be how to gain his share of attention and esteem from his parents and siblings. As various ways of gaining recognition are exhausted by older siblings, the younger ones have to find new ways of gaining recognition.

Men find her charming, but she may be too emotional and willful to make a stable marriage. Politically, she tends to be erratic, switching from one side to another for purely emotional reasons.

Many people, of course, do not fit neatly into this scheme of eight positions. One may be a middle child, for example, and be younger than some siblings but older than others. And even if one is the youngest or the oldest, one may have both male and female siblings. Not having any siblings of the opposite sex is suspected of having important effects upon the individual's personality regardless of his position in the family.

Age difference is another factor that complicates sibling relationships. The study found that if a child is more than six years older or younger than his nearest sibling, he has many characteristics of an only child. Only children seem to be in a category by themselves. They may have trouble dealing with peers of either sex, and more than any other type they remain childless in marriage.

Complications aside, the study is attempting to verify the hypothesis that a person's adult relationships tend to duplicate his early sibling relationships. In other words, having learned to deal with his siblings in certain ways, a person will tend to apply the same ways to his dealings with peers when he grows up.

This hypothesis can be tested by the adult peer relationship in which success or failure is most obvious: marriage. If the hypothesis is correct, a marriage of complementary persons—for example, a younger brother of sisters and an older sister of brothers—will have a better chance of success than a conflicting match—for example, a younger brother of brothers and a younger sister of sisters. A study of 2000 couples in Nuremberg and Zürich seemed to confirm this prediction. Most of the couples who obtained divorces were mismatched by sibling position, and not one of them was perfectly complementary according to that standard.

In contrast to the sibling, the only child does not need to compete with other children for parental recognition. However, he is more dependent on his parents for recognition than are children with brothers or sisters. Like firstborn children, only children are achievers and tend to have high self-esteem.

THE PEER GROUP

Many types of peer groups form during middle childhood. In school, groups are chosen for various activities; out of school, neighborhood groups roam the streets. Formally organized groups are brought together for the Little League, Boy Scouts and Girl Scouts, and dancing, art, and music lessons.

But whether the groups are formal or informal, most of them are composed of members of the same sex, particularly when children are six to ten years old.

Figure 12.2. Boys and girls still play together in this neighborhood group, but in a few years it may be impossible to bring them together even to have their picture taken.

Boys' groups tease girls' groups, and girls' groups pointedly ignore boys' groups. Sometimes a group of boys makes war on a group of girls. Perhaps children at this stage are making sure of their sex-role identities by rejecting the opposite sex and engaging only in activities that they see as typical for their own sex. Whether this polarization will continue in force if sexual stereotypes break down in our culture cannot be foreseen.

Informal peer groups in middle childhood, boys' and girls' alike, often take on the qualities of a gang. They have leaders, a code of their own, and a set of values and norms.

Group Norms

What happens when two groups of boys are formed at summer camp by putting them in separate living quarters? In only five days, each group takes a name and establishes a code of behavior and a system of punishment. The boys in the two groups may share some activities, but friendships will develop only within the living quarters (Sherif and Sherif, 1953).

Norms spring up rapidly in groups of school-age children because the individual is making a major gain in his ability to understand rules. He realizes that they

NORMS

Norms are the standards that serve to guide and regulate the actions of group members. They are established both by large groups such as entire cultures and by the many smaller groups within a culture. Norms may be codified and enforced by some official authority, as are the laws of a state, but most of them operate informally through the force of custom and habit.

Values are more general, broad, and abstract than norms. The value system of a culture or an individual is a set of moral beliefs to which that society or person subscribes. Norms are much more clearly tied to day-to-day living, and they are much more specific in their prescriptions than values are. Norms may even contradict the stated values of a society: the ideology of our culture, for example, holds that human beings are more important than objects; but most people in our society feel that a man who kills another in defense of his property is justified, and our laws support the norm rather than the value.

Norms are often divided into three types: folkways, mores (pronounced MORE-ays), and laws. Most of the patterns of everyday behavior are determined by culturally learned *folkways,* all the little habits that have developed over a long period of time to tell us what to do from minute to minute. These include the actions that we assume to be natural because they are so natural for us, although they vary from one society to another. The number of meals that are eaten in a day, conventions of appropriate dress, the postures that are used for sitting or standing in conversation with family and with guests—all of these are among the folkways of a society.

Mores regulate the behavior that is felt to be essential to the social welfare of the group and about which the group has strong moral feelings. Violation of mores invokes strong disapproval and can result in the ostracism of the offending individual. Violation of a folkway, on the other hand, is considered to be relatively inconsequential. Rules about sexual behavior or about the necessity for members of a society to engage in productive work are among the mores of a culture.

Laws provide the structure of formal enforcement of mores in societies where there are many groups and interests and where improved means of transportation and communication increase the interaction among these groups. Law provides a consistent way of judging and punishing those who violate the important mores. In the large secular societies that make up most of the industrialized world, a specialized group within the society has as its full-time vocation the enforcement of the law.

Children learn the norms of the various groups to which they belong through a process of living within these standards and being taught, largely by example, how to behave. Ordinarily a child's first models are his parents and his siblings; as his social circle widens, he learns new norms from his peers and from other adults. Much of the socialization process is informal and automatic. From the rules of baseball to the notion that girls do not shout, the child absorbs his culture's expectations long before he is intellectually mature enough to assess them or subscribe to them consciously.

The norms of a society can be violated in three ways: by criminal behavior, by rebellion, and by innovation. The criminal disregards the norm even though he and the society agree that it is legitimate. He simply chooses to disobey the rules, and if he is caught he expects to be punished. A man who robs a bank is not usually expressing anything more philosophically profound than a desire to violate a custom of his culture for his own gain. The rebel, on the other hand, rejects the entire normative system and by his behavior declares that the rules of his society are not acceptable to him. The psychotic who completely withdraws from social contact into world of fantasy is probably also expressing such rebellion. The political revolutionary too is declaring a basic disagreement with his cultural norms when he calls for the overthrow of the existing government.

The innovator rejects specific normative elements but attempts to maintain some of the norms of the group and to retain his identity within the group. Many of the individuals involved in the women's liberation movement, for example, advocate basic changes in our society's norms with regard to the behavior of women, but they do not necessarily reject the entire existing social order or even any of its other norms.

are not simply "there"—handed down by tradition or adult authority—but that people make rules and can change them if they wish. Because it is a new discovery, it is exciting to develop his own rules in cooperation with his peers.

The development of norms seems to be stimulated by other factors as well. In the experiment known as Robber's Cave (Sherif, et al., 1961), twenty-two fifth-grade boys were divided into two groups at camp, but neither group knew of the other's presence. Norms did develop in each group, but they multiplied and became much stronger after the groups "accidentally" discovered each other. Perhaps peer groups establish norms in order to create an identity for the group members and distinguish them from outsiders. This explanation might also apply to the exclusiveness of boys' and girls' groups.

Games

According to Gesell (1949), children eight and nine years old are filled with energy. They play running and chasing games such as hide-and-seek and ring-o-levio. They also establish secret societies and hiding places, and invent rituals. They invent secret passwords and talk in Pig Latin, supposedly known only by members of the in-group. Some of this behavior can be seen as an attempt to mimic certain conventions in the adult world.

As the child gets older, the manner of his play changes. Instead of indulging constantly in rough-housing and simple games, he attempts to perfect his skills at baseball, chess, and walking on stilts. His interest shifts from the social aspects of the game to becoming good at it.

There is a surprisingly long historical continuity in children's games and play. Certain games, rhymes, superstitions (for example, not stepping on the crack in

Figure 12.3. Learning football skills does not preclude a certain amount of goofing off.

the sidewalk), and rituals have been passed on from one generation of children to the next for hundreds of years (Opie and Opie, 1959). To some extent the games are constantly being modified, but the continuities, particularly in England and Scotland, are quite striking. What is even more remarkable is that many children forget the lore as they grow older, yet the forms are always being learned by younger children and thus persist for generations.

Solidarity Against Grownups

One of the most obvious features of peer groups in middle childhood is their independence from adults. The extent to which children resist adult values and authority varies a great deal. One extreme is that of the delinquent gang, where the norms of the group stand in opposition to adult authority and call for pranks or illegal and dangerous acts. Members are often required, sometimes as an initiation, to do things that are antisocial, and if they fail to do so they are ostracized. One report (Redl and Windeman, 1951) on groups of disturbed preadolescent boys notes:

> Like all systems of tyranny the delinquent gang has a chronic ''loyalty board'' operating. . . . The mere wish, for instance, to enjoy adult counselor love openly or to allow oneself to be seen in a ''friendly private talk'' with such an adult would send shivers up a would-be toughie's spine.

In some instances, youngsters are forced into a delinquent group and threatened with harm if they try to stay out. Once they are in, however, they gain a feeling of protection, even of security and identity (Alexander, 1964). Whether or not a preadolescent joins a delinquent gang depends, of course, on many factors. One is the extent to which he identifies with his parents and other adults. If these connections are strong, there is a good chance that the child will have the inner strength to resist the pressures of the gang. If he comes from a broken home, however, or one that is inadequate in other ways, or if he lives in a dangerous, gang-ridden neighborhood, the pressures from peers will probably be harder to resist.

Fortunately, delinquent gang behavior is the exception rather than the rule for most preadolescents. Extreme resistance to adult authority is not typical. Studies have shown that conformity to peer influences in six to eight year olds was actually positively correlated with conformity to adult influence as well (Crandall, et al., 1958). This would indicate that a sort of general conformability may make children susceptible to both peer and adult influences.

Another study (Harris and Tseng, 1957) surveyed children of a wide range of ages and found generally positive attitudes toward both peers and adults. The study also discovered a slight decrease in positive attitudes toward parents during middle childhood, which might be the result of increased peer identification or of seeing parents more realistically, not as superhuman beings. Other researchers

(Witryol and Calkins, 1958) have found an increase from fourth- to fifth-grade age groups in children's agreement with dares or challenges to adult authority. From the research done so far, therefore, it would be difficult to draw conclusions about the extent to which peer groups in middle childhood form alliances against adults.

Group Variables

The type of exchanges that take place between members of a group are affected by many factors, including the size of the group. In a study (Hare, 1952) of Boy Scout meetings it was found that agreement was greater in a group of five members than in a group of twelve members, and the leader's opinion influenced the small group more than it did the large group. In the large group, the leader's skill at running the discussion was a very important factor in obtaining a group decision. Members of the large group felt that their individual opinions were less important, and they tended more than the small-group members to band together in factions. The small group was clearly more cohesive.

Another element influencing peer-group behavior is the nature of the activity in which the group is engaged. In a study of preadolescent boys at camp (Gump, Schoggen, and Redl, 1957), it was found that more aggressive behavior occurred when the group was involved in vigorous physical activities such as swimming than when they were doing quiet things such as crafts. Helping actions occurred more often during quiet periods. The activity of one member often prompts the others to do the same thing: when one person starts throwing objects, everyone else may catch the fever, and soon the air is thick with flying objects.

Leadership

Adult-led groups can differ markedly according to the kind of leadership the adult provides. A famous series of studies (Lewin, Lippit, and White, 1938; Lippit and White, 1943) distinguished three kinds of adult leadership and measured their effects on groups of eleven year old boys. There were democratic leaders, who let the boys decide on many activities for themselves yet retained some control over the boys' behavior; there were laissez-faire leaders, who did not interfere with the boys at all; and there were authoritarian leaders, who sternly dictated what the boys should do and controlled every aspect of the situation.

As might be guessed, the authoritarian leaders created a great deal of aggression in their group. This aggression was directed toward outsiders, toward other group members, and toward the leader himself. Also, when the authoritarian leader was absent for a short period, the group tended to fall apart; there was little motivation to accomplish a task. In the laissez-faire group there were expressions of irritability among members at times, perhaps because the lack of direction led to relatively low group cohesiveness. The democratic group, on the other hand, tended to be fairly cohesive and task-oriented. Its members often sought the approval of each other and of the leader.

Status in the Group

Status is the dimension of peer acceptance or rejection and peer approval or disapproval. A person who is highly accepted and approved by his peers is said to have high status, and a person with low acceptance and approval is said to have low status.

Not surprisingly, studies have found that children who like their peers are liked by them. Acceptance was found to be associated with friendliness and an outgoing character (Bonney and Powell, 1953), with kindness as perceived by others (Smith, 1950), and with lack of withdrawal (Winder and Rau, 1962). Another study (Campbell and Yarrow, 1961) showed that popular children tended to be more sensitive to others' motives than did unpopular children. The popular children were able to make complicated inferences about why various peers did certain things. Leaders especially were found to be very attuned to others' feelings and actions. Although high sociability is generally associated with acceptance, at least one study (Elkins, 1958) indicates that for twelve to fifteen year olds low sociability is not a usual reason for rejection by peers.

Another factor in acceptance is the child's correct perception of his own status. Research (Goslin, 1962) has found that unpopular children show a wider discrepancy between their self-ratings and the ratings given to them by others in the group. These children also differed from the group in their ratings of others. Thus, it would seem that sensitivity to status within the group does have a relation to popularity.

One possible explanation of why sensitivity to status brings popularity is that if a child is sensitive to many aspects of other people, including their status, he can easily take their roles and thus will be well liked. Children who are less skilled at role-taking would be less liked and would interact less with peers.

"...and you're to give your big brother the same respect you would give a regular sitter."

If it is true that role-taking, which is largely a cognitive ability, is associated with peer acceptance, then other cognitive traits might also be related to popularity. Many studies have been made of the relationship between popularity and IQ, and almost all of them found a positive relationship between the two.

Friendship

On what basis are friendships made? Age and sex are important in middle childhood, and so is living in the same neighborhood, but the personality factors are not so clear. We might ask, for example, whether status influences children in their choice

Figure 12.4. Sharing a mutual interest makes for close friendship.

of close friends. One study (Sells and Roff, 1967) found no significant correlation of the status of the choosers and the chosen, but another study (Tagiuri, Kogan, and Long, 1958), this one of boys in a private school, found that in choices of roommates there was a similarity in status between chooser and chosen. We can only conclude that more research is needed before this question can be answered.

Are friends made on the basis of similar personalities, or do opposites attract? One investigation (Davitz, 1955) showed that a child sees the person he chooses for a friend as having the same characteristics that he believes himself to have. However, when similarity was independently assessed, the person the child liked most was not really more similar to him than the person he liked least. One might ask, then: Do children choose friends on the grounds of similarity, or do they perceive others as similar because they are friends?

In any case, it does seem that for most personality traits, similarity between friends is the rule. For some traits, however, opposites may attract. One study (Hilkevitch, 1960) found that eighth-grade boys who were labeled by others as attention-seekers tended to associate with boys who would share attention and be supportive of them. Pairs of girls, on the other hand, tended to be much more similar to each other in every way.

Socialization and the Peer Group

One of the major functions of the peer groups is the socialization of the child. Within the group the child learns what is acceptable in his society and what is not. He learns how to win respect and how to achieve his goals without alienating others. Thus, the peer group continues the process of socialization that begins in the home.

Many studies have been made of the ways in which peer groups influence their members and of the ways in which the members are prone to influence. One classic study (Berenda, 1950), which measured the extent to which children of different ages conform to false judgments when pressure is exerted on them by peers, found that they conform most often when the pressure is exerted by peers whom they believe to be very competent. The period of greatest conformity was found to be between the ages of seven and ten years.

Other studies (McConnell, 1963; Iscoe, Willing, and Harvey, 1963) have supported the theory that conformity is at its highest during middle childhood. One explanation for such findings is provided by the theories of Piaget, who maintains that in middle childhood the individual becomes much better at grasping rules and taking the role of the other. She can step outside of her own limited viewpoint, see many aspects of a situation including the views of others, and try out various solutions to a problem. These developments make the child more susceptible to outside influence on her judgment. This may change in the adolescent years, when the child's mind becomes freer to range through many theoretical possibilities. Situational factors, including suggestion by peers, may have less influence on her then.

CHILDREN AND DEATH

Death is extremely difficult for children to understand, and adults often find themselves unable to handle the questions children ask when a loved one dies. Answers such as "Daddy's gone away" or "Daddy's gone to heaven" only lead to additional questions: "Where did Daddy go? Why did he have to leave?"

It is also a mistake to explain it in terms of sleep. A child who is told that dying is like going to sleep is likely to fear that he too may not wake up if he goes to sleep. It should be made clear that death, unlike sleep, is permanent and irrevocable. Although this is a difficult concept for the child to grasp, it may prevent a disturbing and awkward scene later on, when the child may claim to have seen or spoken to the dead person.

It is not uncommon for a child to blame himself for the death of a parent. Unable to understand what has happened, the child wonders if it was something he did wrong that made the parent leave. Alternatively, he may transfer his feelings of guilt to the surviving parent: Why didn't Mommy make Daddy stay?

Some psychologists have proposed the use of play therapy to help children come to terms with their feelings of loss. By using dolls to represent friends and family members, for example, a mother can act out her husband's death and show the child how various people are affected by it. Realizing that his parent's death is not anyone's fault is the child's first important step toward accepting what has happened.

Probably the most important factor in a child's adjustment to the death of a parent is the attitude and emotional response of the surviving parent. A child's confusion can only be intensified when his mother pretends that everything is all right during the day but cries herself to sleep at night. The parent who does not openly share her grief does her child a disservice. By isolating the child, she deprives him of the parent which he so desperately needs at this time.

On the other hand, parents should not go too far in the opposite direction. A father who tells his young daughter that she must take her mother's place as the woman of the house is asking more than most children can give. A parent who has lost his spouse must be both mother and father to the child. The child needs to be reassured that her surviving parent is capable of protecting and taking care of her. Although added responsibilities may become necessary and may even serve as valuable therapy, they should not be imposed at the cost of the child's feeling of security nor at the cost of her childhood.

Birth order in the family has also been shown to influence proneness to conformity (Schacter, 1959). Firstborn children tend to change their opinions to conform to false group norms more than do later-born children, except when a large incentive is offered for a correct answer. Then firstborns will tend to be more independent in responding than the later-borns.

Among the other variables that have been studied in connection with conformity are IQ, sex, and such group factors as the size of the group exerting pressure and the perceived competence and attractiveness of the group or person influencing the individual. No significant correlations between IQ and conformity have been found for children in the middle years. This finding conflicts with the widely held commonsense belief that more intelligent children are necessarily more independent than less intelligent children. On the variable of sex, it has been found in some studies that girls in middle childhood are more conforming than boys (Iscoe et al., 1963). However, in certain situations boys will be more conforming than girls, particularly when "masculine" emotions and motives are involved, such as in sports or situations that call for aggressiveness.

With respect to the variable of group size, a study (Hare, 1952) has shown that members of a group tend to form a consensus more easily when the group is small. On the question of the status or attractiveness of the source of influence, a researcher (Gelfand, 1962) found that children are more conforming to peers whom they perceive as being more competent than themselves. Another study (Harvey and Rutherford, 1957) established that children who found themselves agreeing with low-status peers and disagreeing with high-status peers tended to shift their opinions more often than children who agreed with high-status peers and disagreed with low-status peers.

Racial Awareness and Prejudice

Children may be quite conscious of racial differences without being prejudiced. The awareness of racial differences begins as early as age four, regardless of whether the children are reared in an integrated or a segregated environment. The development of racial prejudice—the feeling that one race is inferior or superior—depends on many factors.

Racial prejudice in the home, even if unspoken, has an undoubted effect on the child. If white parents shun blacks or members of other minorities at school events or public meetings, children will sense that something is unacceptable about them. Some psychiatrists (Poussaint and Comer, 1972) recommend that parents be honest with their children about any racist feelings they might have and discuss

Figure 12.5. Interracial friendships can be spoiled by prejudice, but not by simple awareness of racial differences.

them openly. This way, parents may become better aware of their own attitudes, and children will be able to think about them rationally.

Another source of prejudice in children is exposure to racism in the attitudes of other children, adults other than his parents, and books, magazines, and newspapers. It is impossible to shield children from these influences, but parents can deal with them by talking about them openly as the child comes across them.

As long as racial prejudice exists in many children, we should try to understand its effects. According to several studies (Clark and Clark, 1947; Morland, 1958), black children's race awareness is accompanied by preference for the white race and ambivalence toward their own race. With the rise of the movements of blacks and other minority groups, however, it seems likely that self-disparagement on the part of blacks and other minorities may be decreasing. At least there are competing attitudes in the minds of many black children, and to the extent that their homes and schools foster racial pride, they should become increasingly free of self-devaluation.

THE SCHOOL

School can show children the need for discipline and give them the joy of accomplishment. Unfortunately, it can also shake some children's self-confidence and give them an inferior image of themselves. There are many variables that affect success or failure in schooling, and a great deal has been written about each of them. Two factors that are currently under intense discussion are teaching methods and the personalities of teachers.

Teaching Methods

One broad approach to directing teaching methods regards the teacher as a *facilitator*—that is, the teacher does not attempt to teach strictly defined lessons or bits of knowledge but rather tries to provide the students with materials and methods they can use to learn at their own rate and according to their own interests. A good description of this type of teaching is found in Herbert Kohl's *36 children* (1967). Instead of teaching his whole sixth-grade class lessons in reading and math, Kohl brought in lots of books, art materials, and play materials, then spent his time trying to establish an atmosphere in which the children were free to explore the objects and their own fantasies as well. Under his warm encouragement, they soon developed various projects of their own and made remarkable progress in language and thinking abilities.

John Holt, author of *How children learn* (1970), also subscribes to a version of this method, particularly with very young children. He maintains that the child can be easily hurt and discouraged when he comes up against something he does not know and cannot figure out. If the teacher does not try to force the child to learn but just lets him experiment with books or materials on his own, he will eventually acquire the basic learning skills and a taste for knowledge as well. This will happen, Holt believes, because children are naturally curious. What the teacher must do is be available to help when the child asks for help, and get out of the child's way at other times. One of Holt's anecdotes illustrates this:

> . . . every now and then Lisa would come to a word she could neither figure out, nor guess, nor skip. On this day she found such a word. Slowly she climbed out of her chair and, holding the book, came toward me. I looked at her as she came. She had a set, stern expression on her face. Pointing to a word in her book, she asked, "What does it say?" Her look seemed to say very distinctly, "Now please don't ask me a lot of silly questions, like 'What do you think it says?' or 'Have you tried sounding it out?' or anything like that. If I could do those, I wouldn't be here asking. Just tell me what the word says; that will be enough." I told her. She nodded, went back to her chair, and continued reading.

Holt cautions that getting out of the child's way does not mean neglecting him or ignoring his requests for information or help. He observes that if the child repeatedly fails to get a response from the people in his world, he will soon stop trying to get a response—that is, he will stop asking questions. In effect, he will give up on learning. Thus, the task of the teacher is not to obstruct the child's own learning pattern, but to be there when needed.

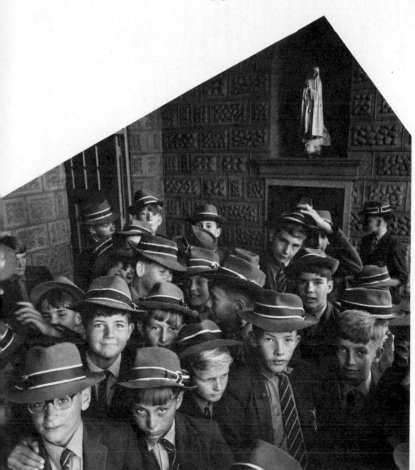

Figure 12.6 Some educators ask whether a traditional structured education, such as the one received in this boys' school, is the best way for children to learn.

Another school of thought about teaching methods takes its cue from the theories of Piaget. This approach assumes that the child can master a particular skill only when he has reached the appropriate stage of cognitive development. A course of instruction should be carefully planned, therefore, to suit the child at each stage of cognitive development. Learning can thus proceed with a minimum of frustration. This approach does not necessarily conflict with the open-classroom approach advocated by Kohl, inasmuch as both let the child proceed on his own and at his own rate. In the Piagetian approach, however, the situation is more carefully structured in order to increase the child's chances of successful learning.

Of course, either tendency—structure or lack of it—can be taken to extremes. As Erikson (1968) points out, teachers can make the school a miniature version of an oppressive and comfortless adulthood, full of duties for the child, organized to the last detail, and clocked to the last second. The child in this situation may learn a sense of duty, but he learns it because it is imposed on him from the outside. He learns it to please authority, not to please himself.

The other extreme is freedom carried to the point of chaos. As the child is only told to do what he wants, he receives no direction and is left confused amid all his choices.

Teachers

It would be easy to conclude that there are two types of teacher—open and structured. But teachers, like pupils, are individuals, each with his own mixture of personal characteristics.

One quality that a good teacher must have is respect for his pupils. He must not attempt to humiliate them or violate their sense of self in any way. Instead, he must do all he can to help them grow, never forgetting that his efforts must be made for their sakes, and not just to feather his own cap.

Some respectful teachers prefer structured situations in which everyone, including the teacher, knows just where he stands and where he is headed. Other equally respectful teachers work more comfortably in a very loose situation: an open classroom with few set routines and a lot of space—physical, intellectual, and emotional—in which to move around.

An anxious teacher may be harmful to the child if he communicates his anxiety to the child. If the child senses anxiety in the teacher, he may begin to adopt the teacher's feeling that the classroom, and by extension the whole world, is a difficult and threatening place. His sense of security will be weakened.

Different types of teachers will use different methods to establish and maintain discipline in a classroom. The anxious teacher may be very demanding, may need to have everything exactly the way he plans it, and if things go wrong may become flustered and angry. Some teachers maintain discipline by threat of punishment, and others rely more on demonstrating appreciation for their students' accomplishments.

References

Alexander, C. N. Consensus and mutual attraction in natural cliques: A study of adolescent drinkers. *American Journal of Sociology*, 1964, *69*, 395–403.

Aronfreed, J. *Conduct and conscience.* New York: Academic Press, 1968.

Bandura, A., and Walters, R. H. *Aggression.* In Stevens, H. W. (Ed.), *Yearbook of the National Society for the Study of Education.* Chicago: University of Chicago Press, 1963.

Berenda, R. W. *The influence of the group on the judgments of children.* New York: King's Crown Press, 1950.

Bonney, M. E., and Powell, J. Differences in social behaviour between sociometrically high and sociometrically low children. *Journal of Educational Research*, 1953, *46*, 481–495.

Bossard, J., and Boll, E. *The sociology of child development.* New York: Harper, 1960.

Bowlby, J. Childhood mourning and psychiatric illness. In P. Lomas (Ed.), *The predicament of the family.* London: Hogarth Press, 1967.

Bronfenbrenner, U. Some familial antecedents of responsibility and leadership in adolescents. In L. Petrullo and R. L. Brown (Eds.), *Leadership and interpersonal behavior,* New York: Holt, 1961.

Brown, F. Depression and childhood bereavement. *Journal of Mental Science*, 1961.

Campbell, J. D., and Yarrow, M. R. Perceptual and behavioral correlates of social effectiveness. *Sociometry*, 1961, *24*, 1–20.

Clark, K. B., and Clark, M. P. Racial identity and preferences in Negro children. In T. Newcomb and E. L. Hartley (Eds.), *Readings in social psychology.* New York: Henry Holt, 1947.

Crandall, V. J., Orleans, S., Preston, A., and Rabson, A. The development of social compliance in young children. *Child Development*, 1958, *29*, 429–443.

Davitz, J. R. Social perception and sociometric choice in children. *Journal of Abnormal Social Psychology*, 1955, *50*, 173–176.

Dodson, F. *How to father.* Los Angeles: Nash, 1974.

Elkins, D. Some factors related to the choice status of ninety eighth-grade children in a school society. *Genetic Psychology Monograph*, 1958, *58*, 207–272.

Erikson, E. *Identity, youth and change.* New York: Norton, 1968.

Gelfand, D. M. The influence of self-esteem on rate of verbal conditioning and social matching behaviour. *Journal of Abnormal Social Psychology*, 1962, *65*, 259–265.

Gesell, A., and Ilg, F. *Child development.* New York: Harper, 1949.

Ginott, H. How to drive our children sane. *Life*, January, 1972.

Goslin, P. A. Accuracy of self-perception and social acceptance. *Sociometry*, 1962, *65*, 283–296.

Gump, P., Schoggen, P., and Redl, F. The camp milieu and its immediate effects. *Journal of Social Issues*, 1957, *13*, 40–46.

Hare, A. P. Small group discussions with partcipatory and supervisory leadership. *Journal of Abnormal Psychology*, 1953, *48*, 273–275.

Hare, A. P. A study of interaction and consensus in different-sized groups. *American Sociology Review*, 1952, *17*, 261–267.

Harris, D. D., and Tseng, S. Children's attitudes toward peers and parents as revealed by sentence cor 'etions. *Child development*, 1957, *28*, 401–411.

Harvey, O. J., and Rutherford, J. Status in the informal group; influence and influencability at differing age levels. *Child Development*, 1957, *28*, 377–385.

Hilkevitch, R. R. Social interactional processes: A quantitative study. *Psychology Report*, 1960, *7*, 195–201.

Holt, J. *How children learn.* New York: Dell, 1970.

Iscoe, I., Willing, M., and Harvey J. Modification of children's judgments by a simulated group technique: A normative study. *Child Development*, 1963, *34*, 963–978.

Klein, C. *The single parent experience.* New York: Avon, 1973.

Kohl, H. *36 children.* New York: New American Library, 1967.

Lewin, K., Lippitt, R., and White, R. K. Patterns of aggressive behaviour in experimentally-created "social climates." *Journal of Social Psychology*, 1938, *10*, 271–299.

Lippitt, R., and White, R. K. The "social climate" of children's groups. In R. G. Barker, J. S. Korinen, and H. F. Wright (Eds.), *Child behavior and development.* New York: McGraw-Hill, 1943.

McConnell, T. Suggestibility in children as a function of chronological age. *Journal of Abnormal Social Psychology,* 1963, *67,* 286–289.

McCord, W., McCord, J., and Howard, A. Familial correlates of aggression in non-delinquent male children. *Journal of Abnormal and Social Psychology,* 1961, *62,* 79–93.

Morland, J. K. Racial recognition by nursery-school children in Lynchburg, Virginia. *Social Forces,* 1958, *37,* 132–137.

New York Times, "14% of U.S. children under 18 being raised by mothers alone." August 8, 1974, p. 14.

Opie, I., and Opie, P. *The language and lore of children.* London: Oxford University Press, 1959.

Poussaint, A. F., and Comer, J. F. What white parents should know about children and prejudice. *Redbook,* May, 1972.

Redl, F., and Wineman, D. *Children who hate.* New York: Free Press, 1951.

Schachter, S. *The psychology of affiliation.* Palo Alto: Stanford University Press, 1959.

Sells, S. B., and Roff, M. Peer acceptance and rejection and personality development. Final report, Project No. 0E-0417, United States Department of Health, Education and Welfare, 1967.

Sherif, M., Harvey, O. J., White, B. J., Hood, W. R., and Sherif, C. W. *Intergroup conflict and cooperation: The robbers cave experiment.* Norman: University of Oklahoma Press, 1961.

Sherif, M., and Sherif, C. W. *Groups in harmony and tension.* New York: Harper, 1953.

Smith, G. H. Sociometric study of best-liked and least-liked children. *Elementary School Journal,* 1950, *51,* 77–85.

Sullivan, H. S. *The interpersonal theory of psychiatry.* New York: Norton, 1953.

Tagiuri, R., Kogan, N., and Long, L. M. K. Differentiation of sociometric and status relations in a group. *Psychology Report,* 1958, *4,* 523–526.

Toman, W. *Family constellation: Its effects on personality and social behavior.* New York: Springer, 1969.

Winder, C. L., and Rau, L. Parental attitudes associated with social deviance in preadolescent boys. *Journal of Abnormal Social Psychology,* 1962, *64,* 418–424.

Witryol, S. L., and Calkins, J. E. Marginal social values of rural school children. *Journal of Genetic Psychology,* 1958, *64,* 418–424.

SUMMARY

1   The attitude of parents toward their child affects the child's behavior toward others. Loving parents produce loving children; hostile parents, hostile children. Correlations have been found between punitiveness and rejection by parents and lack of internal controls and aggression in children. Parents can hurt the child's social development by exercising too little or too much control over his behavior, or by being unduly protective.

2   The loss of a parent often affects the child's social adjustment. Studies show a correlation between loss of a parent and delinquency. Suppressed grief in children may turn up as depression in later life.

3   Interactions with siblings affect the way children relate to schoolmates and teachers. Children tend to adopt a pattern of behavior which will gain them their desired share of attention from parents and siblings. The only child does not have to compete with siblings for the attention of parents, and like the firstborn child, he tends to have high self-esteem.

4   Peer groups in middle childhood are usually composed of members of the same sex. Norms arise rapidly in any new peer group, partly because the members are at an age to understand and make rules and partly because they want their group to be distinct from other groups. As children grow older, their interest in game-playing shifts from the social aspects of the game to the development of skills. Certain games have been played by children without much change for centuries.

5   The characteristic independence of peer groups from the adult world takes an extreme form in delinquent gangs, which give children a sense of belonging and identity. Children whose relationship with parents is satisfactory are less likely to yield to peer-group pressure. Peer-group behavior is influenced by the size of the group and the nature of its activity. The character of groups led by adults is strongly influenced by the character of the adult leader—whether he is authoritarian, democratic, or laissez-faire.

6   Status in the group depends on the degree of acceptance by other members. Factors in acceptance are friendliness, an outgoing personality, and the child's perception of his own status. Generally, children form friendships with those who have traits similar to their own.

7

Children begin to be aware of racial differences at about age four. They become prejudiced in middle childhood through the influence of parents, other children and adults, and attitudes expressed in the popular media.

8

One approach to teaching sees the teacher as facilitator in an atmosphere where children are free to make their own explorations, whereas a more structured approach aims to increase the child's chances for success. Regardless of approach, regard for the child's self-esteem is essential in a teacher.

FURTHER READINGS

Ginott, H. *Between parent and child.* New York: Macmillan, 1968.
　　Ginott's understanding of preadolescent and adolescent problems won him wide respect as a clinical psychologist. Here, with many examples, he shows how adults unconsciously damage self-esteem, undermine integrity, and create hostility.

Golding, W. *Lord of the flies.* New York: Coward-McCann, 1962.
　　A powerful novel about the influence of peer group conformity on preadolescents. English schoolboys stranded on an uninhabited island become savages under the control of a bullying leader as they turn against the dissenting loner who is the tragic hero of the book.

Holt, J. *How children fail.* New York: Pitman, 1968.
　　Holt maintains that few schools meet children's needs. He writes that children fall short of their learning potential when they are afraid of displeasing adults, bored, or confused, and describes the ways that they use to meet or to escape demands made on them by adults in school.

Homan, W. D. *Child sense.* New York: Basic Books, 1969.
　　A book by a pediatrician that stresses the parental role in personality development. In Homan's view, the most important educational force in the formation of character is the child's imitation or rejection of his parents. The book has separate discussions on younger children and older children.

Jencks, C. *Inequality: A reassessment of family and schooling in America.* New York: Basic Books, 1972.
　　Jencks and associates at the Center for Educational Policy Research who contributed to this book arrive at the conclusion that educational reform cannot bring about economic or social equality. Their research suggests that children are more influenced by the family and the street than by the school. Jencks recommends a long-term restructuring of the entire social system.

Part **5**
ADOLESCENCE

Then finally they reached the place she had been looking for. "This is it! See that sign that says PRIVATE? We got to climb the bob-wire fence and then take that path there—see!"

The woods were very quiet. Slick pine needles covered the ground. Within a few minutes they had reached the creek. The water was brown and swift. Cool. There was no sound except from the water and a breeze singing high up in the pine trees. It was like the deep, quiet woods made them timid, and they walked softly along the bank beside the creek.

"Don't it look pretty."

Harry laughed. "What makes you whisper? Listen here!" He clapped his hand over his mouth and gave a long Indian whoop that echoed back at them. "Come on. Let's jump in the water and cool off."

"Aren't you hungry?"

"O.K. Then we'll eat first. We'll eat half the lunch now and half later on when we come out."

She unwrapped the jelly sandwiches. When they were finished Harry balled the papers neatly and stuffed them into a hollow tree stump. Then he took his shorts and went down the path. She shucked off her clothes behind a bush and struggled into Hazel's bathing-suit. The suit was too small and cut her between the legs.

"You ready?" Harry hollered.

She heard a splash in the water and when she reached the bank Harry was already swimming. "Don't dive yet until I find out if there are any stumps or shallow places," he said. She just looked at his head bobbing in the water. She had never intended to dive, anyway. She couldn't even swim. She had been in swimming only a few times in her life—and then she always wore water-wings or stayed out of parts that were over her head. But it would be sissy to tell

Harry. She was embarrassed. All of a sudden she told a tale:

"I don't dive any more. I used to dive, high dive, all the time. But once I busted my head open, so I can't dive any more." She thought for a minute. "It was a double jack-knife dive I was doing. And when I came up there was blood all in the water. But I didn't think anything about it and just began to do swimming tricks. These people were hollering at me. Then I found out where all this blood in the water was coming from. And I never have swam good since."

Harry scrambled up the bank. "Gosh! I never heard about that."

She meant to add on to the tale to make it sound more reasonable, but instead she just looked at Harry. His skin was light brown and the water made it shining. There were hairs on his chest and legs. In the tight trunks he seemed very naked. Without his glasses his face was wider and more hand-some. His eyes were wet and blue. He was looking at her and it was like suddenly they got embarrassed.

"The water's about ten feet deep except over on the other bank, and there it's shallow."

"Less us get going. I bet that cold water feels good."

She wasn't scared. She felt the same as if she had got caught at the top of a very high tree and there was nothing to do but just climb down the best way she could—a dead-calm feeling. She edged off the bank and was in the ice-cold water. She held to a root until it broke in her hands and then she began to swim. Once she choked and went under, but she kept going and didn't lose any face. She swam and reached the other side of the bank where she could touch bottom. Then she felt good. She smacked the water with her fists and called out crazy words to make echoes.

"Watch here!"

Harry shimmied up a tall, thin little tree. The trunk was limber and when he reached the top it swayed down with him. He dropped into the water.

"Me too! Watch me do it!"

"That's a sapling."

She was as good a climber as anybody on the block. She copied exactly what he had done and hit the water with a hard smack. She could swim, too. Now she could swim O.K.

They played follow the leader and ran up and down the bank and jumped in the cold brown water. They hollered and jumped and climbed. They played around for maybe two hours. Then they were standing on the bank and they both looked at each other and there didn't seem to be anything new to do. Suddenly she said:

"Have you ever swam naked?"

The woods was very quiet and for a min-ute he did not answer. He was cold. His tit-ties had turned hard and purple. His lips were purple and his teeth chattered. "I—I don't think so."

This excitement was in her, and she said something she didn't mean to say. "I would if you would. I dare you to."

Harry slicked back the dark, wet bangs of his hair. "O.K."

They both took off their bathing-suits. Harry had his back to her. He stumbled and his ears were red. Then they turned toward each other. Maybe it was half an hour they stood there—maybe not more than a minute.

Harry pulled a leaf from a tree and tore it to pieces. "We better get dressed."

All through the picnic dinner neither of them spoke. They spread the dinner on the ground. Harry divided everything in half. There was the hot, sleepy feeling of a sum-mer afternoon. In the deep woods they could hear no sound except the slow flowing of the water and the songbirds. Harry held his stuffed egg and mashed the yellow with his thumb. What did that make her remember? She heard herself breathe.

Then he looked up over her shoulder. "Listen here. I think you're so pretty, Mick. I never did think so before. I don't mean I thought you were very ugly—I just mean that—"

She threw a pine cone in the water. "Maybe we better start back if we want to be home before dark."

"No," he said. "Let's lie down. Just for a minute."

He brought handfuls of pine needles and leaves and gray moss. She sucked her knee and watched him. Her fists were tight and it was like she was tense all over.

"Now we can sleep and be fresh for the trip home."

They lay on the soft bed and looked up at the dark-green pine clumps against the sky. A bird sang a sad, clear song she had never heard before. One high note like an oboe—and then it sank down five tones and called again. The song was sad as a question without words.

"I love that bird," Harry said. "I think it's a vireo."

"I wish we was at the ocean. On the beach and watching the ships far out on the water. You went to the beach one summer—exactly what is it like?"

His voice was rough and low. "Well—there are the waves. Sometimes blue and sometimes green, and in the bright sun they look glassy. And on the sand you can pick up these little shells. Like the kind we brought back in a cigar box. And over the water are these white gulls. We were at the Gulf of Mexico—these cool bay breezes blew all the time and there it's never baking hot like it is here. Always—"

"Snow," Mick said, "That's what I want to see. Cold, white drifts of snow like in pictures. Blizzards. White, cold snow that keeps falling soft and falls on and on and on through all the winter. Snow like in Alaska."

They both turned at the same time. They were close against each other. She felt him trembling and her fists were tight enough to crack. "Oh, God," he kept saying over and over. It was like her head was broke off from her body and thrown away. And her eyes looked up straight into the blinding sun while she counted something in her mind. And then this was the way.

This was how it was.

—Carson McCullers
The Heart Is a Lonely Hunter

13
Growing into Adulthood

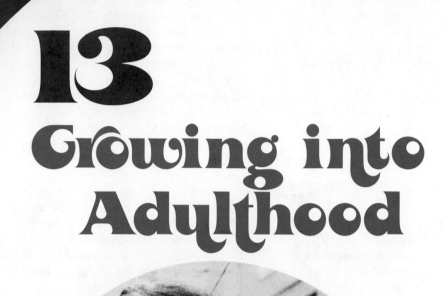

Adolescence is the bridge between childhood and adulthood. It is a time of rapid development: of growing to sexual maturity, discovering one's real self, defining personal values, and finding one's own vocational and social directions. It is also a time of testing: of pushing against one's own capabilities and the limitations imposed by adults.

The framework for individual development in the adolescent period varies from place to place. In the United States, an adolescent in the rural West does not make quite the same transition to adulthood as an adolescent growing up in Boston or New York; and the aborigine in Australia becomes an adult in a way that is altogether different from that of the urban adolescent in Sydney. In general, nonindustrial societies expect people to spend fewer years in school and to marry earlier than do industrialized societies, and thus the period of transition is shorter in nonindustrial parts of the world.

There are, of course, some changes that take place in every person beyond his twelfth birthday no matter where he grows up. Other changes seem to be at least as social as they are biological, and it is sometimes difficult to draw a clear line between them. The onset of adolescence in every culture, however, is heralded by certain physical and sexual changes.

PHYSICAL AND SEXUAL DEVELOPMENT

Some people confuse the terms *adolescence* and *puberty*. *Adolescence* can roughly be defined as the period from the onset of puberty to adulthood. *Puberty* is the shorter period of adolescence during which an individual reaches sexual maturity. Puberty lasts from two to four years and is marked by great physical and psychological changes: a person's body becomes capable of functioning sexually, and his attitudes and behavior become more mature. Sexual maturity is achieved by mid-adolescence.

The outward signs of the development of sex organs and a mature body type are not the first physical changes that herald the developmental stage called adolescence. Many months before these outward signs become visible, the body is changing in subtle ways, particularly in its hormonal makeup. This prepares the way for sexual maturity and the ability to procreate.

Physical Growth

Human beings grow most rapidly at two times during their lives: before they are six months old and then again during adolescence. The second period of accelerated growth is often called the adolescent growth spurt. This spectacular growth has inspired some famous passages in literature, such as this one by Victor Hugo:

> It happened that Marius broke off his daily walk in the Luxembourg, without exactly knowing why, and was nearly six months without setting foot in the garden. One day, however, he returned to it; it was a beauteous summer's day, and Marius was joyous as men are when the weather is fine. . . .
>
> He went straight to "his" walk, and when he reached the end he noticed the well-known couple seated on the same bench, but when he drew near he found that, while it was the same man, it did not seem to be the same girl. The person he now saw was a tall and lovely creature, possessing the charming outlines of the woman at the precise moment when they are still combined with the most simple graces of the child. . . .
>
> At first Marius thought it was another daughter of the gentleman's, a sister of the former. But when the invariable habit of his walk brought him again to the bench, and he examined her attentively, he perceived that it was the same girl. In six months the child had become a woman, that was all, and nothing was more frequent than this phenomenon. There is a moment in which girls become roses instantly—yesterday you left them children, today you find them objects of anxiety (*Les Miserables*).

Adolescents grow both in height and weight, with the increase in height preceding the increase in weight. As they gain weight the amount and distribution of fat in their body changes, and the proportion of bone and muscle tissue increases. Throughout the entire period of adolescence, height increases by 25 percent, and weight increases by 50 percent.

Figure 13.1. The body achieves full maturity in shape and size during adolescence.

In girls, the adolescent growth spurt usually begins between the ages of eight and eleven and reaches a peak at an average of twelve and a half years. Then growth slows down and usually ceases completely between the ages of fifteen and eighteen. The growth spurt in boys usually begins later than it does in girls and lasts for a longer time. For boys, it begins between the ages of eleven and fourteen, reaches a peak at about age fifteen, and slowly declines until the age of nineteen or twenty. During the period of maximum growth, girls grow about three and a half inches in one year and put on about eleven pounds. Boys grow four to five inches a year and gain twelve to fourteen pounds.

Changes in body proportion accompany the changes in height and weight. One of the most noticeable changes is in the trunk of the body. The trunk widens in the hips and shoulders, and the waistline drops. Boys tend to broaden mostly in the shoulders, whereas girls' hips widen more than their shoulders. One of the earliest changes in both boys and girls is the addition of a layer of fat in the hips and the legs. This fat soon disappears in the boy but remains with the girl. The additional height gained in adolescence is primarily the result of increased length of the trunk, not the legs. At first, however, the neck, arms, and legs grow more rapidly than the trunk, and this gives the young adolescent an awkward, disproportionate appearance. Hands and feet have a growth spurt about a year before the arms and legs, and they add to the young adolescent's ungainly figure. The hands, feet, and head are the first body parts to reach their mature size.

Head circumference increases by less than one inch during adolescence, but the face changes markedly. It grows first in length, with the upper part of the face changing before the lower part. As the face lengthens, it becomes broader as well, and the nose and chin become more prominent. Boys' faces become more angular, girls' faces more oval.

Heredity and nutrition influence the timing of the adolescent growth spurt in several ways, one of the most important being their effect on the secretion of hormones by the endocrine glands. A growth hormone released by the pituitary gland is primarily responsible for the rapid growth at the beginning of adolescence. The thyroid gland aids in this development by releasing hormones that permit the conversion of food into tissues and energy. The gonads—the ovaries in the female and the testes in the male—are stimulated by hormones secreted from the adrenal glands and the pituitary. It is the gonads that bring about sexual development, and they play an important role in stimulating the physical development that occurs before the visible signs of puberty appear.

"Gosh, Roger, I can certainly consider myself lucky being shipwrecked with a person like you, I guess."

The first menstruation often is used to mark the beginning of puberty in the girl, but even before it occurs, the sex organs have begun to develop, and the **secondary sex characteristics**—the nongenital physical features that distinguish men from women—are appearing. In the boy, the appearance of semen, pubic hair, a lower voice, and growth of the penis and testes are often used as signs of the onset of puberty, but certain other physical changes occur first. About one to two years before the outward signs of puberty appear, the gonads begin to secrete hormones—androgen in boys and estrogen in girls—that start to bring about the striking physical and mental changes of adolescence.

Puberty can be divided into three stages. In the *prepubescent* stage, the secondary sex characteristics begin to develop, but the reproductive organs do not yet function. In the *pubescent* stage, the secondary sex characteristics continue to develop, and the reproductive organs become capable of producing ova and sperm. In the *postpubescent* stage, the secondary sex characteristics are well developed and the sex organs are capable of adult functioning. About 50 percent of all girls reach the pubescent stage by the age of thirteen, whereas 50 percent of all boys do not reach it until about fifteen. The other 50 percent of all boys and girls are equally divided between the early and the later maturers.

The wide range in ages of reaching sexual maturity is the result of variations in the functioning of the endocrine glands, particularly the pituitary and the gonads. The functioning of these glands is influenced by heredity as well as by the general health of the individual and social and environmental conditions. Children whose parents mature early or late tend to follow the parental genetic example. Children in the Temperate Zone tend to mature earlier than those in the Tropical Zones or the Arctic, and children in urban areas tend to mature sooner than children from rural areas. Girls who have a relatively large amount of protein in their diets tend to mature earlier than average, whereas girls whose diet consists primarily of carbohydrates tend to mature later.

Children who mature early are likely to be large for their age and to have a broad body build, whereas late maturers are smaller than average and have a more slender build. The child who is a later maturer usually matures more rapidly once he gets started; puberty tends to last longer for the early maturer.

Primary sex characteristics

Though the male testes are present at birth, they are only about 10 percent of their mature size. During the first year or two of puberty, the testes grow rapidly. Their growth then slows, and they do not reach mature size until the age of twenty or twenty-one.

Shortly after the testes begin to develop, the penis begins to grow in length, and there is a simultaneous enlargement of the seminal ducts and the prostate gland. Though the penis is capable of erection by means of contact and manipulation from birth on, only during adolescence does it begin to erect spontaneously or in response to sexually provocative sights, sounds, or thoughts.

The female's uterus, fallopian tubes, and vagina grow rapidly from the onset of puberty to the age of about sixteen. The ovaries grow during this period, too, and though they begin to function in the middle of puberty, they do not reach full adult size until the age of twenty or twenty-one. The ovaries produce ova and secrete the hormones needed for pregnancy, menstruation, and the development of the secondary sex characteristics.

One of the most obvious signs that a girl has reached puberty is the beginning of menstruation. The normal range of age at which menstruation first occurs is ten to seventeen years, and in the United States the average age for the **menarche,** or onset of menstruation, is thirteen. About 75 percent of all girls reach menarche between the ages of twelve and fourteen.

Following menarche, menstruation comes only at irregular intervals. For six months to a year or more, ovulation usually does not occur. Headaches, backaches, and cramps frequently accompany the early menstrual periods, and the girl feels tired, depressed, and irritable. As menstruation becomes more regular, these physical and psychological symptoms often diminish or disappear entirely.

Secondary sex characteristics

The secondary sex characteristics—breasts, body hair, the voice change—are not directly related to reproduction, but they are important in making members of one sex appealing to members of the other sex. The first secondary sex characteristic to appear on the male is sparse patches of lightly colored, straight pubic hair, which develop about one year after the testes and penis begin to increase in size. Within a year or two, the pubic hair takes on its characteristic dark, curly appearance. Axillary (underarm) hair and facial hair begin to appear when the pubic hair has almost fully grown in. Like the pubic hair, this hair at first is lightly colored, fine, and sparse. Few boys find that they need to shave before they are sixteen or seventeen. Hair also appears on the arms, legs, and shoulders, and later on the chest. Body hair continues to develop for some time, often into adulthood. The amount and density of hair is determined by heredity.

Boys' skin becomes coarser and thicker during puberty, and the pores enlarge. The *sebaceous*, or fatty, glands in the skin become active at this time and produce an oily secretion, as boys suffering from teenage acne know all too well. The sweat glands in the armpits begin to function even before the axillary hair appears, and the amount and odor of perspiration increase.

Perhaps the most noticeable change in puberty is the voice change. Usually by the time a boy is thirteen, his voice has become husky. Only later, at about age sixteen or seventeen, does it begin to crack. This squeaky voice lasts for a year or two, until the voice change is complete. The voice change results from male hormones causing the larynx to enlarge and the vocal cords to lengthen. Later in adolescence the male voice drops an octave or more in pitch, increases in volume, and develops a more even tonal quality.

Girls' secondary sex characteristics generally develop in the same sequence as those of the boy. The first indication of approaching sexual maturity is a change in the shape of the hips. Their increase in width and roundness is caused in part by the enlargement of the pelvic bone and in part by the development of a layer of subcutaneous fat.

Soon after a girl's hips begin to develop, her breasts begin to grow. The first stage of breast development is known as the bud stage, in which the nipple elevates slightly and the surrounding areola becomes fuller. This occurs at an average age of ten or eleven. Before the menarche, there is an increase in the amount of fat underlying the nipple and the areola, and the breast rises in a conical shape. After the menarche, the breasts become larger and rounder with the development of the mammary glands.

Figure 13.2. Breasts and beard usually reach full development after puberty.

Changing growth patterns

Children in widely separated parts of the world seem to be reaching puberty earlier than their parents did, and they are growing taller and heavier as well. What are the causes of these trends? Is it likely that humankind will become a race of giants?

Records show that in the United States, a young man will, on the average, be one inch taller and ten pounds heavier than his father. A young woman will probably be almost an inch taller than her mother, two pounds heavier, and will reach menarche ten months earlier than her mother did. Today's adolescent is also reaching full adult height earlier than his ancestors did. A century ago boys did not reach full height until age twenty-three or twenty-four, but now an adolescent boy stops growing around the age of eighteen or nineteen. At the turn of the century girls reached full height at the age of eighteen, whereas the modern girl stops growing at age sixteen. This increase in physical size can be easily demonstrated by examining the clothing and furnishings of past generations. A modern family would find the furniture of a house in colonial Williamsburg far too small. The armor worn by medieval warriors would cramp a modern boy of twelve. The first colonists who settled in Jamestown were, on the average, less than five feet tall.

In addition to increasing in height and weight, recent generations also develop earlier than their ancestors did, so that puberty begins at a younger age. This is not a recent phenomenon, nor is it confined to the United States. Children in such diverse areas of the world as China, New Zealand, Italy, and Poland are reaching maturity earlier, and the trend seems to be operating in all populations of these countries. Many studies in recent years have used the menarche as the criterion for tracing this trend. In Scandinavia, England, and America the age at menarche has been getting steadily earlier at the rate of one-third to one-half year per decade, and it is continuing to arrive earlier. In 1840 Norwegian girls reached menarche at an average age of seventeen. Since then menarche has arrived about four months earlier per decade, and today Norwegian girls begin to menstruate before their thirteenth birthday, on average.

With these physical changes has come a correspondingly earlier age at which social and intellectual maturity is achieved. Children become interested in the opposite sex and courtship earlier than their parents did. Parental reaction to this fact can be summed up in the often-heard phrase, "When I was your age. . . ." Sometimes parents do not realize that when they were adolescents they may have been less mature—physically as well as socially—than their children are at the same chronological age.

No one factor can be singled out as the root of these changes. Several environmental factors and hybrid vigor are probably involved. It has been said that the invention of the bicycle and the advent of the steam engine heralded the trend. Before the 1800s people were limited in the means of traveling outside the community to find mates. Neighbors thus tended to intermarry, and a limited number of genetic patterns were transmitted to their offspring. As people's travel horizons broadened and they began to marry more distant neighbors, however, new

Figure 13.3. If adolescents look as though they are maturing sooner than ever, it is because they are. The trend toward earlier development has been recorded in many countries.

genes were introduced into each village. The result is believed to be a hybrid vigor, similar in ways to the larger species of corn and other vegetables that have been developed through crossbreeding.

Improved diet in the twentieth century has often been cited as a cause of the trend. Improvements in agricultural technology have increased crop yields and the caloric intake in much of the world, as well as the vitamin, protein, and mineral content of the food cultivated. Throughout history children of the upper classes have always tended to be larger and to reach maturity faster than children of the lower classes. Upper-class children are growing bigger and maturing sooner these days, but children of poorer families have shown a more striking change.

Immunization, a lower incidence of serious childhood diseases, and better general health care, especially during the prenatal period, are probably factors in promoting growth and maturity among all classes, as are increased play time for children and better climate control. The recent trend toward smaller families may also be a factor. Children in small families tend to be larger and better developed than children in large families.

Will these trends continue indefinitely? Animal species other than man seem to have an upper limit on body size, so anthropologists predict that man's size too will eventually stabilize. While the earlier onset of puberty is not logically related to increases in height and weight, there is some correlation between the two. The earlier age at which menarche is appearing seems to be leveling off in recent years, especially among the upper socioeconomic classes. Earlier puberty may or may not be caused by such factors as increased life span and better health care, although these undoubtedly contribute to increases in size.

Sexual Behavior

All cultures define standards of acceptable sexual behavior for their members and enforce conformity by social sanctions. Traditional American standards condemn adolescent sexual expression and extol the virtues of premarital chastity. These values are not universally shared by other cultures. In one study (Ehrmann, 1961) of 158 societies, 70 percent were found to be tolerant of sexual intercourse between unmarried individuals. Margaret Mead (1928) found that the Samoans consider the concept of celibacy meaningless. They do not censure the premarital activity of untitled girls. Only the wives and daughters of chiefs may not engage in love affairs. A Samoan girl's first love affair, often with an older man, is considered the high point of her sexual pleasure.

Even among Western cultures the standards for acceptable expression of adolescent sexuality vary a great deal. In Spain, where women have a decidedly subordinate role, many girls are sheltered from the world and from interaction with men until the time of their marriage. In traditional Spanish families it is still not uncommon for a relative to be present when a girl meets a suitor. In France, on the other hand, many boys are instructed in the art of love-making by an older woman, who finds the boy's inexperience attractive. Later the boy may teach a young woman about sexuality (Bettelheim, 1963).

American society has succeeded in limiting the sexual activity of the adolescent by various means, the most important of which is the double standard. Some sexual activity is acceptable in boys—indeed, they are half expected to sow their wild oats—but many people believe that girls should restrict their sexual activity to marriage. The illogic of such a position (with whom, after all, are the boys to have their sexual experiences if all of the girls remain virgin?) and its blatant sexism have not prevented the double standard from enduring in the teachings of many parents. At the same time, discussions of sexual matters in our culture have become so much more open in recent years that adolescents are hearing another double message: they are told simultaneously that sex is the most wonderful, exciting, and important thing in the world and that they are not to indulge. It seems inevitable to many observers that these changes in American sexual attitudes will affect the sexual behavior of the adolescent.

It is difficult to gather reliable data about sexual behavior in any culture where so many contradictory attitudes prevail. The first systematic studies of sexual behavior were the Kinsey Reports, published by psychologist Alfred Kinsey and his colleagues in 1948 and 1953. Kinsey found that nine out of ten boys and four out of ten girls masturbated and that masturbation was more common among the present younger generation than among the older generation when they were young. Kinsey also found that at least 70 percent of the male population had had sexual intercourse at least once by age twenty. About half of all women had had premarital sexual intercourse by age thirty, but only 21 percent had experienced coitus at twenty. Later studies indicate that in the 1960s and early 1970s, 58 percent to 65 percent of unmarried college men had experienced sexual intercourse (McCary, 1973), and the number of unmarried college women who had experienced inter-course increased to 35 percent to 50 percent (Bell, 1971).

The double standard has apparently become less effective in preventing young women, at least those in college, from participating in the same sexual experiences as their male peers.

> For women a clear consciousness of sexual urges exists and a majority of college women will have experiences of heavy petting, will approve of premarital coitus when in love or a meaningful relationship exists between partners, and a substantial minority (perhaps majority by senior year) will have engaged in premarital coitus. College women thus are having more sexual experiences, earlier, and probably with more partners than was true of the pre-1960 students (Davis, 1971).

Are attitudes toward sex changing?

American society, especially in the mass communication media, has created the illusion that we are living in a "now" generation, where spontaneity is desirable and inhibitions are to be cast off. Thus many adolescents believe that more sexual activity is taking place than is actually the case, and they sometimes feel pressured to participate. Actually, it is difficult to measure how much sexual mores have changed, although many magazines and films present a world that ignores the standards held up to most adolescents by their parents and teachers. This conflict adds to the confusion of the adolescent searching for his sexual identity and to the difficulties of parents who try to set rules and standards for their children.

GENERATION GAP

There are indications that the "generation gap," which seemed an unbridgeable chasm in the 1960s, may be closing—or at least that a convenient bypass has been found. Recent attitude studies (Yankelovich, 1973) suggest, however, that a gap is opening between college and noncollege educated youths, especially among women.

The most striking differences were found in women between the ages of sixteen and twenty-five. College education did seem to have some effect on the values expressed by young men, but not as much as on those expressed by women. For example, when the men interviewed by the researchers were asked whether they would give priority to self-fulfillment or to economic security in choosing a job, approximately half college men and half the noncollege men opted for self-fulfillment. Among women, however, 62 percent of the college educated and only 41 percent of those without college experience opted for self-fulfillment. Of the 1726 women interviewed, exactly half the noncollege but only 42 percent of the college women judged work to be an important value.

The study suggests that attitudes toward marriage and child rearing have changed dramatically among women. Roughly one-third of both college and noncollege men believed having children to be an important personal value, whereas 35 percent of the college women expressed this value as compared to 50 percent of the noncollege women. However, 50 percent of the noncollege women and 62 percent of the college women admitted that they looked forward to marriage.

One factor that may help explain this finding is the differing concepts of marriage held by members of the two groups. College women often envision marriage as a position from which they can explore new personal relationships and career opportunities, whereas noncollege women often view it as a dead-end road to perpetual childbearing and housework.

The women's attitudes toward marriage may reflect their different conceptions of sexual roles as well. Only 36 percent of the college women believed that a woman's place is in the home, whereas 53 percent of the noncollege women agreed with that view. Furthermore, 79 percent of the noncollege women believed that it is important for a man to be a good provider, and only 56 percent of the noncollege women concurred.

Sexually liberated attitudes were evident among all the women, but more strikingly among the better educated. Eighty-three percent of the college women and 67 percent of the noncollege women agreed that a woman should be free to take the initiative in sex. Sixty-two percent of the noncollege women and 41 percent of the college women believed that it is morally wrong to have children out of wedlock.

There has always been some discrepancy between what parents approve and what their children do, especially in relation to sexual behavior. At a time when traditional sexual values are being called into question, this discrepancy can be increased because the parents themselves may be questioning their own sexual mores. Parents may be less comfortable laying down the old rules than in previous generations even though they may be emotionally committed to traditional sexual values. The adolescent who feels that his parents disapprove of premarital sexual experience is liable to feel some anxiety and guilt about his experiences if they violate the parental norms, and the parents are liable to feel less sure of their own position, no matter what official line they take. Thus, what seems to be a major shift in American attitudes about sexual behavior increases the difficulties of both parents and adolescents in dealing with this sensitive issue.

Varying Rates of Development

Early-maturing boys are taller, heavier, and more muscular than their age mates. They tend to excel at sports, achieve popularity, and become leaders in student government and extracurricular activities. Early-maturing boys also tend to be more interested in girls and gain the advantage of acquiring social graces early. In adult life they are likely to be more successful socially and vocationally, and to be more conventional in career and lifestyle choices.

Early-maturing girls are faced with the problem that few other girls and almost no boys are as tall and well developed as they are. Friends may avoid them simply because they are bigger. Early-maturing girls tend to date older boys until their age group catches up with them.

Late-maturing boys are smaller and less well developed than almost everyone in their age group. They may lack interest in dating, and when they do become interested in girls they often lack social graces or are rebuffed by the prettiest and most popular girls. Late-maturing boys tend to participate in extracurricular activities such as band, chess club, or the school newspaper where their lack of physical maturity is not a drawback. In adult life they tend to be insightful, independent, and less conventionally successful. Little has been written about the late-maturing girl, perhaps because they mature before many of the boys. Late-maturing girls do not face the problems that confront the late-maturing boys, but they may be at some social disadvantage if they are less attractive to boys than other girls are.

All adolescents are concerned with developing a body type that is appropriate to their sex. Boys want to look like football players, and girls like fashion models. Girls tend to be more concerned with physical development than boys, and their appearance and self-concept are more closely bound together. Status in girls' groups and popularity with boys depend in large part on physical appearance, and they equate their chances of success in adult life with their body image. Boys, on the other hand, tend to derive status from athletic achievement and the popularity that accompanies athletic prowess in most schools.

COGNITIVE DEVELOPMENT

One of the major tasks of early adolescence is the achievement of abstract thought. The adolescent grows from a child who focuses primarily on his own immediate concerns to a young adult who can reason abstractly and deal with problems in a wide variety of contexts.

Before adolescence a child is largely concerned with the here and now, with what is apparent to his senses, and with problems that can be solved by trial and error. During adolescence the individual's ability to deal with problems on an abstract level, to form hypotheses, and to reason from propositions that are contrary to fact grows to full adult capacity. By late adolescence and early adulthood, most people have developed their full reasoning powers. In adult life, an individual strives for greater depth of understanding, but his powers of thought will not improve.

Formal Operations

It is not until what Piaget calls the **period of formal operations**—the stage of cognitive development that is reached between the ages of eleven and fifteen—that a person can think flexibly enough about the world to consider abstract universals such as humanity, acceleration, and justice, and to conceive of their intrinsic qualities. Children develop the ability to generalize before the age of eleven, but they are not yet ready to think abstractly. They can, for example, group several different yellow items together but cannot abstract from them the concept of yellowness.

By the age of fifteen, most of us can conceive of yellowness and of the shapes that constitute the subject matter of geometry. We can also arrive at several possible conclusions when given a hypothesis, whereas a child would see only the obvious

PIAGET'S PERIODS OF COGNITIVE DEVELOPMENT

Sensorimotor Period (birth to 24 months)

Preoperational Period (2 to 7 years)

Concrete Operational Period (7 to 11 years)

Formal Operational Period (11 years on)

Realizes that classes are not only groups of concrete objects but may also be conceived of—and operated on in thought—as abstract or formal entities.
1. Imagines several alternative explanations of the same phenomenon.
2. Operates with propositions that are contrary to fact.
3. Operates with symbols that stand for nothing in the individual's own experience, but have an abstract definition.
4. Operates with symbols of symbols. Understands metaphor.

Figure 13.4. When the individual reaches the stage of formal operations he can use symbols to stand for other symbols, as in algebra.

conclusion. A child shown a picture of a car wrecked in an accident, for example, may simply conclude that the car went into a skid and hit a tree. An adolescent can propose several possible causes for the accident—faulty brakes, wet road, or drowsy driver.

According to Piaget, a second characteristic that sets the thinking of adolescents apart from that of children is the ability to conceive of terms outside the realm of their own experience and the information given. The adolescent can also deal with propositions that are contrary to fact. If a child is given the proposition that water is lighter than air, he is likely to reply that air is lighter, whereas the adolescent can grasp the proposition as a hypothesis and reason from it. This capacity to deal with the possible as well as the actual liberates him and gives him his first opportunity to reflect on ideas. Since he is no longer bound by actual occurrences and data from the sensory world, he is free to jump from proposition to proposition and from hypothesis to hypothesis and gain greater insight into many ideas and theories. His interest in theoretical problems not related to everyday life and his ability to hypothesize new solutions increase throughout adolescence.

Piaget also found that the individual's ability to deal with symbols develops significantly during the stage of formal operations. He becomes able to understand political cartoons and metaphors for the first time. His ability to use symbols for other symbols, as in algebra, first appears during this stage.

During late adolescence and early adulthood the ability to acquire and utilize knowledge reaches its peak efficiency. Scores on tests that measure high-level mental processes, such as mathematical ability and analogies, tend to peak in late adolescence and decline thereafter, while scores on tests that measure the amount of knowledge tend to increase with age. It has also been found that tests administered in adolescence are better predictors of adult intellectual functioning than tests given earlier in life.

The adolescent's increased freedom in forming hypotheses often causes him difficulty in making decisions. He sees that not one but many alternatives are open to him, and this leads him to doubt his judgment. It often leads to external conflict, too, especially with his parents and other authority figures. He challenges adult decisions, demanding to know the reasoning behind the decisions but also wanting to present the virtues of his opinion and the opinions of his peers. He is not likely to accept a decision without questions and some debate. He is also likely to challenge religious and social values.

The adolescent's interest in theoretical ideas also leads him to construct ideal families, societies, and religions. He sees that there are alternatives to the way things are presently done, and he is anxious to find a means to end human suffering and poverty, social inequity, and false beliefs. Utopian solutions to the world's problems—planned communities, Eastern religions, and new forms of consciousness—find many adherents in the adolescent group. Many hours and late nights are spent debating the validity of such utopian ideals, and some adolescents become involved in groups committed to their practical applications.

Adolescents caught up in idealism often place their ideals before family values. They may be outraged to find adults indulging in a few "harmless" or "pragmatic" vices while recommending virtue to young people, or practicing discrimination while invoking justice. The adolescents who take offense at such hypocrisy may rebel against the social structure in an intellectual sense, but usually they have no means to carry out the remedies they conceive. The long nights spent in discussing ideal solutions seldom lead to concrete action or active participation in social movements. As the adolescent approaches young adulthood, he usually accepts the reality of social conditions and seeks to solve the preexisting problems rather than creating idealized structures.

A more earthy example of the adolescent tendency to idealize life is the teenage crush. Most crushes are brief because nobody can live up to the ideal.

Postconventional Morality

The adolescent's newly found ability to reason abstractly increases the range of her moral judgment. She may become aware of potential conflicts among socially acceptable standards, and between individual rights and social standards or laws. In terms of Lawrence Kohlberg's levels of moral development, the criteria of stage 4 ("law and order" morality) cannot resolve these conflicts; the adolescent may recognize that society's rules can be mutually inconsistent and that the rules can be used to violate individual rights (almost everything that Hitler did was perfectly legal, for example). If she recognizes the inadequacy of stage 4, she will reach for the next level of moral development, the level that Kohlberg calls **postconventional** morality, although most adolescents (and many adults) remain at the conventional level of morality in the majority of their judgments.

At the level of postconventional morality, the individual defines moral values and principles apart from the authority of the groups or persons holding these principles and apart from her own identity with these groups. At this level, an individual controls her decisions internally; that is, she bases her decisions on her own evaluation and standards of what is right, rather than by conforming to social standards.

The postconventional level is divided into two distinct stages: the social-contract legalistic orientation and the universal ethical principle orientation. In the social-contract legalistic orientation (Kohlberg's stage 5), moral action is defined in terms of individual rights and in terms of standards that have been wittingly agreed to by the whole society. Although the person at this stage has an awareness of values and opinions, her emphasis is on the procedural rules for reaching a consensus and the legal point of view that results from consensus. She believes that if a law is inequitable, it must be changed in a democratic and constitutional manner and in accordance with social utility, not by breaking a law to make a test case, as did many civil rights workers in the 1960s. The American government and the Constitution operate at this level of morality.

The universal ethical principle orientation (Kohlberg's stage 6) recognizes right as defined by the individual conscience in accordance with self-chosen ethical principles. These principles are abstract, and they include justice, the equality of human rights, and respect for the dignity of human beings as individual persons.

People tend to prefer the highest level of moral development that they can

KOHLBERG'S LEVELS OF MORAL DEVELOPMENT

Level I: Preconventional Morality (Early Middle Childhood)

Level II: Conventional Morality (Late Middle Childhood)
Level III: Postconventional Morality (Adolescence)[a]

At this level the individual makes choices on the basis of principles that he has thought through, accepted, and internalized. Right behavior is the behavior that conforms to these principles, regardless of immediate social praise or blame.

Stage 5 morality focuses on the value of the social contract and on basic human rights that do not need to be earned. The "law and order" emphasis of Stage 4 gives way to a concern for the creation of good laws, rules that will maximize the welfare of the individual.

Stage 6 is the level of the morality of individual conscience. Right behavior produces a feeling of being right with oneself; a person can obey the law and still feel guilty if he has violated his own principles. The rights of humanity independent of rules of civil society are acknowledged, and human beings are seen as ends in themselves.

[a]Kohlberg found that about 23 percent of all moral judgments made by sixteen year olds are at this level.

comprehend. They often can comprehend stages a notch or so above the one on which they operate, though they cannot verbally express the higher stages or apply them to their own behavior. Their preference for a higher level of morality is basic to the expectation of moral leadership in the United States. Most people operate at the conventional level of morality, whereas leadership is expected to be at the postconventional level.

An adolescent may be at any level of moral development—preconventional, conventional, or postconventional—and act at that level in most situations but at another level in other situations. An individual at the postconventional level is most likely to slip back to the conventional level when her support of individual rights conflicts with rules formulated by an authority figure. For example, a person may be opposed morally to racial discrimination and yet may fail to uphold the rights of another when such an action would lead her into a confrontation with a school authority. Such backsliding is not unusual during a period when an individual's values and beliefs are in a stage of reformation. Though an individual may backslide and then regain her highest level, Kohlberg believes that progress always takes place in the same sequence of levels. Some people, Kohlberg admits, never reach the postconventional level of morality. They operate at the conventional or preconventional level throughout their lives.

Researchers (Hahn et al., 1968) conducted a survey of Berkeley students who were about to decide whether or not to join a sit-in to demand political freedom of communication. Students at the stage of social-contract orientation maintained that students came to Berkeley with a knowledge of the rules, and that if they did not agree with the rules, they could enroll in another college. Only about 50 percent of these students sat in the Administration Building as a form of protest. Students at the universal ethical principle stage found the issue clear-cut, and about 80 percent of them sat in to demonstrate their belief in the principle of political freedom of communication. Only about 10 percent of the students at the conventional stage of morality joined the sit-in. It is interesting to note, however, that of the students who were still at the preconventional level of morality, more than 60 percent joined the sit-in. These hedonistic students evidently joined just for the fun of it.

Concept of Time

Young children have great difficulty in handling concepts of time. A very young child is likely to define time as "what the clock tells." As children grow older, they can more easily deal with events in the immediate past and the near future, but they basically live in the present and are primarily concerned with the attainment of short-term goals. The child may fantasize about what he might do in years hence, but he cannot differentiate between fantasy and goals that can be realized.

It is only with the onset of Piaget's stage of formal operations that the individual has the ability to think realistically about future possibilities and adult roles that he might assume. According to Piaget, time becomes a reality for the adolescent because he can trace it back to the past and into the future and transcend the reality of the present moment. Future plans become as real to him as present goals and can be dealt with at a realistic level.

Adolescents also become aware of longer periods of time—years and decades—and of the processes of growth, aging, and death. They can realistically conceive that their parents were once young and not married to each other and that they themselves will become adults, marry, grow old, and eventually die.

Self-Concept

Human beings are aware of themselves. They are aware of their past and future, of death, and of other people—friends, enemies, and strangers. Because a person is aware of his own life and ultimate death, he must establish a firm identity and a purpose and meaning for his life. Without an adequate concept of himself, he will feel anxious and may fall into social isolation and despair.

The question "Who am I?" looms large before the adolescent. With the ability to think abstractly comes the adolescent's ability to reflect on his own thoughts and the thoughts of others—that is, the ability to be introspective. He sees himself as a member of society and is seeking a definition and a role in life—a **self-concept**.

The adolescent's tendency to evaluate his personality and appearance from the vantage point of others is notorious. Like the child he is egocentric, but in a different way. The child is not terribly concerned about other people's reactions to his behavior and appearance, whereas the adolescent constantly evaluates himself and anticipates the reactions of others as admiring or critical. He believes that other people are as preoccupied with his appearance and behavior as he himself is, and he judges his world primarily by the reaction he receives.

In a way, the adolescent is constructing an imaginary audience. It is imaginary because he is usually not the focus of attention, though his overly developed self-consciousness leads him to think he is. The imaginary audience serves a dual purpose. First, the adolescent projects his self-criticism onto the audience he creates in his mind, and then he judges the audience's reaction to him. Second, the imaginary audience is a form of self-admiration in that the person projects the image that he believes to be attractive—be it a new form of dress or a position on a social issue—and that he believes will appeal to his peers. When young people meet, each one is playing to the imaginary audience and simultaneously is an actor to himself and an audience to others. The testing of images takes the place of substantial interpersonal communication.

Related to the adolescent's self-consciousness in groups is his belief that his feelings and thoughts are unique—that no one has ever had such exquisite experiences or suffered such intense agony. At the same time, the adolescent recognizes that his thoughts are private and that he can say things that are in opposition to his feelings. The child who fabricates usually comes to believe what he says; he does not lie in order to erect a screen between himself and society. The adolescent, on the other hand, sees the possibility of creating a fabrication that will serve as

Figure 13.5. The group is the adolescent's prime theater of activity. It may take him away from schoolwork, but it also prepares him for an adult life of interaction with many different kinds of people.

a social disguise behind which to hide his thoughts and wishes. He may, for example, affect a flippant, cynical sense of humor to hide his shyness. Or he may go out for football to compensate for genuine academic interest that might lead to his being labeled a "brain." This sort of fabrication ranges from politeness and tact to deceit and exploitation.

The development of a sense of humor is one of the more obvious accomplishments of adolescence. One psychologist (Allport, 1937, 1961) has called the development of humor the core of the mature personality and the most striking correlate of insight. When an individual is certain of his self-concept, he can perceive the incongruities of life and laugh at himself without feeling threatened.

The development of the sense of humor has been correlated with Piaget's stages of development (Zigler, 1967). At the age of fourteen, the adolescent's increased capacity for abstract thought permits a more sophisticated level of humor. Though much of the humor is still corny, ridiculing, or smutty, humor based on self-appraisal becomes more frequent and acceptable.

THE SOCIETY OF ADOLESCENTS

Parents and the mass media have much to say about the "youth culture" or the "adolescent subculture." Does such an adolescent society exist? Or has the adult population merely created a convenient stereotype as a means of explaining adolescent behavior?

Insofar as adolescents organize certain features of American culture and make them specifically their own—haircuts, clothing, music, and the like—it is true that they have created their own society. But this separation is not necessarily a revolt against institutions or norms. It is more often just the way adolescents articulate their own needs and create a context in which to work out mutual problems.

In nonindustrialized cultures adolescents usually do not separate into a distinct group with an identity and values that differ from the society as a whole. Most adolescents in these cultures live in small communities and do not attend school on a regular basis, but instead work beside their parents in maintaining the family. They form friendships insofar as work and free time permit, but such friendship groups are not comparable to the adolescent society in the United States.

Instead, adolescents in these cultures are permitted to participate to some extent in the society of adults. In Samoa, for example, adolescent girls are admitted to the *Aualama,* the organization of untitled women, and boys join the *Aumaga,* the organization of untitled men. The ceremonial life of the village centers around these groups, and much of the work in them is allotted to the young unmarried members (Mead, 1928).

One exception to this generalization is the play association of the Hausa of Northern Nigeria. Children form same-sex play groups under leaders of their own choice, and by imitative play learn fundamental etiquette and political behavior. When individuals marry, they withdraw from the association and assume adult roles. But because of the small membership in these groups, they cannot be equated with adolescent groups in the United States.

In the United States, adolescent society focuses upon the school. The regional high school is usually the first place that adolescents are massed together in a large enough group to create their own social world. School is the place where the adolescents spend most of their time, in classes and extracurricular activities. In this environment they create a miniworld in which to seek answers to many of the conflicts that mark this period, the search for self-identity and values in particular. Experiences are shared, common problems are discussed, and individual achievement is measured.

Popularity and success within the peer group are almost always more important to the adolescent than academic achievement, although in some schools and in

Figure 13.6 "People are looking at me. They're judging the way I look and act."—This thought haunts the self-conscious adolescent.

certain groups within most schools peer approval requires doing well in academic activities. For younger adolescents, homework and class projects may take second place to extracurricular activities, social events, and visits to friends. Even enrollment in courses may depend on whether one's friends are enrolled. Older adolescents who are college bound often become intensely involved in the competition for admission to their first-choice college, and status in the senior year may be measured to a large degree by the student's college acceptance letters.

Adolescents often prefer the company of their peers to that of their family, but it should not be forgotten that this can also be true of children and adults. The adolescent's social milieu is a large one. He relates socially not only with his many acquaintances but also with relative strangers. Thus, adolescent society serves as a bridge to the adult world, where he will be confronted with the wide variety of colleagues and occupations of our mobile society. The peer interaction involved in extracurricular activities also mirrors the procedures by which organizations operate in the adult world. Student government and other activities create power hierarchies, and the adolescent learns how to deal with them.

Authority in many adolescent organizations, however, tends to be lateral rather than vertical. That is, adolescents tend to diffuse authority among group members and are reluctant to assume positions of authority over their peers. They see their interrelationships more as a brotherhood than a vertical power arrangement.

Adolescent society differs from adult society in other ways too, but these differences are mainly superficial. For example, adolescent society thrives on fads, distinctive modes of dress, and slang. Feeling that they are not fully accepted as individuals in adult society, they create a group identity that gives them a sense of belonging to the larger world. Despite these shows of distinctiveness, however, researchers (Bandura, 1964) have shown that the normal adolescent does not differ significantly in moral attitudes from his parents. In most cases he conforms to their standards of achievement and their vocational preferences.

Composition of the Peer Group

In the prepubescent period, children band together in same-sex gangs. These gangs are really extensions of the childhood gang. In a year or so, the gang becomes a unisex *clique* as interest in the opposite sex increases. This clique usually forms an informal association with a clique of the opposite sex. Individual dating is initiated by the leaders of the cliques.

The clique provides a setting for intimate personal relationships that formerly were found primarily in the family. Clique members are bound together by geographic proximity, education, heterosexual interest, degree of social and personal maturity, and similar social backgrounds as well as by mutual interests and a similar academic orientation. There is little cutting across social class lines in clique membership, though an athlete from a minority background is sometimes admitted to the leading boys' clique.

Around the clique is the larger and less rigidly defined *crowd*. The crowd is held together by its orientation to the future, the social background of its members, and their personality types. An adolescent knows which crowd everyone belongs to, even if he does not know the individual members. To belong to the crowd, one must first belong to a clique. Members of the leading crowd occupy the most desirable positions in the school, such as student government officers and cheerleaders. In later adolescence the crowd disappears and is replaced by cliques of couples going steady.

In addition to belonging to crowds and cliques, adolescents have one or two close friends. Friendships are based on more intimate and intense feelings than clique relationships. Interaction is more open and honest and less self-conscious, and there is less role-playing to gain social acceptance. The individual does not hesitate to show his doubts, anxieties, and resentments. Friendships are usually based on similar social backgrounds, interests, and personality types. Friendships between wildly different personality types are rare.

Popularity

Membership in the clique and the crowd is determined by popularity. Lack of popularity—or peer-group approval—can be excruciatingly painful. Whatever their social class, all adolescents want to be popular.

One researcher (Ringness, 1967) found that possession of a pleasing personality was the most crucial factor in achieving popularity. Athletic prowess, scholarship, knowledge of popular culture, and other attributes may supplement personality qualities in achieving popularity, but in themselves, they are not sufficient for peer acceptance. Many studies (Tryon, 1939; Bonney, 1946) have tried to identify the components that constitute a pleasing personality. Liking other people; being tolerant, flexible, and sympathetic; being lively, cheerful, good-natured, and possessed of a sense of humor; acting naturally and being self-confident without being conceited; possessing initiative and drive; and planning for group activities are among the components identified.

Some personality types are more likely than others to be rejected. The person who is ill at ease and lacks self-confidence may try to disguise his discomfort by aggressiveness or conceit. Being timid, nervous, or withdrawn also alienates other people, as does making excessive demands for attention.

It has long been thought that academic success precludes popularity, especially for girls, but one observer (Ringness, 1967) found the contrary to be true: about half the subjects in his study admired good students. In fact, the adolescent who does poorly in school may feel inadequate and develop behavioral patterns that lead to rejection by the peer group. Youngsters who were popular in childhood generally continue to be popular in adolescence. Their popularity, in part, derives from beginning adolescence with a relatively stable self-concept.

Parents encourage their children to achieve popularity and success with peers, and teachers tend to reward popular students. This is perhaps unfortunate, for in rewarding popularity, they are reinforcing conformity to peer-group values rather than initiative in other areas.

Conformity

Strictly speaking, *conformity* is simply observing the norms of one's society or subgroup. This is not always as easy as it sounds, however, because the many norms of the society and the peer group sometimes conflict with each other. Ultimately, the individual must choose among them and adopt only the ones that suit him personally. A child learns the norms by the age of eleven or twelve. Then in adolescence he begins to evaluate them in relationship to himself and his evolving value system.

Figure 13.7. Conformity can be a strain at times.

Researchers (Costanzo and Shaw, 1966) have used Piagetian cognitive development theory to measure the degree of conformity in adolescence. They found that with the onset of pubescence the child becomes aware of rules and relies on them for patterns of behavior. At the formal operational stage of development the child is uncertain of his own values and judgments, and when he is in doubt, he follows the behavioral patterns and values of his peer group. By later adolescence and young adulthood, the individual has learned to select standards of conformity and to be confident of his own judgments, even when the majority disagrees.

An individual shows an increased tendency to conform in threatening situations. One study recruited sixty-four college girls for an experiment that was said to involve painful shocks. Before the experiment was performed, the girls sought information from others to help them evaluate their emotions and opinions, and in the experiment they tended to conform to the group opinion. The implications of this study can be extended to normal adolescent behavior: perhaps adolescents develop solidarity with their peers as a means of coping with the threatening adult world. Under constant threat of the dire consequences of dropping out of school, getting poor grades, getting their names in police records, and the like, adolescents may feel the safest thing to do is to follow the group (Rainsey, 1967).

THE FAMILY

The importance of the adolescent's peers in her development is partly the result of changes that occur in her relationships with her family during this period. Adolescence is the time when children prepare themselves to leave the family and move out into the world as autonomous adults. The transition from childhood to adulthood requires that the adolescent and her family find ways of separating from each other. "At adolescence the interaction of parent and child is conditioned by their mututal knowledge, however dimly and remotely held, of the child's eventual departure. The family's task is to rehearse the child for [this departure]" (Douvan, 1966).

The developing sexuality of the adolescent—those physical and psychological changes that define this period and influence so many of her peer relationships—are also at the heart of the changes that occur in her relationships with her family. Difficulties inevitably arise because the child becomes a sexually mature person while she is still living within the structure of the family. The same feelings of competition with the same-sex parent and desire for the opposite-sex parent that aroused impossible fantasies in the five year old now present a much more graphic dilemma: the adolescent girl is no longer a child, and she needs to see herself as a competent and appealing woman without becoming too alarmed by the potential for expressing her sexuality within the family unit. Part of the search for intimacies among her peers is motivated by a need to find sexual competition and sexual intimacy outside the family, where incest is not a threat.

This dilemma is felt by many parents as well. The figure of a father who is overly concerned with the young men who come courting his daughter is often found in television comedy; the heart of his difficulty may be his own attraction for the young woman his daughter has become. Similarly, a mother's overly strict concern for her daughter's sexual purity may be rooted in feelings of competition with the daughter. The adolescent must find a way out of this situation, a socially acceptable means to satisfy her adult needs outside of the family.

The overriding task of adolescence, then, is to achieve autonomy. The drive for independence has motivated the child in many previous stages of development, but now in adolescence it is finally achieved. At the end of this period the person is out of the family and functioning as an individual with his own lifestyle, activities, and values.

Adolescent autonomy develops in three areas: emotions, behavior, and values (Douvan, 1966). Emotional autonomy occurs when the person has resolved his infantile attachments to his parents, when he has found ways to satisfy his needs for affection and intimacy outside of the home. Behavioral autonomy comes gradually as the person is given or demands and wins the right to make decisions about his own behavior—from whether he can wear jeans to a party to which college he will attend and what vocation he will choose. Value autonomy occurs when the person has constructed his own set of values—his sense of right and wrong, his commitment or lack of it to a given religious tradition, and so on—that are not simply borrowed from or reactions against those of his parents but developed out of his own inner sense of himself. Many people continue to struggle for value autonomy long after they have left their parents' homes. A young mother, for example, may find herself scolding her child in exactly the same tone of voice that her mother used years before—and suddenly realize that her value system is still very much a reflection of her mother in spite of the fact that intellectually she would defend a different set of values.

Adolescence makes new demands on parents as well as children. Some parents have such a strong investment in their role as a parent that they find it difficult to let the child grow up. Others find the normal growth struggles of their adolescent so painful that they want to turn the child out of the house before he is ready or able to go. Learning to relate to one's children as adults is difficult in the best of circumstances, and often both the parent and the child require years of patience and understanding before they achieve a comfortable adult relationship. Sometimes the basis for real understanding is reached when the child himself becomes a parent and is able to see the parent's point of view for the first time.

Economic Influences

Despite radical changes in the structure of the American family in the last 100 years, there is overwhelming evidence of similarity between parents' social class and the social class of the children's peer group, and between parents' religious and moral values and those of their children. Parents and children are also of the same mind when it comes to educational plans, social aspirations, political preferences, and racial views.

Nonetheless, significant changes in the conflict between the generations have occurred in the last century, and in large measure they stem from changes in the economic role of the family. Until about the 1880s American adolescents worked

ADOLESCENT EMOTIONALISM

It is a rare adolescent who thinks his parents understand him. No less rare is the parent who appreciates the odd and seemingly irrational statements and actions of her teenage son or daughter. The years of adolescence are often characterized by rebellious, quarrelsome, sulky, and highly emotional behavior. They are difficult years for everyone involved.

Some of the emotional stress associated with adolescence is thought to stem from physical discomfort. The "growing pains" of adolescence reflect the body's difficulty in adjusting to the sudden spurts of growth that bones and muscles undergo after puberty. The adolescent may experience dull aches and pains that make him grouchy and irritable, though he is often unaware of the source of his irritation.

Hormonal changes in the adolescent may contribute to his changing temperament. Menstruation, maturing of the sex organs, and the growth of body hair are dramatic changes brought about by normal glandular development. Adolescents tend to be extremely self-conscious about and generally preoccupied with their bodies. They may talk, read, and fantasize endlessly about sex. Although comparing breast size among girls and penis size among boys is not uncommon among friends, many adolescents become excessively modest and go to great lengths to avoid showing bodies they believe to be underdeveloped. Girls may find it especially difficult to adjust to the rapid changes that occur just before the first menstruation.

Having sexual emotions aroused by mere sights or thoughts is a new and frightening experience for many adolescents. Not recognized as an adult by society, the adolescent is placed in an extremely awkward situation insofar as his budding sexuality is concerned. He has no socially acceptable outlet for his sexual desires, and the guilt associated with "dirty books," masturbation, and petting, not to mention more straightforward sexual behavior, only intensifies his doubts and anxieties about his body and emotions.

The adolescent may turn to his peers for understanding, yet find it impossible to discuss his problems openly even with his closest friends. Most adolescents need to spend a great deal of time alone just thinking and relaxing.

Adolescents want to be like their peers and yet different. While struggling to establish his individuality, the adolescent wishes to be "normal"—to look, act, and think like the rest of the crowd. Highly sensitive to every personal deviation, he may become quite upset because he is taller, shorter, fatter, or skinnier than the majority of his friends. It does little good to tell the unhappy person that he is just "going through

alongside their parents and contributed to the economic support of the family, as adolescents in many nonindustrial areas of the world still do. The boy served as an apprentice to his father and was expected to take over when he became mature. He contributed his physical strength and learned his father's trade or helped on the farm. The girl helped with household chores and looked forward to the day

a stage," that his voice will stop squeaking, or that his acne will eventually disappear.

Is there a universal adolescent temperament? Many anthropologists doubt it. Margaret Mead discovered that in Samoa, where adolescents are relatively free to enjoy sexual relations, they rarely experience the stress and tension associated with adolescence in the United States.

In our society, however, it takes much patience, tolerance, and understanding on the part of enlightened and loving parents to mitigate the emotional distress of adolescence.

when she would have her own home and family. Whenever the child was needed for work in the fields or at the shop, he simply skipped school.

The situation is very different today. Adolescents no longer contribute to the family income, but instead are supported for more and more years. Though adolescents are capable of working to increase their social autonomy, today's labor market has no demand for them. The energy and emotion that a child once invested in family-related work has passed into the school and peer-group relations. Where once the the child worked through adolescent problems and grew to maturity within the family structure, he now achieves autonomy and defines his self-concept outside

---

HOW ELMTOWN WAS STUDIED

When sociologists, anthropologists, and psychologists undertake the study of human behavior, they are often concerned with subjective data. We cannot predict what a person will feel or do in a given situation as certainly as we can predict what will happen when two chemicals are mixed at a given temperature and pressure. How, then, does the social scientist go about conducting a study?

August B. Hollingshead's study of the youth of Elmtown is a classic example of sociological research. "Elmtown" is the fictional name of a real town chosen by a University of Chicago group as a typical midwestern American community. In the spring of 1941, Hollingshead was invited to participate in a sociological study of the youth of Elmtown.

The first three months of Hollingshead's project were devoted to preparing for the intensive field work that was to follow. Much of this time was spent visiting Elmtown and getting a general idea of the history, population, and socioeconomic structure of the town. Then Hollingshead and his family moved into a house near the local high school.

The next step was to formulate the specific hypothesis to be investigated. Extensive reading convinced Hollingshead that little research had been done in the sociocultural aspects of adolescent behavior. He thus arrived at his working hypothesis, namely that "the social behavior of adolescents appears to be related functionally to the positions their families occupy in the social structure of the community."

Hollingshead then proceeded to outline the general nature of his task. His study would involve the observation of adolescents, the collection of data pertaining to community institutions, and finally the analysis of these data in relation to the social position of the adolescents' families. Hollingshead began to focus his attention on the school, the church, the local government and the public and private lives of the people of Elmtown.

In choosing his adolescent subjects, Hollingshead attempted to include boys and girls representative of the entire local population. Of the original 735 subjects, half were boys and half girls for each age level from thirteen to nineteen years. All were white and 96 percent were born in the Midwest. All the national groups living in Elmtown were represented in the sam-

the home. In industrialized societies the period of adolescence has been prolonged by the extension of education. Today's jobs demand more years of specialized training, and the adolescent must forego financial independence and social autonomy if he is to prepare for meaningful and financially rewarding life work.

SOCIAL CLASS INFLUENCES

A classic study of social class and youth was presented in *Elmtown's Youth* (Hollingshead, 1949). The children studied were divided into five classes (upper,

ple population.

Hollingshead and his wife then proceeded to familiarize the people of Elmtown with the project and win their trust and confidence. Securing the cooperation of local school authorities, ministers, and other community leaders greatly facilitated the gathering of data pertaining to everyday life in Elmtown. Before long, the Hollingsheads had become active members of the community.

The Hollingsheads quickly established a rapport with the youth of Elmtown. As they discovered that the Hollingsheads could be trusted not to betray confidences and not to offer unsolicited moral advice, the young Elmtowners welcomed them to parties, poker games, and various local hangouts. These casual encounters provided the researchers with many valuable insights.

Apart from first-hand observation, the Hollingsheads obtained most of their data from the examination of public records and from personal interviews. By studying back issues of the *Elmtown Bugle* and records of the police, courts, and local tax bureau, the researchers gathered information that the Elmtowners themselves might have

been reluctant to divulge. Approximately 1600 people were eventually interviewed. Interviews were conducted on the job, in the schools, in the home, and on the street.

The type of interview used varied according to the person and the situation. Some involved the asking of direct questions, and others took the form of casual conversation. When no notes were taken or when the subject requested that his remarks be kept ''off the record,'' the researchers wrote down the conversation as soon afterwards as possible. Accuracy and thoroughness were prime considerations.

The final stage of the study involved the social stratification of Elmtown families and the numerical analysis of the resulting data. After extensive research, the Hollingsheads succeeded in dividing the families of Elmtown into five basic socioeconomic classes. They were then able to convert their findings into statistical evidence based on a comparison of each individual family. In this way, the Hollingsheads were able to determine the extent to which adolescent behavior was related to social status in a typical midwestern town in the 1940s.

upper-middle, lower-middle, upper-lower, and lower-lower) and these classes were found to make substantial differences in the upbringing and attitudes of the children. In the upper and upper-middle classes, for example, where parents encouraged their children to maintain their position in society, education and personal self-realization were prized because they served this purpose. The lower-middle class, on the other hand, believed that self-realization was largely a matter of individual initiative; parents in this class did not try to promote their children's upward mobility through education. The upper-lower and lower-lower classes were characterized by apathy and resignation. They had little interest in education, nor did they believe that individual initiative would lead to upward mobility. This negative attitude was transmitted to their children, who, in turn, became underachievers in school.

The lower-class adolescents in Hollingshead's study were found to be more defiant of authority than middle-class adolescents and readier to engage in physical fights. The lower-class adolescent had little social interaction with peers in the more affluent classes. Few crossed class lines to be admitted into cliques, and few participated in activities outside the school, such as Boy Scouts.

Job opportunities for lower-class youth were also limited. The jobs they did find were mostly menial, demanded little knowledge, and paid poorly. Absenteeism was high, and this reinforced the image of the lower-class youth as undependable. Adult members of this class, having had similar work experience, communicated their negative attitude to their offspring.

A later study (Havighurst, 1954) found that low-income children have less difficulty in achieving emotional independence from their parents than affluent children because low-income parents show less protective concern and have less contact with their children. Middle-class youth have more parental support and counseling in occupational choice and social affairs than do lower-class youth. This parental support, however, makes it more difficult for the adolescent to free himself from parental control. Middle-class parents supervise their children's training and the development of their interests, and this conditions the children to accept adult authority and to adopt adult social standards.

The Problems of Affluence

Socioeconomic affluence has an important effect on the way an individual copes with the problems and challenges of adolescence. Deviant behavior was once assumed to be mostly limited to low-income adolescents, but recently there seems to have been a trend toward emotional instability and delinquent behavior among adolescents of the affluent classes.

Ideally, financial security and material abundance should create optimal conditions for the physical and emotional development of youth. Too many material goods, however, may lead to emotional poverty in an adolescent if it deprives him of the experience of coping with reasonable amounts of frustration. A frequently cited factor in the emotional poverty of affluent youth is that parents tend to fill their children's lives with lessons of all kinds and to permit activities that they believe will lead to their children's popularity. By the time these children reach adolescence, they may be unable to look forward to new experiences that are socially acceptable. Thus, many turn to deviant behavior.

Many affluent adolescents tend to conform rigidly to peer-group standards. Having been indoctrinated by their parents' efforts to keep up with the Joneses, they attach great importance to achieving popularity in school, to good grades and leadership positions. Affluence enables the adolescent to acquire the status symbols needed to achieve popularity without much trouble. Some adolescents, on the other hand, lack the drive to achieve because they have known nothing but economic security. They demand material goods but show no interest in work. After their college years, however, most of them enter a vocation that requires intellectual effort and emotional commitment.

References

Allport, G. W. *Personality: A psychological interpretation.* New York: Holt, 1937.

Allport, G. W. *Pattern and growth in personality.* New York: Holt, 1961.

Bandura, Albert. The stormy decade, fact or fiction? *Psychology in the Schools,* 1964, *1,* 244–341.

Bell, R. R. *Marriage and family interaction.* Homewood, Ill.: Dorsey, 1971.

Bettelheim, Bruno. The problem of generations. In Erik H. Erikson, Ed., *Youth and challenge.* New York: Basic Books, 1963.

Bonney, M. E. A sociometric study of some factors of mutual friendships on the elementary, secondary, and college levels. *Sociometry,* 1946, *9,* 21–47.

Costanzo, Philip, and Shaw, Marvin E. Conformity as a function of age level. *Child Development,* 1966, *37,* 967–975.

Davis, K. E. Sex on campus: Is there a revolution? *Medical Aspects of Human Sexuality,* January, 1971.

Douvan, Elizabeth and Adelson, Joseph. *The adolescent experience.* New York: Wiley, 1966.

Ehrmann, W. Premarital sexual intercourse. In *The encyclopedia of sexual behavior.* Vol. II. A. Ellis and A. Abarbanel (Eds.) New York: Hawthorn, 1961.

Hahn, N., Smith, M. B., and Block, T. Political-social behavior, family background, and personality correlates of adolescent moral judgment. *Journal of Personality and Social Psychology,* 1968, *10,* 103–201.

Havighurst, R. J. *Developmental tasks and education.* New York: Longmans Green, 1954.

Hollingshead, A. B. *Elmtown's Youth.* New York: Wiley, 1949.

Kinsey, A. C., Pomeroy, W. B., and Martin, C. C. *Sexual behavior in the human male.* Philadelphia: W. B. Saunders, 1948.

Kinsey, A. C., Pomeroy, W. B., and Martin, C. C. *Sexual behavior in the human female.* Philadelphia: W. B. Saunders, 1953.

McCary, J. L. *Human sexuality.* 2d ed. New York: D. Van Nostrand, 1973.

Mead, M. *Coming of age in Samoa.* New York: William Morrow, 1928.

Rainsey, C. E. *Problems of youth.* Belmont, Calif.: Dickenson, 1967.

Ringness, T. A. Identification patterns, motivation, and school achievement of bright junior high school boys. *Journal of Educational Psychology,* 1967, *58,* 93–102.

Tryon, C. M. Evaluation of adolescent personality by adolescents. *Monograph of Social Research and Child Development,* 1939, *4,* No. 4.

Yankelovich, Daniel. Study reported in Brozen, N. Widening gap in views registered between college and noncollege women. *New York Times,* May 22, 1974, p. 45.

Zigler, E. F. Cognitive challenge as a factor in children's humor appreciation. *Journal of Personality and Social Psychology,* 1967, *6,* 332–336.

SUMMARY

1 Even before the sex organs show an outward change, hormonal changes are preparing the body for adulthood. A dramatic change then takes place in height, weight, and body proportions. These are affected by heredity and nutrition, along with secretion of hormones by the endocrine glands.

2 Puberty is the period during which an individual reaches sexual maturity. In the prepubescent stage, secondary sex characteristics begin to develop. In the pubescent stage, the reproductive organs become capable of producing ova or sperm. In the postpubescent stage, the sex organs are capable of adult functioning. Spontaneous erection in the male in response to sights, sounds, and thoughts first occurs during adolescence. The appearance of breasts and menstruation in girls, body hair in both sexes, and voice change in boys herald sexual maturity.

3 Traditional American values require that adolescents postpone sexual intercourse until after marriage, although this prohibition is more strictly applied to girls than to boys. Recent research indicates that more than half of the college men in America and more than a third of the college women do not conform to this standard. Changing attitudes toward sexual expression create conflicts for both adolescents and their parents since the parents may be less sure of their own values and the adolescent may feel anxiety and guilt if he violates his parents' norms.

4 Abstract thinking starts in early adolescence in what Piaget calls the stage of formal operations. The individual reaches the peak of his thinking powers in late adolescence. His ability to consider many alternatives leads him to question his own ideas and challenge authority figures and traditional beliefs. Because he can understand such concepts as freedom and justice, he may achieve what Kohlberg calls the postconventional level of moral development.

5 Family relationships are complicated during adolescence by the developing sexuality of the adolescent. The overriding task of the young person is to develop autonomy in his emotions, behavior, and values so that he can become independent.

6 There is still a strong similarity between adolescents' values and goals and those of their parents, despite conflicts over independence. Adolescent culture represents the need to work out mutual problems. Fads are perhaps a way of rejecting the adult world's concern over the future. Popularity within the peer group is usually more important to younger adolescents than academic achievement. They tend to be conformist, and to form cliques and crowds, but to have only one or two close friends.

FURTHER READINGS

Caprio, F. S., and Caprio, F. B. *Parents and teenagers*. New York: Citadel, 1968.
This book by a psychologist and his son is directed at both adolescents and parents. The first part, for parents, deals with such matters as improving communication, attitudes toward dating, and the use of the family car. The second half advises teenagers on dealing with problem parents, developing confidence, and coping with sex, among other things.

Keniston, K. *The uncommited*. New York: Harcourt Brace Jovanovich, 1965.
In one of the most discussed books of the late sixties, Keniston examines the alienation of American youth. What he has to say about tensions created by social change, the shattering of traditional social values, and noncommitment as a way of life is still relevant.

Rubin, I., and Kirkendall, L. A. (Eds.) *Sex in the adolescent years*. New York: Association Press, 1968.
Selections from the writings of various authorities. In addition to sex and related problems in normal adolescence, the book deals with such special cases as the late maturer and the handicapped. Areas of discussion include homosexuality, drugs, pregnancy, and alcohol.

Semmons, J. P., and Krantz, K. E. (Eds.) *The adolescent experience*. New York: Macmillan, 1970.
A handbook designed for adults who counsel youth. Comprehensive discussions by many contributors of the sexual and social development of adolescents, reproductive physiology and anatomy, problems of sexual identity, and sociomedical aspects of adolescent behavior, including pregnancy, abortion, venereal disease, and drug use.

Tanner, J. M., Taylor, G. R., and the editors of Time-Life Books. *Growth*. New York: Time-Life, 1965.
A well-illustrated book about human growth with clear explanations of physical changes in adolescence, including the role of hormones. There are cross-cultural comparisons of adolescent growth and some psychological observations.

14
Culture and Identity

Many things have changed since *Rebel Without a Cause* first hit the movie houses, but not the portrayal in film, literature, and song of the sensitive adolescent struggling against a heedless adult world that is seemingly out to stifle, cheat, and corrupt him. Of course, the sorrows and longings of "youth," as adolescence used to be called, have been celebrated for hundreds of years, and modern psychologists and sociologists were seeking the causes of adolescent storm and stress before James Dean could ride a tricycle. In the 1920s, for example, psychologist G. Stanley Hall described adolescence as a particularly difficult period of development because at that stage the individual must contend with painfully conflicting emotions. Many other psychologists, including Anna Freud (1969), have continued to emphasize the crises that individuals undergo in adolescence.

Some psychologists, however, are of a different persuasion. One of them (Bandura, 1964) suggests that the crisis of adolescence may be caused, or at least aggravated, by the popular stereotype of adolescence as a time of crisis. He found the behavior of most individuals in adolescence to be consistent with their earlier behavior—those who were troubled before were also troubled in adolescence. He found, too, that conflict between the adolescent and his family could be avoided by beginning his training for independence in childhood. The accomplishment of certain developmental tasks in childhood has also been found (Eisenberg, 1965) to promise a relatively crisis-free transition to adulthood.

While some theorists doubt that adolescence is necessarily a time of crisis, others ask if it is really a stage of growing up at all. When a person is fully grown physically, capable of sexual reproduction, and capable of abstract thought, he is simply an adult; why call him anything else? If these three important changes do not make a person an adult, then what does?

No answer to this question is provided by biology or the study of cognitive development; that is, there are no epochal changes of a physical or intellectual nature that occur when a person is in his late teens or early twenties. The answer, if any, must come from other quarters. To educators and employers, a person is not an adult until he has completed his schooling; to landlords and bankers, a person is not an adult until he has achieved financial independence; and to the state, a person is not an adult until he has reached the statutory age.

But anthropologists have found that there are many societies in which the "statutory age" of adulthood corresponds closely to the age of puberty. In these societies, adult work begins as soon as the person is physically ready for it, and "financial independence" is meaningless because the economy of the society is not based on specialization and exchange. In these societies adolescence does not exist. Indeed, at many periods in our own civilization's past, there was little or no interval between puberty and marriage, work, and citizenship.

This does not mean, however, that the requirements of modern industrial society are arbitrary. In order to do adult work in our highly specialized, technological economy, a person needs a great deal of education—more, in the prevailing view, than can be crammed into the years before puberty. And in order to vote wisely in an election or reach a fair decision on a jury, a person needs both an extensive education and more experience of the world than a thirteen year old could be expected to have. Some critics have argued that the importance of schooling is overestimated and the capacities of teenagers grossly underestimated, but they have made next to no dent in the general belief that our society has good reasons for withholding adult status until the individual is close to twenty.

Thus, extended adolescence does exist in industrial societies, even though it is only a consequence of that particular culture. It takes a variety of forms within each industrial nation. Some people have children while still in their teens, whereas others never have any children at all; some drop out of high school and get a job, whereas others are supported by their parents through college and graduate school; and some know their vocational goals, preferences in life-style, and social and religious values without hesitation, whereas others spend many years trying to find themselves. There are also subtle differences between one industrial nation and the next in their general patterns of adolescence. One theorist (Wylie, 1961) believes that French adolescents grow up in a different atmosphere from that of their American counterparts because French society perceives its own rules as a framework projected onto what would otherwise be social chaos. French people realize that this framework is largely artificial, but they expect each other to abide by it for the sake of mutual convenience. Americans, on the other hand, believe that the individual discovers the rules that govern a naturally ordered reality. Each adolescent is expected to define his own limits as he explores the forces that govern his world. Because the French adolescent has already learned to accept culturally defined social limitations, he does not rebel against the image he has of himself as an adult, whereas the American adolescent must learn to recognize social expectations at the same time as he is trying to work out his personal self-realization.

Figure 14.1. The importance of establishing an identity is no secret to this teenager.

RITES OF PASSAGE

At the age of thirteen, Jewish boys all over the world participate in the ceremony of *bar mitzvah* and announce to the world: "Today I am a man." From this day on they are eligible to participate in the rituals of the adult religious community. In most other Western groups, however, a lad of thirteen is still considered very much a child.

In fact, there is no clearly defined line that separates children from adults in secular American society, though the physical changes of puberty mark the biological end of childhood. Most people would agree that shaving and menstruating are things done by adults and not by children. Getting a driver's license, graduating from high school or college, embarking on a career, and getting married are all steps that contribute to the achievement of adult status in our society; yet, the end of adolescence is never clearly defined. We even hear some people accused of prolonging their adolescence indefinitely.

In most non-Western societies, the entrance into adulthood is unmistakably defined. At a specified age, the individual is permitted to participate in a ritual or series of rituals that qualify him to assume an adult role in his society. Anthropologists refer to the procedure whereby the child becomes an adult member of his culture as *rites of passage,* or puberty rites.

Although the original meaning and function of ancient puberty rites are shrouded in the mists of time, we do know something about the role of these rites in surviving nonliterate societies. The rites generally entail familiarizing the pubescent male with the secret traditions and folkways of the society. Often they involve mutilation of the body, and most especially of the sexual organs. By initiating the young man into adult society, the elders secure their own position of power, unite the tribe, and insure the continuation of traditional social behavior.

In some societies, the rites continue throughout most of the individual's adult life. Among the Karadjeri of Australia, for example, initiation is an extremely complex and drawn-out affair that begins at puberty and ends only when the man finally achieves the status of an elder.

Initiation begins for the Karadjeri youth when he is covered with human blood at the age of twelve. Two weeks

IDENTITY

In an industrial society, with its many opportunities and its great variety of adult roles, the individual is obliged to form for herself a stable, coherent identity that she and others can be comfortable with. Adolescence is the first of many times that she will be faced with the questions that define us as persons: Who am I? What do I care about? What do I want to do with my life? Throughout the crises and changes of adulthood—marriage, parenthood, a new job, separation from one's children, old age—the individual has to rework his or her notion of identity. The identity that is formed in adolescence is a dynamic, mobile construction that will change and grow as the person does.

later, after a hole has been bored through his nasal septum and a feather inserted, he achieves the status of *nimamu.* After the passage of a year or two, the *nimamu* is ready to undergo his first major puberty ritual, an elaborate circumcision ceremony that lasts for several days. At the conclusion of this ritual—after much singing, dancing, self-mutilation, weeping, throwing of boomerangs, drinking of blood, and, ultimately, the circumcision itself—the young man becomes *miangu.* It is not for another year or two that the *miangu* undergoes subincision, the ritual slitting of the urethra. This ritual, during which blood from the young man's wound is used to draw designs on his back, confers upon the youth the status of *djamununggur.*

In the years that follow, the young Karadjeri continues to participate in a series of rituals that serve to elevate his status gradually in the community. By eating particular foods, reciting certain words, and wearing special garments, he is slowly familiarized with the traditions and sacred objects known to the elders. Initiation culminates several years after marriage when the man is permitted to participate at a feast where he is shown the *pirmal,* inscribed wooden boards that are the tribe's most sacred objects. Even after a man has participated in this feast, his prestige continues to grow throughout his life until he eventually achieves the status of an elder.

The elaborate rituals of the Karadjeri are closely linked to the tribe's ancient history. Each of the initiation customs harkens back to the legend of the Bagadjimbiri, the mythical superhuman race from whom the Karadjeri trace their ancestry. Throughout his initiation, the young man gains more and more insight into the history and customs of his people and their ancestors.

Recently, some psychoanalysts have proposed that puberty rites reflect a fundamental envy by men of the sexual organs and functions of women. Because they do not menstruate, adolescent boys do not experience any clear-cut proof of their sexual maturity. It has been suggested that mutilation of the genitals, stopping up of the anus, and other common puberty rituals are symbolic expressions of the male's desire to share in the procreative power of the female.

The process of identity formation has been studied by Erik Erikson (1968), who theorizes that it consists of two stages in adolescence. In the first stage, the individual seeks an answer to the question "Who am I?" Uncomfortable with her physical and sexual development and unsure of her judgment and social roles, she becomes preoccupied with who she really is and what she appears to be in the eyes of others. Often she adopts the tactic of emulating heroines and committing her faith to ideals. In the service of these women and ideals, she believes it would be worthwhile to prove herself trustworthy, and she clings to them in the hope that they will prove constant while she is undergoing the rapid changes of adolescence. Some individuals, however, fear the finality of making commitments; they may express their need for faith in loud and cynical mistrust.

At this stage of identity formation, conformity to the peer group may be intense. The adolescent may identify so completely with the heroines of the peer group that she seems to lose her own emerging identity. By trying out various characteristics on her peers and observing the reaction she gets, she hopes to clarify her own idea of herself. At the same time, she is somewhat intimidated by the many possibilities of the future and the conflicting values offered by society, but by identifying temporarily with stereotyped peer group values, she gains time to sort out her own values and aspirations. She may switch abruptly from utter devotion to someone or something to a complete abandonment of her commitment. She must test the extremes, Erikson believes, before she can settle on a steady course.

When the process of identity formation at this stage is completed, Erikson (1950) concludes, the individual will be "confident that he possesses an inner sameness and continuity that are matched by the sameness and continuity of his meaning for others." Then he enters what Erikson calls the stage of intimacy. Intimacy is the capacity to commit one's self to someone or something and to develop the ethical strength to abide by such commitments, even when they require painful sacrifice and compromise. Many people achieve this stage for the first time before they are out of school; others live through it in their twenties or enter it only after a crisis later in their adult lives.

Dependence and Independence

One of the major tasks of adolescence is to become independent of the family and peer group. The developing adolescent must outgrow his childhood status; he must show other people, particularly his parents, that he is becoming an independent person with an identity that is distinct from that of his family.

In early adolescence few serious problems arise in the family because the adolescent is not interested in the same things as his parents. Before long, however, the adolescent begins to share many of his parents' pursuits and concerns; he becomes less interested in baseball and airplanes, perhaps, and more interested in girls and cars. When it comes to these things, his parents are not willing to leave him alone. He may resist the limitations they place on him in such matters, but he still needs their advice, guidance, and approval.

He may also need their economic support to get through school. One observer (Adelson, 1964) has suggested that the long period of financial dependency may lead parents and adolescents to avoid conflict on genuine issues. Instead, conflict centers on trivial matters, such as clothes and haircuts, so as to forestall the expression of serious antagonisms.

Values

As adolescents fight against their dependency on parents and other authority figures, they may be attracted to mythologies and ideologies that seem to offer some order and authority to replace those they have rejected. The ideologies that most appeal to them tend to be rigid and authoritarian—predictable systems that impose a framework in which the adolescent can work out details of his life. It is important

ERIKSON'S CRISES IN PSYCHOSOCIAL DEVELOPMENT

Basic Trust versus Basic Mistrust (first year of life)

Autonomy versus Shame and Doubt (second year of life)

Initiative versus Guilt (the preschool years)

Industry versus Inferiority (middle childhood)

Identity versus Role Confusion (adolescence)

The adolescent is in a period of questioning that comes with his rapid physical growth and sexual maturation at a time when he has established a first level of competence in the world of tools. The chief concern of the young person in this period is his identity, which he feels as a need to know how other people see him in comparison with the way he sees himself. He also needs to find a career commitment to use the skills that he has acquired in middle childhood.

Role confusion threatens as the adolescent has doubts about his sexual identity or, more commonly, feels ambivalent about occupational identity. To compensate for role confusion, the adolescent may overidentify and become completely committed to some fashionable hero or ideal for a time. Another kind of reaction is to seek relief in young love, where the adolescent forms his own identity in a close relationship with a peer. Role confusion accounts for the clannishness and conformity of adolescence: being unsure of who he is, the young person has little tolerance for differences in others.

Intimacy versus Isolation (young adulthood)

Generativity versus Stagnation (prime of life)

Ego Integrity versus Despair (old age)

to the adolescent to know where he stands; with the help of an inflexible system of values, he can be certain of his own position. Gradually, however, as he becomes more confident of his own judgment, rigid systems are usually replaced by a looser, more flexible point of view.

But does the adolescent progress as far as he potentially could in developing individual values? One observer (Friedenberg, 1959) believes that pressures for conformity with his peers overwhelm the adolescent and prevent the full development of his own values. Few adults try to counteract these pressures by challenging the adolescent's immature values, perhaps because they do not have anything better to offer, or because they cannot communicate their own values clearly, or because they wish to avoid conflict. Yet a well-reasoned dialogue between the generations about differing moral values is indispensable for full personal development.

Despite the lack of challenge and dialogue, most adolescents are intensely concerned with developing a personal value system. Relatively few, however, are actively involved in social movements. At the height of the period of demonstrations in the 1960s, a study (Allport, 1968) found that most college students seldom worried about national welfare or the fate of mankind. What they were really concerned with was obtaining a rich, full life for themselves.

The political attitudes of adolescents have been correlated with their cognitive and moral development in a study (Adelson and O'Neil, 1966) that asked subjects to respond to a hypothetical situation in which 1,000 people become dissatisfied with their government and go to a fictional island to form a new government. Thirteen year olds found it hard to imagine the consequences of such an action. Fifteen year olds found it difficult to visualize the community that might evolve and to think of the services that the new government might provide for its citizens. They tended also to be intolerant of civil liberties and to favor an authoritarian form of government. After the age of fifteen, the subjects of the study were able to perceive that law can promote the general good and produce social and moral benefits. They were able to understand the idea of a contract between the citizens and the state. They recognized both the individual's right to freedom and the necessity for restraints on actions that infringe the rights of others or threaten social order.

VOCATIONAL CHOICE

One of the most difficult and potentially frustrating tasks of adolescence is the choice of a career. In the distant past, vocational "choice" was really a matter of social dictate. A craftsman's son had few alternatives but to assume his father's profession; a peasant's son could only aspire to those vocations that were appropriate to his social class; and women had no socially approved options beyond the roles of household manager, wife, and mother. In nearly all cases, personal needs and desires were subordinated to the demands of a rigidly structured society.

Today, the adolescent enjoys a comparatively wide margin of freedom in the choice of a career, but by virtue of this freedom, vocational decision making has become more problematical than ever. For example, in terms of skills and interests a youth may be best suited to working as a garage mechanic, but his father may want the boy to take advantage of greater educational opportunities and perhaps become a lawyer or doctor. The conflict resulting from parental expectations may be further aggravated if the youth desires the salary and status of a doctor or lawyer but not the job itself. In some cases multiple job interests also complicate the situation. An adolescent may be torn among professions as disparate as those of a paleontologist, a golfer, and a business executive. The act of choosing one of these careers may be obstructed not only by the desire for all of them, but also by the fear that he will not prove talented enough once the choice is made. Finally, we must consider the fact that although there is a large variety of jobs in our society, relatively few of them are appealing to adolescents. Therefore, competition is severe, rejections are inevitable, and vocational "choice" may necessarily become vocational compromise.

The adolescent who is struggling to deal with vocational choices can take some comfort in the fact that many adults are experiencing a similar struggle. Changing vocations during adult life has become fairly common, especially among women whose first vocation was raising their children.

Figure 14.2. Which will you have: a life of getting up early every morning to do the chores? Or a life upon the stage? Despite appearances, the answer is an individual matter.

Preadolescent Preparation

The world of work is first delineated by the family. Parents provide the first models of what workers do and how one feels about work. The socioeconomic level of the family largely determines the vocational aspirations and attitudes of the child because ideas about the kinds of work available to the child and notions of the emotional significance of a person's job are determined to a large extent by the economic and social level of family and friends. It is usual for the children of professionals to enter the professions, for example, and for parents who are unemployed or underemployed to pass these difficulties on to their children both by example and because of the economic realities of their lives.

Long before the child is aware of the need to choose a career and years before he begins to make decisions about his vocation, he develops personality aspects that strongly influence this process. One of the most central aspects has been called *coping behavior* (Murphy, 1962). This is the personality characteristic that determines the way the child deals with his environment. It is developed through the child's efforts to fulfill his needs by exploring and participating in his surroundings instead of avoiding them and thus to increase his ability to deal with his environment and his confidence in that ability. If a child is successful in learning coping behavior, he will be able to deal effectively with work-related decisions when the time comes. Parents and teachers can help young children prepare for vocational decisions by encouraging them to develop good work habits, helping them to think about and make personal plans, and giving them practice in making decisions that are appropriate to the child's level of development.

One study (Ginzberg, 1951) of the processes involved in a child's decisions about work divides it up into three developmental stages, the first of which begins early in childhood. In the fantasy stage, up to about age eleven, the child assumes that he can enter any career. His thinking about the work he wants to do is purely subjective, unrelated to the realities of the work itself or to his own abilities to perform the work. The second stage, called the tentative period, includes children from age eleven to seventeen. In this stage the child gradually becomes aware of the fact that certain qualifications are required for certain kinds of work and that these correlate with personal qualities and abilities. He develops a more realistic idea of what is involved in doing various kinds of work and comes to understand that there are training requirements for specific jobs. An important realization of this period is the understanding that personal values influence vocational decisions.

In the third stage, called the realistic choice period, the person begins to devise a workable plan for his career choice. This plan requires a synthesis of subjective and objective considerations, bringing together what the person wants to do and what it is possible for him to do within the limitations of his abilities, his economic situation, and so on. Three phases are included in this planning: exploration, in which the person attempts to find out more about specific job areas through discussions with counselors, work-related experiences (in a job after school, for example) and so on; crystallization, in which the child prepares to commit himself to a vocational choice; and specification, in which the child selects a particular occupation.

Although his sample of young women was too small to make any confident generalizations, the researcher made some interesting conjectures about the special difficulties that adolescent girls experience in selecting a particular occupation. He theorized that young women find it difficult to come to a final commitment about work because they feel that a woman's vocational choices are greatly influenced by her marital prospects and the economic situation of her future husband. Since most seventeen year olds do not have clear marital plans, young women are likely to be more tentative in their vocational decision making and to feel unresolved about this choice. They may, for example, find it difficult to imagine and plan for an occupational life until they know whether or not they will be married at the end of their career training.

In another study of the developmental process involved in making a career choice, the researcher (Havighurst, 1964) developed a pattern of decision making that parallels Erikson's psychosocial tasks. The system might be summarized as follows:

Age 5–10	The child identifies with the worker. His concept of working is part of his ego ideal.
Age 10–15	The child develops basic working habits and learns how to use his time and energy in order to complete tasks.
Age 15–25	The person gains a worker identity by choosing a vocation and preparing for it.
Age 25–40	The person becomes productive by perfecting the skills of his chosen vocation.

Notice that the developmental process envisioned here takes about thirty-five years and represents a major thread in the growth from early childhood into adulthood. Making a vocational choice is a long and complex process, and the factors that influence it are developed through much of an individual's life. This is one of the reasons why changing vocations in adult life is felt by many to be so terribly difficult. It also helps to point out the importance of helping the adolescent to make a wise decision in his initial commitment.

Vocational Counseling

The complexity and increasing rate of change in today's job market makes the work of the vocational counselor both more important and more difficult than ever before. Many jobs are unappealing to youth, and many more unknown to them. In an era of extensive specialization, not even a guidance counselor will know all the types of jobs that are available. Furthermore, new job categories open up

Figure 14.3. A young draftswoman. Drafting has traditionally been a man's occupation, though women are well suited for it.

continually, while others become obsolete. An adolescent, therefore, is faced not only with determining whether he will still be interested in his profession years after he has made the choice, but also whether that particular job has a viable future.

For example, one junior high school student many years ago expressed a deep interest in electronics engineering, and her guidance counselor informed her that the field was burgeoning with lucrative opportunities. Six years later, by the time she was entering college, the student was obliged to consider alternative career choices—not because her previous interest had waned, but because she believed that her aptitude in math was not strong enough. Perhaps this was just as well, for by the time she graduated, a high percentage of electronics engineers were out of work and the electronics job market was glutted with applicants.

This example serves to introduce a specific aspect of the job problem for young women. It is significant that in her adolescence the would-be engineer received few positive and many negative reactions to her proposed career choice simply because she was female. Moreover, she received little direction in choosing subjects that would have prepared her for a college engineering program. It is true that today, more than ever, women are entering professions that hitherto have been dominated by men. But their educational and professional opportunities are still not on par with those of men; and they do not receive the kind of psychological, emotional, and intellectual preparation needed to compete successfully in the job market.

By the time she reaches adolescence, a young woman has already been subtly infused with society's notion that a "real" woman is one who is married, raising a family, and perhaps doing some sort of volunteer work. If she does enter a profession, the pressures on her are disproportionately higher than those on her male counterparts:

> Paradoxically, while women must not "succeed," when they *do* succeed at anything, they have still failed if they're not successful at *everything*. If a woman accomplishes a valuable task, she still has failed if she (unlike man) has, for example, abandoned the care of her children or her looks in order to do so (Chesler, 1972).

It is only fair to note that males are similarly conditioned for certain roles and until recently have been discouraged from entering "female" professions, such as nursing. For women, however, self-realization through work and social activism is a more difficult problem, one that adolescent females are becoming more aware of. The dream of entering a male-oriented profession may involve considerable struggle and frustration before it is realized, and the adolescent may fear that she is neither intellectually nor emotionally prepared for the task.

Vocational choice, then, may be complicated by a variety of personal and extrapersonal factors. Although no perfect solution to the problem exists, some guidance in choosing a career is available, and present research into the subject may result in even more effective guidance in the future. In an effort to help the adolescent make his career decisions, some high schools offer a course in vocational planning. Students also take aptitude tests that are administered and evaluated by trained vocational psychologists in various high schools and universities. These tests give at least some indication of a student's fundamental abilities and skills (mechanical, spatial, conceptual, etc.) and often disclose interests the student may not have been previously aware of. One study (Osipow, 1968) suggests using these tests and other statistical information in devising giant matrices that would correlate a broad range of individual abilities and personality traits with appropriate occupations. A student could then use these matrices in selecting a career for which he seems well suited.

Perhaps most helpful to adolescents are the individual counseling programs offered by many schools, church youth clubs, and government agencies. However, the need for these programs—especially among low-income adolescents who receive little or no guidance from their own families—often exceeds their availability; there simply are not enough counselors who can provide the time and quality of guidance that many young people require. A partial solution at least to the problem of time and limited facilities is group career orientation. Lectures on vocational opportunities and planning that are offered by universities, the armed services, corporation representatives, and independent service groups cannot possibly equal the value of individual counseling, but they can at least stimulate interest, broaden the youth's understanding of the job market, and give him a realistic conception of the training and skills he would need in various fields. Some group career workshops and lectures are specifically geared to the vocational problems of women. They often try to provide encouragement, along with much useful information, to adolescents who are planning careers, to women who wish to change careers, and to women who are entering the job market for the first time.

As a supplement to or substitute for any of these sources of vocational guidance, the adolescent can start his own "self-help" program. Federal, state, and local government agencies often supply vocational pamphlets upon request. These may contain general information about careers or describe vocational opportunities in specific regions. Also, the public library has books on careers, some of them quite interesting in their use of fictional stories to convey all sorts of information about a given profession. Finally, no matter where else he turns, the adolescent will have to consult with himself. To the best of his ability, he will have to probe for his truest impulses and desires and measure the strength of his commitment to a particular career, while at the same time realizing that no decision he makes is irreversible.

ALIENATION

If the adolescent fails to achieve a positive identity, he may become alienated. In Erikson's terminology, this unhappy state is known as *identity confusion;* Erikson illustrates it with a line from Arthur Miller's play *Death of a Salesman,* in which the young man Biff cries out, "I just can't take hold, Mom, I just can't take hold of some kind of life." The inability to take hold of life, to form an integrated sense of self, will restrict a person to a life of feeling isolated from society and may lead to doubt, sexual insecurity, and lack of autonomy.

Virtually all adolescents experience temporary identity confusion as part of growing up. Most adolescents outgrow it as they move into adulthood. **Alienation** results only when the individual never manages to form an integrated identity, and then he may feel like a stranger—an alien—in his own world. In severe cases he may become mentally ill. Most adolescents overcome temporary identity confusion in the course of normal development. Erikson suggests that during periods of identity confusion parents should be tolerant and understanding. They can also give reasonable guidance and help the adolescent find new opportunities to explore human behavior and interaction.

Many psychologists and psychiatrists have emphasized the social and cultural factors that hinder the adolescent's identity formation. One of them (Erich Fromm, 1941, 1956, 1961) perceives man's nature as being in conflict with our present civilization. It is this basic incompatibility that tends to cast man into isolation. Because society places its highest values on money and power, the personal development of the individual is often thwarted, and the adolescent encounters many stumbling blocks in his quest for identity. Another theorist (Friedenberg, 1959, 1965) sees self-definition as the most important task in developing identity and personal autonomy. An individual can achieve self-definition only through steady contact with and repeated testing by adults whose values are firmly rooted. The greatest obstacle to the adolescent's full personal development is American society's "melting pot" concept of education, in which individuality and creativity are suppressed and a premium is placed on conformity. In this view, the pressure for "group adjustment" is the adolescent's greatest obstacle to achievement of self-definition. The rigid authoritarianism of the secondary schools is blamed for punishing and frustrating creativity and uniqueness.

The late writer Paul Goodman (1956, 1964) spoke persuasively about society's disregard for the adolescent and its setting aside of personal values in favor of material rewards. In a society where the individual has ceased to be important, the adolescent lacks models with whom to identify and is almost certain to encounter difficulties in achieving an integrated identity. There is no identity without a feeling

Figure 14.4. The "freak" goes to considerable lengths to dissociate himself from the "system."

of self-worth, Goodman believed, and this cannot be realized without a sense of accomplishment; but society denies the adolescent any opportunity for meaningful accomplishment. Faced with this prospect, some adolescents choose to drop out of society rather than contribute to their own alienation.

Dropouts and Activists

Some adolescents experience alienation when they become aware of injustice and inequality in their society and become disillusioned with the "system." Coming at a time when the individual is normally struggling against dependency on his parents, this awareness leads him to blame his parents, along with the rest of the adult world, for "selling out" to achieve success in a materialistic and corrupt society. He rejects the social and political values of his parents wholesale, and, despairing of any meaningful change within the society around him, drops out of it to seek rewards in subjective experience. This social dropping-out may take the form of withdrawing psychologically from the world of adult authority or of actually leaving home and school to live a new life-style among his peers.

Although he may not at first understand the values of the subculture he decides to identify with, he will probably adopt its dress and manners and may even experiment with drugs, mysticism, and other varieties of "consciousness-raising" experience.

In contrast to the dropout, who has rejected his parents' values, the activist often shares many of his parents' social and political values but rejects one aspect of his culture, such as war, discrimination, or commercialism. Activists have a fundamental faith in their society, but they believe that many of its ideals have not been implemented and that it is time for drastic reforms. The activist often comes from an upper-middle-class home, where he was taught liberal values. He sees, however, that after these values were accepted by society, they seldom were put into effect. His activism, as he sees it, is an attempt to make these values work, to make changes within the system so that its benefits can be available to all. Some of the most popular causes among activists have been putting an end to racial discrimination and the Vietnam War and aiding the American Indian and exploited agricultural workers.

The Black Adolescent

Although many blacks, through education and perseverance, have achieved middle- or upper-class status, the majority remain poor and minimally educated. The alienation of the black adolescent is usually the direct result of racial discrimination, of being denied opportunities that would equip him for a place in a predominantly white society. Research (Miller, 1959) has found that this sense of being excluded may appear as early as age ten or eleven among slum children. The feeling of being an outcast is steadily intensified as a multitude of career opportunities and other rewards of the society are dangled before the adolescent while his peers assure him that such opportunities were never meant for him. This negative reinforcement and passive acceptance of the "black role" in society has kept a high proportion of blacks from completing high school.

Identity confusion may be a particularly painful state for the black adolescent, bound up as it is with his heightened awareness of privation and futility. With intensified efforts to achieve civil rights, new career opportunities have opened up for blacks, but a large number of black adolescents continue to drop out. The civil rights movement has also brought about a new awareness of black culture—black history, black art, black fashions—which allows blacks to take pride in their African as well as their American heritage. Teaching children that "black is beautiful" and at the same time pressing for expanded opportunities and rewards may do much to give the black adolescent a more secure sense of identity and ease his transition into functioning and productive adulthood.

Alienation From the Family

In all levels of society increased pressures have brought about a loosening of family ties in recent years. In lower economic groups the constant struggle to cope with squalor and disease puts a strain on family relationships, and at the upper economic levels increased affluence and the quest for ever more affluence may bring pressures that make family life haphazard and minimal. With one or both parents often absent from the home because of business or social commitments, the child spends much of his time with others of his own age who may influence him more than his family does.

By his early teens it is apparent to a child that the intense concern of the adult world with acquiring skills and attaining material rewards is not matched by a like concern for human or social values. Although he is likely to identify with the values of his society, he sees only the discrepancy between what his elders profess and what they practice. He has gained no experience in using society's institutions to remedy its ills and injustices. His education may have exposed him to social values, but without constant reinforcement through example and the opportunities to participate in their application, he will remain unable to use these values in solving human problems or in forming a stable personal identity.

PROBLEM BEHAVIOR

Except for dropping out of school, most of the asocial behavior and mental health problems exhibited by adolescents are not the exclusive domain of that age group. Certainly adolescents have no monopoly over drug abuse and alcoholism, and such problems as depression, schizophrenia, and obesity cut across all age levels. Child psychologists and other social scientists disagree about whether these problems have specific characteristics when they originate in adolescence, but most agree that the developmental crises of adolescence—the physical and psychological upheavals that

THE DRIVE-IN

They must have been familiar sights, walking around the shopping plaza in their shorts and flat ballerina slippers that always scuffed on the sidewalk, with charm bracelets jingling on their thin wrists; they would lean together to whisper and laugh secretly if someone passed who amused or interested them. Connie had long dark blond hair that drew anyone's eye to it, and she wore part of it pulled up on her head and puffed out and the rest of it she let fall down her back. She wore a pull-over jersey blouse that looked one way when she was at home and another way when she was away from home. Everything about her had two sides to it, one for home and one for anywhere that was not home: her walk, which could be childlike and bobbing, or languid enough to make anyone think she was hearing music in her head; her mouth, which was pale and smirking most of the time, but bright and pink on these evenings out; her laugh, which was cynical and drawling at home—"Ha, ha, very funny,"—but highpitched and nervous anywhere else, like the jingling of the charms on her bracelet.

Sometimes they did go shopping or to a movie, but sometimes they went across the highway, ducking fast across the busy road, to a drive-in restaurant where older kids hung out. The restaurant was shaped like a big bottle, though squatter than a real bottle, and on its cap was a revolving figure of a grinning boy holding a hamburger aloft. One night in midsummer they ran across, breathless with daring, and right away someone leaned out a car window and invited them over, but it was just a boy from high school they didn't like. It made them feel good to be able to ignore him. They went up through the maze of parked and cruising cars to the bright-lit, fly-infested restaurant, their faces pleased and expectant as if they were entering a sacred building that loomed up out of the night to give them what haven and blessing they yearned for. They sat at the counter and crossed their legs at the ankles, their thin shoulders rigid with excitement, and listened to the music that made everything so good: the music was always in the background, like music at a church service; it was something to depend upon.

A boy named Eddie came in to talk with them. He sat backwards on his stool, turning himself jerkily around in semicircles and then stopping and turning back again, and after a while he asked Connie if she would like something to eat. She said she would and so she tapped her friend's arm on her way out—her friend pulled her face up into a brave, droll look—and Connie said she would meet her at eleven, across the way. "I just hate to leave her like that," Connie said earnestly, but the boy said that she wouldn't be alone for long. So they went out to his car, and on the way Connie couldn't help but let her eyes wander over the windshields and faces all around her, her face gleaming with a joy that had nothing to do with Eddie or even this place; it might have been the music. She drew her shoulders up and sucked in her breath with the pure pleasure of being alive.

From *The Wheel of Love and Other Stories* by Joyce Carol Oates. New York: Fawcett Books, 1970.

young people go through during this period—do make the teenager more susceptible to some of these disorders than he might be at other times of life.

Some of the problems that may cause serious concern also occur to a lesser degree without becoming serious conditions or long-term pathological syndromes. Obesity, for example, is not uncommon in adolescence, but it is usually transient and not severe. Like many adults, teenagers have periods of depression; wide swings of mood are considered normal in adolescents. At some point many teenagers in the United States experiment with drugs or alcohol and are little the worse for it. Unfortunately, however, in a few cases these problems become chronic (permanent) or entail severe psychological effects or social implications.

Disorders

The adolescent is subject to nearly all of the mental and emotional upsets and social maladjustments that the adult is. These run the gamut from neuroses (anxiety, phobias, obsessions, and compulsions) to psychoses (such as schizophrenia). Many youngsters troubled by psychiatric disorders do poorly academically and drop out of school. Some turn to drugs; others act out their problems through such asocial behavior as sexual promiscuity and criminal acts. And, of course, unless detected and treated, psychiatric disorders during the adolescent years will continue into adulthood and can impair normal psychic functioning throughout a person's life.

Schizophrenia

Schizophrenia, often thought of by the layman as "split personality," is actually a complicated psychosis characterized by an inability to relate to one's environment. Contrasting systems (hence the concept of split personality) are typical of schizophrenic behavior. On the one hand, the schizophrenic is inactive, seems indifferent to the world around him, and is frequently lost in reverie; on the other, he will be hypersensitive and subject to emotional outbreaks and manifestations of anxiety, panic, and profound depression. Schizophrenia may be severe—permanently impairing personality development, social adjustment, and mental function, and usually requiring that the patient be institutionalized; but there are also mild forms. Remission of symptoms and sometimes even a complete cure are possible.

Psychiatrists are becoming increasingly aware of schizophrenic behavior in teenagers. The problem of diagnosing this disorder in adolescence is that the usual ego changes that occur during puberty resemble those of early schizophrenia. The schizophrenic adolescent becomes increasingly seclusive, has disconcerting fluctuations in mood, is edgy, is sometimes lost in fantasy, is sometimes aggressive with his siblings and impertinent to his parents, and fluctuates between deep depression and euphoric exultation. All of these behavior patterns can occur in normal adolescents. The difference seems to be that the healthy adolescent remains in touch with reality. His behavior is only selectively disturbed (he may, for example, display deviant behavior at home or at school, but adjust well elsewhere), whereas the behavior of the schizophrenic is more or less uninfluenced by time and place.

Adolescent schizophrenia is usually treated somewhat differently from adult schizophrenia. There tends to be greater use of special drugs that act upon the central nervous system, as a supplement to psychotherapy. Most psychiatrists suggest that, whenever possible, the teenage schizophrenic be kept at home or in a small institution or clinic rather than in a large, impersonal institution. The importance of continuing a patient's schooling or vocational training is also emphasized.

Depression

Although melancholy or dejected feelings are quite usual during adolescence, depression sometimes becomes a more severe condition, and as such it is considered to be neurotic or psychotic. One severe form of this psychiatric disorder is known as *manic-depressive* psychosis; it is characterized by drastic mood swings from elation to depression. These changes in mood may be either random or cyclical, and they are often accompanied by delusions or hallucinations. The manic periods are manifested by elation or irritability, overtalkativeness, flight of ideas, and increased physical activity. The depressive periods are characterized by melancholy, mental and physical retardation, inhibition, apathy, feelings of worthlessness, insomnia, and a preoccupation with suicide.

Psychiatrists disagree about the degree to which manic-depressive behavior occurs in adolescence. As with the symptoms of schizophrenia, it is sometimes difficult to distinguish normal shifts in mood from abnormal ones. Although true manic-depressive reactions are rare before fifteen years of age, the syndrome does seem to be more common in adolescents over fifteen than was formerly thought.

One researcher into this problem (Toolan, 1962) believes that the most accurate way to describe depressive illness in adolescents is in terms of "depressive equivalents," a set of symptoms that add up to depressed behavior. The chief of these symptoms are boredom and restlessness, fatigue, hypochondriasis (imaginary ill health), preoccupation with the body, and difficulty in concentrating. The depressed teenager may have a devalued self-image, which frequently leads to antisocial behavior that only produces further depression and guilt and reinforces the adolescent's belief that he is bad, ugly, or inferior.

It is frequently difficult for parents, counselors, and others who work with teenagers to determine when depression is normal and when it should be considered a symptom of mental illness. As is the case with schizophrenic behavior, a depressed condition can be considered potentially abnormal when it occurs in inappropriate circumstances, when it persists for unduly long periods, or when the adolescent seems totally incapable of dealing with his depressed feelings. In such cases, psychiatric help should be sought. Psychotherapy seems to be the chief tool for treating the condition in teenagers. Antidepressant drugs and electroshock treatments, which are often administered to depressed adults with good results, seem to be less effective with adolescents. The depressed teenager usually recognizes that he is troubled, is eager to obtain help, and frequently responds quite well to therapy.

Figure 14.5. Normal adolescent depression.
When depression becomes so severe as to
be pathological, it is not likely to make
such a romantic photograph.

Eating disturbances

Obesity and excessive thinness may appear to be strictly physical problems, but in adolescence in particular, these conditions sometimes either result from or lead to emotional disturbance. The physiological factors that may influence abnormal body size include genetic predisposition, disordered regulatory mechanisms of the metabolism, endocrine malfunctioning, and an excessive endowment of fat cells from early childhood. Obesity may occur purely as a result of any of these conditions, but it is frequently seen in people having psychiatric problems as well.

Adolescent overweight may be a temporary state, aggravated by the physiological imbalances that occur during puberty; as long as it does not profoundly lower the self-esteem and body-image of the adolescent, it is not a cause for great concern. When, however, obesity becomes chronic or develops into an emotional disturbance as well as a physical condition, it requires medical and, frequently, psychiatric treatment.

The excessively overweight person with severe emotional problems is thought by many psychiatrists to have suffered interference with or inadequate satisfaction of oral drives during infancy. Psychoanalysis has shown that because of these frustrated drives, the compulsive eater may symbolically equate food with an insatiable craving for unobtainable love. Food may also function as a substitute for sexual gratification. In other cases, eating may be a form of self-indulgence or, conversely, a means of punishing forbidden impulses. A preoccupation with food may also be related to an adolescent's need to cling to his parents or, on the other hand, a wish to reject them. The list of psychological factors that might be involved in obesity could, in fact, be almost endless, but one writer on the subject (Bruch, 1961) feels that there is a more basic underlying reason for eating disturbances. She believes that the fundamental problem of seriously over- or underweight people is an inability to recognize one's own bodily needs—essentially, an inability to differentiate hunger from satiety—and that this incapacity stems from a child's earliest eating experiences.

> If . . . a mother's reaction [to her child's hunger] is continuously inappropriate, be it neglectful, oversolicitous, inhibiting, or indiscriminately permissive, the outcome for the child will be a perplexing confusion. When he is older he will not be able to discriminate between being hungry and being sated, or suffering from some other discomfort. At the extremes of eating disorders, one finds the grotesquely obese person who is haunted by the fear of starvation and the emaciated anorexic who is oblivious to the pangs of hunger and the weakness, fatigue, and other symptoms characteristic of chronic undernutrition.

According to this view, treatment of eating disturbances must begin with teaching the patient to be aware of and to distinguish between bodily impulses. He must be trained to recognize both hunger signals and signals of satiety and to respond to them in a discriminating way. Unless this is done, neither special diets nor psychotherapy will enable the patient to overcome his eating problems.

Up to this point, we have been discussing how eating disturbances arise at least in part from emotional problems. There is another side to the coin—the influence that obesity can have on the person's mental health. "Western culture is so hostile and derogatory to even mild degrees of overweight that every obese person faces some problems in his social relations, adolescents in particular, all of whom are struggling for self-respect" (Bruch, 1961). Many overweight teenagers suffer real ego damage as a result of cultural pressures to be thin. The attitude that "thin is beautiful" is also one of the chief factors in the early stages of the development of the condition known as *anorexia nervosa*, which, though fairly uncommon, chiefly affects teenage girls. This condition, one of the few psychiatric illnesses that can result in death, is characterized by voluntary restriction of food intake in a neurotic pursuit of thinness that results in emaciation and undernutrition. The anorexic characteristically attempts to deny all feelings of hunger and assuages any pangs by a variety of methods, including occupying herself by feeding others (when she is preparing meals for her family, for instance, she redirects her desire for food), drinking large amounts of water and low-calorie fluids, or actually eating but then inducing vomiting. Gradually, after months of starvation, hunger frequently almost disappears. Sufferers from this mental disorder tend to deny almost frantically that they are fatigued or that their skeletonlike appearance is abnormal. These starving adolescents almost always end up in the hospital, where the disease is recognized as the full-blown neurotic syndrome that it is. Treatment is complicated; two-thirds of the patients recover or improve, one-quarter relapse, and seven percent die.

Dropouts

Those American youths who fail to complete a high school education are commonly termed educational dropouts. There is disagreement not only about how many there are, who they are, and why they withdraw from school, but also over whether the situation is a cause for as much concern as it has been given in the past decade. Some think that solving the dropout problem is of critical importance to human development, whereas others feel that the policy of encouraging young people to complete their education is really an evasion of the more critical issues of racial discrimination and increased unemployment among the young.

One estimate (Dentler, 1964) indicates that in 1975 approximately 30 percent of all students enrolled in school will fail to complete high school, but that only about 15 percent will be voluntary dropouts (the other 15 percent either having died or having withdrawn for physical, mental, or emotional reasons). Regardless of whose statistics are used, it is safe to say that the overall odds that the American student will graduate have improved substantially over the last several decades.

But what about those who do not graduate? The profile of the average high school dropout indicates that he is usually a low school achiever, frequently below grade for his age. He tends to participate very little in extracurricular student activities. The chances are good that he is a member of a racial minority group. The average dropout comes from a low-income family in which the parents have low levels of educational and occupational attainment. Dropouts' families are frequently disorganized, sometimes with the father absent.

Studies have shown that what happens to the dropout when he leaves school is quite predictable—he perpetuates the cycle. Secure employment is the key to attaining a higher standard of living, and whether or not it should be so, a high school diploma has become a prerequisite for finding almost any niche in the labor force. Nongraduates have a much higher unemployment rate in today's automated society than do high school graduates. Thus the dropout tends to be doomed to economic failure and resultant social discrimination.

What can be done about this? Some educators and others concerned about the problem have suggested that in addition to urging students in the strongest possible terms and with the greatest possible inducements to get their high school diplomas, alternate forms of education—more and better technical schools, for example—should be established to give young people the skills necessary to become economically valuable members of society. Until this is done, they say, there will continue to be dropouts from our essentially academically oriented schools.

Delinquency

The term "juvenile delinquency," which was widely used in the 1950s and 1960s, is much less frequently heard today. This is not, however, because delinquent behavior has abated in recent years; rather, it is because we now tend to place antisocial teenage behavior in more concrete categories. It seems to be part of a trend to treat teenagers more like adults and to identify and deal with individual adolescent problems in a specific way.

A few decades ago, every boy was expected to steal watermelons and push over outdoor toilets at Halloween. These acts were condoned on the basis of the generalization that "boys will be boys." Today, there is a growing tendency to consider theft as theft, whether the object stolen is a watermelon or some other item, and to class acts similar to pushing over outdoor toilets as vandalism. (Ramsey 1967)

Figure 14.6. The high school dropout may not seem to lack self-confidence, but he often has a history of low achievement in school.

Along with this growing tendency to call a spade a spade and to deal with it as such seems to be a decrease in societal concern and governmental interference with individual adolescent-parent relationships. Whereas the most frequently lodged charge against teenage girls in the 1950s was "ungovernability" (which quite often amounted to no more than sneaking out of the house in the face of parental prohibition to meet a boyfriend), law-enforcement officers today are increasingly reluctant to spend time and resources trying to mediate family quarrels.

A delinquent act is now considered to be any act that violates the property rights or physical well-being of others and which, if it were committed by an adult, would be considered a crime.

Adolescent criminal behavior

Teenage offenses run the gamut from vandalism to murder. Recent statistics showed that 25 percent of the muggings and robberies reported in New York City were committed by people under the age of sixteen. It is clear that adults have no monopoly on hard-core crime. The profile of the juvenile offender in the United States has changed radically in the past twenty-five years. The following description (Merrill, 1947) of the average juvenile delinquent's background was set forth some time ago. Delinquents were thought to:

1. Come from homes in which the relationship between the parents is not cohesive and "good."
2. Come from homes in which discipline is lax, in which the parents use physical punishment, and in which the parents less often use reasoning as a method of control.
3. Come from parents who themselves have criminal records.
4. Have a lower average intelligence.
5. Have feelings of being unloved and rejected.

Not all of these characteristics are valid today, if indeed they ever really were. A more recent study (Pine, 1966) asserts that a significant number of juvenile crimes are committed by middle- and upper-income teenagers and, in fact, that upward social mobility is a breeding ground for the development of delinquent behavior.

Juvenile criminals are made, not born, and most social scientists who have studied the problem do feel that the home environment is the chief factor in influencing the development of delinquent behavior. Frequently cited are the lack of a strong father figure (a situation that is most common in both lower- and upper-income families) and inadequate parental love and attention. Peer group pressure also plays a significant part in adolescent criminality.

The means of dealing with juvenile offenders in our society seem to be largely unsatisfactory. Placing them in so-called "reform" schools is still the most common correctional measure taken with teenage criminals. Such institutions purport to rehabilitate the teenage delinquent but not infrequently end up functioning as schools for the further mastery of criminal techniques.

WHAT IS A GROWN-UP?

The generation of children who become adolescents in the 1950s lived in a world in which the official definition of an adult was fairly clear. A grown-up was a person who had made some major decisions about the direction of his or her life and had settled into a relatively predictable pattern of living. Men had jobs, careers to which they were committed, in companies or professions where they would work their way up to positions of importance. Women had children and houses to mind; they might also have jobs or other significant outside interests, but their main vocation for their adult lives was the maintenance of a home for their family.

Along with these clear economic and social roles, adults were expected to have the emotional stability that comes from knowing what you are doing. Grown-ups were people who had figured out who they were; their values were defined, and they lived in a world where they could take control of their lives; they had the power, ability, know-how, and self-confidence to get what they wanted. Adults were genuinely respected; many young people looked forward to adulthood as the best time of their lives. One chose a career, got married, bought a house and had children in a progression that was seen as both inevitable and desirable.

There is no question, of course, that part of that notion of adulthood was always a myth. The idealized grown-up who has all the answers and can be counted on to manage things is a necessary figure for most small children, who like to be assured that not everyone is helpless as they are; in fact, many of us can recall the day when we first learned to our dismay that our parents were not perfect. In the 1950s however, the fiction that most adults are stable, settled, and happy seemed to persist after childhood, despite the fact that few people had ever met anyone even approaching this ideal.

The generation entering adolescence in the 1970s seems to have a very different perspective on the adult world. Their idea of a grown-up includes few illusions. They are coming of age during a period in which adults and adult decisions are being called sharply into question. They have never known a time in which confidence was not being battered by one crisis or another—Vietnam, Kent State, Attica, the Near East, or Watergate. Today's young people have good reason to wonder whether the grown-ups of their world are in control of anything.

Some observers insist that the adolescents of the 1970s are really not so very different from those of the 1950s or 1930s. It is said that young people have always been critical of their elders, but that they come around as they grow up and become very much like their parents in the end. Others believe that fundamental changes are occurring in the relationships between the generations. Margaret Mead, for example, insists that "a profound disturbance is occurring in the relationships between the strong and the weak, the possessors and the dispossessed, elder and younger, and those who have knowledge and skill and those who lack them. The secure belief that those who knew had authority over those who did not has been shaken" (1970).

Mead theorizes that there are three kinds of cultures: postfigurative, in which children learn from their elders and ancestors; cofigurative, in which children learn from their peers; and prefigurative, in which children teach adults and have no clear model for themselves. Our world, Mead believes, is entering a prefigurative phase.

In postfigurative cultures, such as most nonindustrial societies, the authoritative models for behavior and values comes from past tradition. The fundamental assumption of people living in such a culture is that nothing really changes; and in fact change is so slow that there really is great continuity in their lives.

In a cofigurative society, by contrast, members of each generation learn values and ways of behaving from their peers. The young find models among their own age-mates because there has been an abrupt change in the culture in which the family lives or the family has emigrated from one country to another. The elders carry the old tradition with them, but their children reject that tradition—and treat the elders with less respect—because their knowledge is not useful in the new land.

In a prefigurative culture, which Mead believes is exemplified by contemporary American society, children cannot learn useful behavior and values from their parents because the changes in the world have made their elders' beliefs and practices obsolete in their own time. Children have no models because no one knows what the world of the future will be like.

Even very recently, the elders could say: "You know, I have been young and *you* have never been old." But today's young people can reply, "You have never been young in the world I am young in, and you never can be." . . . These young dissidents realize the critical need for immediate world action on problems that affect the whole world. What they want is, in some way, to begin all over again. The idea of orderly, developmental change is lost for this generation of young, who cannot take over the past from their elders, but can only repudiate what their elders are doing now. The past for them is a colossal, unintelligible failure and the future may hold nothing but the destruction of the planet. The sense the young have [is] that their elders do not understand the modern world. . . . (Mead 1970).

In such a culture, the young must necessarily look to the future for their models of adult behavior; their definition of a grown-up cannot be realized or even known until they are grown.

Many adults today are candid enough to acknowledge that they do not know how to solve their own problems or the problems of the larger community. The one thing that seems certain is that our lives will contine to change and that traditional models will become less and less useful to the generations to come. Adolescents, therefore, cannot be sure they want to become adults, inasmuch as adulthood is no longer defined by tradition. Mead thinks the new symbol of what life will be like is the unborn child, for whom we have great hope and care but whom we cannot know until he is born.

Teenage drug abuse

Although it does not strictly fit the description of a delinquent act given above (that is, the violation of the property rights or the physical well-being of another), the use of alcohol and other drugs by an adolescent is considered delinquent behavior in that it is punishable by law. Using alcohol is legal for adults, of course, and many teenagers resent the double standard. Our judicial system attempts to shelter the young by making adult "vices" especially forbidden to minors, but such laws can have the opposite of their intended effect if they make the forbidden behavior especially attractive. There is some evidence that using alcohol may cause adolescents to commit other illegal acts, but this is undoubtedly also true of adults. The larger question of whether the law ought to proscribe any behavior that harms no one but the participants is one which legal authorities are beginning to ask as it becomes more and more difficult for them to enforce certain of these laws.

The use of drugs other than alcohol by American teenagers was practically nonexistent before World War II; since then it has increased steadily until reaching a peak in recent years. What began as a practice almost exclusively of lower-class slum dwellers spread in the 1960s to middle- and upper-class people. What proportions illegal drug use has reached is unknown, but its incidence is declining somewhat and it is being replaced to some degree by the consumption of the less expensive and more easily accessible alcoholic beverages.

References

Adelson, J. The mystique of adolescence. *Psychiatry*, 1964, *27*, 1–5.

Adelson, J., and O'Neil, R. P. Growth of political ideas in adolescence: the sense of community. *Journal of Personality and Social Psychology*, 1966, *4*, 295–306.

Allport, W. *The person in psychology.* Boston: Beacon, 1968.

Bandura, A. The stormy decade: Fact or fiction. *Psychology in the School*, 1964, *1*, 224–231.

Bruch, H. Transformation of oral impulses in eating disorders. *Psychiatry Quarterly*, 1961, *35*, 458.

Chesler, P. *Woman and madness.* New York: Doubleday, 1972.

Dentler, R. A. Dropouts, automation, and the cities. *Teachers College Record*, 1964, *65*, 475–483.

Eisenberg, L. A developmental approach to adolescence. *Children*, 1965, *12*, 131–135.

Erikson, E. *Childhood and society.* New York: Norton, 1950.

Erikson, E. *Identity: Youth and crisis.* New York: Norton, 1968.

Freud, A. Adolescence as a developmental disturbance. In Caplan and Lebovici (Eds.), *Adolescence.* New York: Basic, 1969.

Friedenberg, E. Z. *Vanishing adolescence.* Boston: Beacon, 1959.

Friedenberg, E. Z. *The dignity of youth and other atavisms.* Boston: Beacon, 1965.

Fromm, E. *Escape from freedom.* New York: Rinehart, 1941.

Fromm, E. *The art of loving.* New York: Harper, 1956.

Fromm, E. *May man prevail.* New York: Doubleday, 1961.

Ginzberg, E., et al. *Occupational choice.* New York: Columbia University Press, 1951.

Goodman, P. *Growing up absurd.* New York: Random, 1956.

Goodman, P. *Compulsory mis-education.* New York: Horizon, 1964.

Havighurst, R. J. Youth in exploration and man emergent. In H. Borrow (Ed.), *Man in a world of work.* Boston: Houghton Mifflin, 1964.

Mead, M. *Culture and commitment: A study of the generation gap.* Garden City, N.Y.: Doubleday, 1970.

Merrill, M. A. *Problems of child delinquency.* 1972 reprint of 1942 ed: Westport, Conn.: Greenwood.

Miller, W. *This cool world.* Boston: Little, Brown, 1959.

Murphy, L. B. *The widening world of childhood, the paths toward mastery.* New York: Basic Books, 1962.

Osipow, S. H. *Theories of career development.* New York: Appleton, 1968.

Pine, G. J. The affluent delinquent. *Phi Delta Kappan,* 1966, *48* (4), 138–143.

Ramsey, C. E. *Problems of youth:* A social problems perspective. Encino, Calif.: Dickenson, 1967.

Toolan, J. M. Depression in children and adolescents. *American Journal of Orthopsychiatry,* 1962, *22,* 404–415.

Wylie, L. Youth in France and the United States. In Erik Erikson (Ed.), *The challenge of youth.* New York: Basic, 1961.

SUMMARY

1 There is no major biological or mental difference between adolescence and adulthood, and some societies regard puberty as the beginning of adulthood. In our society, adult status is granted at about age twenty, when the individual is presumed to have the education and experience to make responsible decisions.

2 The adolescent search for identity is described by Erikson as a struggle to form a continuous identity out of a welter of possible roles. One of the adolescent's most important tasks is to establish his independence from his parents.

3 Because adolescents have a wide variety of vocational choices, the decision is often a difficult one, though guidance counseling and publications on different vocations can be a great help. Sexual stereotyping creates problems for females in search of a career.

4 Failure to find an identity may result in alienation. Dropping out and activism are two forms of alienation found in idealistic adolescents.

5 Adolescents are prone to many of the same social and psychological problems as adults, including drug abuse and crime. Young offenders are responsible for a disproportionate amount of the crime committed in the United States.

FURTHER READINGS

Chapin, W. *Wasted: The story of my son's drug addiction.* New York: McGraw-Hill, 1972.
> A father's account of drug abuse by a middle-class youth and the family's struggle to understand and deal with it. Mark Chapin started smoking marijuana at fourteen and moved on to LSD and amphetamines. He was in a mental hospital when the book was written.

LeShan, E. J. *The conspiracy against childhood.* New York: Atheneum, 1967.
> Decrying the demand for "ever-accelerated learning at an ever-earlier age," this prominent child psychologist charges that children are being forced into premature adulthood. In trying to stuff them with knowledge, we are neglecting to develop them into whole human beings, she asserts. She urges a reassessment of educational priorities and cautions against "the Montessori madness."

Montessori, M. *The absorbent mind.* New York: Holt, 1968.
> "Education from birth" is the principle on which Montessori based the prekindergarten methods of teaching that brought her world renown. In this book based on her lectures, Montessori makes it clear that education involves much more than the inculcation of information and that to reform education, man must first reform himself. The process needs to be instituted in the first three years of life.

Schreiber, D. *Profile of the school dropout.* New York: Random House, 1967.
> Every year almost a million youths drop out of school into a world where jobs are limited for the unskilled and uneducated. In this symposium of educators, school administrators, and psychologists, the emphasis is on society's failures and on the problems and possibilities of American education. Contributors include Paul Goodman, Bruno Bettleheim, and Martin Deutsch.

Smith, B. *No language but a cry.* Boston: Beacon, 1964.
> Based on studies of thirty-two children selected as normal in infancy and followed for twelve years, this book views development as a process of continuing struggle for mastery over new problems. To understand the child, we need to understand what it is he is coping with and why he acts as he does. An interesting account of research methods and detailed case histories are included.

Willings, S. B. *Hassling.* Boston: Little-Brown, 1970.
> This book about adolescent rebellion against society reports events in a high school in Palo Alto, California, from 1967 to 1969. Dissent, demonstrations, and confrontations arose over the Vietnam war, race relations, the draft, drugs, black power, and student power.

Epilogue
The Study
of Child
Development

The growth of child development as a scientific discipline was stimulated by the changing intellectual and social ideas of the nineteenth century. In that period, the desire to improve the total welfare of the child—his upbringing, education, health and legal status—reflected a general spirit of humanitarian reform in both the United States and Britain.

Also contributing to a favorable climate for child development research was Darwin's *The Origin of Species* (1859). The theory of evolution, supported by substantial biological data, indirectly shattered the static concept of personality which had influenced thinking for many years—a concept which denied the possibility of individual growth and change. Darwin's work lent credence to the idea of developmental processes, which begin at conception and are operative throughout a person's life. The behavior and personality of the adult human being could be viewed from the perspective of his growth and development from infancy.

Until the twentieth century, however, systematic studies and empirical data on child development were nonexistent. Those working with children in guidance clinics and schools proceeded with good intentions but with little scientific knowledge to guide them in the kind of care and training they provided. The way children actually developed, the ways in which their personalities were formed, and the importance of learning were topics that still required substantial research.

The course of that research is marked by several interesting controversies, one of which concerns the origin of human knowledge. This issue had been the subject of centuries of debate, but it became especially relevant to the field of child development. Was the mind equipped with innate ideas and structures which determined the knowledge one acquired? Or did one's knowledge derive from his perceptions of the outside world? And therefore, should parents and teachers concentrate on helping the child develop those potentialities that, as they develop from within, will enable him to gain knowledge of the world? Or should they devote their efforts toward controlling the child's experiences in order to impress upon him the most important and valuable associations among them? Investigators from a variety of scientific disciplines have focused their attention on these and numerous other questions, and their studies have laid the foundation of the science of child development.

Very few children sit down at the piano and, with no previous instruction, pick out a tune. On the other hand, many children practice diligently for years and never learn to play well. How much of musical ability—or any other ability—is inborn talent? How much comes through learning?

EMERGENCE OF CHILD DEVELOPMENT

It was not until the 1920s and 1930s that child development began to emerge as a distinct field of study. Professionals interested in devoting themselves to this field formed the Society for Research in Child Development in 1933. On practical grounds there had been little need for such a discipline before, inasmuch as the United States had almost no nursery schools, no child guidance clinics (with the notable exception of the Institute for Juvenile Research in Chicago), few parent education programs, and no broadly organized child research centers until the 1920s (Frank, 1962). Then, as centers for the study of children were established, directors came from a variety of disciplines, for the field was so new that there were as yet no child development specialists. But knowledge, methodology, and theory accumulated rapidly, and a new discipline was created out of many fields and schools of thought.

As a recent study illustrates (Sears, 1974), several influences shaped the modern field of child development in the twentieth century. One of the earliest proponents of child-study was G. Stanley Hall (1844–1924), an American psychologist who emphasized the importance of biological factors in human development. Approaching child development from a scientific point of view, Hall attempted to compile normative information about the behavior, interests, emotions, imagination, habits, and preferences of children through the use of questionnaires. His method of inquiry proved unreliable since the samples used were not clearly specified, there was no standard procedure for collecting data, and the responses given to the questionnaires may have been unduly influenced by the attitudes of those administering them. Nevertheless, Hall's work inspired others to use alternate testing techniques in a field which had previously lacked scientific data, and the result was a vast amount of information concerning all areas of child development.

Hall also exposed many American psychologists to Freud's theory of psychosexual development. Through Freud's work and that of later analysts such as Erik Erikson, who widened the scope of Freud's original concepts, psychoanalysis helped mold the theoretical basis of child development research. It also helped stimulate research in anthropology, a field which would eventually exert a rival influence on child development. The work of anthropologists Bronislaw Malinowski and Margaret Mead, for example, showed that many developmental problems, such as the "adolescent crisis," which traditional psychoanalysis regarded as universal phenomena, were in fact common only to Western cultures. Subsequent cross-cultural research has broadened the perspective on child development and served as an important means of testing theories on the subject.

The growth of child development as a scientific discipline has also been strongly affected by behavioral psychology, especially in the United States. John B. Watson, who initiated behavioral studies and experimentation at the beginning of this century, claimed that human behavior and learning were reflex responses to environmental conditioning, and that behavior could therefore be molded. He

The current generation of anthropologists is contributing valuable information on child rearing to the
study of child development.

and later behaviorists, who utilized new and improved techniques of investigation
(some of them borrowed from anthropology) explored the relationship between
personality formation and child-rearing. Behavior modification techniques which
derived from these years of research have had a significant impact on child development theory and American teaching practices.

The contrast between Freudian psychoanalysis and behavior theory—the
former emphasizing the importance of instincts and innate drives in molding
behavior and the latter stressing the influence of the environment and the importance of learned patterns of behavior—highlights an old controversy often
termed "nature versus nurture." Early in the century, advocates of a genetic
approach to understanding human behavior and learning initiated studies dealing
with hereditary influences. In one such study (Goddard, 1913) intellectual capacity was traced through ten generations of a single family, the Kallikaks. The
father had mated with two women, one a feeble-minded barmaid and the other
a woman of normal intelligence. The majority of children whose lineage was
traced to the barmaid liaison were found to be inferior in terms of social and
educational achievement to children of the other strain—implying to the researchers that members of the former group were the victims of inherited intellectual defects. The evidence of subsequent comparative studies of parents and

children, and siblings and twins provided further support for the genetic interpretation of variations in intelligence. But neither the geneticists nor those who have stressed the importance of social and environmental factors on intelligence have conclusively settled the controversy.

In the 1920s, approximately the same time that studies in both genetic inheritance and behavioral psychology were adding new dimensions to child development research, a German scientist named Kurt Lewin was formulating his own distinctive theory of child behavior. Influenced by a background in physics and Gestalt theory, Lewin viewed the relationship between the child and his environment (or the "organism" and the "field," to use Lewin's terminology) as a dynamic interplay of forces. Behavior patterns were shaped by neither the child nor his environment alone, but rather a tension between these two.

Lewin's work was less serviceable to child development theorists than the longitudinal studies which were also initiated in the 1920s. These studies filled a gap left by the stage theories of psychoanalysis and the learning theories of the behaviorists by providing information about the growth of individuals—not just a group average—over a specified period of years; that is, longitudinal studies measure an individual's growth and change at successive stages in his life.

Major Contemporary Theorists

Today, the study of child development is being carried out by means of research projects designed to explore specific problems, many of which have been described in this book. The data gained from this research is used to constantly refine and modify existing theories so that they are in accordance with available empirical evidence. We have mentioned some of these theories before, in connection with various stages of the child's development. Now we can compare the emphasis and approach of each of them in the field as a whole.

Piaget's theory

For Jean Piaget the most important problem in child development is the origins of knowledge in the child. Piaget focused on the interaction between the child and his environment and studied the ways in which a child develops his sense of time, space, number, and causality. The model for his explanation of this process is biological adaptation. Piaget was an expert on fresh-water mollusks in his teens and received a doctorate in biology when he was twenty-two.

There are two essential features of biological adaptation that Piaget uses in his model of human development. The first is the constant application of old structures to new functions and, through this, the development of new structures to fulfill other functions. In this way, development is solidly rooted in what already exists and displays a continuity with the past. Second, these adaptations are never isolated behaviors, but part of a total system of dynamic equilibrium where all structures adapt in order to maintain a balance among themselves and between themselves and their environment.

Piaget's search for the processes which work toward equilibrium involved him in an exploration of the structures that emerge at each level in the child's development. Once he has identified these structures he shows how they adapt both to environmental demands and to each other. For example, the structure referred to as the sucking reflex is adapted specifically to the nipple. But, as Piaget observed, the infant tries to satisfy his sucking need on any objects, such as a pacifier, which are available to him. That is, he generalizes his use of the structure. When the infant learns to reach for objects or, at breast-feeding times, to find his mother's nipple more quickly, he has in effect learned to modify the structure in order to deal more effectively with his environment.

Werner's theory

The Austrian-educated Heinz Werner began his career teaching courses on embryology and neurology. He repeatedly drew on this background for analogies that would illustrate and clarify his concepts of psychological development. Like Piaget, he emphasizes the interdependence of various aspects of human behavior and the relation between human behavior and the total environmental context in which it occurs. While Piaget concentrates on the growing individual organism, Werner has developed a theory embracing all developmental processes—social, cultural, and biological—using the same general principles.

For Werner, developmental changes—whether they take place in an embryo, in an adult human organism, or in society—follow what he calls the *orthogenetic* principle: development takes place in the same direction and through the same stages in every organism despite differing external conditions. It proceeds from a state of relative lack of differentiation to a state of increasing differentiation, articulation, and organization at several levels.

The developing organism's behavior at first is *syncretic*—its qualities are fused, though they are striving toward being separate and distinct. For example, the emotions of the infant develop from a primitive, generalized excitement into the two differentiated feelings of joy and distress. Then distress is differentiated still further into the two emotions of fear and anger. Werner sees the transition from syncretic to discrete as never completely accomplished, so that some syncretism always remains a part of adult experience.

Werner also observes that behavior is initially diffuse and gradually becomes more *articulate*. For example, a child drawing a box may correctly show the sides as separate from the top; but if he attempts to show all the sides at once, he is failing to articulate the coordination of the parts.

Werner believes the functioning of an organism at an early developmental stage is both *rigid* and *labile*. A child displays rigidity when she repeats the same action over and over without any alteration. At the same time, she may do some

things quite haphazardly, and here her behavior is labile, or uncontrolled. For the child to develop into an adult she must learn to differentiate between situations that require control and situations that require spontaneity. Once this has been learned, the child's responses have become adult, that is, flexible and stable.

At first, then, the organism's behavior can be described as undifferentiated, syncretic, diffuse, rigid, and unstable. Through development it becomes increasingly differentiated, articulated, flexible, and organized at many levels. In this way the organism becomes better adapted to meet the demands of a complex environment.

Freud's theory

The Viennese physician Sigmund Freud began investigating psychological problems when his research on the nervous system uncovered disorders that had no apparent physiological basis. These investigations led him to make certain observations about human development. Freud believed that a child's growth occurs in biologically-determined stages and is shaped by basic instinctual forces, and that the way in which he handles his experiences and conflicts during these stages will affect him in maturity. Werner and Piaget see a diffuse organization of potential structures in the newborn child that, on contact with the outside world, develop toward adulthood; Freud found in the neonate a hotbed of emotional drives that had to be reconciled with the requirements of his social environment. Freud felt that the drives of the child, if left unchecked, threatened the very fabric of civilization.

Behaviorism and social learning theory

For behavioral psychologists, people *are* only what they *do.* Mental processes that cannot be observed are considered irrelevant to psychology. B. F. Skinner has said that "emotions" are only fictional causes to which we attribute behavior. Behaviorism limits its study to objective, observable behavior; describes behavioral change in terms of stimulus and response; and tests hypotheses in controlled experiments. Skinner (1953) says that behaviorists

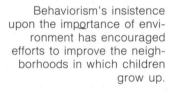

Behaviorism's insistence upon the importance of environment has encouraged efforts to improve the neighborhoods in which children grow up.

. . . undertake to predict and control the behavior of the individual organism. This is our "dependent variable"—the effect for which we are to find the cause. Our "independent variables"—the causes of behavior—are external conditions of which behavior is a function. Relations between the two—the "cause-and-effect relationships" in behavior—are the laws of science. A synthesis of these laws expressed in quantitative terms yields a comprehensive picture of the organism as a behaving system.

Skinner has never attempted such a synthesis or proposed a comprehensive theory of development, but in his view a child's development is a building process, with the bricks of experience being constantly added one on top of another to form the person.

Behaviorism has provided the basic principles—learning and reinforcement—used by another school of psychological thought known as *social learning theory*. Social learning theorists can be distinguished from the behaviorists because their model includes some of the problems raised by Freud. However, many of the concepts vital to Freud's thinking, such as the subconscious and the basic instinctual drives, are not integrated into social learning theory.

Many of the formulations of social learning theory are still being modified; however, most social learning theorists recognize the role of anxiety in learning. They see dependency as the root of nearly all socialization and aggression as an energy that is gradually channeled into socially acceptable behavior.

Even from this brief description it can be seen that the major schools of developmental psychology differ not only in their philosophical antecedents, but also in what they think is important about children. Piaget has focused on the area of cognition—the acquisition and functions of intelligence. The boundaries of Freudian interest encompass the birth, expression, and repression of human emotions in society. And for Skinner the lines of inquiry are drawn so that only the observable actions of the individual—that is, his behavior—are included. These differences in perspective have produced a variety of theories of child development and a collection of prescriptions for the care and education of children that sometimes overlap and sometimes contradict each other.

There is no one generally accepted theory of child development. The science of medicine has progressed to the point that there is some general agreement about the best way to treat certain physical diseases, but there is much less agreement in the science of child development about how to handle, for example, the learning difficulties of a six year old. What you do depends partly on what theories you believe, and thus far no single theory has been so successful in solving the problems of children and explaining their behavior that it has significantly diminished the value of other theories.

RESEARCH IN CHILD DEVELOPMENT

Because children are so often perceived as uncomplicated little people—and perhaps also because we have all been children—we tend to take our "knowledge" about them for granted. We "know" that three year old Leslie can't understand our adult conversation, that twelve year old Steven will outgrow his awkwardness, and that adolescent masturbation is harmless. The difference between what the child development researcher knows about children and what the rest of us know is, simply, that the researcher takes nothing for granted. He usually has certain ideas about a given topic or problem, but he makes no claims to their validity until he has compared these ideas with factual data.

In seeking the data which he needs to test his ideas, the scientific researcher confronts the problem of structuring his investigation so that it provides him with the most accurate information possible. Undoubtedly, his conceptions about the phenomena he wishes to study will affect his selection and organization of facts and the connections he perceives among them; but the researcher's conceptions must not jeopardize the accuracy of his facts. Therefore, he uses empirical methods of investigation which will enable him to approach the phenomena under study as objectively as possible.

The first thing that a researcher must do in an investigation is to determine what the problem is—that is, specify what phenomena and what relationships he wants to study. This may seem obvious, but if the statement of the problem is precise enough, it gives the researcher an idea of how to start.

The researcher usually phrases the problem as a question, using words that are as unambiguous as possible. Suppose, for example, that he has been working with delinquent children and he discovers from talking with them that many of them seem to be quite ingenious in their misbehavior. The researcher wonders if there is some connection between creativity and delinquency. He might pose the question this way: What is the relation between creativity (as measured by a test of creativity) and delinquent behavior (as indicated by arrest records) for youths between the ages of 10 and 14.

Notice that the question tells the researcher what to study and at the same time suggests how he could conduct his investigation. Another quality of good problem statements is that they imply procedures to be used in finding the answer. In this case the study will involve giving a creativity test to a certain group of children. The question is posed in a way that suggests that it can be answered by what is called **empirical** testing, that is, by observation or experimentation.

Another important characteristic of scientific problem statements is that they contain no value judgments: the scientist is not interested in whether the relation to be studied is good or bad, right or wrong, democratic or authoritarian. These qualities of relations may be important, but they are not measurable by the methods of science.

After the researcher has stated the problem, he can then review the studies that already have been done in the area to be investigated. He may discover that someone else has already done research on a similar problem. He may find some suggestions for new procedures—a test that has recently been devised to measure creativity in children between the ages of 13 and 17, for example, that he can adapt for the subjects he has in mind. He may learn about a colleague who is

*"Play set or no play set, he has two Navy destroyers
waiting in mid-ocean for further orders."*

Drawing by Hoff; copr. 1955 The New Yorker Magazine, Inc.

working on intelligence and delinquency. This survey of the existing literature will
help the researcher to sharpen his conception of the problem.

Constructing Hypotheses

The next step is the construction of a **hypothesis**, a conjecture about the relation
between two or more phenomena. Like the problem statement, the hypothesis should
imply the means that will be used to test the relation, but it is stated in declarative
form: it tells what the researcher thinks the relation is. The problem statement
in our previous example could be restated as a hypothesis this way: Children who
commit delinquent acts have higher creativity scores than children who do not
commit delinquent acts.

Notice that the hypothesis is not about creativity alone or delinquent behavior alone; it is about the relation between them. And the statement is made in such a way that it suggests what the researcher can do to discover whether the hypothesis is true. Assuming that methods can be found to measure the various aspects of the hypothesis (assuming, for example, that delinquent children can be located and tested for creativity), the hypothesis can be proven or disproven.

The objects of scientific study are often called **variables**; in psychology, the variables are the particular human features to be studied—people's social class, for example, or their sex, age, aggressive behavior, or anxiety. In research that involves statistical description and calculation, the variables are the aspects to which numbers are assigned. One can measure levels of aggression, theoretically at least, and assign the numbers 1 through 10 to varying levels of aggressive behavior; all sorts of mathematical computations can then be done with the numbers.

There are two kinds of variables: independent and dependent. The **independent** variable is the presumed cause of the relation given in the hypothesis; it is the variable that is manipulated or varied by the researcher. The **dependent** variable is the presumed effect of the relation; it should vary with changes in the independent variable. A study might be done, for example, in which the hypothesis was that achievement in school depends upon attitudes towards teachers. In this case, the attitudes would be the independent variable, and the achievement would be the dependent variable.

If the hypothesis is empirical—that is, if it contains variables that are to be observed or tested—the research design must include **operational definitions** of each of the variables. Operational definitions assign meanings to variables by describing activities that the researcher performs to measure the variables. An operational definition of frustration could be the description of the behavior of children placed in a room where they could see but not touch a selection of toys that were placed behind a wire mesh (Kerlinger, 1964). The operational definition tells the researcher what to observe.

Research Methods

After the hypothesis has been constructed, the researcher designs a study using the set of methods and techniques that are best suited to the nature and scope of his study. The research method chosen depends on the variables being tested: some hypotheses lend themselves to experimental methods; others can best be tested by the ex post facto, historical, or descriptive method.

Experimentation is a research method in which the researcher has direct control over at least one of the independent variables. He manipulates that variable and observes the dependent variable to see if it changes as he changes the independent variable. Suppose, for example, that a researcher proposes this hypothesis: Increasing the frustration experience of three year olds will increase their aggressive behavior. He defines frustration operationally as the condition of three year olds when they are offered an attractive toy which is then suddenly withdrawn;

aggression is operationally defined as the number of times the subjects hit or push other children in a given time period. The researcher can design an experiment in which a group of three year olds are observed in a playroom, exposed to the frustrating experience, and then observed again. The observers record the incidence of aggressive behavior before and after the frustrating experience. In this case, aggressive behavior, the dependent variable, is assumed to be caused by the experimentally induced frustration, the independent variable. The experimenter can manipulate the degree of frustration to see if he can vary the amount of resultant aggression.

In many areas of child development study the experimental method cannot be used because the independent variable is not under the control of the researcher. In a study that attempts to determine the relation between intelligence and aggressive behavior, for example, the following hypothesis might be constructed: Ten year olds who score above 110 on the Stanford–Binet IQ test exhibit less aggressive behavior than ten year olds who score 110 or below. In this case, intelligence is the independent variable—it cannot be manipulated by the researcher. All he can do is measure it and correlate it to behavior. The method used in such studies is called *ex post facto;* it varies from the experimental method in that the researcher observes the dependent variable and then attempts to account for it by conjecturing about the independent variable retrospectively. Because the researcher cannot control the independent variable, he cannot be sure that it is the cause of the change in the dependent variable. (Perhaps ten year olds with IQs above 110 have some other characteristic in common that affects their aggressive behavior.) For this reason, ex post facto research is not considered to be as scientifically accurate as experimental research.

Historical research investigates variables that have occurred in the past. A historical study might be made, for example, of the disciplinary measures used by parents in the United States during the decade from 1920 to 1930. Good historical research depends on the use of **primary** sources—the original records of past events and experiences, such as eyewitness descriptions, photographs, diaries, and so on. The historical data collected in such studies can be particularly useful in drawing comparisons with other periods and in giving perspective to current events.

Descriptive research involves the collection of data about a particular characteristic of the subjects under study. This method of investigation produces profiles of a given group in terms of specific phenomena—the height and weight patterns of fifteen year olds, for example. Descriptive data is useful in that it tells what people of a particular age, sex, cultural group, and so on are like in terms of one characteristic or another. It also provides a basis for comparison in developmental studies.

Children as subjects

Many of the special problems in child development research are the result of the characteristic nature of the subjects being studied, the children. It has been said that children as research subjects fall somewhere between animals and adults (Mussen, 1960). Like animal subjects, very young children are unable to understand verbal directions. Research with infants must be structured by nonverbal means; for example, different visual patterns are used to test attention span. The behavior of very young subjects is seen as a reaction rather than a communication; one can observe that a three month old child smiles under certain conditions, but the child cannot tell you why she is smiling.

With older children verbal communication can be used, but the researcher must remember that these subjects will not necessarily communicate in the same ways that adults would. A child may misunderstand directions, lose interest in the experimental task, or become sidetracked by his fascination with the appara-

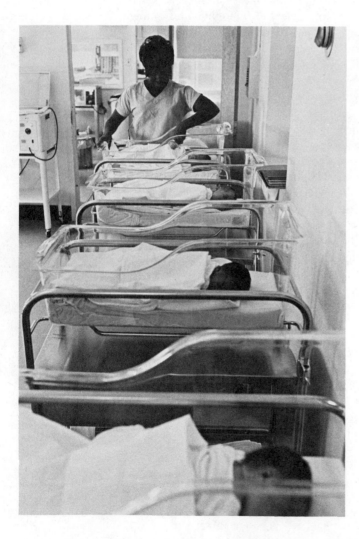

Physical studies of children may be conducted in schools, if the school has the necessary medical records or facilities, but much more frequently they are made with the cooperation of physicians, clinics, and hospitals. University hospitals in particular are likely to have their own research staffs whose business it is to keep track of such things as the incidence of bed wetting in the pediatric ward and the factors influencing it. Specialized children's hospitals are a major source of data for researchers in child development.

tus being used in the study. Child development researchers must design their studies with the special characteristics of children in mind.

In addition to the procedural difficulties that arise in studies with children, child development research raises some special ethical problems. Unlike adult subjects, children cannot accept responsibility for their participation in research. Often it is difficult to explain the intention of research to a child. In addition, research procedures may be upsetting to a child; sometimes, in fact, they are deliberately so, as when part of the experimental design is to place the subject in a stressful situation. Obtaining the consent of the child's parents simply transfers the required ethical judgment from the researcher to another adult. We will return to these ethical considerations later in our discussion.

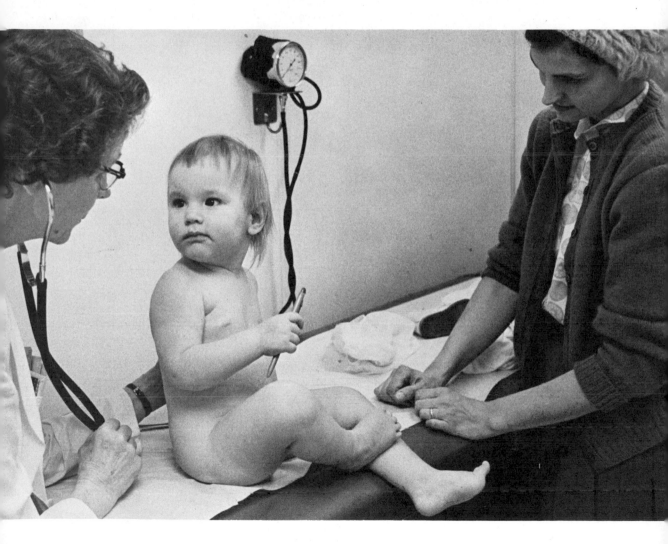

Research Procedures

The information generated in psychological research is based on knowledge about some *sample* of the population from which conclusions are drawn about the entire population. In **sampling**, the researcher takes a portion of the population to represent the entire population: he studies ten or fifty or three hundred infants, and he says that his conclusions apply to all infants like those in the study.

In selecting sample subjects, the researcher can use the principles of random selection to insure that every member of the population being studied has the same chance of being chosen for the study. *Random sampling* produces an unbiased sample of the population that may be taken to represent the entire group. In effect, random sampling gives the researcher a group of subjects whose independent variables are statistically equivalent to those of the population from which they are taken.

Suppose that a study is planned to determine the effect of a reading readiness program on kindergarten children. If the subjects are selected through random-sampling techniques, they are likely to have the same range of reading readiness skills at the beginning of the study as the entire group of all kindergarteners: some of the children will be very ready to read, some will lack the ability to make certain visual discriminations necessary for reading, and so on. The randomly selected sample group will have these characteristics in proportions that can be statistically related to the proportions in the population as a whole. This means that if the researcher manipulates one variable of the reading readiness of his sample group, he can measure the degree to which the same manipulation will affect the population as a whole. Using the principles of random selection to choose subject populations allows the researcher to know how confidently he can generalize the results of his research.

In addition to choosing his sample according to statistical principles that will insure, insofar as possible, that the results of his research will be generally applicable, the researcher also needs to use good measuring instruments in his study. Measurement simply means the "assignment of numbers to represent properties" (Kerlinger, 1964). Measuring some variables, such as age, height, and weight, is fairly easy because the properties of these variables are usually expressed numerically. Behavioral properties such as hostility or problem-solving ability are much more difficult to measure because they are based on an inference that a particular observable behavior indicates the property (that the number of times a child hits another child in playgroup indicates the child's level of hostility, for example).

Measuring instruments must be reliable if the data produced in a study are to be accurate. *Reliability* means that if a researcher measures the same phenomenon today, tomorrow, and next week, he will get the same numbers. It also means that if someone else uses the same measuring instrument in a duplicate study ten years from now, the results will be the same.

In constructing a test to be used to measure creativity, for example, a researcher needs to devise an instrument in which errors in the administration of the test, in the scoring of the test, in the variety of test items chosen for a particular form, and so on are minimal. He develops an accurate, reliable instrument by trying out the test items separately and eliminating the ones that produce inconsistent scores. A reliable test uses language that is unambiguous, so that everyone who takes it understands the questions in the same way; it contains enough items to reduce the effect of chance error; it states directions clearly and is administered under standard conditions. Such a test will give the same results in successive trials with the same population.

Measuring instruments must also be valid if they are to produce useful data. The measurement has validity if it really measures what it says it does. Valid measurement of a physical characteristic such as height is fairly easy because the measurement is direct, but many psychological variables cannot be measured so directly. When a variable is one that must be inferred from behavior, such as frustration, the researcher needs to ask whether the behavior he measures actually demonstrates that variable. For example, suppose a four year old builds towers with her blocks and then knocks all the towers over. Is she expressing aggression, hostility, frustration, or the happy exuberance that comes from her realization that she can control her environment? How can the researcher determine what the behavior means? This question must be answered before research results can be validly applied to behavior outside of the research situation.

There are several different types of validity. An example of one type is a good measuring device, such as a test, that contains a representative sample of the properties that make up the variable being measured; such a device is said to have *content validity*. Suppose you want to measure mathematical ability. The best way to do it is to determine all of the characteristics that make up this ability and then to construct a test that includes all of the characteristics.

The validity of an instrument can also be checked by comparing the measurement results with some other, external outcome; this is called *predictive* or *concurrent validity*, depending on whether the outcome used for comparison occurs in the future or at the same time. A valid reading-readiness test, for example, would predict with accuracy whether a child is prepared to learn to read.

The most important kind of validity in psychological research is called *construct validity*. It is an empirical method for determining what factors account for the results that are obtained in research. Construct validation inquires into the meaning of the variables being studied. One method of construct validation is to compare the results of the research with other studies that are designed to measure the same variables, but this method can be used only if other valid measures already exist. Alternatively, the validity of the research can be checked by breaking down the results into their various properties, testing those properties, and then correlating the scores with the results obtained in the original research. If one theorized, for example, that sociability includes the properties of being liked by one's friends, being active in social events, and having a good sense of humor, one could devise research to determine sociability and then correlate the results with separate tests of those three properties.

It is possible for a measuring instrument to be reliable and not be valid. If we say that a creativity test is reliable, all we are saying is that it will produce the same scores if administered under the same conditions. If we say that the test is valid, we are saying that it actually measures the creative quality. Good research requires instruments that are both reliable and valid.

Data Collection

Researchers gather information about the problems they study in a variety of ways. The method of data collection is determined by the nature of the problem and is suggested by the wording of the research hypothesis. Research in child development often relies upon observation for data collection, but interviews, objective tests, and other methods are also used.

Observation of behavior involves, very simply, watching what subjects do and say. It may take place in a laboratory in which the environment is highly controlled

Will these children play just as they would if they were not being observed?

Written tests have been
designed for children
of all ages.

by the researcher or in a natural environment. The laboratory is used when the variable being investigated cannot be found—or adequately controlled—in a natural setting. Both in the laboratory and in a natural setting the researchers make every effort to keep the subject's behavior from being influenced by the observation itself. They also strive to attain reliability by having all the observers record what they see on standard forms and by comparing the reports of two observers watching the same thing.

The chief problem with the observation method is that the observer may introduce his bias into the recording of the behavior. This problem can be alleviated by careful construction of instruments that clearly define the behavior to be recorded. Rather than asking an observer to record incidences of dependency on the teacher in a classroom situation, for example, the researcher may ask that the observer note every time a child asks permission from the teacher before the child does something. The second record would be much more objective than the first.

A second problem inherent in observation is that the observer may change the behavior of the subjects simply because he is observing. The presence of the observer should be as unobtrusive and nonjudgmental as possible, especially in studies involving a natural environment.

Interviews and questionnaires are another means of data collection. In these techniques, the researcher asks the subjects direct questions either verbally or in written form. Oral interviews can be used effectively in collecting data from children because the interviewer can adapt his questions to the child, rephrasing or explaining when the child does not understand. Interviews can be highly structured situations in which the wording, order, and time given to answer each question is fixed, or they may be more flexible and open-ended. Questionnaires are useful for collecting the data of descriptive research, such as a census, but some information cannot be easily obtained from a questionnaire form because people are unable or unwilling to give the information to the researcher.

Numerous objective tests have been devised to measure intelligence, aptitudes for a wide variety of skills, achievement in general and specific areas of knowledge, and personality and attitudes. Most of these are paper and pencil tests in which the subject is asked to respond to questions by choosing one answer from a small number of possibilities. The researcher then makes inferences about the subject from his responses. Because the tests are so structured and the possible responses are so limited, there is usually great agreement among researchers in the inferences that are made from them. Objective tests are useful starting points for obtaining information about a subject, and they are often administered in counseling or

---

PERSONALITY TESTS

Because the assessment of individual personalities is so important to employers, the armed forces, and educational institutions, personality testing has become a regular function of clinical psychology. Many different techniques are used. One of them, the *interview,* is simply a face-to-face talk between the subject and the interviewer. The interview may be structured or unstructured—that is, the questions may be prepared in advance or they may be guided by the course of the conversation. In another technique, the *situational* test, the subject is observed either in a natural situation or in a situation arranged by the observer. Another technique, the *inventory,* is a very common test that usually involves a list of statements to which the subject is asked to respond. For example, he may be asked to reply ''always,'' ''sometimes,'' or ''never'' to statements such as ''People pick on me'' or ''I would rather watch television than go to a party.''

Projective tests are those in which the subject is prompted to project his own fears, aspirations, and attitudes onto an ambiguous shape or drawing.

In the Rorschach inkblot test, for example, the subject is shown ten inkblot cards one at a time and asked to say whatever the inkblot brings to his mind. The psychologist trained in administering the test then assesses the subject's personality on the basis of his responses.

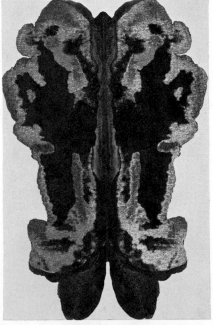

diagnostic situations as a first step to be followed by personal interview. Intelligence, aptitude, and achievement tests have been standardized for our culture and educational systems; the best of these tests are highly reliable and generally valid. The use of personality and attitude measures is also widespread, although some professionals consider them less valid than other kinds of objective tests (Kerlinger, 1964).

Among other methods for collecting research data are various projective measures, which require the subject to respond by making a choice, a completion, an association, or some other expression; sociometry, which measures communication and interaction patterns of groups of people; and content analysis, which involves studying communications such as television programs by measuring given aspects of their content (the kinds of violence portrayed in a particular series about police work, for example).

Results

The unprocessed information that an investigator gathers in research is called the *raw data* of the study. At the end of an observational study of behavior, for example, the researcher would have a collection of recording forms filled out by observers. If the study is purely descriptive, the raw data is the information sought by the study and needs only to be codified as the end product of the research. A study to determine the IQ scores of all the seventh graders in a particular school system is essentially complete when all the test scores have been calculated; the raw data (the scores) is all the information sought in this study. Certain computations may be made with the scores, such as finding the average IQ, but the study does not require that any inferences be made from the data gathered.

In much psychological research, however, the raw data is not the end product of the study. If the research begins with a hypothesis, the researcher collects data and then returns to his hypothesis to see whether the data confirm it. Often this means that he will try to determine whether his results are significant—that is, could not have happened by chance. Suppose that the study has shown a relation between frustration and aggression; increasing frustration leads to an increase in aggression. The instruments used to measure the variables have been found to be both reliable and valid. Nevertheless, it is possible that the relation between the variables is the result of chance rather than the result of the experimental manipulation of the independent variable. The researcher subjects his data to statistical analyses that show how likely it is that his results could have been obtained by chance. If these analyses show that the increased aggression of the subjects in the study was far greater than the aggression that would have occurred by chance, then the researcher can infer that the aggression was caused by the increase in frustration.

Once the raw data has been analyzed statistically, the researcher may then go on to draw conclusions from his study, saying what he thinks the results mean. He may also wish to relate the results of his research to other studies and to the larger theoretical constructs in child development.

Sampling techniques, which usually comprise a necessary part of any research design, ideally permit the researcher to generalize his results and apply his conclusions to the population under study. In practice, however, a researcher may encounter a number of problems using this method of investigation. For one thing, obtaining a random sample may entail considerable expense and time, especially since randomly chosen subjects may be involved in any of a variety of professions or personal activities which interfere with the study procedure. A researcher may have difficulty in obtaining samples which are large enough or which are truly representative; or he himself may misjudge the degree to which important variables in the population under study are represented in his sample group. Furthermore, if the sample survey format includes questionnaires and interviews, the researcher must also contend with problems of inaccuracy and insufficient information—members of the sample group may not fully understand the questions asked; they may give what they believe are "expected," rather than true, responses; or they may simply make up answers to questions about which they have no particular opinion. Therefore, it often becomes necessary to use other methods of research to test the data obtained from sampling.

ETHICAL CONSIDERATIONS

Any research involving human subjects raises ethical questions. Child development research requires special attention to ethical considerations because children are generally considered to be more vulnerable than adults and because it is often difficult to communicate with children as one would with adults. The American Psychological Association has adopted certain ethical principles for the conduct of research with human subjects, including the following:

> Ethical practice requires the investigator to inform the participant of all features of the research that reasonably might be expected to influence willingness to participate. . . .
> When the methodological requirements of the study necessitate concealment or deception, the investigator is required to ensure the participant's understanding of the reasons for this action [after the study has been completed]. . . .
> Ethical research practice requires the investigator to respect the individual's freedom to decline to participate in research or to discontinue participation at any time.
> The ethical investigator protects participants from physical and mental discomfort, harm, and danger. If the risk of such consequences exists, the investigator is required to inform the participants of that fact, secure consent before proceeding, and take all possible means to minimize distress.
> After the data are collected, ethical practice requires the investigator to provide the participant with a full clarification of the nature of the study and to remove any misconceptions that may have arisen (American Psychological Association, 1973).

The difficulties in applying these principles to children who participate in research are obvious. A child is not capable of giving her consent for her participation in research. Permission must be obtained from the child's parents or guardians, and the researcher must explain to them the nature of the research and of any risk of stress or harm to the child. Where the research design permits full disclosure of these matters to the subject, the ethical researcher will explain them to the child as well, using language that the child can understand. With preschool children, the explanation of the research procedure can often be expressed in terms of a game that the investigator wants the child to play.

Many psychologists condemn the practice of deceiving a research participant. These professionals feel that experiments in which the researcher must lie to the subject are not worth doing (Mussen, 1960). In child development research, there is surely no justification for deceiving the person who gives consent for the child's participation in the research since telling the parents will not automatically affect the child's behavior in the study.

The widespread belief that children are less able to handle stress than adults has been neither supported nor denied by current experimental evidence (Mussen, 1960), but the right of the participant to be protected from harm is universally applied.

This right is considered so vital that the U.S. Department of Health, Education, and Welfare subjects all applications for research grants involving human subjects to a stringent committee review.

> This review shall determine that the rights and welfare of the subjects involved are adequately protected, that the risks to an individual are outweighed by the potential benefits to him or by the importance of the knowledge to be gained, and that informed consent is to be obtained by methods that are adequate and appropriate (U.S. Department of Health, Education, and Welfare, 1971).

In designing his study, the researcher should be aware of the need to minimize both short-term and long-term adverse effects on the subjects; in explaining the experiment to the child's parents, he must be frank about the level of anxiety, frustration, or whatever that will be involved, and he should be in a position to predict the effects of this discomfort on the child. After the experiment has been performed, it may also be necessary to explain to the child (in the child's terms) the reasons for the discomfort in the experiment. The researcher might sit down with the child, for example, and encourage her to express her feelings about the experience so that all concerned will be aware of the child's perception and better able to relieve any difficulties that have arisen.

What Is Child Development For?

One of the ethical considerations mentioned in the previous section concerned whether or not the "potential benefits" and information derived from any given research project warranted risk-taking when human subjects were involved. This question of applicability brings us back to an important point mentioned in our introduction: child development studies were nourished by a deep interest in the welfare of children, and were intended to serve an immediately practical purpose. Since those formative years, developmental research has become more scientifically sophisticated and theoretical, but the problems it must confront are still rooted in the social environment. The question therefore remains, "How should the knowledge gained by the study of child development be used?"

Before addressing ourselves to this question and the conflicting responses it has brought forth, let us briefly consider the influence of child development studies on past social policy. As we noted, much of the early research focused on specific problems of child welfare and effected changes in areas such as child-

Should the behavior modifying techniques
developed by science be used to engineer
conformity?

rearing, education, and the institutionalization of mentally-retarded and delinquent
children. But most of the research, especially of the past twenty years, has affected attitudes—it has not produced striking changes in social practice. As a matter of fact, research in developmental psychology since World War II has rarely
applied itself to particular social problems; instead it has focused primarily on
laboratory experimentation and general theories of child development and behavior
(Sears, 1974).

Today however, a variety of groups are pressuring developmental scientists
for research which will produce immediately beneficial results. Some of these
people naively assume that child development studies can offer solutions to complex social problems which are as dramatic and conclusive as the vaccines against
disease developed by medical researchers. And each of these groups which are
demanding relevant research—government, community activists, educators, psy-

chologists, parents, and even children themselves—have their own conflicting, and sometimes simplistic, theories concerning problem areas such as drug abuse, delinquency, and educational training.

At one extreme on the continuum of such viewpoints concerning social problems are those who believe that children should be allowed to grow and develop on their own, without interference from science or government. These people maintain that social planners who, for example, are trying to improve schooling in ghetto areas and who support federal funding of community projects for child welfare are simply wasting time and money on problems which should be left to run their own course.

At the other extreme are certain behavioral psychologists like B. F. Skinner who advocate strenuous social planning. Skinner has written a novel about a community in which the principles of psychology are used to bring up children who are peaceable, cooperative, and cheerful. In this community, called Walden Two, the children are trained in self-control, among other things. In Skinner's view, social problems could be virtually eradicated through behavioral conditioning and scientifically designed institutions which reinforce only those values which are beneficial to society.

But which values are most beneficial to society? Even if all people were to accept the *idea* of a program of social policy designed to control all the variables affecting child development, could they possibly agree on who would engineer such a program?

In New Jersey, the State Department of Education has proposed a system which is intended to provide each student with a "thorough and efficient" education through the use of behavior modification experiments, school busing, and the recording and analysis of each child's progress and level of development. Similar programs have been implemented in other school systems across the nation. Educational Improvement Centers, initially funded by the federal government and presently in limited operation, are intended for gathering data on each student's personal background and continually developing and evaluating educational policy.

Not unexpectedly, this proposal has aroused considerable controversy. Many parents have charged that behavioral scientists, with the sanction of the federal government, are trying to control the mind and behavior of children, that they are teaching children to challenge their parents' attitudes and values, and are programming children with their own value system.

This controversy is not untypical. The use of scientific knowledge in social planning probably always will involve conflicts between members of different groups who have their own opinions concerning how and when such knowledge should be applied. And perhaps this is as it should be. No one group is better able than all others to deal with the problems of our society. The field of child development has always been receptive to contributions from a variety of sources. It has little to gain from power struggles, and much to lose if the dialogue between concerned parties were to end.

References

American Psychological Association. *Ethical principles in the conduct of research with human participants.* Washington, D.C.: American Psychological Association, 1973.

Darwin, C. R. *Origin of species.* London: 1859.

Frank, L. The beginnings of child development and family life education in the twentieth century. *Merrill-Palmer Quarterly*, 1962, *8*(4), 7–28.

Goddard, H. H. *The Kallikak family.* New York: Macmillan, 1913.

Kerlinger, F. N. *Foundations of behavioral research.* New York: Holt, 1964.

Mussen, P. H. (Ed.) *Handbook of research methods in child development.* New York: Wiley, 1960.

Sears, R. R. Your ancients revisited: A history of child development. In E. M. Hetherington (Ed.) *Review of child development research.* Vol. 5. Chicago: University of Chicago Press, 1974.

Skinner, B. F. *Science and human behavior.* New York: Macmillan, 1953.

U.S. Department of Health, Education, and Welfare, *The Institutional Guide to DHEW Policy on Protection of Human Subjects*, DHEW Publication No. (NIH) 72–102, December 1, 1971.

488

SUMMARY

1   There has been a historical debate among theorists as to the most important factor involved in the acquisition of knowledge. Most German and French theorists have emphasized inherent mental developments and structures, while the American and English school of thought has held that experience is the most important factor.

2   Charles Darwin's *Origin of Species* was instrumental in bringing to light the importance of developmental processes for rearing and education. The close of the nineteenth century saw psychologists compiling data on the mental functions of both adults and children.

3   The contemporary study of child development has been affected by many influences, including that of G. Stanley Hall, who obtained vast quantities of information and statistics in a field that had little of this data before. Some other influences were psychoanalysis, anthropology, behaviorism, and the longitudinal study.

4   Psychologists use a sample—a relatively small portion of the population in question—to draw conclusions about the population as a whole. Random choice of subjects for a research project can insure an unbiased sample. If the sample is unbiased, it will have all the same pertinent characteristics—and in the same proportions—as the whole population.

5   If a measuring instrument is reliable, it will produce the same results under the same conditions in future trials. If it is valid, it will measure the properties that it is supposed to measure. A valid test of intelligence, for example, would measure the abilities identified as elements of intelligence, and not English comprehension, motivation to please authorities, or other factors.

6   Data is collected in several ways, including observation, objective tests, or direct interviews. Data collection through observation requires the researcher to watch what the subjects say or do and to record the number of times a certain activity occurs. In a direct interview, the investigator asks questions of a subject face to face. The objective method involves a set of written questions.

7   The American Psychological Association maintains a series of ethical principles for the conduct of research with human beings. An investigator must inform the participants of all aspects of the research project. The participant may decline to participate in the research, or discontinue participation at any time. If a research project necessitates concealment or deception, the investigator must explain the reason for such action at the completion of the study. The investigator is required to protect all participants from mental or physical harm.

FURTHER READINGS

Ariès. *Centuries of childhood: A social history of family life.* Robert Baldick (Trans.). New York: Vintage, 1962.

This fascinating history of childhood from early medieval to modern times includes discussions of children's games, dress, social behavior, and education. It also traces the development of the family from the fourteenth century to the present. Ariès makes extensive use of primary sources such as paintings and diaries, and his history is full of rich detail about the lives of children in earlier times.

Asimov, Isaac. *The Intelligent Man's Guide to Science.* New York: Basic Books, 1963.

These two volumes, the first of which deals with the physical sciences and the second with the biological sciences, cover both the content and the methodology of the various sciences. Especially useful as a popular introduction for readers who feel that science is too abstract, difficult, and mysterious for them to understand.

Bronfenbrenner, U. (Ed.). *Influences on human development.* Hinsdale, Illinois: Dryden, 1972.

A collection of readings in child development that covers a broad range of topics and includes many examples of the use of statistics in research. Among the many topics covered are early deprivation, the effects of television violence on children, group upbringing experiments, birth order in relation to achievement, and the socialization of student activists.

Downie, N. M., and Heath, R. W. *Basic statistical methods.* (3rd ed.) New York: Harper, 1970.

This text sets forth the statistical methods most commonly used by psychologists in research. It includes instructions and exercises that enable the beginning student of statistics to master the computations involved and to relate statistical analysis to various research designs.

Huxley, A. *Brave new world.* New York: Harper, 1939.

Central London in the year 2450 is a culture based on sexual promiscuity, conspicuous consumption, and the fulfillment of every conditioned desire—a society in which, as the World State slogan teaches, "everyone is happy now." Children are created in test tubes and programmed before and after birth to fill their prescribed places in society. Huxley's vision is savagely satirical and still relevant.

Murphy, L. M. *The widening world of childhood.* New York: Basic Books, 1960.

An examination of causal factors in mental illness from early childhood to adolescence. For those requiring help, Smith reviews home, state, and community mental services. He discusses community preventive services—a growing need.

Page 118   Copyright © 1966 by John Updike. Reprinted from MIDPOINT AND OTHER POEMS, by John Updike, by permission of Alfred A. Knopf, Inc.

page 157   From "The Fathering Instinct: Working Fathers" by Andy Clayton. Reprinted with permission from *Ms.* magazine.

Part 3 opener From MEMORIES OF A DUTIFUL DAUGHTER by Simone de Beauvoir. Copyright © pages 207–208 1959 by World Publishing Company. Reprinted with permission of Libraire Gallimard, Paris, France.

Part 4 opener Excerpt from Chapter 3 ("We played robbers . . . a Sunday-school.") in THE ADVEN- pages 301–302 TURES OF HUCKLEBERRY FINN by Samuel L. Clemens (Harper & Row).

Page 306   © 1973 by The New York Times Company. Reprinted by permission.

Part 5 opener From THE HEART IS A LONELY HUNTER by Carson McCullers. Copyright 1940 and pages 389–391 © 1967 by Carson McCullers. Reprinted by permission of the publisher, Houghton Mifflin Company.

page 446   Reprinted from THE WHEEL OF LOVE by Joyce Carol Oates by permission of the pub- lisher, Vanguard Press. Inc. Copyright, © 1970, 1969, 1968, 1967, 1966, 1965, by Joyce Carol Oates.

Picture Credits

Chapter one
opener, pages 6–7 Alycia Smith Butler
     page 18 Kathryn Abbe
       31 Rodelinde Albrecht
       33 Alycia Smith Butler

Chapter two
opener,
pages 38–39   Kathryn Abbe
     page 40 Photograph by Ken Heyman
       43 Photograph by Ken Heyman
       49 Kathryn Abbe

Chapter three
opener,
pages 66–67   Alycia Smith Butler
    page 72–73 Courtesy of the University of Iowa
       75 Reprinted from RADIOGRAPHIC ATLAS OF SKELETAL OF THE HAND AND WRIST, SECOND EDITION by William Walter Greulich and S. Idell Pyle with the permission of the publishers, Stanford University Press. Copyright © 1950 and 1959 by the Board of Trustees of the Leland Stanford Junior University.
       83 Kathryn Abbe

348–349   Alycia Smith Butler

355   Leif Skoogfors from Woodfin Camp

Chapter twelve

pages 360–361   Photograph by Ken Heyman

page 366   Winston Vargas/Photo Researchers, Inc.

370   Joseph Szabo

372   Kathryn Abbe

375   Copyright © 1970 by Stanley and Janice Berenstain. Reprinted with permission of The Sterling Lord Agency, Inc.

376   Kathryn Abbe

379   Dan Budnik from Woodfin Camp

381   Thomas Hopker from Woodfin Camp

Chapter thirteen

pages 392–393   Thomas Hopker from Woodfin Camp

page 395   Ellen Pines from Woodfin Camp

396   Drawing by Opie; © 1963 The New Yorker Magazine, Inc.

399   Joseph Szabo

401   Joseph Szabo

407   Kathryn Abbe

412   Sylvia Johnson from Woodfin Camp

414   Joseph Szabo

417   Joseph Szabo

421   Tim Eagan from Woodfin Camp

Chapter fourteen

page 428   Kathryn Abbe

429   Joseph Szabo

431   George Gardner/Photo Researchers, Inc.

437   Rohn Engh/Photo Researchers, Inc.

437   Kathryn Abbe

440   Sylvia Johnson/Woodfin Camp

443   Jill Freedman/Photo Researchers, Inc.

449   Joseph Szabo

452   Joseph Szabo

Epilogue, page 460   Alycia Smith Butler

page 462   Orville Andrews/Photo Researchers, Inc.

464   George Roger/Magnum Photos

467   Drawing by C E M; © 1961 The New Yorker Magazine, Inc.

468   Photograph by Ken Heyman

471   Drawing by Hoff; Copr. 1955 The New Yorker Magazine, Inc.

474   Rapho Guillumette Pictures

475   Rapho Guillumette Pictures

478   Alycia Smith Butler

479   Kathryn Abbe

481   Christa Armstrong/Rapho Guillumette

485   Joseph Szabo

GLOSSARY

Abortion. The spontaneous or induced expulsion of a human fetus.

Accommodation. Jean Piaget's term for the modification of a structure to deal with the demands of the environment.

Adaptation. The process of cognitive growth which, according to Jean Piaget, modifies psychological structures to suit the environment.

Adolescence. The period from the onset of puberty to adulthood.

Age equivalent. The average age at which a child reaches a particular developmental stage.

Aggression. Hostile action or feelings, especially those caused by frustration.

Alienation. The feeling of being separated or withdrawn, especially from personal and/or social relationships or from one's culture.

Alleles. The differing forms of any given gene, which give different instructions for the form a characteristic should take.

Amniotic sac. A thin membrane enclosing the embryo and filled with a fluid in which the embryo is immersed.

Androgyny. The varying distribution of the characteristics of both sexes in one person.

Anoxia. A condition in which the brain does not receive enough oxygen to allow it to develop or function properly.

Assimilation. Jean Piaget's term for the tendency of an organism to use a structure or ability once it is available.

Anxiety. An uneasiness of mind experienced as apprehension or fear, often related to concern about some impending event. Feelings of anxiety are appropriate in some circumstances; however, the term is usually used to refer to inappropriate apprehension aroused by self-doubt.

Attention. Selective response to environmental stimuli according to one's needs and interests.

Attention span. The length of time during which a person focuses on a given object or task.

Autism. A nearly total withdrawal from reality and escape into fantasy.

Autonomy. The quality of being able to make one's own choices.

Calcification. The step after ossification in bone formation, during which the bones are hardened through the deposit of calcium salts.

Centration. The tendency to center attention on a single feature of an object or situation.

Cephalocaudal. Refers to the sequence of body growth in which development occurs first at the head and then moves downward through the rest of the body, part by part.

Cesarean birth. Delivery through a surgical incision into the mother's abdomen and uterus.

Childhood psychosis. Severe emotional disturbance in children.

Classical conditioning. A learning procedure in which the response caused by one stimulus is transferred to a previously neutral stimulus.

Cognition. The process of knowing, including perception, thinking, and problem solving, regarded by Jean Piaget as a form of biological adaptation.

Colic. A syndrome characterized by a distention of the abdomen, apparently resulting in severe pain and causing a baby to cry violently and continuously; also, used loosely to describe the symptoms of infants who have regular or prolonged bouts of paroxysmal crying during their first few months.

Compulsion. An irrational, repeated activity which arises when one can no longer control an anxiety or attempts to satisfy an obsession.

Concrete operational period. The third of Jean Piaget's stages of cognitive development (from seven to eleven years of age), characterized by the child's ability to retrace his thoughts and to view things in a variety of ways.

Conditioning. The process of evoking a specific response by presenting a particular stimulus.

Conformity. Behaving according to established social rules or norms.

Congenital. Refers to a characteristic a person is born with, even if it does not become apparent until later.

Critical period. The phase in prenatal development when the body part or organ system is growing most rapidly.

Cross-cultural studies. The observance of the effect of the same environmental stimulus on behavior in different cultures.

Decentration. Jean Piaget's term for the ability to shift the center of one's attention.

Dependence. Reliance on others for information, support, and emotional comfort.

Descriptive research. Research involving the collection of data about a particular characteristic of the subjects under study.

Developmental age. A measure of the degree of a person's physiological maturity. Contrasted with chronological age, which indicates how long a person has lived.

Dilation. The first of the three stages of labor, usually lasting from two to sixteen or more hours, during which contractions begin to occur.

Discrimination. The ability to recognize the distinctive features of similar but nonidentical things.

DNA (Deoxyribonucleic acid). The most important substance in the nucleus of the zygote, this acid constitutes the genetic "blueprint" for the new individual.

Down's syndrome. The form of mental retardation known as mongolism, caused by the failure of the paired chromosomes to separate properly when an egg or sperm is formed and characterized by limited intelligence, a skin fold at the corner of the eyes, a broad nose, and a protruding tongue.

Egocentrism. Concern with one's own activity or needs.

Embryonic period. The second of the three stages of gestation, at the end of which many body systems are in operation and the embryo begins to resemble the human form.

Empirical testing. Testing that relies on observation or experimentation for its answers.

Experimentation. A research method in which the researcher has direct control over at least one of the independent variables.

Expulsion. The second stage in labor, during which the baby is expelled through the cervix.

Fantasy. Creative imagination, often involving a substitution in which one object or situation stands for another.

Fetal period. The third of the three stages of gestation, during which body systems reach full development.

Fontanelles. The soft areas of connective tissue on the skull of the newborn.

Formal operational period. The fourth of Jean Piaget's stages of cognitive development (from eleven to fifteen years of age), characterized by the child's development of abstract thought.

Gene. The element in the chromosomes that transmits a hereditary character.

Gestation. The prenatal phase of life, lasting an average of 266 days in humans.

Gonad. The primary sex gland, ovaries in the female and testes in the male.

Growth curve. A statistical curve derived from plotting weight and height against chronological age for comparison of an individual child's growth pattern with the average rate of growth.

Heterozygous. Refers to an individual who has both one dominant and one recessive gene for a given trait.

Historical research. Research that investigates variables that have occurred in the past.

Homozygous. Refers to an individual whose two genes for a given trait are both either dominant or recessive.

Hormone. One of the many chemicals produced by the endocrine glands and causing physical or psychological changes.

Hysteria. A psychoneurotic condition sometimes characterized by a tic or loss of function due to anxiety.

Identity confusion. Erik Erikson's term for the condition resulting from an adolescent's failure to achieve a positive identity, sometimes evidenced by feelings of alienation.

Imitation. The modeling of one's actions on those of another, one of the fundamental ways a child learns.

Imprinting. A fixed response, or instinctive programming, in the young of social species.

Learning. The process by which one acquires or modifies a pattern of behavior.

Longitudinal study. The study, over a long period of time, of several variables in the same person.

Mean. The average arrived at by adding up all the figures in a study and then dividing the sum by the number of figures.

Median. The average, or middle point, below which half the cases in a statistical study fall.

Meiosis. The process of cell division, or reduction division, by which human sperm and egg cells are produced.

Mitosis. The process of cell division by which the body produces new cells in order to maintain growth and good health.

Monozygotic twins. Identical twins developed from a single zygote.

Morpheme. The smallest part of a word that conveys meaning and cannot be further subdivided without destroying the meaning; the units into which phonemes are arranged to make a language.

Mutation. A change in genetic structure affecting physical development, biochemistry, or behavior.

Obsession. A persistent and disturbing preoccupation.

Operant conditioning. A learning method developed by B. F. Skinner in which the response precedes the stimulus.

Operation. A process, according to Jean Piaget, that changes its object.

Organization. The process of cognitive growth which, according to Jean Piaget, integrates one psychological structure with another.

Orthogenetic. Refers to Heinz Werner's theory of the sequence of development which takes place in the same direction and through the same stages in every organism despite differing external conditions.

Ossification. The process of bone formation, starting from a few locations and spreading outward from those locations.

Peer group. Those who are members of one's social group, especially in cultures in which membership is determined by age or status, and by whom one is treated as an equal.

Period of the embryo. The second of the three principal stages of gestation, during which the blastocyst is implanted in the uterus wall.

Period of the fetus. The third of the three principal stages of gestation, during which body systems advance and the fetus grows rapidly.

Phobia. Excessive fear aroused by a particular object or situation and characterized by an extreme desire to avoid the object.

Phoneme. The smallest unit of sound that has meaning in the language.

Placenta. The disk-shaped mass of tissue that serves as a two-way filter between the bloodstreams of the mother and the embryo.

Placental stage. The third and final stage of labor, during which the placenta and the attached membranes and cord (the afterbirth) are expelled from the uterus.

Postpubescent stage. The third stage of puberty, at which time the sex organs are capable of adult functioning.

Preimplantation period. The first of the three stages of gestation, during which all cells are exact replicas of the zygote.

Prematurity. Refers to the delivery of a fetus before the normal gestation period has been completed.

Preoperational period. The second of Jean Piaget's stages of cognitive development (from two to seven years of age), characterized by the child's development of symbolic representation.

Prepubescent stage. The first stage of puberty, during which the secondary sex characteristics begin to develop, but the reproductive organs do not yet function.

Proximodistal. Refers to the sequence of body growth in which development occurs first at the center of the body and later at the extremities.

Psycholinguistics. The study of the learning, use, and understanding of language.

Puberty. The period of adolescence during which an individual reaches sexual maturity.

Pubescent stage. The second stage of puberty, during which the reproductive organs become capable of producing ova or sperm.

Reflex. An involuntary motor response to a specific stimulus.

Regression. Reversion to an earlier stage, especially behaving in a manner more suitable to a younger age.

Reinforcement. The reward that motivates learning. According to a fundamental tenet of behavioral psychology, when an action is followed by a satisfying consequence, that action tends to be done more often.

Rh factor. A substance present in the red blood cells of most people and causing antigenic reactions when the mother's blood is Rh negative and the fetus' blood is Rh positive.

Rites of passage. The procedures whereby a child becomes an adult member of his culture. Also called puberty rites.

Schemata (plural of *schema*). Jean Piaget's term for the combination of perceptual impressions into a coherent plan.

Schizophrenia. A general term for disturbances that have a detachment from reality at their core; more precisely a complicated psychosis characterized by inability to relate to one's environment.

Secondary sex characteristics. The physical features other than the genitals that distinguish men from women.

Self-concept. One's definition of oneself including a person's mental image of his physical self, his expectations about his own behavior, and other such expressions of the person's sense of himself.

Sensorimotor period. The first of Jean Piaget's stages of cognitive development (from birth to two years), characterized by the child's organization of his perceptions and exploration of his environment.

Sensory deprivation. Lack of normal sensory stimuli, which can account for early childhood difficulties due to impaired perceptual and sensory abilities.

Sex role. Masculine or feminine behavior patterns as defined by any given society.

Socialization. The process that guides the growth of our social personalities, allowing us to become reasonably acceptable and effective members of society.

Somatotyping. W. H. Sheldon's system of grouping body types into the categories of endomorph (soft and rounded), mesomorph (well-muscled), and ectomorph (thin and frail), each of these somatotypes correlating with certain personality traits.

Sutures. The places where the skull bones of infants touch.

Syncretic. Refers to a developing organism's initial behavior, its qualities being fused though striving toward being separate and distinct.

Teratogens. The environmental agents that produce abnormalities in the developing fetus.

Teratology. The study of congenital abnormalities caused by prenatal environmental influences.

Toxemia. Blood poisoning, which, when developed by pregnant women, can cause premature birth or anoxia in the baby.

Umbilical cord. The link between the embryo and the placenta through which the embryo takes nourishment and oxygen and releases waste products.

Zygote. The fertilized egg, the first cell in which the father's genes are joined with the mother's.